ISLAM AND GLOBAL DIALOGUE

Today, the World's religions are challenged by factions that preach religious exclusivism and theologies of hate. As 9/11 tragically demonstrated, Islam has been hijacked and used by extremists and global terrorists. Islam and Global Dialogue *is a major contribution toward the promotion of mutual understanding, religious pluralism, and tolerance and thus in the reassertion of religion's role in promoting global peace rather than conflict.*

> John L. Esposito, University Professor of Religion and
> International Affairs, and Islamic Studies,
> Georgetown University, USA

In a period of bloody confrontations and religious radicalisms that nourish the self-styled clash of civilisations, it is necessary to read these pluralistic reflections on the matter by a brilliant group of Jewish, Christian and Muslim intellectuals and scholars. The book is a meritorious effort to promote dialogue and peace.

> Juan Goytisolo, Marrakesh

This essential book conclusively disposes of the vicious mythology that the religious faiths are doomed to fight each other.

> Dan Plesch, Birkbeck College, and the United Services Institute, UK

At a time when the world is becoming increasingly interdependent, multi-cultural and multi-religious, the concept of religious pluralism is under assault as a result of hatred, prejudice and misunderstanding from both religious exclusivists and dogmatic secularists.

In this important and timely book, twenty internationally acclaimed scholars and leading religious thinkers respond to contemporary challenges in different ways. Some discuss the idea of a dialogue of civilisations: others explore the interfaith principles and ethical resources of their own spiritual traditions. All of them reject the notion that any single religion can claim a monopoly of wisdom; all are committed to the ideal of a just and peaceful society in which people of different religions and cultures can happily coexist. More space is given here to Islam than to Judaism and Christianity because, as a result of negative stereotypes, it is the most misunderstood of the major world religions. HRH Prince Hassan bin Talal of Jordan contributes the Foreword.

For Mansur and Muin

Islam and Global Dialogue
Religious Pluralism and the Pursuit of Peace

Edited by

ROGER BOASE
Queen Mary College, University of London, UK

Foreword by
HRH PRINCE HASSAN BIN TALAL

ASHGATE

Published by
Ashgate Publishing Limited
Gower House
Croft Road
Aldershot
Hants GU11 3HR
England

Ashgate Publishing Company
Suite 420
101 Cherry Street
Burlington, VT 05401-4405
USA

Ashgate website: http://www.ashgate.com

British Library Cataloguing in Publication Data
Islam and global dialogue: religious pluralism and the pursuit of peace
 1. Religious pluralism – Islam 2. Religious pluralism 3. Culture conflict –
 Religious aspects – Islam 4. Culture conflict – Religious aspects 5. East and West
 I. Boase, Roger
 297.2'8

Library of Congress Cataloging-in-Publication Data
Islam and global dialogue : religious pluralism and the pursuit of peace / edited by
Roger Boase ; with a foreword by HRH Prince Hassan bin Talal.
   p. cm.
 Includes bibliographical references and index.
 ISBN 0-7546-5307-2 (hardcover : alk. paper)
 1. Religious pluralism--Islam. 2. Islam--Universality. 3. Peace--Religious
 aspects--Islam. I. Boase, Roger.

 BP190.5.R44I73 2005
 297.2'8--dc22
                                                                          2005003006
ISBN-10: 0 7546 5307 2
ISBN-13: 978-0-7546-5307-3

Reprinted 2006

Typeset by Tradespools, Frome, Somerset
Printed and bound in England by Antony Rowe Ltd, Chippenham, Wiltshire

Contents

v

Part Three   Jewish, Christian, and Muslim Responses to
Religious Diversity

Postscript

Bismillah ar-rahman ar-rahim
In the name of God, Most Merciful, Most Compassionate
(*Al-Fatihah* – The Opening)

Our Father in the heavens
Hallowed be Thy name
(The Lord's Prayer)

Exalted and hallowed be His great Name
in the world which He created according to His will
(Opening words of the *Kaddish*, the Jewish prayer for the dead)

There is no god but God
(*La ilaha illa'llah*)

Holy are You,
and awe-inspiring is Your Name;
and beside You there is no God.
You are praised, O Lord, the holy God
(*Amidah*, stanza 3, ancient Palestinian version)

When I call aloud the name of the Lord,
You shall respond, "Great is our God"
(Deuteronomy 32:3)

Allahu Akbar
God is Great
(*Takbir*)

Allah is my Lord and your Lord, so worship Him.
This is a straight path.
(Words of Jesus in the Qur'an, 3:51; 19:36)

May He who makes peace in His high heavens
make peace for us and for all Israel.
And say: Amen
(Last lines of the *Kaddish*, repeated twice)

As-salamu 'alaykum wa rahmatullah wa barakatuhu
Peace be upon you and God's mercy and blessings
(Muslim greeting and petition for peace,
repeated twice after every cycle of prayer)

List of Contributors

HRH Prince Hassan bin Talal, the former Crown Prince of Jordan, younger brother of His Majesty the late King Hussein, and a direct descendant of the Prophet Muhammad, is renowned for his work in promoting interreligious and intercultural understanding. He is Chairman of the Arab Thought Forum, Moderator of the World Conference on Religion and Peace, and Vice-Chairman of the Foundation for Interreligious and Intercultural Research and Dialogue (Geneva). He is the author of *A Study on Jerusalem* (1979), *Palestinian Self-Determination* (1981), *Search for Peace* (1984), *Christianity in the Arab World* (1994), *Continuity, Innovation and Change: Selected Essays* (2001), and joint author of *To be a Muslim* (2004).

Khaled Abou El Fadl is one of the leading authorities in Islamic law in the United States. He was trained in Islamic legal sciences in Egypt, Kuwait, and the United States. He is currently Professor of Law at the UCLA School of Law. Previously he has taught at the University of Texas, Yale Law School, and Princeton University. He teaches courses in Islamic Law, Immigration Law, Human Rights, and International and National Security Law. He is a member of the Board of Human Rights Watch and a member of the Lawyer's Committee for Human Rights. He often serves as an expert witness in international litigation involving Middle Eastern law, and in cases involving immigration law, terrorism, and political asylum claims. His recent books include *Islam and the Challenge of Democracy* (2004), *The Place of Tolerance in Islam* (2002), *Conference of the Books: The Search for Beauty in Islam* (2001), *And God Knows the Soldiers: The Authoritative and Authoritarian in Islamic Discourses* (2001), *Speaking in God's Name: Islamic Law, Authority and Women* (2001), and *Rebellion and Violence in Islamic Law* (2001).

Akbar S. Ahmed holds the Ibn Khaldun Chair of Islamic Studies at American University, Washington DC, and was named the 2004 District of Columbia Professor of the Year by the Carnegie Foundation. A former Pakistani ambassador to London and Fellow of Selwyn College, Cambridge, his works include *Pakhtun Economy and Society* (1980), *Discovering Islam* (1988), which was the basis of the BBC six-part television series *Living Islam* (1993), *Postmodernism and Islam* (1992), *Jinnah, Pakistan and Islamic Identity* (1997), *Islam Today: A Short Introduction to the Muslim World* (1999), and *Islam Under Siege* (2003). With Brian Forst, he has co-edited *After Terror: Promoting Dialogue among Civilizations* (2005). He is the executive producer and co-scriptwriter of the film *Jinnah* (1997). With Dr Judea Pearl, father of slain *Wall Street Journal* reporter Daniel Pearl, Dr Ahmed has been engaged in public dialogues across the USA and the UK.

Mahmoud M. Ayoub is Professor of Islamic Studies at Temple University, Philadelphia, USA. Since 1999, Dr Ayoub has participated in the US Department of State's Middle East programme. He is Chief Editor of Tabataba'i's *Qur'an Commentary al-Mizan*, under the aegis of the Alawi Foundation, and a consultant editor of the journal *Islam and Christian-Muslim Relations*. His books include *The Qur'an and its Interpreters*, vols 1 (1984) and 2 (1992), *Dirasat fi al-'Alaqat al-Masihiyyah al-Islamiyyah* (Studies in Christian-Muslim Relations) (2000), *Crisis of Muslim History: Religion and Politics in Early Islam* (2003), and *Islam in Faith and History* (2004).

Tony Bayfield is Chief Executive of the Reform Synagogues of Great Britain, Director of The Sternberg Centre for Judaism in North West London, and a Co-President of the Council of Christians and Jews. He is the founder editor of the quarterly journal *MANNA: The Voice of Living Judaism*. His publications include *Dialogue with a Difference* (1992), a book on Jewish-Christian relations, published jointly with Marcus Braybrooke, and *He Kissed Him and They Wept* (2001), which also explores interfaith relations. He has been co-convenor of a unique Jewish-Christian-Muslim dialogue group for the last decade.

Wendell Berry is a native of Henry County, Kentucky, where he farms, teaches, and writes. He is the author of over forty volumes of essays, poems, stories, and novels, for which he has received many awards. He is a former professor of English at the University of Kentucky and a past fellow of both the Guggenheim Foundation and the Rockefeller Foundation. His books of essays include *Standing on Earth: Selected Essays* (1991) and *In the Presence of Fear: Three Essays for a Changed World* (2001).

Roger Boase is a Research Fellow in the Department of Hispanic Studies, Queen Mary College, University of London, and formerly a professor at the University of Fez, Morocco. He is the author of *The Origin and Meaning of Courtly Love* (1977), *The Troubadour Revival* (1978), and with Aisha Ahmad, *Pashtun Tales from the Pakistan-Afghan Frontier* (2003). Important articles include "Arab Influences on European Love-Poetry", in *The Legacy of Muslim Spain*, ed. Salma Jayyusi (1992), "Excerpts from the Epistle on the Spirit of Holiness", in *Muhyiddin ibn 'Arabi: A Commemorative Volume* (1993), "Autobiography of a Muslim Convert: Anselm Turmeda (*c.*1353–*c.*1430)", *Al-Masaq*, vol. 9 (1996–97), 45–98, and "The Muslim Expulsion from Spain", *History Today*, April 2002.

John Bowden was for more than thirty years, until his retirement in 2000, editor and managing director of SCM Press, one of the world's leading English-language publishers of books on theology and religion. An Anglican priest and former university lecturer, deeply committed to interfaith work, he has translated more than 200 books from German, Dutch, French and Italian, and since 1990 has translated all the works of Hans Küng. He is the author of *Jesus the Unanswered Questions* (1988), and editor of a large encyclopaedic work entitled *Christianity: A Complete Guide* (Continuum, 2005).

Marcus Braybrooke is an Anglican vicar who has been involved in interfaith work for over thirty-five years. He was one of the founders of the Three Faiths Forum and of the International Interfaith Centre. He has been Executive Director of the Council of Christians and Jews, co-editor of the journal *World Faiths Insight*, and President of the World Congress of Faiths. He is the author of *Time to Meet* (1990), *Pilgrimage of Hope and Faith* (1992), *A Wider Vision* (1996), *Faith and Interfaith in a Global Age* (1998), *Christian-Jewish Dialogue: The Next Steps* (2000), *What We Can Learn from Hinduism* (2002), *What We Can Learn from Islam* (2002), *1000 World Prayers* (2003), and with Kamran Mofid, *Sustaining the Common Good: Bringing Economics and Theology Together* (2005).

Robert Dickson Crane is Chairman of the Center for Understanding Islam, Chairman of the Crescent University Foundation, President of the Center for Policy Research, Washington, Virginia, and Associate Editor of the new online magazine, *The American Muslim*. President Reagan appointed Dr Crane US Ambassador to the United Arab Emirates in 1981. From 1963 to 1968, he was a personal adviser to Richard Nixon, who appointed him in 1969 to be Deputy Director of the National Security Council in the White House. Dr Crane was Director of Publications in the International Institute of Islamic Thought (1986–88) and Director of the Legal Division in the American Muslim Council (1992–94).

William Dalrymple is a writer and historian, Fellow of the Royal Society of Literature and the Royal Asiatic Society, and author of several highly acclaimed bestsellers: *In Xanadu* (1990), *City of Djinns* (1994), *From the Holy Mountain: A Journey in the Shadow of Byzantium* (1997), *The Age of Kali: Indian Travels & Encounters* (1998), a collection of essays on India, *Sacred India* (1999), and *The White Mughals: Love and Betrayal in Eighteenth-Century India* (2002).

Diana L. Eck is Professor of Comparative Religion and Indian Studies at Harvard University. Her work on India includes the books *Banaras, City of Light* (1982) and *Darsan: Seeing the Divine Image in India*. (1981, rev. 1996). Eck's book, *Encountering God* (1993), addresses issues of religious diversity. *A New Religious America* (2001) is an account of the changing religious map of the USA. Since 1991, Eck has been running The Pluralism Project at Harvard, which produced *World Religions in Boston: A Guide to Communities and Resources* (1994), and an interactive CD-ROM, *On Common Ground: World Religions in America* (1997).

Frank Julian Gelli grew up in Rome, where he worked as a journalist, drama critic, and playwright. In 1973 he came to England as correspondent of the drama magazine *Sipario*. He holds degrees in philosophy, theology, and education from Birkbeck College and King's College, University of London. He was a Chaplain of the Church of St Nicholas, Ankara, Turkey (1989–91), and then Curate of Kensington until 1999, when he devoted himself full-time to writing and interfaith work. He is the founder of the Arkadash Network, a spiritual fellowship of reconciliation and friendship between Muslims and Christians. He has recently written a book on the Prophet Muhammad and is currently working on another on Jesus in the Sufi tradition.

Fred Halliday has since 1983 been teaching at the International Relations Department of the London School of Economics, where he has held a Chair since 1985. He has been Fellow of Transnational Institute, Amsterdam and Washington (1974–82), and Chairman of the Research Committee of the Royal Institute of International Affairs (1989–92). He is a member of the Advisory Council of the Foreign Policy Centre and a Fellow of the British Academy. His books include *Iran: Dictatorship and Development* (1978), *The Making of the Second Cold War* (1983), *Arabs in Exile, Yemeni Communities in Urban Britain* (1993), *Rethinking International Relations* (1994), *Islam and the Myth of Confrontation* (1996), *Revolution and World Politics: The Rise and Fall of the Sixth Great Power* (1999), *Nation and Religion in the Middle East* (2000), *The World at 2000* (2000), *Two Hours that Shook the World* (2001), and *The International Relations of the Middle East* (2004).

Jeremy Henzell-Thomas is Director of the Book Foundation, a British charity engaged in the publication of key Islamic texts, the development of resources for Islamic education, and the sponsorship of Islamic art. He was the first Chair of FAIR, the Forum Against Islamophobia and Racism, founded in 2001, and has also served on the Executive Committee of the Association of Muslim Social Scientists (UK). Recent publications include *The Language of Islamophobia* (2001), *Passing Between the Clashing Rocks: The Heroic Quest for a Common and Inclusive Identity* (2004), and various articles in the online resource, *The American Muslim*, of which he is a contributing editor.

Murad Wilfried Hofmann is a prolific writer on Islam, and a former German ambassador to Algeria (1987–90) and Morocco (1990–94), who reverted to Islam in 1980. Educated at Munich University and Harvard Law School, he served as Director of NATO and Defence Affairs in the German Foreign Office (1979–83), and Director of Information for NATO in Brussels (1983–87). His publications in English include *Islam: The Alternative* (1993), *Journey to Makkah* (1998), *Islam 2000* (1996), *Religion on the Rise: Islam in the Third Millennium* (2001), *Journey to Islam: Diary of a German Diplomat, 1951–2000* (2001), and *Modern Islamic Polity in the Making* (2001).

Muhammad Legenhausen, a native of New York, received his PhD in philosophy from Rice University in Texas, in 1983, the same year in which he converted to Islam. He taught philosophy at Texas Southern University (1979–89), and since then has lectured on philosophy and religious studies in Tehran and Qom. He has published numerous articles that have appeared in English, Farsi, Arabic, and Indonesian, and is the author of *Islam and Religious Pluralism* (1999), and *Contemporary Topics of Islamic Thought* (2000).

Francis Robinson was Vice-Principal of Royal Holloway, University of London, where he is Professor of the History of South Asia. He was Visiting

Professor at EHESS, Paris, South Asia Programme, and the University of Washington, Seattle, Middle East Programme (1982–86). He has been President of the Royal Asiatic Society (1982–86, 2003–). His publications include *Atlas of the Islamic World since 1500* (1982), *The Cambridge Encyclopedia of India, Pakistan, Bangladesh, Sri Lanka, Nepal, Bhutan and the Maldives* (ed.) (1989), *The Cambridge Illustrated History of the Islamic World* (ed.) (1996), *Islam and Muslim History in South Asia* (2000), *The 'Ulama of Farangi Mahall and Islamic Culture in South Asia* (2001).

Jonathan Sacks is Chief Rabbi of the United Hebrew Congregations of the Commonwealth and Visiting Professor of Theology at Kings' College London. He was formerly Principal of Jews' College, London. He is a frequent contributor to radio, television, and the national press. In 1990 he delivered the BBC Reith Lectures on 'The Persistence of Faith'. His publications include *Tradition in an Untraditional Age* (1990), *Persistence of Faith* (1991), *Arguments for the Sake of Heaven* (1991), *Crisis and Covenant* (1992), *One People?* (1993), *Will We Have Jewish Grandchildren?* (1994), *Community of Faith* (1995), *The Politics of Hope* (1997, rev. 2000), *Morals and Markets* (1999), *Celebrating Life* (2000, rev. 2004), *Radical Then, Radical Now* (2001), *The Dignity of Difference* (2002), *The Chief Rabbi's Haggadah* (2003), and *From Optimism to Hope* (2004).

Norman Solomon is a member of the Oxford University Teaching and Research Centre in Hebrew and Jewish Studies. He was the Founder Director of the Centre for the Study of Judaism and Jewish-Christian Relations at the Selly Oak Colleges, Birmingham (1983–94), and is Adviser to the International Council of Christians and Jews (1988–). His publications include *Judaism and World Religion* (1991), *The Analytic Movement: Hayyim Soloveitchik and his School* (1993), *A Very Short Introduction to Judaism* (1996), and *Historical Dictionary of Judaism* (1998). He was editor of the quarterly *Christian Jewish Relations* for the Institute of Jewish Affairs, London (1985–91).

Antony T. Sullivan is an Associate at the Center for Middle Eastern and North African Studies at the University of Michigan, and a Senior Fellow at the Fund for American Studies in Washington, DC. He also serves as Director of Faculty in Greece for the International Institute for Political and Economic Studies (IIPES). He has played a major role in bringing together Muslim intellectuals and their western counterparts to address contemporary challenges facing the West and the Islamic world. In 2005, Sullivan became Chief Middle East correspondent for Stratfor.com. In addition to more than eighty scholarly articles, Sullivan is the author of *Thomas-Robert Bugeaud, France and Algeria, 1784–1849* (1983), and *Palestinian Universities Under Occupation* (1988). He is a contributor to *The Rushdie File*, eds Lisa Appignanesi and Sara Maitland (1990), *World History: 1500 to the Present*, ed. David McComb (1993), *Islam and the West: A Dialog*, eds Imad-ad-Dean Ahmad and Ahmed Yousef (1998), and *Globalization: Prospects for Peace, Prosperity and World Order*, ed. Tim Kolly (2002).

Foreword

HRH Prince Hassan bin Talal

Although this new century has begun so darkly for any proponent of peace, it has also seen a great increase in exchanges across cultural and spiritual borders. One result is that investigative views, as represented by the authors of the essays in this volume, have become prominent markers of ways forward to a more peaceful engagement with each other. They show that differences of opinion need not mean differences of approach, and that civilised dialogue within cultures and traditions is as necessary and as enlightening as dialogue between them.

Ironically, our greatest certainty now is that we face unpredictable times. The communications revolution has introduced ever more politicised roles for media and educational policy, while the density and movements of the world's population seem sure to shift according to ongoing changes in birth-rates and economic developments. New concepts in the developed world, such as Euro-Islam or government-defined citizenship exams, have provoked many to re-examine the relationships between national, regional, cultural, and religious identities, while, in developing countries, issues such as the "brain drain", suggested links between poverty and violence, and struggles for independence should alert us to be prepared for major and unexpected changes to come.

In this atmosphere, our most powerful tool for grasping and, ultimately, directing events is effective communication. By comprehending each other's insights, we can identify common ground on which to start building towards each other with the ideals and habits of peacefulness towards one universal civilisation. This does not mean that we have to agree on all points. Recognising and appreciating the culture of "the other" need not involve negating one's own culture. I believe in Professor Mircea Malitza's "one world of ten thousand cultures." However, we must be clear about the need to better human conditions, and it is not only acceptable but also preferable that our methods, so long as they consistently deliver improved conditions, should differ. By respecting cultural and religious diversity, while at the same time recognising the importance of universal human values and international humanitarian norms, as well as the concept of global sustainability, an alternative ought to be found to the feared hegemonic and homogenic globalisation process.

Scholarship and knowledge, reason and experience, are powerful tools for building bridges across the divisions between peoples' assumptions and educations. Still, once bridges are built, they serve no purpose unless people are persuaded that they can benefit from them. It is necessary to explain, as this volume also sets out to do, the reasons why we must cross bridges, meet on them, widen and strengthen them, and even build homes upon them. This book of scholarship and knowledge maps many bridges open for use, along with places suitable for new construction. It remains to build creatively, attractively, and flexibly – and encourage people to walk across.

Preface

Before the atrocity now known by the abbreviation 9/11, Islam was already receiving a bad press as a result of bloody conflicts in many parts of the world – notably Palestine, Chechnya, and Kashmir, but after that date Islam has become, for many people, a synonym for fanaticism and terrorism. The chief aim of this book is to promote mutual understanding between Jews, Christians, and Muslims, and to demonstrate that there is no contradiction between Islam and the concept of religious pluralism. It is hoped that, by stimulating further thoughts and discussions, these essays will be useful to all those around the world who are engaged in the task of constructing a more just and humane world in which religious and cultural diversity will be respected.

It needs to be stressed that there is nothing inherently violent about Islam as a religion. Indeed quite the reverse. As anyone with any knowledge of Arabic will tell you, the word *islam,* which is generally defined as "submission to the will of God", derives from the same root as *salam,* "peace". War, in certain circumstances, is a duty, but it can never be "holy" and it is governed by a strict code of conduct that forbids, for example, the killing of women and children. The striving denoted by the verb *jahada* is primarily spiritual or moral, as in God's admonition to the Prophet: "Strive hard against the deniers of the truth and the hypocrites" (9:73).[1] Other passages indicate that the Qur'an itself is the instrument with which believers must strive against those who disbelieve (25:52; 66:9). As Dr Seyyed Hossein Nasr says, concerning the concept of *jihad,* "its translation into 'holy war', combined with the erroneous notion of Islam prevalent in the West as the 'religion of the sword', has helped to eclipse its inner and spiritual significance" (1987: 28).[2] All external forms of struggle – and these include fighting ignorance and injustice – are worthless if they are not accompanied by the inner struggle, or greater *jihad,* against evil and the whims of the ego. The Prophet Muhammad is reported to have said: "If a man engaged in battle entertains in his heart a desire to obtain out of the war only a rope to tether his camel, his reward shall be forfeited." A soldier is not a *mujahid* if he is motivated by hatred, or revenge, or personal ambition, or the pursuit of worldly gain, and there is a well-known story that the Prophet Muhammad's son-in-law 'Ali ibn Abi Talib felt obliged to refrain from killing a man who spat at him to avoid the sin of killing his enemy in anger.

Only self-defence, in the widest sense, including the defence of religious freedom, makes force permissible for Muslims. If people did not have such a right to fight, then "monasteries and churches and synagogues and mosques, in which God's name is much remembered, would surely have been destroyed by now" (Qur'an, 22:40). However, it is also written: "whoever pardons [his foe] and makes peace, his reward rests with God" (42:40), and "if they incline

xvii

towards peace, incline thou also to it and place thy trust in God " (8:61). Those who have been unjustly driven from their homelands have a duty to fight (Nasr 1987: 27–33). However, when the opportunity for peace arises, Muslims are encouraged to be forgiving and to seek reconciliation, for mercy and compassion are God's chief attributes, and it may be that "God will bring about affection between you and some of those whom you now face as enemies (60:7). According to one Prophetic tradition, to settle a dispute between people is more excellent than fasting, charity, and prayer. On the basis of the above definition of a just war, readers can easily figure out which recent and continuing conflicts may legitimately fall into the *jihad* category.

There is a widespread fallacy that without religion there would be no more wars. But, as the Chief Rabbi Jonathan Sacks so rightly says in his book *The Dignity of Difference*, "If religion is not part of a solution, it will certainly be part of the problem" (2002: 9). The present recourse to violence throughout the world is symptomatic of a general moral crisis, a spiritual bankruptcy, and increasing social injustice. The fact that religious extremism is rooted in genuine grievances does not make it any less an aberration contrary to the whole spirit of Islam. With the decline of traditional knowledge and the dissemination of Western secular values, the ecumenical and mystical aspects of Islam are not only unfamiliar to the majority of non-Muslims but they are not properly understood by the average Muslim, even though they are clearly expressed in the Qur'an. This is why the time has come for Muslims and non-Muslims to join together in an intellectual and ecumenical *jihad*. It is only by "the stockpiling of trust" through interreligious dialogue that we can lay the foundations of a more peaceful world.[3]

How can we live in peace and avoid the clashes of culture or civilisation that are being widely predicted unless we recover the unity of the pluralistic vision that is at the heart of all the great spiritual traditions? From every quarter, this vision is now under threat. Not only did people of many nations and faiths die in the suicidal attacks on New York and Washington, but since then, as a direct or indirect consequence of this event, thousands of other innocent people have died in Afghanistan, Palestine, Kashmir, Chechnya, and elsewhere, and the whole world has become a much more dangerous place: increasingly interdependent, multi-cultural, and multi-religious, but at the same time increasingly polarised. Furthermore, in the countries listed above and, more recently, in Iraq, military force has been used as a first resort instead of engaging in patient diplomacy or employing methods compatible with ethical principles and international law.

Never, in the history of the human race, has there been simultaneously such a capacity for mutual understanding and such a capacity for global destruction, such a wealth of information and yet such a dearth of wisdom and understanding. Despite the increasing interdependence of all nations, both economic and ecological, the astonishing new means of communication at our disposal, and the revolutionary growth of computer technology, enabling us to store an almost infinite quantity of data, there is as much fear, hatred, prejudice, insecurity, ignorance, and misunderstanding – as much lack of real communication – as ever before.

This book grew out of a paper, which I wrote in the summer of 2001, on Islam and religious pluralism.[4] After 9/11 my determination to correct some of the negative stereotypes of Islam took on a new urgency.[5] Islam itself was in the dock. At first I thought of inviting responses from scholars of many different religious persuasions, provided that their approach to religious diversity could be defined as open or broadly pluralistic. However, there was not space within a single volume to do justice to all the major religions. So it was decided that the book should be confined to the three Abrahamic faiths: Judaism, Christianity, and Islam. Since these are sibling religious traditions, competing with one another and sharing much of the same Scripture, this gives the book a sharper focus.

I would like to thank His Royal Highness Prince Hassan bin Talal of Jordan, one of the most eloquent and learned exponents of the need for mutual understanding between the People of the Book, for finding time to write the Foreword, and of course I wish to thank the distinguished scholars who have generously collaborated with me on this project.

Ayman Ahwal, Carol Bebawi, Hugh Boulter, Dr Robert Crane, Dr Murad Hofmann, the late Dr Michael Hooker, the Reverend Canon Dr Michael Ipgrave, Dr Leonard Lewisohn, the Reverend Dr David Marshall, Mehri Niknam, the Reverend Alan Race, Nancy Roberts, Daoud Rosser-Owen, Dr Ataullah Siddiqi, Dr Tony Sullivan and Dr Seif I. Tag el-Din all deserve special thanks for their advice or help at different stages in the genesis of the book.

I am grateful to Sarah Lloyd of Ashgate Publishing for agreeing to publish this work, the late Shaykh Abdullah Sirr-Dan al-Jamal (John Ross), who introduced me to the ecumenical aspect of Islam many years ago, the late Michael Scott of Tangier, who was a walking encyclopaedia of esoteric knowledge, the late Peter Talbot-Wilcox, whose World Faiths Study Group I attended for a time, Rabbi Dr Jonathan Magonet, Principal of Leo-Baeck College, who invited me to participate in a Jewish-Christian-Muslim dialogue group which has been meeting since 1992, and the Naqshbandi spiritual master, Shaykh Muhammad Nazim Adil al-Qibrisi.

Above all, I am indebted to my wife Aisha for her moral support and constant encouragement.

Roger Boase
Remembrance Day 2004

Notes

1 Qur'anic quotations, with Surah and Ayah numbers, are generally based on Muhammad Asad (1980).
2 Footnotes have been kept to a minimum by referring to books in the Bibliography by the author's name, followed by the date of publication and the page reference.
3 Diana L. Eck, *Minutes, Sixth Meeting of the Working Group of Dialogue with People of Living Faiths* (Geneva: World Council of Churches, 1985), p. 30; cited in Smock, 2002: 7.

4   For details, see below endnote 1, p. 262.
5   See my article, "The Need to Explain", *MANNA: The Voice of Living Judaism*,
    no. 75 (Spring 2002), 6–7.

Introduction

The concept of religious pluralism, in particular the notion that no single religion can claim a monopoly of the truth, has gained wide currency during the last two decades as people have become increasingly aware of the need to break down barriers of mutual prejudice by engaging in interfaith and intercultural dialogue. Now, however, as a result of recent political events, this concept – and the interpretation of religion and culture that it presupposes – is increasingly under assault. The language of dialogue is being eroded by the self-fulfilling prophecy of a "clash of civilisations" and the nightmare of "total war".[1] This is a book of essays by Jewish, Christian, and Muslim scholars who believe in the ecumenical imperative and who respond to the challenge of religious diversity by exploring the interfaith principles and ethical resources of their own spiritual traditions. What unites them is a commitment to the vision of a just, peaceful, and multi-religious society – a vision to which all human beings can respond, whether or not they believe in the existence of God. More space is here given to Islam than any other religion because the ecumenical message of the Qur'an is not well understood.

Part One begins with an essay by the Reverend John Bowden, explaining the importance of interfaith dialogue between Jews, Christians, and Muslims. He first outlines the context of any contemporary discussion of religious pluralism, a term which he deliberately avoids defining in any systematic way. He then examines the significance of religious pluralism for the Abrahamic faiths, considering in particular the problems raised by the modern and post-modern world-view influenced by the European Enlightenment (a convenient short-hand for a complex of scientific and ethical achievements, such as modern technology and the UN Declaration of Human Rights which have their roots in the eighteenth century).[2] After discussing questions of truth in belief, he moves to the sphere of ethical values, and ends by indicating the challenges to all three faiths.

The second essay is by Professor Diana Eck who runs the Pluralism Project at Harvard University. This essay on "Exclusivism, Inclusivism, and Pluralism" comes from her book *Encountering God* (1993). Although it is a chapter in that book, it really stands on its own as an independent essay. I have placed it in this opening section because it offers a strong defence of the pluralistic approach to religious diversity and defines the three key terms used by most of the contributors to this collection.

In the third essay, Muhammad Legenhausen, an American Muslim who lives in the holy city of Qom, distinguishes between seven different types of religious pluralism and offers a critique of the ideas of John Hick. This essay is important for two reasons: first, some of the criticism that he levels against

1

Christian or liberal pluralism is persuasive; and second, although he follows the Shi'ah tradition, he expresses views about the attitude of Islam to other religions that are based on authoritative sources and are probably shared by many Muslims, although they are not entirely consistent with the more open position of other Muslim contributors to this compilation.

At this stage, I shall briefly define the terms exclusivism, inclusivism, and pluralism. The Reverend Alan Race was the first to elaborate these three general approaches to religion in his book *Christians and Religious Pluralism* (1983), although he did so in a Christian context.[3] The exclusivist rejects the truth claims of other religions in the belief that only his or her religion is true; for such a person no other religion may be a source of salvation or divine grace. The inclusivist is more broad-minded: he or she would concede that sparks of spiritual truth may be found in other religions, and would acknowledge the need for tolerance, mutual respect, and peaceful cooperation between people of different faiths; but such a person would consider other religious traditions to be in some way inferior, incomplete, or deficient. The pluralist believes that "no one creed has a monopoly of spiritual truth; no one civilization encompasses all the spiritual, ethical, and artistic expressions of mankind."[4] Such a person seeks to understand each religion on its own terms as an expression of the Divine, or path to the Divine. Religious pluralism is therefore not a neutral or descriptive term for the phenomenon of religious diversity but an ideal to strive for and a positive evaluative response to this phenomenon. It is, moreover, a response that requires great humility: "Pluralism means coming to terms with the truth claims of the other and an adjustment of one's own claims to truth. Pluralism requires a degree of 'epistemological modesty', and is uncommon in the historical record of all religions and in the doctrines of virtually all faiths."[5]

Islam is generally regarded as a religion that is hardly compatible with a pluralistic theology or a pluralistic vision of society. Muslims themselves are obviously partly to blame for this because many of them have little knowledge of, or respect for, religions other than their own. Worse still, they tend to take pride in their ignorance, forgetting that, as the Prophet Muhammad said: "Knowledge is the lost property of the believer and he should reclaim it wherever he finds it." Many of them also respond to a growing sense of social alienation, associated with globalisation, poverty, political injustice, and other genuine grievances, by reducing Islam to a militant political ideology that closely conforms to the Islamophobic view of Islam so dear to the media pundits.

Muslims have failed to publicise the pluralistic vision that is at the heart of Islam because it is a vision that many of them have lost. There may also be some hesitation about using the word "pluralism",[6] which seems to undermine the central Islamic principle of unity, or *tawhid*. Yet, as Dr Murad Hofmann says, "it is essential that the Western media and those who exert an influence on public opinion should be made aware of the true Islamic model of religious pluralism."[7] Since, for Muslims, religious diversity is divinely ordained (Qur'an, 5:48), Muslims are not only bound to respect and understand other spiritual paths in the interests of peace, justice, love, and social harmony, but they are also bound to do so in pursuit of the truth.

In today's increasingly interdependent and multi-religious world, it is vitally important to recover a sense of the sacred, to refute those who regard religion itself as inevitably divisive, and to rediscover the ecumenical and ethical principles that have been taught by all great spiritual teachers. It is not simply a matter of respecting religious differences; we have to recover the practical spiritual wisdom that unites us and makes us human. The Prophet Muhammad taught that not only all human beings but also "All creatures of God form the family of God and he is the best loved of God who loves His family best" (*Mishkat*, I, p. 247). His son-in-law Imam 'Ali urged the Governor of Egypt to remember that his subjects are "brothers in humanity before they are your brothers in religion" and should be treated with mercy, love, and kindness. As Martin Luther King said, "our loyalties must become ecumenical rather than sectional. Every nation must now develop an overriding loyalty to mankind as a whole in order to preserve the best in their individual societies" (King 1967: 190).

Every great civilisation in the past has been based on a religious tradition.[8] Modern Western civilisation has discarded, or attempted to discard, this solid basis, offering itself as a model for "backward societies" to emulate, even though many of the capitalist or neo-liberal values upon which it is based, such as individualism, relativism, materialism, sensationalism, the obsession with security, the expansion of appetites and desires into needs and rights, and the idea of productivity as an end in itself, are hollow and do not bring real happiness or satisfaction. It is certainly ironic that the modern West, which now threatens to swallow up all other cultural traditions and world-views, is deeply divided and insecure, despite its enormous wealth and power; fear, stimulated by the media and certain interest groups, is causing people to lose faith in the possibility of a free and peaceful multi-ethnic, multi-cultural, and multi-religious society. If we seek to bolt the doors and close all the windows, it is obvious that the knocking will only grow louder.[9] Peace cannot be preserved by means of war because, as Wendell Berry writes, "One cannot reduce terror by holding over the world the threat of what one most fears" (2003: 10).

Among remedies that have been proposed for the spiritual, moral, political, and ecological crisis in which we find ourselves are the following: the concept of a dialogue of civilisations[10] (advocated by Anwar Ibrahim at an international seminar on Islam and Confucianism in Kuala Lumpur in 1995 and by Muhammad Khatami, President of Iran, at the United Nations General Assembly in 1998); the possibility of reconciling economics with religion and morality so that globalisation may serve the good of the whole of humanity, instead of the interests of a small dominant minority,[11] and the project of establishing a global ethic, initiated by Hans Küng at the Parliament of the Worlds' Religions in 1993.

Religious scholars generally agree that people are capable of building their self-identities on the basis of what they hold in common with the "other" rather than, as Huntington (1996) would have it, on the basis of differences, fears, and tribal loyalties. They feel that the tendency to grade civilisations or cultures in a hierarchy according to Western criteria is obsolete. Instead of thinking of the world in terms of seven or eight civilisational groups defending their selfish and partial interests, "it would be far better to establish the mental framework for a world organization serving the interests of the human species as a whole" (Marti 2001). This is what religious leaders from around the world sought to do in 1993 when they agreed that, to prevent global order from degenerating into either chaos or tyranny, it was imperative to formulate a global ethic, representing the core moral values of the religions of the world, or "the necessary minimum of shared ethical values, basic attitudes or standards, to which all regions, nations and interest groups can subscribe" (Küng 2003: 11).

The fundamental demand of this global ethic is that every human being, regardless of age, sex, race, physical or mental ability, religion, or nationality, possesses an inalienable dignity and must be treated humanely. This demand is based on the so-called Golden Rule. As the Chicago Declaration states:

> There is a principle which is found and has persisted in many religious and ethical traditions of humankind for thousands of years: *What you do not wish done to yourself, do not do to others.* Or, in positive terms: *What you wish done to yourself, do to others!* This should be the irrevocable, unconditional norm for all areas of life, for families and communities, for races, nations, and religions. (Küng and Kuschel 1993: 23–4).

Four simple commandments derive from the practical application of the Golden Rule: "Have respect for life! Deal honestly and fairly! Speak and act truthfully! Respect and love one another!"[12] The goal of these directives is to transform consciousness: "Earth cannot be changed for the better unless we achieve a transformation in the consciousness of individuals and in public life" (Küng and Kuschel 1993: 34). Or, to cite the Qur'an, "God does not change the condition of people until they change that which is within their inner selves" (13:11).

In recent years various institutions have discussed the applicability of this global ethic.[13] It is hoped that this ethic will find its practical implementation in concerted efforts to monitor and prevent the proliferation of nuclear, chemical, and biological weapons, to introduce measures to halt global warming and to protect the environment from pollution and commercial exploitation, to support and expand the work of the International Criminal Court, to tackle the problems of poverty and world debt, and to redress the injustice that has been done to those who have been denied their political rights. In 1983 the global crisis seemed desperate: "The world is in agony ... Peace eludes us ... the planet is being destroyed ... neighbours live in fear ... children die!" (Küng and Kuschel 1993: 13). How much worse the situation now seems!

First of all, it is important to refute the immoral and illegal concept of unilaterally determined pre-emptive self-defence[14] and the paradoxical notion that liberal and democratic values can, and should, be imposed by force. We must counter the arguments of those who prepared the groundwork for neo-imperialism in the post-9/11 period, and who have said that we should celebrate "the intellectual wreckage of the liberal conceit of safety through international law administered by international institutions".[15] If the prediction of a "clash of civilisations" – or more accurately a "clash of barbarisms" – may prove to be wrong, or at any rate somewhat exaggerated, it will not be thanks to the military policies of the US administration, which have only assisted in the recruitment of suicide bombers in several dozen countries, but to the massive popular anti-war movement across the world, supported by leading world figures, such as the Pope, the Dalai Lama, and Nelson Mandela, and to those nations that have stressed the need to work within the framework of international regulations. Some credit should also be given to the many people around the world who have sought in different ways to promote civilisational or intercultural dialogue.

The essays in Part Two of this book are about Islam and the West and the idea of a dialogue of civilisations. To understand the roots of the present global crisis, it is necessary to know about the history of relations between the West and the Muslim peoples of the world. Professor Francis Robinson gives us a brilliant synopsis of this history, explaining how the changing balance of power, the memory of the Crusades, and the colonial experience produced resentment and a sense of loss, which led to the emergence of Islamic revivalist or reformist groups with a political agenda in many parts of the Muslim world.[16] Since, however, Muslims and Christians have a common Semitic and Hellenic inheritance, Robinson reflects that there are grounds for concord as well as conflict.

William Dalrymple, travelling in space and time, takes us back much earlier, giving us a glimpse of the Middle East before the intervention of crusaders and colonisers. He evokes the daily life of Christian saints and ascetics in the Middle East and the Eastern Byzantine world in the sixth century after Christ, just before the spread of Islam, by using a contemporary travel account and his first-hand experiences as source material with which to illuminate the past. Following in the footsteps of the monk John Moschos, Darymple is surprised to discover how many aspects and practices of the early Christian church have been preserved in Islam. Although saddened by the decline of Christian monasticism, he finds several places in the Middle East and the Levant where Christians and Muslims are fellow pilgrims, and he bears personal witness to the essential kinship between Judaism, Christianity, and Islam.

Professor Akbar Ahmed discusses the two competing ideas about relations between the "Western" and Islamic worlds, namely that of an inevitable clash and that of a dialogue, within the context of 9/11, and he does so with reference to the concept of globalisation and Ibn Khaldun's analysis of the way civilisations decline due to a breakdown in social cohesion. He gives a good account of the reasons for mutual distrust between the West and the Muslim world and the re-emergence of religion as a factor shaping political events. He sees the clash of civilisations as a dangerous self-fulfilling prophecy if people do not engage seriously in the task of building bridges.

Professor Fred Halliday offers some healthy and subtle reflections on the dubious theory of a clash of civilisations in an essay based on a lecture that he gave in Tunis in 1997, soon after the publication of Huntington's famous book. He discusses how difficult it is to define what is meant by a culture or a civilisation when traditions and historical narratives are being constantly reinvented, and he points out that, as a result of globalisation and global interdependence, there is no such thing as a society or culture untouched by outside influences. He advocates the need for intelligent counter-arguments to Huntington's thesis, refuting his fatalism with regard to global dialogue and his belief that international institutions and universalist principles have become in some way irrelevant.

In a paper originally given in 2002 at the time of the publication of his book *The Dignity of Difference*, Rabbi Dr Jonathan Sacks offers some profound thoughts on why, with the decline of ideology, religion has become such a divisive force in many parts of the contemporary world, and why paradoxically religion, or rather a religious paradigm that values diversity and rejects both tribalism and universalism, is also the best and only true antidote to war, violence, and intolerance.

Dr Antony Sullivan argues that, for the good of humanity and in the interests of world peace, the aggressive ideological foreign policies of Christian fundamentalists and neo-conservatives must be replaced by traditional cultural conservatism. It is within such a framework, he suggests, that Jews, Christians, and Muslims can rediscover their communalities and face together the challenge of radical secularism. He finds strong support for his politically incorrect views in the writings of Peter Kreeft and Russell A. Kirk. He also proposes that Western civilisation should be designated as "Abrahamic" rather than "Judeo-Christian", and he fully endorses the condemnation by Muslim scholars of violence and terrorism using traditional Islamic criteria.

Dr Robert Crane is worried by the role that professional Islamophobes have played in demonising Islam and promoting the paradigm of a clash of civilisations. He argues that American Muslims – and, one might add, Muslims throughout the world – have been challenged by the terrorists of 9/11 to prove that they are not collectively guilty and that their religion is not a source of fanatical extremism. In his view, the real worldwide clash is not between civilisations or religions, but within each civilisation between extremists of all kinds. He maintains that the principles of America's Founding Fathers are entirely consistent with the universal principles of Islamic law, and he proposes that Muslims must join traditionalists of all faiths in formulating a common vision for America and for the whole world in order to bring about civilisational renewal.

Dr Khaled Abou El Fadl finds that there are methodological flaws in the paradigm of a clash of civilisations, and argues that the terrorist activities and extremist ideas of Usama bin Ladin and his followers reflect a sense of alienation from modernity, on the one hand, and from the Islamic heritage, on the other, neither of which they properly understand. In his view, the theory of a clash of civilisations only aggravates the siege mentality of such groups, whose puritanical self-righteousness reflects the influence of Wahhabi and Salafi schools of thought.

Part Three, "Jewish, Christian, and Muslim Responses to Religious Diversity", begins with a lecture delivered at the Sternberg Centre for Judaism on 3 May 2002 in memory of Sir Francis Younghusband, founder of the World Congress of Faiths. Rabbi Tony Bayfield cleverly employs a literary device in order to give vent to his indignation, anguish, and despair: he assumes the part of the prosecuting angel before the court of heaven in order to indict the sibling traditions of Judaism, Christianity, and Islam for being indirectly and jointly responsible for the atrocity of 9/11.

Rabbi Dr Norman Solomon suggests how Jews might create a "theological space" for dialogue with Christians and Muslims. After discussing traditional attitudes of Jews to non-Jews, he mentions how Christianity and Islam were later accommodated within Jewish theology as religions that were preparations for the coming of the expected Messiah. He then cites the rare example of the Jewish Yemeni neo-Platonist Netanel ibn Fayyumi (d. *c*. 1164), who recognised the authenticity of the Qur'anic revelation and the concept of the universality of revelation. It is only recently, he concludes, chiefly as a result of the impact of modernity, that Jews, Christians, and Muslims have begun to abandon their "absolutist claims" and are embarking on a journey of self-discovery and a discovery of "the other" in dialogue.

The Reverend Marcus Braybrooke, who has been a member, founder, or chairman of nearly every interfaith organisation in Britain, urges people of all faiths to recognise that "each faith has a precious gift to share with the world" because each conveys a message that is both unique and universal. He gives a useful summary of the Christian inheritance of exclusivism which still colours interfaith relations, and cites a few examples of Christians who have rejected this inheritance; he gives his own definition of the terms "exclusivism", "inclusivism", and "pluralism", and explains how certain seemingly exclusivist biblical passages might be differently understood.

Father Frank Julian Gelli suggests that the concept of the Hidden God, active in the world in a variety of ways, is the best way to interpret the phenomenon of religious diversity. His general conclusion is that the difficulties associated with universalist and exclusivist truth-claims, genuine doctrinal differences, and irrational ancestral fears can only be resolved by the mystery of divine love.

Dr Murad Wilfried Hofmann gives a lucid analysis of religious pluralism and Islam. First, he discusses how perceptions of Islam have changed with the hardening of stereotypes since 9/11, and attempts to predict what may happen to Muslim minorities in the future if they reject social integration as the world becomes more polarised. Second, he summarises the Qur'anic model of religious pluralism. Third, he refutes those who would accuse him of empty theorising by comparing the history of Muslim-Christian-Jewish coexistence in Muslim Spain and elsewhere with the Christian record of intolerance, backed by an exclusivist theology. Then, after explaining the juridical status of Jews and Christians in an Islamic state, he ends with some thoughts about the ecumenical prospects of Islam.

My own contribution covers some of the same ground as the previous paper, but from a different angle. I interpret the 9/11 terrorist attacks and the manner in which the US government has subsequently responded to those attacks as assaults upon the very concept of religious pluralism. I explain why we would be wrong to imagine that Islam is inherently violent or intolerant and why we need to abandon the language of confrontation. I give an outline of the interfaith principles that are found in the Qur'an and discuss some ecumenical and ecological aspects of Islam.

Dr Jeremy Henzell-Thomas, drawing on his knowledge of linguistics and semantics, challenges the pessimistic doctrine of a clash of civilisations by identifying certain quintessentially Anglo-Saxon values that are associated with the Islamic idea of "the middle way" – moderation, tolerance, the concept of fair play, and the balance between reason and faith.

Professor Mahmoud M. Ayoub gives a brief account of religious and cultural pluralism in the Qur'an, which he feels is now threatened by the process of globalisation. He explains the confusion that has arisen as a result of the different levels of meaning in the word *islam*, referring, on the one hand, to a universal attitude of submission to the will of the Divine, and, on the other hand, to an institutionalised religion, bound by a juridical code of law. He touches on the question of whether the concept of the People of the Book can be expanded to include Zoroastrianism, Buddhism, and other faiths.[17]

The final essay is by the American visionary, conservationist, poet, and novelist Wendell Berry. War, he rightly says, is always a failure and modern warfare is so devastating that there can be no winners and no losers. I would add that military superiority is, in any case, no guarantee of security when the enemy uses guerrilla or terrorist tactics. Berry condemns the hypocrisy of those leaders who claim the moral right to manufacture and sell weapons of mass destruction while, at the same time, denying the right of their enemies to possess such weapons. How, he asks, can "internationalised capitalism", which destroys cultural diversity and squanders the earth's human and natural resources for the sake of short-term gain, serve the professed aim of national self-defence? How can peace be guaranteed by acts of violence? These are some of the disturbing questions that he raises. It is to be hoped that the essays in this book will, in some small measure, contribute to the cause of peace and make amends for the failure of war.

Notes

1   Richard Perle writes "If we just let our vision of the world go forth, and we embrace it entirely, and we don't try to piece together clever diplomacy, but just wage a total war ... our children will sing great songs about us years from now" (*Green Left Weekly*, 12 December 2001, cited in Pilger 2002: 9–10).

2   Norman Solomon once called the modern critical approach inherited from the Enlightenment "the third dialogue partner" (Bayfield and Braybrooke 1992: 147). The heritage of the Enlightenment, or the civilisation of modernity, has now become an invisible fourth presence in any interfaith encounter between the People of the Book.

3   Alan Race also discusses this typology of responses to religious diversity in *Interfaith Encounter* (2001: 21–42).

4   Sacks 2002: 62. Unfortunately this is one of the passages that the Chief Rabbi has been persuaded to delete from later editions of his book.

5   David Gordis, "John Paul II and the Jews", in Sherwin and Kasimow 1999: 131.

6 Non-Christians do not often use this word (Forward 2001: 44).

7 See below, pp. 237–8.

8 See Nasr 1989: 65–86, and Akram 2002. Traditional non-European languages do not have a word for "tradition" because in the pre-modern age people were so immersed in tradition that they had no need of the concept.

9 See *The Penguin Krishnamurti Reader,* ed. Mary Lutyens (Harmondsworth: Penguin Books, 1970), p. 97.

10 The first to coin this phrase may have been the French Muslim Roger Garaudy in the title of his book *Pour un dialogue des civilisations* (1977).

11 See Mofid 2002, Braybrooke and Mofid 2005. Dr Mofid offers an alternative to the globalisation of inequality and the globalisation of religious extremism. He argues that the economic, moral, and spiritual crises that the world is experiencing are interlinked and can only be resolved by replacing neo-liberal economics by economic globalisation for the good of humanity. In his opinion, "economics as traditionally taught – as he was taught – is simply inadequate to the profound material and spiritual challenges of the age" (Comments made by Dr James Piscatori at the launch of Dr Mofid's book *Globalisation For the Common Good,* Plater College, Oxford, 9 March 2002).

12 These are mentioned in the brochure of his exhibition, *World Religions, Universal Peace, Global Ethic,* opened at the German Embassy, London, on 17 May 2001, sponsored by the Weisfeld Foundation; see Küng and Kuschel 1993: 24–34. The Golden Rule is found in Zoroastrianism, Judaism, Buddhism, Taoism, Confucianism, Hinduism, Christianity, Islam, and the Baha'i faith.

13 See the InterAction Council's *A Universal Declaration of Human Responsibilities* (1997) (Swidler 1998: 52–66), the *Earth Charter* (2000), produced by The Earth Council, Costa Rica: <http://www.earthcharter.org/draft/charter.htm>, and the *Call to Our Guiding Institutions* (1999), issued by the Council for a Parliament of the World's Religions (Barney 1999: 108).

14 See Robert Kagan, *The Coming Anarchy: Shattering the Dream of the Post Cold War* (New York: Random House, 2000).

15 Richard Perle, "Thank God for the Death of the UN", *The Guardian,* 21 March 2003.

16 Throughout Muslim history there have been puritanical revivalist movements, such as the Kharijites who assassinated the fourth Caliph 'Ali in 661 CE and questioned the legitimacy of the Ummayad dynasty. But the modern phenomenon of Islamic revivalism – the conviction that a literalist interpretation of the Qur'an, combined with a strict adherence to the Sunnah (the example of the Prophet Muhammad), or a return to basic principles (*usuliyyah*), will resolve all the woes of the Islamic world – began in the eighteenth century as a response to Western colonialism and the challenge of modernity. This movement became increasingly militant in the 1960s when many of their leaders were tortured or executed. Some would regard religious "fundamentalism" in general is an expression of resistance to globalisation: see Tony Bayfield, "Religious Diversity and Resistence to the Globalization of Western Values", editorial, *MANNA* (October 2002). The expanding global hegemony of the USA may produce a backlash that will slow down the process of globalisation. John Gray suggests that a "partly deglobalized world would be a less tidy and more genuinely diverse world" and also "a safer world"; see "The End of Globalization", *Resurgence,* no. 212 (May/June 2002), 19–20.

17 See Shah-Kazemi (2002). In this important paper on the unity of mysticism, omitted from this book for reasons of space, he discusses key passages in the

Qur'an that are a source of inspiration for interfaith dialogue, drawing upon traditional Sufi commentators, such as Ibn al-'Arabi, 'Abd al-Razzaq Kashani, al-Ghazzali, and Jalal al-Din Rumi.

PART ONE
DEFINING THE ISSUE

He who knows one religion ... knows none.

Max Müller

Beware of being bound up by a particular creed and rejecting others as unbelief! Try to make yourself a prime matter for all forms of religious belief. God is greater and wider than to be confined to one particular creed to the exclusion of others. For He says, "Wherever you turn, there is the Face of God" Qur'an, 2:115.

Ibn 'Arabi

We not only need to understand one another, we need one another to understand ourselves.

Jean Halperin

We are like little fish with their mouths open wanting to swallow the ocean.

Shaykh Nazim al-Qibrisi

Man is ... the only animal that has the True Religion – several of them. He is the only animal that loves his neighbour as himself and cuts his throat, if his theology isn't straight. He has made a graveyard of the globe in trying his honest best to smooth his brother's path to happiness and heaven.

Mark Twain

Chapter 1

Religious Pluralism and the Heritage of the Enlightenment[1]

John Bowden

What is Religious Pluralism?

For almost 1500 years the three great monotheistic faiths – Judaism, Christianity, and Islam – have lived together, for better or worse, in relationships ranging from mutual respect and toleration to persecution. Moreover, the world into which they came knew of yet other religions, even if the Abrahamic faiths often dismissed these in disparaging terms as idolatry or superstition, and more new religions have emerged, or have been discovered, during the course of their history. So there is a sense in which religious pluralism as a phenomenon has always been with us.

There has been religious pluralism in a second sense, too. Neither Judaism, nor Christianity, nor Islam is a monolithic block. Within each faith, as it has developed, differences of opinion and tradition, not to mention geographical and cultural factors, have led to variant and often rival forms of belief and practice, and to divisions of greater or lesser severity. So there is also religious pluralism within each of the monotheistic faiths.

However, the religious pluralism that has become such a major issue at the beginning of the twenty-first century differs quite substantially from these two other forms. What sets it apart is the rise of a tradition, rooted in the eighteenth-century European Enlightenment, which has shaped so many features of the present-day world. From that tradition developed what is often called "secularisation", originally the withdrawal of areas of life from religious control, and the autonomy of the natural sciences. An autonomous scientific approach has had success in so many areas of theory and practice that it has been claimed that it possesses a method and an explanation which can be extended to all areas of life and knowledge, and this in turn has established widely a world-view which assumes that its standpoint is the one from which everything else must be looked at.

Those who adopt this standpoint emphasise in particular that it is essentially a relative one: there is relativity in all things, not only in science but also in history and in cultural values, including religion. They point out that in the cultural sphere the natural way of explaining things is in terms of how they came to be, that this process of coming into being is essentially historical, that values are created over the course of time rather than received from some absolute source, and that therefore there are no absolutes. In this context,

13

"religious pluralism" is a term which simply describes the fact that there are many different religions; how one understands the existence of these religions depends on the standpoint one adopts. But the existence of this religious diversity inevitably tells against absoluteness. Those who adopt this new standpoint, which lies outside all religions and holds itself to be autonomous, note that the very fact that more than one religion lays claim to absoluteness demonstrates the relativity of the claims to absoluteness: the claim to absoluteness can thus be explained, for example, as the characteristic of a particular type of faith community. That community is saying something about itself and its attitude, but the actual claim cannot be universalised in the strict sense. This all-pervasive relativism lies at the heart of the real problem of religious pluralism as posed today, and it is a very perplexing and serious one.

Religion, Truth, and Tolerance

The tradition that began with the European Enlightenment showed consider-able hostility to religion, and with the theoretical and practical successes of the natural sciences, it began to look in some areas as if religious belief had had its day. Since the resources of science and technology gave Europe, and later the United States, the power to expand, colonise, and control large areas of the world, "Enlightenment" attitudes also spread far beyond the lands of their origin and even seemed to be shaping a new global consciousness. As late as the 1960s, there was widespread talk of "the death of God" and a totally secular world.

However, religious belief has refused to die, and in many respects today it seems as strong as ever. In Judaism, Christianity, and Islam there is a resurgence of groups who have turned their back on many aspects of the modern world (though it is proving impossible for them to reject all the fruits of the Enlightenment): the so-called "fundamentalists" (not a happy term, which raises all kinds of problems, but one which has become almost indispensable shorthand). New religions of every kind, often taking the form of sects, have mushroomed, and there is a renewed recognition, in a world that has become so problematical and so threatening, of a human need for a religious dimension.

"Fundamentalists" are, by nature, intolerant of those who differ from them, because they are convinced that they are the ones who embody the true faith in their beliefs and practices. But they are not the only ones to be involved in what could almost be said to be a religious revival. Elsewhere there is widespread interest in religions of every kind, as part of an apparent spiritual hunger for something more than the material. However, there seems to be little interest or concern in the truth-content of this kind of religion. While respect for religious feelings has become an important part of the social code which is enforced in many Western democratic countries, it is hard to find anywhere any wider discussion outside more narrowly academic circles of what might be the truth of any religious beliefs in a modern context. As a result, for example, in "New Age" religion, many of those types of beliefs which Judaism, Christianity, and

Islam once dismissed as superstition or idolatry are enjoying an equal status with the great faiths in predominantly secular societies.

Respect for religious feelings is clearly not enough. Religious feelings do not just drop down to us from heaven; psychologists (themselves part of the Enlightenment tradition!) have shown us how many religious leanings stem from the earliest, primitive experiences of the human race, and how one of the important roles of the great faiths like Judaism, Christianity, or Islam has been to counter them or purge them. Thus the conflict between true religion and fake religion is still very much alive in our age. Here the great faiths may even welcome the help of insights from the Enlightenment to resolve it. At all events, the question of truth in religion is not one that can be avoided, and in the present climate merely to lay claim to truth in a way which is not open to discussion, or to dismiss the truth-question as irrelevant or unanswerable, is not enough.

Equally, it is not enough to leave unquestioned the account of itself given by the Enlightenment tradition. Impressive though many of its scientific achievements may have been, the problems it has caused are becoming increasingly evident – so evident that, in some religious traditions, there are increasing moves to belittle it or to reject it. But there is no going back in history and unmaking the Enlightenment: the questions that it raises go too deep for those who have been introduced to them to be able to forget that they were ever asked.

Religious Pluralism and the Abrahamic Faiths

At this point it is necessary to move on from the general to the more specific. What specific questions does religious pluralism pose for Jews, Christians, and Muslims, and how should they respond to these questions?

Here it may be helpful to look at two particularly important issues. How are Jews, Christians, and Muslims to understand one another – and those of yet other faiths in a world of religious pluralism? And second, how should Jews, Christians, and Muslims react to one another in a world so strongly dominated by the legacy of the Western European Enlightenment?

These are far from being theoretical questions. There is, as noted in the previous section, a widespread feeling that many important beliefs, practices, customs, and values are being destroyed by the modern scientific culture which is sweeping the world, and that there is a concern to offer alternatives which make for richer and fuller lives, and are truer to the nature of the world and humankind. Yet conflicting solutions are only too likely to be ineffective and to make things worse rather than better. So mutual understanding and the sharing of insights and action, particularly between the great faiths, is an essential prelude to effective action.

One does not have to go along with all of Professor Hans Küng's often admirable insights and arguments at least to endorse a statement the succinctness of which has yet to be bettered:

No peace among the nations without peace among the religions.
No peace among the religions without dialogue between the religions.
No dialogue between the religions without investigation of the foundation of the religions.

More Investigation

If those of different faiths are to understand one another better, nothing is more important to strive for than deeper knowledge through encounter, shared experience, and study. Happily one of the most heartening developments of recent years has been the steady increase in dialogues between Jews, Christians, and Muslims, between Jews and Christians, Christians and Muslims, and Jews and Muslims, at a variety of levels.

Particularly important here is a deeper knowledge of the history of one's own faith and that of others. It is important to know about the times when, say Jews and Muslims lived harmoniously together in Spain, or when relations between Christians and Jews in Central Europe were atrocious, not to apportion praise or blame, but simply to understand how we have treated one another in the past. A Christian's understanding can be enriched by looking, say, at the comparatively primitive state of Western Europe at the beginning of the Middle Ages with the eyes of a Muslim living at the heart of the Arab world. An understanding of present-day attitudes of Muslims can be deepened by looking more closely, say, at the impact on them of the experiences of the last century and the early years of this one.

Investigations of this kind will inevitably lead to those issues and arguments which move believers most: disagreements over the fundamentals of faith, that is, beliefs, practices, sacred scripture. The types of disagreement differ, depending on the faith, but they do exist in each faith. At this point the questions may well rightly move beyond those which can appropriately and profitably be raised in discussions involving those outside the faith in which they arise, but they can certainly be examined in another important context: self-criticism.

Self-Criticism

In the history, and indeed in the present condition, of Judaism, Christianity, and Islam, there is much for which each faith has good reason to feel ashamed. The gap between ideal and reality has often been considerable, and there have been disastrous failures. In the past, these failures have been identified and castigated within the faith itself by those who have not felt responsible for them and blamed them on "the others", and have also been singled out for hostile attacks by those of other faiths. All this has reinforced a sense of self-righteousness and has hardly improved matters.

But the failures remain, and in some way or another it is necessary to come to terms with them. Self-criticism is not an exercise in which members of any faith have engaged in publicly to any great extent, and it asks a great deal of anyone who ventures on it, but if mutual understanding is to grow it is vitally necessary; indeed, self-criticism is perhaps the most important thing that the great faiths have to learn in a pluralist world in which so much is open to public examination and comment and in which the acquisition of knowledge cannot be restricted. At the very least, expressions of self-criticism, even if they arouse opposition among the faith concerned, do send out messages to those who are working for a wider reconciliation and give them some hope that a more generous relationship between faiths may be achieved. Those who feel able to recognise their own failings may be more ready to recognise the failings of others for what they are.

But by what criteria is self-criticism to be engaged in? Is it possible to engage in self-criticism simply on the basis of one's own tradition? Is it just that one's own faith has failed to live up to its best ideals and teachings? Is not self-criticism also prompted by the recognition that other faiths have better insights in particular areas which need to be taken into account? And above all, is it not prompted by the fact that those standing in the Enlightenment tradition, outside any specifically religious faith at all, have seen things to which religious believers have been blind? The role of women in society is a particularly demanding test case here.

The Relevance of the Enlightenment

Wherever one turns, the Enlightenment and its consequences inevitably keep resurfacing. The question of self-criticism, which has just been raised, brings up the issue of Enlightenment values, such as human rights, a concept which, while understandably problematical to some faiths, as we shall see, is nevertheless regarded by many as a major achievement in the modern world.

But the Enlightenment also becomes an issue in other far less controversial areas, such as the study of faiths, which were mentioned above. It is important to know the history of our faiths, their traditions, the origin of their fundamental beliefs. But how is that to be done? For any one living in our world by the methods pioneered by the Enlightenment, these methods have had enormous success in digging up the secrets of the past, in discovering sacred sites from antiquity, in reconstructing past cultural worlds, in tracing the development of past conflicts, in identifying new documentary sources and dating them, in purifying the tradition, in establishing reliable texts of sacred scriptures, in giving voices suppressed by victorious opponents a new hearing. And all this has been widely welcomed.

But where do we call a halt? What happens when critical methods are applied to the very processes by which sacred scripture, tradition, and dogma were established, casting doubts on the legitimacy of the development? What happens if these methods become an acid that eats away at the very concept of sacred scripture, tradition, and dogma?

This is a question with which, by virtue of their particular history, Christianity and Judaism have lived for many centuries, and which Islam, by virtue of its very different history, has largely been spared. But it is a question that is hard to ignore: once you begin on the slippery slope of the investigation of the past by Enlightenment methods, where do you stop? The historical-critical examination of their holy scripture is something which Christians and Jews have long since accepted and attempted to come to terms with, with varying degrees of success; so far its application within Islam has been largely resisted.

Is that a good thing? Is it a weakness? What criteria do we use for arriving at our judgement? Here again it becomes all too evident what a grip the Enlightenment has on us. Can an appeal to divine revelation alone still be enough when, as we saw above, the very plurality of such appeals itself poses a problem? These are questions that will continue to hang over all faiths. But it could be argued that there are more urgent practical matters to consider, particularly given the breakdown of moral values that is now so evident a mark of many modern societies. How is religious pluralism to be regarded against this background?

A Global Ethic

The attempts to develop a "global ethic", as evidenced in the Declaration toward a Global Ethic, approved by The Parliament of the World's Religions in Chicago in 1993, and taken further by the writings of Professor Hans Küng of Tübingen and his Global Ethic Foundation, are an important step forward. The conviction underlying this approach is that an enormous amount could be achieved for the human race if the great religions, their leaders and teachers, with all the means and possibilities at their disposal, were to lend their support to the promotion of ethical demands fundamental to all religions, such as "You shall not kill", "You shall not steal", "You shall not lie", "You shall not commit sexual immorality".

The vision is a noble one and has been widely endorsed. Moreover, the approach adopted – avoiding points of dissent and controversy, and starting from established consensus – might seem, at first sight, to avoid some of the problems touched on earlier. However, as soon as the four "irrevocable directives" begin to be filled out, criticisms have already been expressed, and when these criticisms are examined closely, it can be seen that the severest of them claim that, despite the good intentions of the basic approach, it is still very influenced by Western, Enlightenment ideals.

Moreover, Hans Küng has made it clear that, in his view, in all religions, one should always ask self-critically what the original nature of that religion really was – his expectation apparently being that if one could get back to this "original nature", the religions would prove to be closer to one another than they often seem. Here again, the "Enlightenment" questions that have been outlined above become unavoidable. Indeed, as we have seen, they are already raised in the very concept of "self-criticism", since criticism requires criteria – and where are those criteria to be drawn from?

So in the end, in a pluralistic world, it is clear that there is a need not only for an exploration of how the faiths can be a greater moral force, but also of how their moral values relate to those which have been established since the Enlightenment, for example, in the United Nations Declaration of Human Rights. To dismiss this as a typically "Western" document, as has often happened, is not to say very much unless a serious attempt is made to build on the positive statements in it and to formulate its valuable insights in a more satisfactory way.

If progress is going to be made, much is going to be required of the representatives of the great faiths. First of all, patience, tolerance, and understanding are going to be needed, a spirit of cooperation which takes into account all the factors which have been described above and a will to achieve something better. But second, and even more difficult, there will be a need not only to engage in courteous dialogue but also to be ready to engage in argument, to tackle differences, and indeed change. What is needed in the future has been put particularly well by the distinguished German scientist Carl Friedrich von Weizsäcker, so it is with his words that I shall end:

An encounter between the leading experiences of the cultures of the world is inescapable. The Western Enlightenment has conquered Asia; it dominates technocratic Japan, Communist China, and India as a representative democracy and growing economy – all of them, with all their problems. But thinking people in the West often long for the meditative experience of the East. Esoteric sects often have stronger wills than the churches, the membership of which is constantly decreasing.

So we are directed towards the experience of history. Human history is an incomplete advance over the very short period of a few millennia. Where it is leading is uncertain. Total catastrophe is possible, as we see today more clearly than ever before. A completion has increasingly been dreamed of.

Religion is incomplete. The Enlightenment is incomplete. Religion today can take the next necessary step only if it is quite serious about the Enlightenment. The Enlightenment can take the next necessary step only if it is quite serious about religion.

In view of this, how can we treat the differences in ethical norms, the pointers towards inner experiences, and the theologies which interpret both of these? At the beginning of work on the project of a global ethic, for good pragmatic reasons, the differences are first being allowed to stand, in a spirit of tolerance.

But tolerance is not the permanent solution. When there is tolerance, two different legitimate principles are often allowed to stand without differentiation. Co-humanity is essentially tolerant of actual dealings between human beings; indeed, it loves difference as an expression of the richness of humanity. No two people are the same, nor should they be; no two cultures are the same, nor should they be. But recognised truth is essentially intolerant of recognised error. It can tolerate the error as the view of a fellow human being, but it cannot recognise it. The Buddha said: "If you reject the insight of my teaching, you must follow your insight." That is the legitimate, indeed necessary, tolerance of the *quest for* truth. For me, as a scientist, that is spoken from the heart. But that does not mean that science relativises the truth that is sought. Only when you have recognised the insight of my teaching as true should you follow my teaching. And I, as a scientist, as a matter of course allow you to refute me if you can. Since people with religious questions seek truth, they will not ultimately go along with the tolerance which is initially accepted in the global ethic. Religion is incomplete. The true religious task will also prove to lie both in a global ethic and beyond a mere global ethic. All theologies will be fundamentally changed.

(Küng 1996: 73–4)

Note

1   This paper was requested by the Interfaith Foundation for a conference in Amman, Jordan, in November 1997, on "Religious Perspectives on Pluralism". I was asked to write it from a perspective that should be equally accessible to Jews, Christians, and Muslims.

Chapter 2

Is Our God Listening? Exclusivism, Inclusivism, and Pluralism[1]

Diana L. Eck

Is Our God Listening?

In Chaim Potok's novel *The Book of Lights*, a young rabbi from Brooklyn, on leave from his post in Korea during the Korean War, travels for the first time in Japan. One afternoon he stands with a Jewish friend before what is perhaps a Shinto shrine with a clear mirror in the sanctum or perhaps a Buddhist shrine with an image of the Bodhisattva of Compassion. We are not told which, and it really does not matter. The altar is lit by the soft light of a tall lamp. Sunlight streams in the door. The two young men observe with fascination a man standing before the altar, his hands pressed together before him, his eyes closed. He is rocking slightly. He is clearly engaged in what we would call prayer. The rabbi turns to his companion and says,

> "Do you think our God is listening to him, John?"
> "I don't know, chappy. I never thought of it."
> "Neither did I until now. If He's not listening, why not? If He is listening, then – well, what are we all about, John?"[2]

Is "our God" listening to the prayers of people of other faiths? If not, why not? What kind of God would that be? Would the one we Christians and Jews speak of as maker of heaven and earth not give ear to the prayer of a man so earnestly, so deeply in prayer? On the other hand, if God is listening, what are we all about? Who are we as a people who cherish our own special relationship with God? If we conclude that "our God" is not listening, then we had better ask how we are to speak of God at all as people of faith in a world of many faiths. But if we suspect that "our God" is listening, then how are we to speak of ourselves as people of faith among other peoples of faith?

Is our God listening? It is a disarmingly simple question, a Sunday school question, not the sort most proper academic theologians would care to pursue. But this simple question leads us into the most profound theological, social, and political issues of our time. We all know that this is not solely a question about God's ears, the capacity of God to listen, or the destiny of our prayers. It is a question about the destiny of our human community and our capacity to listen with openness and empathy to people of faith very different from ourselves. It is a question about how we, whoever we are, understand the religious faith of others.

The question of religious difference elicits a variety of responses. A collection of Gandhi's writings on religion is published under the title *All Religions are True* (1962), and that assertion is certainly one way of responding to difference. At the other end of the spectrum, there are those that assert that all religions are false and are fundamentally misguided – look at the wars and violence, the atrocities perpetrated in the name of God. A third option is to insist that one religion is true and the rest are false. Or one might claim that one religion is true and the others are partially true. Most of us have operative ideas about the diversity of religious traditions that fall somewhere along this spectrum. We carry these ideas along with us as we encounter people whose religious faith is different from ours. Even those who consider themselves quite secular employ some such set of evaluative ideas about religions in order to interpret the meaning of religion and of religious difference. We also carry with us notions of what it means for something to be true – literally true, metaphorically true, true for us, universally true.

While the interpretation of religious difference and plurality has long been a question, the close proximity of people of many races, cultures, and religions in urban environments has decisively shaped our response to this question today. In 1966, Harvey Cox began *The Secular City* with the observation that "the rise of urban civilization and the collapse of traditional religion are the two main hallmarks of our era and are closely related" (1966: 1). In the urban environment from which the gods have fled, he argued, secularism was the dominant world-view, relativising and bypassing religion, rendering it irrelevant and a private affair. In 1985, Harvey Cox noted "the return of religion" with *Religion in the Secular City*. The demise of religion had been prematurely announced. Suddenly there were Jerry Falwell and the Moral Majority; one in five adults in the United States weighed in with the Gallup Poll as an Evangelical or Pentecostal Christian.

In the "secular city" of the 1990s, we would have to report the rise of religions, in the plural. We just might be tempted to turn Cox's sentence wholly around and postulate that today the collapse of urban civilization and the rise of traditional religions are the two main hallmarks of our era. It is not that secularism is now no longer an issue, for the privatisation and relativisation of religion is still a reality to contend with. The challenge today, however, is not so much secularism, but pluralism. If one of the great issues of the secular city was anonymity, the great issue of the multi-cultural city is identity – ethnic, racial, and religious identity, African-American, Caucasian, Asian, Hispanic, Buddhist, Muslim.

In both the urban and global contexts we rub up against the new textures of religious diversity with increasing frequency. The question "Is our God listening?" poses, in a blunt way, the challenge of our encounter with real difference. Responses to this question take theological, social, and political forms. There are many types of responses, but we will explore just three possibilities, indicative of the range of interpretation within almost every religious tradition.

First, there is the exclusivist response: our own community, our tradition, our understanding of reality, our encounter with God, is the one and only truth, excluding all others. Second, there is the inclusivist response: there are, indeed, many communities, traditions, and truths, but our own way of seeing things is the culmination of the others, superior to the others, or at least wide enough to include the others under our universal canopy and in our own terms. A third response is that of the pluralist: truth is not the exclusive or inclusive possession of any one tradition or community. Therefore the diversity of communities, traditions, understandings of the truth, and visions of God is not an obstacle for us to overcome, but an opportunity for our energetic engagement and dialogue with one another. It does not mean giving up our commitments; rather, it means opening up those commitments to the give-and-take of mutual discovery, understanding, and, indeed, transformation.

Put in terms of our question, in the view of the exclusivist, "our God" is not listening to those of other faiths. For the inclusivist, "our God" is indeed listening, but it is our God as *we* understand God who does the listening. The pluralist might say "our God" is listening, but he or she would also say that God is not ours, God is our way of speaking of a Reality that cannot be encompassed by any one religious tradition, including our own.

The most significant difference between the inclusivist and the pluralist is the self-consciousness of one's understanding of the world and God. If we are inclusivists, we include others in a world-view we already know and on the terms we have already set. If we are pluralists, we recognise the limits of the world we already know and we seek to understand others in their own terms, not just on ours.

Mere plurality – diversity – is not pluralism, though often the two words are used as if they were interchangeable. We can interpret diversity as exclusivists, as inclusivists, or as pluralists. One might argue that the greatest religious tensions in the world in the early twenty-first century are not found between the Western and the Eastern traditions, between the prophetic and the mystical traditions, or indeed between any one religion and another; they are the tensions that stretch between those at opposite ends of the spectrum in each and every religious tradition. Exclusivists and pluralists – fundamentalists and liberals, wall-builders and bridge-builders – are there in a variety of forms in every religious tradition. *Intra*-religious tension is today as powerful as *inter*-religious tension. Very often the religious conflicts that flare up have less to do with *what* one believes than with *how* one believes what one believes.

The last few years have seen a burst of Christian theological discussion of exclusivism, inclusivism, and pluralism. This is important work because it amply demonstrates the tremendous diversity within Christian thinking. There is no one Christian view of other faiths. Even in the statements of today's churches there is a wide range of Christian interpretation. For example, the 1970 Frankfurt Declaration of the Evangelical Church of Germany explicitly rejected "the false teaching that non-christian religions and world-views are also ways of salvation similar to belief in Christ" (Knitter 1985: 78–9). This declaration is clearly an exclusivist statement. At the other end of the spectrum, members of the United Church of Canada meeting in Naramata, British

Columbia, in 1985 crafted a clearly pluralist statement, insisting, "If there is no salvation outside the church, we reject such a salvation for ourselves. We come to this notion of the salvation of others through being loved by Christ. We would be diminished without the others as others."[3]

Since there are many theologians who have laid out typologies of the various Christian theological positions of exclusivism, inclusivism, and pluralism, I will not do that here in anything but a skeletal and suggestive form. My point is a wider one: that these three ways of thinking about the problem of diversity and difference are not simply Christian theological positions, but are recognisable in the thinking of people of other religious traditions and in the thinking of non-religious people. All of us – Christians, Muslims, Hindus, and others – struggle to interpret the experienced facts of diversity to ourselves and to our communities, and our interpretations have social and political reverberations. Theology is not isolated from its context. If "our God" has no regard for our Muslim neighbours, why should we? Or, put the other way around, if we have no regard for our Muslim neighbours, why should God?

While we may be interested in exclusivism, inclusivism, and pluralism as theological viewpoints, it is all too clear that they are also social and political responses to diversity. We can recognise them in our churches, in our communities, and in our world. And while we speak of exclusivists, inclusivists, and pluralists as if they were entirely different groups of people, let us remember that these ways of thinking about diversity may well be part of the ongoing dialogue within ourselves. Since they represent attitudes, ways of thinking, the move from one position to another is often more of a sliding step than a giant leap. One of the continual challenges and dilemmas in my own writing and thinking is recognising the ways in which I move back and forth along this attitudinal continuum, coming from a context of Hindu-Christian dialogue, understanding myself basically as a pluralist, and yet using what some will see as inclusivist language as I widen and stretch my understanding of God, Christ, and the Holy Spirit to speak of my Christian faith in a new way. I cannot solve this dilemma, but I can warmly issue an invitation to join me in thinking about it.

"In No Other Name ... "

Every time I speak to a church group about religious diversity, someone inevitably raises a hand to confront me with a passage mined from the New Testament to illustrate the exclusivity of Christianity. If she were there, Grandma Eck would certainly have her hand up, too: "It says in the Bible, 'There is salvation in no one else, for there is no other name under heaven given among mortals by which we must be saved.' So how can you speak of the Buddha?" The statement quoted is that of Peter in Acts 4:12. It is true that it says "no other name". In those remarkable days following Pentecost, when the energy of the Holy Spirit made Peter bold in his faith, he healed a man lame from birth, saying, "I have no silver or gold, but what I have I give you; in the name of Jesus Christ of Nazareth, stand up and walk." Peter was asked by the elders and scribes of the temple, "By what power or by what name did you do this?" He was unambiguous. It was not in his own name he had healed the man, nor was it in the name of a foreign god, as the council of elders perhaps suspected. It was in no other name than that of Jesus Christ.

Krister Stendahl has often remarked that phrases such as this one "grow legs and walk around out of context". The words "no other name", despite the spirit of affirmation in which Peter must have uttered them, became words of condemnation: only those who call upon the name of Christ are saved and all others perish and suffer eternal punishment. Actually, Christians have disagreed through the ages on the meaning of "no other name". From the time of Origen in the third century, to John Wesley in the eighteenth century, to C. S. Lewis and Paul Tillich in the twentieth, there have been those who have insisted upon the universality of God's grace and the omnipotence of God to restore all creatures to Godself. And there have likewise been those such as Augustine in the fourth century, John Calvin in the sixteenth century, and the fundamentalists of the twentieth century who have insisted upon the eternal damnation and punishment of unbelievers. In the past few years two books have been published that attempt to summarise the range of meanings implicit in these words. In *No Other Name?*, Paul Knitter (1985) sets forth the array of Christian interpretations of other religions across the Protestant, evangelical, and Catholic spectrums, questions the adequacy of exclusivism as a response to the religious plurality of today, and develops his own pluralistic position. John Sanders's *No Other Name* retains the phrase as a declarative, not a question; it is what the author calls "an investigation into the destiny of the unevangelized", and it also presents a full range of Christian views on the subject.[4]

In the decades and centuries following Jesus' death, many Christians gradually transferred their Spirit-filled affirmations about Christ to affirmations of allegiance to "Christianity" and "the church". Over time, their positive affirmations about Christ somehow became sharply negative judgements about any religious community other than the church. By the time of Cyprian, in the third century, we have the famous dictum *"Extra ecclesiam nulla salus"* – "Outside the church there is no salvation." This church-centred exclusivism dominated Christian thinking for many centuries. In the sixth century, for example, we hear, "There is no doubt that not only all heathens, but also all Jews and all heretics and schismatics who die outside the church will go to that everlasting fire prepared for the devil and his angels" (Knitter 1985: 122). In the early fourteenth century we hear Pope Boniface VIII insist even more strongly on church-centred salvation: "We are required by faith to believe and hold that there is one holy, catholic and apostolic Church; we firmly believe it and unreservedly profess it; outside it there is neither salvation nor remission of sins."[5]

As a Methodist, it is always somewhat disquieting to recall that with the Protestant Reformation, Protestants were also numbered among those who would die outside the church and be plunged into the fires of hell. Gradually the official papal view on the salvation of Protestants began to change, but as late as the 1950s a notorious Catholic chaplain at Harvard, Father Leonard J.

Feeney, fulminated in Harvard Square against both Jews and Protestants in boldly exclusivist terms. "Outside the Catholic Church there is no salvation", meant just that. Finally, after months of heated controversy, Pope Pius XII confirmed in a papal encyclical that Feeney had gone too far, contravening the papal view that those who belong to the church "with implicit desire" might also be eligible for salvation. Father Feeney, unwilling to change his views, was excommunicated in 1953.[6]

Protestants have also had their share of exclusivism. Luther returned the condemnation of the Roman Catholic Church with his own brand of exclusivism. He insisted that all worship apart from Christ is idolatry and that "those who remain outside Christianity, be they heathens, Turks, Jews, or false Christians although they believe in only one true God, yet remain in eternal wrath and perdition".[7] The "false Christians" were Roman Catholics.

The great twentieth-century Protestant theologian Karl Barth takes a different starting-point, insisting that "religion is unbelief. It is a concern, indeed, we must say that it is the one great concern, of godless man."[8] Religion is here opposed to revelation, and revelation is God's initiative; it is Christ alone. All the world's religions are human attempts to grasp at God, to understand God and are set in radical distinction from God's self-offering and self-manifestation. According to Barth, the truth of the Christian message has nothing to do with its structures of "religion", it is the gift of revelation. Barth did not know much of other religious traditions, or of Buddhist, Hindu, and Islamic claims to the gift and the grace of divine revelation. When asked by the Asian theologian D. T. Niles how he knew for certain that Hinduism is "unbelief", given the fact that he had never met a Hindu, Barth is said to have responded, "*A priori* – it is a given; it derives from revelation, not experience."[9] The Dutch theologian Hendrik Kraemer followed Barth, writing forcefully of the "radical discontinuity" between the Gospel and all other religions. In the influential book *The Christian Message in a Non-Christian World*, which Kraemer prepared for the meeting of the International Missionary Council in Tambaram, India, in 1938, he speaks of other religions as but "human attempts to apprehend the totality of existence".[10] He poses two alternative ways of thinking about religious diversity: "The first maintains the continuity between the essential tendencies and aspirations to be found in the ethnic religions and the essential gift of the Christian religion ... The second position stresses the discontinuity, and takes this as the starting-point of its thinking." Kraemer finds the second position "inescapable" and Christian revelation the "sole standard of reference".[11]

Of course, Christianity is not the only religion with an exclusivist streak of interpretation. Not surprisingly, however, the exclusivist position has been most extensively developed by the monotheistic Jewish, Christian, and Muslim traditions, each with its "sole standard of reference". These prophetic Western traditions have uncompromisingly emphasised the oneness of God, the oneness of truth, and the exclusivity of the way to truth and the community of truth.

The idea that the human apprehension of truth is multi-faceted, a view developed so extensively in the traditions originating in India, is quite alien to the monotheistic consciousness of the West. "I am the Lord, and there is no other!" rings like a refrain through the biblical books of Deuteronomy and Isaiah. The Psalmist, too, addresses God in exclusive terms: "You alone are God" (Ps. 86:10), "You alone are the Most High over all the earth" (Ps. 83:18). The exclusivity is reciprocal. God says to Israel, "You alone have I chosen of all the nations on earth!" (Amos 3:2). Even though Jews also affirm the universality of God's covenant with Noah and through him with all humanity, Israel's chosenness and covenant with God through Abraham is finally an exclusive covenant.

Christians pick up on this chosenness, this covenant, transforming the language of the old covenant into a "new covenant" made with humanity through the life, death, and resurrection of Christ. The new covenant is also held to be exclusive: Christ is *the* way, the truth, and the life. Similarly, Muslims affirm the finality of the One God's revelation to the Prophet Muhammad. The *shahadah*, or "testimony" of faith, is a clarion affirmation with an exclusivist ring about it: "There is no God but God and Muhammad is God's messenger." There is nothing that can be likened to or compared to God – no image, no icon, no partner, no incarnation. The human response to this message of God is "the straight path": Islam. And since the One God is universal, so is the path of human righteousness.

It is important to realise, however, that these religious foundations of Western monotheism are not in themselves exclusivist, for they have also been the religious foundations for inclusivists and pluralists. The emphasis on God's oneness, for example, can also lead to a sense of the wideness of God's mercy that undergirds both the inclusivist and the pluralist position. Even so, it is clear that monotheism has often produced the kind of monolithic mindset and dogmatic language that has readily lent itself to exclusivist interpretations. One God alone, one Son of God, one Seal of the Prophets – and none other. And along with the oneness goes onlyness, the sense of surety about God's will that can be seen in groups like the Christian Embassy in Israel, the Gush Emunim, and the Islamic Jihad. Even outside the monotheistic traditions of the West, however, there are strains of exclusivism. In Japan in the thirteenth century, for example, the sectarian Buddhist teacher Nichiren insisted that *only* the name of the Lotus Sutra was salvific. Sheer faith in the name of the Lotus Sutra alone, exclusive of all others, would lead to salvation.

Oneness and *onlyness* are the language of identity. The exclusivist affirms identity in a complex world of plurality by a return to the firm foundations of his or her own tradition and an emphasis on the distinctive identity provided by that tradition. This identity is in part what social theorists call an "oppositional identity", built up over against who we are *not*. Exclusivism is more than simply a conviction about the transformative power of the particular vision one has; it is a conviction about its finality and its absolute priority over competing views. Exclusivism may therefore be the ideological foundation for isolationism. The exclusivist response to diversity, whether theological, social, or political, is to mark ever more clearly the boundaries and borders separating "us" from "them". It is little wonder that exclusion has been one of the tools of racism and ethnocentrism. The series of Asian exclusion acts that erected walls around a Eurocentric idea of the United States were an attempt to define an American identity, as were the 1920s Supreme Court discussions of the meaning of "Caucasian" or "white person" as qualifications for US citizenship. The language of interrelatedness and interdependence that has come increasingly to the fore as nations and peoples struggle with issues of plurality is experienced by the exclusivist as compromising and threatening to identity and to faith.

The very fact of choice can precipitate a sense of threat to identity. My own grandmothers and great-grandmothers made many pioneering choices. Anna Eck pulled up stakes in Sweden. Hilda Fritz left her windswept farm in Iowa for a homestead in the Pacific Northwest. Ida Hokanson Fritz set out for college, the first in her family to do so, and landed a teaching job in the lumber camps of Washington State. But for all the choices they made out of necessity and creativity, they did not have to choose whether to be Christian or Buddhist. They did not even have the opportunity to think about it. At most they chose to be more or less actively Christian. For many people, this is still the case today; for our society as a whole it is not. We *do* have to choose our religious affiliation more actively than those who lived a generation ago. Most of us have some opportunity to know other ways of faith and to see them for what they are: powerful life-changing and world-ordering responses to the Transcendent. I see this opportunity as a positive thing. It is clear, however, that many people experience the fact of difference as a failure of the church's mission to the "lost" and "unreached", and experience choice as threatening. The crisis of belief generated by the plurality of religions and the problems of secular culture has made the certainties of Christian exclusivism, indeed of any kind of exclusivism, more attractive.

Today's exclusivism, with its variety of fundamentalist and chauvinist movements both ethnic and political, may be seen as a widespread revolt against the relativism and secularism of modernity. This does not mean that all "fundamentalists" are conservative or traditional in rejecting the modern world. But they have not made peace with modernity or made themselves at home within it.[12] The Enlightenment heritage of modernity – the inquiry into the sources of Scripture; the critical academic study of society, culture, and religion; the historical comparison of truth claims; the evolutionary claims of science – is by and large rejected by fundamentalists. Religious truth is "a given" and is plain, simple, and clear.

In the United States, the rise of Christian fundamentalism in the 1970s and 1980s grew amidst the threat of burgeoning plurality and choice in virtually every arena of life, including sexuality and religion. Nothing could be taken for granted as a given. One could choose a hometown, an occupation, a "lifestyle", a world-view, and even a religious tradition – choices people in traditional societies do not confront as individuals. In *The Heretical Imperative* (1979), sociologist of religion Peter Berger has pointed out that the word "heresy" has its root in the Greek word for choosing on one's own, apart from the community. Today such individual choice in matters of religion, formerly "heretical", has become the modern imperative. Individual choosing is expected and necessary – even in matters of religion.

A new wave of exclusivism is cresting around the world today. Expressed in social and political life, exclusivism becomes ethnic or religious chauvinism, described in South Asia as communalism. Religious or ethnic identity is the basis on which a group campaigns for its own interests against those others with whom it shares the wider community of a city, state, or nation. As we have observed, identity-based politics is on the rise because it is found to be a successful way of arousing political energy, as was clear with the rise, however brief, of the Moral Majority in the United States, the rise of the Soka Gakkai in Japan, and the Bharatiya Janata Party (BJP) in India.

The new Muslim resurgence has somewhat different roots. The affirmation of Islamic culture against the tide of Western capitalist, materialist culture finds its voice in the new, sometimes strident, assertiveness of Islamic identity. It is little wonder that the old colonial West and its new heir, the United States, are cast in a negative light. Over forty countries with substantial Muslim populations have gained independence since the Second World War and in various ways have found Islam to be the foundation of nation building. And yet the post-colonial era has left social and political problems, and sometimes chaos, that are quite dissonant with the Islamic vision of society. This too stimulates the call to a reassertion of Islamic fundamentals. For most interpreters, these fundamentals do not permit the bifurcation of the world into the "secular" and the "religious", for the *shari'ah*, the Muslim "way", is a whole comprehensive world-view which creates a transnational community and challenges that community to a life of obedience, a life aligned with the truth God has revealed in the Qur'an.

Exclusivism often arises among minorities, or those who have a minority consciousness even if they are not numerical minorities. While some minorities are content to be minorities and to experience themselves as the salt or the leaven that improves the whole, it is nonetheless often the case that the sense of fear and threat that are especially powerful among minorities gives rise to fundamentalist or exclusivist movements. The sense of being pitted against a dominant and engulfing "other" that threatens one's identity leads to the assertion of self over or against the "other" as a form of self-protection. The exclusivism of the early church, the beloved community of which the author of the Gospel of John writes, is a good example of the way in which minority consciousness engenders a very clear sense of boundaries and some strongly exclusivist language.

There are many places where such an exclusivist, fundamentalist, or communalist position is enacted by minorities in public affairs. The sense on the part of Sikhs of being gradually engulfed in a dominant and increasingly secular Indian culture has surely contributed to the anti-Hindu rhetoric of militant Sikhs and the demand for a separate Sikh state of "Khalistan". The militant Jewish leadership of the late Rabbi Kahane and of the Gush Emunim often takes the form of anti-Arab Zionist chauvinism, gaining strength from the sense among Israelis of being under siege in an engulfing Arab world. In both cases, minority consciousness gives rise to an unbending exclusivism. This is even more the case with smaller and less powerful minorities than Jews or Sikhs. In South India and Thailand, for example, the minority Christian churches are often extremely fundamentalist theologically and exclusivist socially, in part because Christians feel they are too few to permit an attitude of openness and interrelatedness without being submerged by the majority culture.

Minority consciousness is not entirely a rational matter of numbers, however. In Sri Lanka, for example, the Buddhist Sinhalese majority has a minority consciousness. Even though the Tamils are a small minority in Sri Lanka itself, the southern Indian state of Tamilnadu, a short distance across the straits, presents a large Tamil population and a wide context of Tamil culture and influence. In India, the recent rise of Hindu chauvinism is fuelled by the sense that Hindus, though they are the majority numerically, have no power in their own land because of the proliferation of special privileges and reservations given to minorities. A new exclusive sense of Hindu identity is in the process of formation.

It is important to note, however, that some numerical minorities do not have an exclusivist consciousness at all. The native peoples of the Americas, for example, while being protective of their rites and lifeways, also see the truth in other ways and paths. Over forty years ago, Chief White Calf of the Blackfeet of Montana offered a critique of Christian exclusivism that was very expressive of Native American attitudes. As an old man, in the summer of 1958 he told the story of creation to one Richard Lancaster, whom he called his son:

> I am Chief White Calf of the Blackfeet, and I am one hundred and one years old, and I give you this story that I got from my father, Last Gun, who got it from the old men of the tribe ... You are my son and I give it to you. Only once before I tried to give this story. There was a missionary and I called him son and gave him a name and tried to give him this story but he would not take it because he said that this is not the way things were in the beginning. But I was not proud to have him for my son because he says there is only one path through the forest and he knows the right path, but I say there are many paths and how can you know the best path unless you have walked them all. He walked too long on one path and he does not know there are other paths. And I am one hundred and one, and I know that sometimes many paths go to the same place.[13]

Deep conviction about one's own path need not be exclusivist. It might be simply the evangelical or neo-orthodox enthusiasm for one's own roots, one's own people, or one's own tradition. Traditions and people of faith are continually revitalised by the return to roots and energy of new revival movements. But exclusivism is not just ardent enthusiasm for one's own tradition. It is coupled with a highly negative attitude toward other traditions. Like the missionary who would not even listen to White Calf's story, the exclusivist does not participate in dialogue, does not listen openly to the testimony of others. Exclusivism has to do not only with how we hold our own convictions, but also with how we regard the convictions of our neighbour. In a world of close neighbours, the exclusivist has a real problem: one will likely meet those neighbours. One might discover they are not anathema after all. Or one might discover that they are equally ardent exclusivists.

Is "our God" listening? The exclusivist, whether Christian, Jewish, or Muslim, feels no qualms in speaking about "our God" or speaking about "the truth". The use of the possessive with reference to God does not seem peculiar. Nor is there reticence in saying that "our God" does not listen, at least appreciatively, to the prayers of others; as Bailey Smith, the president of the Southern Baptist Convention, put it bluntly in 1978, "God Almighty does not hear the prayers of the Jew." The Christian exclusivist insists that the truth of Christ excludes all others: '*Extra ecclesiam nulla salus*' – 'outside the church, no salvation'. This voice has sounded long and loud in the churches – so much so that many imagine it is the only way Christians think about the matter.

"One Great Fellowship of Love"

While the exclusivist response may be the most loudly expressed, most Christians are probably inclusivists. The evangelical message of Christianity is not exclusive, they would argue. No indeed – the invitation is open and the tent of Christ is wide enough for all. As the words of an early twentieth-century Protestant hymn put it, paraphrasing Galatians 3:28, "In Christ there is no east or west, in him no south or north, but one great fellowship of love, throughout the whole wide earth." The hymn was written for an exhibit of the London Mission Society in 1908. At least one strong stream of the mission movement was fed not by an exclusivist theology that deemed all non-Christians to be lost heathen, but by an inclusivist "fulfilment theology" that held non-Christians to be genuine seekers of a truth found fully in Christ. That is, other religious traditions are not so much evil or wrong-headed as incomplete, needing the fulfilment of Christ. In some ways other religious traditions have prepared the way for the Good News of Christ. While not wholly false, they are but partially true. All people of faith are seekers, and Christ, finally, is what they seek. All can be included in the great fellowship of love.

In such a view, the plurality of religions is not experienced as a threat, and "others" are not seen as opponents. Rather, the diversity of peoples and traditions is included in a single world-view that embraces, explains, and supersedes them all. For Christians, inclusivism at its best may mean articulating a sense of the mysterious workings of God and of Christ among people of other faiths. Such a view, however, often hides within it a hierarchical acceptance of plurality, with one's own view of things on top. It is also a hierarchical view that goes, often unreflectively, with power. Everyone is invited in, and we are the ones who put up the tent. Others are gathered in, but on our terms, within our framework, under our canopy, as part of our system.

Is "our God" listening? C. S. Lewis, a Christian inclusivist, would say, "I think that every prayer which is sincerely made even to a false god ... is accepted by the true God and that Christ saves many who do not think they know him."[14] The inclusivist attitude is, of course, much more open than the exclusivist, but the presupposition is that in the end ours is the truth wide enough to include all. Ours are the terms in which truth is stated.

Recall for a moment how, at the close of the World's Parliament of Religions in 1893, John Henry Barrows expressed great satisfaction that each day of the Parliament included the "universal" prayer of Jesus, the Lord's Prayer. J. N. Farquhar, a missionary in India, studied the Hindu tradition with respect, but concluded in his book *The Crown of Hinduism*, published in 1913, that Christ is the fulfilment of the highest aspirations and aims of Hinduism. Not surprisingly, such inclusivism is a way of thinking that is common to people of faith in virtually every tradition. Many a Hindu would surely think of Vedanta as the culmination and crown, not only of Christianity but of all religious paths. And it is common to hear Muslims say, as did a Muslim taxi driver who took me from downtown Washington, DC, to the mosque on Massachusetts Avenue, "To be a good Muslim, you first have to be a good Jew and a good Christian. Islam includes everything that is there in Judaism and Christianity."

There is a dilemma here, for to some extent all religious people are inclusivists in so far as we use our own particular religious language – God, Jesus Christ, the Holy Spirit, the Buddha, Vishnu – and struggle with the limits and meaning of that language. As long as we hold the religious insights of our particular traditions, cast in our particular languages, to be in some sense universal, we cannot avoid speaking at times in an inclusivist way. It is important to recognise this. For instance, my Buddhist friends at the Cambridge Insight Meditation Centre do not perceive their understanding of the nature of human suffering and the potential of human freedom as a peculiarly Buddhist truth, but as a truth about the human condition which is universal and accessible to all who would look clearly at their own experience. "*Ehi passika*", "Come and see", was the invitation of the Buddha. Wake up and see for yourself. For Muslims, the revelation of the Qur'an in the "night of power" is not a parochial revelation meant for the ears of Muslims alone, but a revelation to all people, before which the proper response is *islam*, literally "obedience". For Muslims, aligning one's life with the truth God has revealed, which is what Islam means, makes all believers *muslims* with a small "m". Similarly, when Hindus quote the words of the Rig Veda, "*Ekam sat vipraha bahudha vadanti*" – "Truth is one, but the wise call it by many names", they are not claiming this to be the case only for Hindus, but to be universally true. Similarly, Christians who speak of the Christ event do not speak of a private disclosure of God to Christians alone but of the sanctification of humanity by God, a gift to be claimed by all who will but open their eyes to see it. In the words of Charles Wesley, "The arms of love that circle me would all mankind embrace!"

In the West, inclusivism has taken the particular form of theological supersessionism, as we see clearly in the progression of the prophetic monotheistic traditions from Judaism to Christianity to Islam. We not only come from the same stock, we are perpetually interpreting one another. The Christian tradition contains within its scriptures and traditions an interpretation of Judaism. For a long period, Christian theological orthodoxy held that the Christian community supersedes the Jewish community in a "new covenant" with God. The Muslim tradition, acknowledging the validity and prophecy of the Jewish and Christian traditions, claims to have superseded both of them as the final revelation of God, clarifying the distorted vision of both with the corrective lens of the Qur'an. My Muslim cab driver in Washington was right, in a sense, about Islam including an understanding of the Jewish and Christian traditions. He would no doubt object, however, to the further revelation claimed by Baha' Ullah in Iran in the mid-nineteenth century, just as Christians would reject the post-biblical revelation claimed by the Reverend Sun Myung Moon. No one wants to be superseded.

In my own Methodist tradition, the theological foundation of inclusivism is John Wesley's conviction that universal love is the heartline of the Christian message. No one could say, according to Wesley, that the "heathen and Mahometan" would suffer damnation. Far better to leave this matter to God, "who is the God of the Heathens as well as the Christians, and who hateth nothing that He hath made".[15] And who is this God? Charles Wesley's famous hymn "O Come Thou Traveller Unknown", written on the theme of Jacob wrestling with the unknown God, exclaims, "Pure Universal Love thou art!" The refrain repeats throughout the hymn – "Thy Nature, and thy name, is Love."

On the Catholic side, exclusivism has gradually yielded to an inclusivist view, seeking ways to include in God's salvation those "outside the church". It perhaps began with the discovery of what was called the New World, but which was clearly new only to the newcomers. The indigenous peoples had been there for many centuries and had never heard so much as a whisper of the name of Jesus. How was the church to think of the destiny of their immortal souls? Could a merciful God, whose providence extends throughout all creation, have condemned to hell all these who died outside the church but had never even heard of Christ? Finally, in 1854, the Vatican launched the doctrine that would later be the nemesis of Father Feeney, the doctrine of salvation to those individuals of godly faith handicapped by what was termed "invincible ignorance": "Although juridically speaking they are 'outside' (*extra*) the Catholic Church and formally not its members, yet in a vital sense they are 'inside' (*intra*) ... invisible members of the Catholic Church."[16]

With closer acquaintance, however, it became clear – often through the missionaries who knew them best – that the wisdom of native peoples, Hindu philosophers, and Buddhist monks could not simply be classified as the "invincible ignorance" of those who did not have the opportunity to know Christ. Even when they did have the opportunity to be acquainted with Jesus through the Gospel and the sometimes unappealing witness of the church, they were often not persuaded to cast off their own traditions of wisdom or spirituality. Indeed, the missionaries themselves sometimes glimpsed the wisdom of the Hindus or Buddhists among whom they worked and began to raise questions. The new attitude took a long while to ripen. It was really with the fresh air of Pope John XXIII and the Second Vatican Council (1962–65) that a new strain of inclusive thinking was born. The council drew up a statement, "The Relation of the Church to Non-Christian Religions", known by its first two words as *Nostra Aetate* (Flannery 1975: 738–42). It begins, "In this age of ours, when men are drawing more closely together and the bonds of friendship between different peoples are being strengthened, the Church examines with greater care the relation which she has to non-Christian religions." This remarkable document starts with the affirmation that all people "form but one community", citing the reference of Acts 17 that God made from one stock all the peoples of the earth, in order that they should seek after God and find God. The statement allows that God's "providence and evident goodness, and saving designs extend to all men."

Nostra Aetate is an appreciative statement of the depth of various traditions. Hindus, it affirms, "explore the divine mystery and express it both in the limitless riches of myth and the accurately defined insights of philosophy". Buddhism "testifies to the essential inadequacy of this changing world" and proposes a way of life which leads to liberation. Muslims "highly esteem an upright life and worship God, especially by way of prayer, alms-deeds and fasting". Jews and Christians especially "have a common spiritual heritage", and Jews "remain very dear to God, for the sake of the patriarchs, since God does not take back the gifts He bestowed or the choice He made."

The most quoted paragraph of the document sums up the inclusivist position:

> The Catholic Church rejects nothing of what is true and holy in these religions. She has a high regard for the manner of life and conduct, the precepts and doctrines which, although differing in many ways from her own teaching, nevertheless often reflect a ray of that truth which enlightens all men. Yet she proclaims and is in duty bound to proclaim without fail, Christ who is the way, the truth, and the life (John 14:6). In him, in whom God reconciled all things to Himself (2 Cor. 5:18–19), men find the fullness of their religious life.

Nostra Aetate goes on to affirm that the suffering of Christ was not just for Christians, but for all people, and the cross of Christ is "the sign of God's universal love and the source of all grace". The document says, "We cannot truly pray to God the Father of all if we treat any people in other than brotherly fashion, for all men are created in God's image." The Catholic theologians of Vatican II do not propose that there is salvation outside the church, but do affirm God's "saving designs" and the universality of "general revelation" through which grace is made available to all. Yet in and through all such revelation, it is the cross of Christ that is both "the sign of God's universal love and the source of all grace".

The Catholic theologian Karl Rahner went a step beyond Vatican II in his inclusivism. Like John Wesley, he takes as his starting-point the central message of the Gospel: God's universal love, the gift of God's grace, and God's desire to save all humankind. Rahner uses a splendid word, *heilsoptimismus*, "holy optimism", inviting us to "think optimistically" about the possibilities of salvation outside the church. Among the channels of God's grace, according to Rahner, are the great religions. They are "positively included in God's plan of salvation".[17] Rahner's most famous phrase is "anonymous Christians", by which he means faithful people of non-Christian religions who do not "name the name" of Christ, but who are nonetheless saved by his power and grace, even though they do not know it. Christ is the "constitutive cause" of salvation, and wherever God's saving grace abounds in the world, Christ is present, whether in name or not.

Inclusivism is an appealing way of looking at things and there is much to appreciate in inclusivist viewpoints. Whether it is Christian, Hindu, or Muslim inclusivism, this bent of mind is mostly benign toward other traditions or faiths. The inclusivist does not exclude or condemn others, is not usually chauvinistic, defensive, or self-aggrandising. Granted, an inclusivist uses his or her own language and conception – God's universal love, for the Christian, or perhaps Krishna's omnipresence and omnipotence, for the Hindu – as a way of understanding the other, but would insist that, realistically, we can only understand the world in and through the language and the symbols we have inherited from our own traditions. So in Rahner's inclusivist scheme my Hindu friends are baptised "anonymous Christians" and Muslims are saved by the mediation and grace of Christ, even though this certainly violates their self-understanding. And yet, to be fair, Rahner states explicitly that the term "anonymous Christians" is not intended for dialogue with others, but only for what we might call internal use as Christians set their own understanding aright (Knitter 1985: 128).

There is still something unsettling here. While it preserves the integrity of my own self-understanding, inclusivism often dodges the question of real difference by reducing everything finally to my own terms. The problem with inclusivism is precisely that it uses one language – the religious language of one's own tradition – to make definitive claims about the whole of reality. What about the self-understanding of the Muslim? What about her testimony of faith? What about the Jews who do not speak of being "saved" at all and would object strenuously to the notion of being saved by Christ behind their backs, making them anonymous Christians whether they like it or not? What about the Hindus who would find it an extraordinary theological sleight of hand to attribute all grace to Christ? Mr Gangadaran, my Hindu friend from South India, is a Shaiva Siddhantin. His life is infused with a sense of God's love and grace, as conveyed in the hymns of the Tamil saints, which he sings with as much gusto as any Methodist sings those of Charles Wesley. But the voices of people like Gangadaran do not really count in the Christian inclusivist frame of reference. The inclusivist viewpoint would be challenged by the independent voices of other people of faith, people who do not wish to be obliterated by being included in someone else's scheme and on someone else's terms without being heard in their own right.

The inclusivist viewpoint would also be challenged by the encounter with other inclusivisms. The Muslim, for example, who would argue that all who bow their heads and bend their wills to the one God are *muslims*, with a small "m", is an inclusivist. So is the Buddhist abbott of Mount Hiei in Japan, who, when he met Pope John Paul II, included him in the Buddhist family by pronouncing him a reincarnation of the Buddhist monk Saicho. So was my Hindu friend in Banaras who was certain that I had been a Hindu in my past

life, which explained my affinity for the holy city. So is the Vaishnava Hindu
who sees all truth and all paths as leading up to Krishna. In the Song of God,
the Bhagavad Gita, Krishna vows to receive all prayers offered, to whatever
god, in whatever name, for he is the recipient and lord of all worship:

> I am the way, sustainer, lord,
> witness, shelter, refuge, friend,
> source, dissolution, stability,
> treasure, and unchanging seed.

For those on the receiving end of the inclusivist's zeal, it often feels like a
form of theological imperialism to have their beliefs or prayers swept into the
interpretive schema of another tradition. The inclusivist, however, is often not
aware of how it feels to be "included" in someone else's scheme. Inclusivists
often simply assume, either in innocence or in confidence, that their world-view
ultimately explains the whole. From each inclusivist point of view, it does.
Mission, in its positive sense, whether Christian, Buddhist, or Muslim, is an
outgrowth of such inclusivism – the "other" is not so much dangerous as
immature and in need of further enlightenment. It was this way of thinking that
lay behind Kipling's sense of "the white man's burden" to be the bearer of
civilisation. It was also this thinking that lay behind Swami Vivekananda's
mission to bring spiritual growth to the immature and materialistic West.

Those of us who are English-speaking women readily recognise inclusivist
strategies through our own experience of language. We are said to be included
in terms and locutions that do not mention our name, like the "brotherhood of
man". Women learned the rule of thumb men provided to cope with this
problem: "men", of course, means "men and women", except in those
instances in which it does not mean "men and women". The problem with
inclusivism is clear. Inclusivism is a "majority consciousness", not necessarily
in terms of numbers, but in terms of power. And the consciousness of the
majority is typically "unconscious" because it is not tested and challenged by
dialogue with dissenting voices. The danger of inclusivism is that it does not
hear such voices at all.

The inclusivist, wittingly or unwittingly, thinks of himself or herself as the
norm and uses words that reduce the other to that which is different: non-
Christians, non-whites, non-Western. The economic inclusivist speaks of
"developing" countries, as if all will be well when they are "developed" like us.
The hierarchies built into inclusivism enable the inclusivist to assume
uncritically that racial minorities, or "third-world" peoples, or women will
come someday to share in "the system", and that the system will not change
when they do. Inclusivists want to be inclusive – but only in the house that we
ourselves have built. Such inclusivism can easily become the "communalism of
the majority". Its presuppositions are unchallenged by alternatives. When the
inclusivist really begins to listen to the voices of others, speaking in their own
terms, the whole context of theological thought begins to change along the
continuum toward pluralism.

Is "our God" listening? Of course, "our God" listens to the prayers of all people of faith, but it is "our" God who does the listening in the inclusivist view. We, after all, know perfectly well who God is, and if God is going to listen to the prayers of the Hindu uttered before the granite image of Vishnu, it is the God we know.

"There's a Wideness in God's Mercy"

For the Christian pluralist, there is no such God as "our" God. Humility or simple honesty before God requires that we not limit God to the God we know or to the particular language and image through which we know God. As Wilfred Cantwell Smith has repeatedly put it, God transcends our idea of God. We sing the hymn "There's a wideness in God's mercy, like the wideness of the sea ...." But what does it really mean to take seriously the wideness of God's mercy?

Religiously, the move to pluralism begins for Christians the moment we imagine that the one we call God is greater than our knowledge or understanding of God. It begins the moment we suspect that the God we know in Christ "listens", if we wish to put it that way, to the earnest prayers of people whose religious language and whose God we do not even understand. It is our understanding of the wideness of God's mercy that provides the theological impulse toward pluralism. And, as we shall see, it is also our confidence in Jesus, the Christ, who was open to all people, regardless of religion or status, that pushes Christians into the wider world of faith.

For Christians, to stress God's transcendence does not take away the precious particularity of the Christian tradition, but it does take away our ability to claim the comprehensive, exhaustive universality of our own tradition. There are "other sheep", as Christ himself affirms, who are not of this fold (John 10:16). There are faces of the Divine that must lie beyond what we ourselves have glimpsed from our own sheepfold. It is God's transcendence which drives us to find out what others have known of God, seeking truly to know, as it was put at the Parliament (of World Religions), "how God has revealed himself in the other". It is God's transcendence which drives us to inquire more deeply into the insights of those Buddhists who do not speak of God at all.

In a Christian pluralist perspective, we do not need to build walls to exclude the view of the other, nor do we need to erect a universal canopy capable of gathering all the diverse tribes together under our own roof. We do not need to speak of "anonymous Christians". From a Christian pluralist standpoint, the multiplicity of religious ways is a concomitant of the ultimacy and many-sidedness of God, the one who cannot be limited or encircled by any one tradition. Therefore, the boundaries of our various traditions need not be the places where we halt and contend over our differences, but might well be the places where we meet and catch a glimpse of glory as seen by another.

This does not mean we cease speaking in our own language and adopt some neutral terminology, but it does mean that we cease speaking only to ourselves and in the terms of our own internal Christian conversation. We will speak in the context of interreligious dialogue. For example, as a Christian, I will continue to speak of God, of Christ, and of the Holy Spirit. I may speak of the "wideness of God's mercy", even though the Buddhist will see this as a particularly Christian or theistic way of understanding the grounds for pluralism. The Buddhist will continue to speak of the Buddha and the Dharma, the teachings of the Buddha. And some Buddhists may insist that the "positionless position" of a non-dogmatic Buddhism is what clears the ground for pluralism. But my primary concern will not be to "include" the Buddhist in my terms, but to understand the Buddhist in his or her own terms, to test and broaden my own self-understanding in light of that encounter. Neither of us will speak as if the other did not exist or were not listening or could be absorbed into our own religious world-views. And each of us will begin to understand our own traditions afresh in light of what we have learned from the other.

In the Christian pluralist perspective, the plurality of religions is not interpreted as a "problem" to be overcome. It is a fact of our world. And it is one we must encounter creatively if we are to make sense of the world. People have always and everywhere responded to what Christians would call "God's presence" among them. Perhaps this great human movement of seeking, and of finding, is part of what we speak of as "the providence of God". Saint Paul reminded those to whom he preached in Athens that "from one ancestor God made all nations to inhabit the whole earth, and He allotted the times of their existence and the boundaries of the places where they would live, so that they would search for God and perhaps grope for Him and find Him – though He is not far from each one of us. For 'In Him we live and move and have our being,' as even some of your own poets have said, 'For we too are his offspring.' (Acts 17:26–8).

Despite Paul, there are many Christians who are happy to see people of other faiths as "searching and groping" for God, but are not so sure about the finding. In 1983, at the Vancouver General Assembly of the World Council of Churches, there was a heated debate over a single sentence in a report which recognised "the work of God in the lives of people of other faiths". Is God really at work in the lives and faith of others? Many delegates were not sure. A dozen substitute formulations were offered. There was scarcely time to consider the matter fully at the end of a steamy week in August. Finally, the assembly settled for a watered-down recognition of "God's creative work in the *seeking* for religious truth among people of other faiths".[18] In the confusion of plenary debate, delegates were finally uncertain about the "finding". But the apostle Paul was not uncertain. He did not leave others groping after the Divine. He acknowledged the finding as well as the seeking. How many Christian missionaries, like Paul, have thought to "bring God" to some part of Africa or Asia, only to find that the one they called God was already there. So if there is a "finding", is it not the imperative of the Godward heart to inquire after what has been found?

In January 1990, the World Council of Churches called a theological consultation in the little village of Baar in Switzerland to address the theological confusion among Christians about what it means to speak of God's presence among people of other faiths. Protestant, Catholic, and Orthodox theologians formulated a statement of current thinking on the matter, beginning with an understanding of creation and the implications of affirming God as the creator of heaven and earth:

> We see the plurality of religious traditions as both the result of the manifold ways in which God has related to peoples and nations as well as a manifestation of the richness and diversity of humankind. We affirm that God has been present in their seeking and finding, that where there is truth and wisdom in their teachings, and love and holiness in their living, this, like any wisdom, insight, knowledge, understanding, love and holiness that is found among us, is the gift of the Holy Spirit ...
>
> This conviction that God as creator of all is present and active in the plurality of religions makes it inconceivable to us that God's saving activity could be confined to any one continent, cultural type, or group of peoples. A refusal to take seriously the many and diverse religious testimonies to be found among the nations and peoples of the whole world amounts to disowning the biblical testimony to God as creator of all things and father of all humankind.[19]

In some ways it is not so unlike the Catholic language of *Nostra Aetate*. There is much that is necessarily inclusivist in such a recasting of Christian language. And yet there is an important point of departure here. For if Christians acknowledge – as do those of us who forged this language at Baar – not only the "seeking" but the "finding" of God by people of other faiths, then the encounter with the Hindu or Muslim is truly an opportunity to deepen our knowledge and understanding of the one we call God. It is an occasion for truth-seeking dialogue – to offer our own testimony, to hear the testimonies of others in their own terms, to wrestle with the meaning of one another's terms, and to risk mutual transformation.

Within each tradition there are particular religious resources for the move toward the active, truth-seeking engagement with others that is the distinguishing mark of pluralism. And there are people in each religious tradition attempting to think afresh about their own identity within the context of interreligious dialogue. I speak of what I call "Christian pluralism", exploring the wider world of faith as a Christian. Jews who seek a context for pluralistic thinking often speak of God's ancient and unbroken covenant with the whole of humanity – the covenant with Noah signalled by the rainbow and spanning the earth as the sign of God's universal promise. Muslims also begin with the sovereignty of God, the creator of the universe, the sole judge in matters of truth, and the one who challenges the diverse religious communities to "compete in righteousness". As the Qur'an puts it, "If God had so willed, He would have made all of you one community, but He has not done so that He may test you in what He has given you; so compete in goodness. To God shall you all return and He will tell you the Truth about what you have been disputing" (5:48). Buddhists often refer to the Buddha's teaching of the interdependence of all things and remind us of the Buddha's simple statement about the raft of *dharma*, of religious practice, as a way of crossing the river; it is a vehicle, not an end in itself. Only the fool would reach the far shore and then, out of loyalty to the raft, pack it along with him. Hindus begin with the oneness and transcendence of what they call *Sat* – the Real, Truth. It is that which becomes known to human beings through many names and forms. It is that which human beings can no more comprehend as a whole than the blind men of the parable can comprehend the entirety of the elephant.

The aim of all this religious thinking is not to find the lowest common denominator or the most neutral religious language. Far from it. The aim is to find those particular places within each tradition that provide the open space where we may meet one another in mutual respect and develop, through dialogue, new ways of speaking and listening. The aim is not only mutual understanding, but mutual self-understanding and mutual transformation. As the Jewish scholar Jean Halperin put it at an interreligious consultation held in Mauritius in 1983, "We not only need to understand one another, we need one another to understand ourselves."[20]

The British philosopher and theologian John Hick has been a pioneer in pluralist thinking. He speaks of pluralism as the "Copernican revolution" in contemporary theology. From a "Ptolemaic" Christian inclusivist position in which other traditions of wisdom or devotion were understood to revolve around the sun of the Christian tradition, their validity measured by their distance from the centre, the Christian pluralist makes a radical move, insisting that as we become aware of the traditions of Buddhists or Muslims, we must begin to see that it is God or Ultimate Reality around which our human religious traditions revolve, not any one tradition or way of salvation. As Hick puts it, "We have to realise that the universe of faiths centres upon God, and not upon Christianity or upon any other religion. [God] is the sun, the originative source of light and life, whom all the religions reflect in their own different ways" (1980: 71). For Christians this means that others cannot simply move into our own orbit, but must be seen and appreciated on their own terms, moving, as we ourselves do, around that centre which cannot be fully owned or claimed by any one tradition alone.

The World House: Toward a Practical Understanding of Pluralism

The Copernican revolution is a good image for dramatising the revolution in religious understanding that we are now experiencing. It is as dramatic as Copernicus's discovery that what we thought was at the centre of our universe turned out not to be. God always transcends what we humans can apprehend or understand. No tradition can claim the Holy or the Truth as its private property. As Gandhi put it so succinctly, "Revelation is the exclusive property of no nation, no tribe" (1962: 25).

Every image has its limitations, however, and that of the Copernican revolution and the new solar cosmos is no exception. We know today, for example, that ours is but one of a number of solar systems, so even the heliocentric universe has its limits. Anyway, the paradigm of all the great religions sailing around the centre on their own particular orbits is not entirely satisfactory. It lacks the dynamic interaction of the world in which we live. Our worlds and our world-views are not on separate orbits, but bump up against one another all the time, even collide. People of different religious traditions do not live apart, but are in constant interaction and need, if anything, to be in more intentional interrelation. A theocentricity patterned after the solar system will not carry us far as an image for our new world, for our problem is not only our understanding of Truth, but our relationship to one another. We need a more interactive way of thinking.

If the move toward pluralism begins theologically in the places where people of different traditions find an openness – and even an imperative – toward encounter with one another, it begins historically and culturally with the plain fact of our religious diversity, our cultural proximity to one another, and our human interdependence. In very practical terms, how are we all to live with one another in a climate of mutuality and understanding? Is it even possible? Those who live according to an exclusivist paradigm frankly do not wish to live closely with people of other faiths and would prefer to shut them out – which is increasingly impossible – or to convert others to their own view of the world. Those who appropriate differences, as do the inclusivists, assume that the world-view of others looks very much like their own, and the ground rules are presumed to be "ours". But those who think about life together as pluralists recognise the need for radical new forms of living together and communicating with one another.

What, then, is pluralism? The word has been used so widely and freely as a virtual synonym for such terms as *relativism, subjectivism, multiculturalism*, and *globalism* that we need to stop for a moment and think clearly about what it does and does not mean. Pluralism is but one of several responses to diversity and to modernity. It is an interpretation of plurality, an evaluation of religious and cultural diversity. And finally it is the ability to make a home for oneself and one's neighbours in that multi-faceted reality.

First, pluralism is not the sheer fact of plurality alone, but is active engagement with plurality. Pluralism and plurality are sometimes used as if they were synonymous. But plurality is just diversity, plain and simple – splendid, colourful, maybe even threatening. Diversity does not, however, have to affect me. I can observe it. I can even celebrate diversity, as the cliché goes. But I have to participate in pluralism. I can't just stand by and watch.

Religious and cultural diversity can be found just about everywhere – in Britain and Brazil, in the ethnic enclaves of the former Eastern bloc, in New Delhi and in Denver, in the workplace and in schools. Pluralist models for successfully engaging diverse peoples in an energetic community, however, are relatively rare. In the Elmhurst area of Queens, for example, a *New York Times* reporter found people from eleven countries on a single floor of an apartment building on Justice Avenue. There were immigrants from Korea, Haiti, Vietnam, Nigeria, and India – all living in isolation and fear – each certain that they were the only immigrants there.[21] Diversity to be sure, but not pluralism.

Mere cosmopolitanism should also not be mistaken for pluralism. In Cambridge, Massachusetts – which, like Queens, is highly cosmopolitan – Muslims, Christians, Jews, and Buddhists live along with many people who have no active or passive identification with any religious faith at all. The whole world seems to live in this small city. There is cultural diversity and diversity of style; anyone sitting in the sidewalk cafés of Harvard Square will observe the parade of Cambridge life. But again, the mere presence of wide-ranging religious diversity is not itself pluralism. Religious pluralism requires active positive engagement with the claims of religion and the facts of religious diversity. It involves not the mere recognition of the different religious traditions and the insuring of their legitimate rights, but the active effort to understand difference and commonality through dialogue.

Second, pluralism is not simply tolerance, but also the seeking of under-standing. Tolerance is a deceptive virtue. I do not wish to belittle tolerance, but simply to recognise that it is not a real response to the challenging facts of difference. Tolerance can enable coexistence, but it is certainly no way to be good neighbours. In fact, tolerance often stands in the way of engagement. If as a Christian I tolerate my Muslim neighbour, I am not therefore required to understand her, to seek out what she has to say, to hear about her hopes and dreams, to hear what it meant to her when the words "In the name of Allah, the Merciful, the Compassionate" were whispered into the ear of her newborn child.

Tolerance does not take us far with ideas that challenge our own. For a majority people, tolerance is simply another expression of privilege. As the philosopher Elizabeth Spelman puts it: If one is in a position to allow someone else to do something, one is also in a position to keep that person from doing it. To tolerate your speaking is to refrain from exercising the power I have to keep you from speaking ... And of course I don't have to listen to what you have to say ... Tolerance is easy if those who are asked to express it needn't change a whit.[22]

Tolerance is, of course, a step forward from active hostility. When the mosque in Quincy, Massachusetts was set ablaze by arson, when a mosque in Houston, Texas was fire-bombed at the time of a Middle East airplane hijacking, when the Hindu-Jain temple in Pittsburgh, Pennsylvania was vandalised and the images of the deities smashed, and when a group of youngsters soaped swastikas on windows and cars in Wellesley, Massachu-setts, people called for tolerance – an unquestionable virtue under the circumstances. There are many places in the world where the emergence of a culture of tolerance would be a step forward – where religious, racial, and ethnic rivalries flash into violence in Northern Ireland, in India, in the Sudan or Nigeria, or in Los Angeles or Miami. But tolerance is a long way from pluralism.

As a style of living together, tolerance is too minimal an expectation. Indeed, it may be a passive form of hostility. Christians can tolerate their Jewish neighbours and protect their civil liberties without having to know anything about them and without having to reconsider some of the roots of Christian anti-Semitism. Tolerance alone does nothing to remove our ignorance of one another by building bridges of exchange and dialogue. It does not require us to know anything new, it does not even entertain the fact that we ourselves might change in the process. Tolerance might sustain a temporary and shaky truce, but it will never bring forth a new creation.

Third, pluralism is not simply relativism, but assumes real commitment. In a world of religious pluralism, commitments are not checked at the door. This is a critical point to see plainly, because through a cynical intellectual sleight of hand some critics have linked pluralism with a valueless relativism – an undiscriminating twilight in which "all cats are grey", all perspectives equally viable, and as a result, equally uncompelling. In saying that pluralism is not simply relativism, I do not wish to side with today's slippery critics of relativism, such as Allan Bloom, who stigmatise openness and cultural relativism as new academic dogmas. My main point is to distinguish pluralism from certain kinds of relativism. While there are similarities between pluralism and relativism, the difference between the two is important: relativism assumes a stance of openness; pluralism assumes both openness *and* commitment.

Relativism, like pluralism, is an interpretation of diversity. It is also a word with many meanings. On the whole, relativism simply means that what we know of the world and of truth we can only know through a particular framework. In this, the pluralist would agree – what we speak of as truth is relative to our cultural and historical standpoint as well as the frame of reference through which we see it. What is true is always "true *for*" someone, for there is always a point of view – conditioned in multiple ways by whether one is Christian or Muslim, American or Asian, male or female, rich or poor, a prosperous farmer or a homeless refugee. Matters of truth and value are relative to our conceptual framework and world-view, even those matters of truth that we speak of as divinely ordained.

Relativism, then, to a certain extent is a commonsense interpretation of diversity. It is clear that what I hold as truth is historically relative. If I had lived in the fourteenth century, I would likely have held the world to be flat. What I hold as truth is also culturally and religiously relative. As a Christian, I know that the Muslim who speaks of justice and human community appeals to the authority of the Qur'an as energetically as I appeal to the authority of Jesus or the Bible. It is indisputable that certain "facts" of my childhood learning, such as "Columbus discovered America", were accurate only from a European point of view. From the standpoint of the native peoples of this continent, "the discovery" was perhaps more accurately an invasion. And as for morality, it is clear that in some frames of reference, the Hindu or Jain for instance, any wilful taking of life, including animal life, is rejected; vegetarianism is religiously enjoined and culturally presupposed. Through other frames of reference, including ours in most of the Christian West, there is little religious debate about the moral dimensions of what we should eat. But when it comes to the taking of human life – through war, capital punishment, or abortion – there are religious people lined up on both sides of every argument with evidence to support their views.

A thoughtful relativist is able to point out the many ways in which our cognitive and moral understandings are relative to our historical, cultural, and ideological contexts. So far, the pluralist would be a close cousin. But there are two shades of relativism that are antithetical to pluralism. The first is nihilistic relativism, which denies the very heart of religious truth. One of the common strategies for diffusing the challenge of religious and ideological difference is to insist that there is no ultimate centring value, no one life-compelling truth. For the nihilistic relativist, the impossibility of universalising any one truth claim suggests the emptiness of all truth claims. According to Spelman, the nihilist says, "If I can't maintain my position of privilege by being the sole arbiter of truth, I at least can insist that no one is".[23] If all religions say different things, this only proves that all of them are false. As we well know, nihilistic relativism is not the property of any one culture or continent today. It is a truly worldwide phenomenon, just as religious exclusivism and secular materialism are worldwide phenomena. As Abraham Joshua Heschel puts it, "We must choose between interfaith and inter-nihilism."[24]

The second shade of relativism that must clearly be distinguished from pluralism is a relativism that lacks commitment. There are relativists who are committed Jews, Christians, and Hindus who speak of commitment to "relative absolutes", recognising the relativity of those symbols we hold as "absolute". There are many more, however, who are completely uncommitted, which is why relativism is equated by some critics with *laissez-faire* plurality. Mind you, the uncommitted certainly have a place in the dialogue of a pluralistic world, but the heart of the issue with which we struggle is the difficult, potentially explosive, and potentially vibrant encounter of people with strong and very different commitments. Pluralism can only generate a strong social fabric through the interweaving of commitments. If people perceive pluralism as entailing the relinquishing of their particular religious commitments they are not interested. Neither am I.

Relativism for me and for many others becomes a problem when it means the lack of commitment to any particular community or faith. If everything is more or less true, I do not give my heart to anything in particular. There is no beloved community, no home in the context of which values are tested, no dream of the ongoing transformation of that community. Thus the relativist can remain uncommitted, a perpetual shopper or seeker, set apart from a community of faith, suffering from spiritual ennui. Indeed relativism as a view in itself is often identified with secularism and the disavowal of any religious faith.

The pluralist, on the other hand, stands in a particular community and is willing to be committed to the struggles of that community, even as restless critic. I would argue that there is no such thing as a generic pluralist. There are Christian pluralists, Hindu pluralists, and even avowedly humanistic pluralists – all daring to be themselves, not in isolation from but in relation to one another. Pluralists recognise that others also have communities and commitments. They are unafraid to encounter one another and realise that they must all live with each other's particularities. The challenge for the pluralist is commitment without dogmatism and community without communalism. The theological task, and the task of a pluralist society, is to create the space and the means for the encounter of commitments, not to neutralize all commitment.

The word *credo*, so important in the Christian tradition, does not mean "I believe" in the sense of intellectual assent to this and that proposition. It means "I give my heart to this." It is an expression of my heart's commitment and my life's orientation. Relativism may be an appropriate intellectual answer to the problem of religious diversity – all traditions are relative to history and culture. But it cannot be an adequate answer for most religious people – not for me, nor for my Muslim neighbour who fasts and prays more regularly than I do, nor for my Hindu colleague whose world is made vivid by the presence of Krishna. We live our lives and die our deaths in terms of cherished commitments. We are not relatively committed.

Pluralism is not, then, the kind of radical openness to anything and everything that drains meaning from particularity. It is, however, radical openness to Truth – to God – that seeks to enlarge understanding through dialogue. Pluralism is the complex and unavoidable encounter, difficult as it might be, with the multiple religions and cultures that are the very stuff of our world, some of which may challenge the very ground on which we stand. Unless all of us can encounter one another's religious visions and cultural forms and understand them through dialogue, both critically and self-critically, we cannot begin to live with maturity and integrity in the world house.

Fourth, pluralism is not syncretism, but is based on respect for differences. Syncretism is the creation of a new religion by the fusing of diverse elements of different traditions. There have been many syncretistic religions in history. In the fourth century BCE, the Ptolemaic kings fused Greek and Egyptian elements in the cult of Serapis to aid in the consolidation of empire. In the third century, Mani interwove strands from the Zoroastrian, Buddhist, and Christian traditions to create Manichaeism. The Mughal emperor Akbar's Din-i-Ilahi ("Divine Faith") brought together Hindu and Jain philosophy, Muslim mysticism, and Zoroastrian fire sacrifice in sixteenth-century India. To a certain extent what goes by the name of New Age religion today is an informal religious syncretism, piecing together a package of spiritual aids from Native American ritual, Hindu yoga and Ayurvedic medicine, Buddhist meditation, and Sufi and Christian mysticism. Of course it goes without saying that there is a process of adaptation and enculturation that is part and parcel of every tradition as it enters into the life of new peoples and new cultural contexts. The discussion of whether this is or is not "syncretism" is a long one and hinges too much on terminology to detain us here.

There are some critics who imagine, however, that pluralism is aimed at generating a new syncretistic religion knit together from the most universal or most interesting elements of various world religions. Or that pluralism is a kind of global shopping mall where each individual puts together a basket of appealing religious ideas. Or that pluralism will reduce each tradition to the bland unity of the lowest common denominator. So it is important to say, once again, that pluralism, while not plurality, is based on plurality. A pluralist culture will not flatten out differences, but has respect for differences and the encounter of differences. Its aim is quite the opposite of syncretism. While common language will be crafted out of the give-and-take of dialogue, there is no attempt to make up a common language, to produce a kind of religious Esperanto that all would speak.

There are religious traditions that have an open and somewhat syncretistic flavour today. The Unitarian Universalists, for example, who hold a humanitarian view of Jesus and a wide respect for other religious teachers, often include the prayers and scriptures of many traditions in their worship. The ecclecticism of some Unitarian congregations today includes neo-pagan and neo-Hindu influences as well as a strong Christian universalism. The Baha'is build a similar appreciative stance toward religious diversity into their various temples. In New Delhi, for example, there is a splendid new Baha'i temple built in the shape of a lotus and housing a number of shrines around its central sanctuary, one for each of the religious traditions, all brought together under one roof.

The aim of pluralism, however, is quite different. It is not to create a worldwide temple of all faiths. It is rather to find ways to be distinctively ourselves and yet be in relation to one another. No doubt there is common ground to be discovered along the way; no doubt there are common aspirations to be articulated. But joining together in a new "world religion" based on the lowest common denominator or pieced together from several religious traditions is not the goal of pluralism. In some ways, it is the very antithesis of pluralism.

Fifth, pluralism is based on interreligious dialogue. The isolation or dogmatism of the exclusivist is not open to dialogue. The inclusivist, while open to dialogue, does not really hear the self-understanding of the other. The truth-seeking of the pluralist, however, can be built on no other foundation than the give-and-take of dialogue. There is something we must know – both about the other and about ourselves – that can be found in no other way.

We do not enter into dialogue with the dreamy hope that we will all agree, for the truth is we probably will not. We do not enter into dialogue to produce an agreement, but to produce real relationship, even friendship, which is premised upon mutual understanding, not upon agreement. Christians and Muslims, for example, may find we agree on many things. We share prophets like Abraham and foundational values like justice. But a clear understanding of differences is as precious as the affirmation of similarities.

The language of dialogue is the two-way language of real encounter and it is for this reason that dialogue is the very basis of pluralism. There must be constant communication – meeting, exchange, traffic, criticism, reflection, reparation, renewal. Without dialogue, the diversity of religious traditions, of cultures and ethnic groups, becomes an array of isolated encampments, each with a different flag, meeting only occasionally for formalities or for battle. The swamis, monks, rabbis, and archbishops may meet for an interfaith prayer breakfast, but without real dialogue they become simply icons of diversity, not instruments of relationship. Without dialogue, when violence flares – in Queens or Los Angeles, Southall or New Delhi – there are no bridges of relationship, and as the floodwaters rise it is too late to build them.

A second aim of dialogue is to understand ourselves and our faith more clearly. Dialogue is not a debate between two positions, but a truth-seeking encounter. If Muslims assume that the taking and giving of interest on loans is morally wrong and Christians embedded in a capitalist framework never thought to question the matter, what can we learn from one another? If Buddhists describe the deepest reality without reference to God and Christians cannot imagine religiousness without God, what will each of us learn that is quite new, through the give-and-take of dialogue? The theologian John Cobb has used the phrase "mutual transformation" to describe the way in which dialogue necessarily goes beyond mutual understanding to a new level of mutual self-understanding.[25]

The Sri Lankan Christian theologian Wesley Ariarajah has spoken of dialogue as the "encounter of commitments". When dialogue was first discussed broadly and ecumenically by the Christian churches at the assembly of the World Council of Churches in Nairobi in 1975, there was much heated discussion. A bishop of the Church of Norway led the attack, calling dialogue a betrayal of Christian mission. The church should be engaged in proclaiming the Gospel to the ends of the earth and making disciples of all nations, not in interreligious dialogue, he said. There were many, then and now, who saw dialogue as a sign of weakness of faith. Ariarajah and many others have insisted that quite the opposite is true. What kind of faith refuses to be tested by real encounter with others? What kind of faith grows by speaking and proclaiming without having to listen, perhaps even be challenged, by the voices of others?

Discovering one's own faith is inherently part of the human pilgrimage. What motivates us deeply, what orients us in the world, what nourishes our growth and gives rise to our most cherished values? Every human being must cope with these questions or suffer the anxious drift of avoiding them. But our challenges on the human pilgrimage are not solved once and for all by the unfolding discovery of our own faith, for we encounter other pilgrims of other faiths. Dialogue means taking a vibrant interest in what motivates these other pilgrims, what orients them in the world, what nourishes their growth and gives rise to their most cherished values. To live together we need to know these things about one another and to risk the changes of heart and mind that may well come when we do.

There is a third aim of dialogue. Mutual understanding and mutual transformation are important, but in the world in which we live, the cooperative transformation of our global and local cultures is essential. It is surely one of the most challenging tasks of our time. Buddhists and Hindus, Muslims and Jews, Maoris and Christians have urgent work to do that can only be done together. As Wilfred Cantwell Smith so succinctly put it, "Our vision and our loyalties, as well as our aircraft, must circle the globe."[26]

Notes

1   Reproduced from *Encountering God*, by Diana L. Eck © 1993, 2003: 166–99, with the author's permission and the agreement of Beacon Press, Boston.
2   *The Book of Lights* (New York: Ballantine Books, 1981), pp. 261–2.

3 *Report on the Naramata Consultation on Interfaith Dialogue: Faithfulness in a Pluralistic World* (Division of World Outreach, United Church of Canada, May 1985), p. 2.

4 *No Other Name: An Investigation into the Destiny of the Unevangelized* (Grand Rapids, MI: Eerdmans, 1992).

5 "The Bull *Unam Sanctam, 1302*", in J. F. Clarkson et al. (eds), *The Church Teaches* (St Louis, MO: B. Herder Book Co., 1955), pp. 73–5.

6 See "Letter of the Holy Office to Archbishop Cushing of Boston, 1949", in Clarkson et al., *The Church Teaches*, pp. 118–21. A treatment of the controversy may be found in George B. Pepper, *The Boston Heresy Case in View of the Secularization of Religion* (Lewiston, ME: Edwin Mellen Press, 1988).

7 Quoted and translated from Luther's collected works in Cracknell 1986: 11.

8 *Church Dogmatics* (Edinburgh: T. & T. Clark, 1956), vol. 1, part 2, pp. 299–300. The entirety of Section 17, "The Revelation of God as the Abolition of Religion", concerns this matter.

9 Gerald H. Anderson, "Religion as a Problem for the Christian Mission", in Dawe and Carman 1980: 114.

10 London: Edinburgh House Press, 1938, p. 135.

11 Hendrik Kraemer, "Continuity or Discontinuity", in W. Paton (ed.), *The Authority of the Faith* (Oxford: Oxford University Press, 1939), pp. 13–14, 21.

12 Bruce Lawrence argues effectively that "because modernity is global, so is fundamentalism", in the introduction to his book *Defenders of God* (San Francisco, CA: Harper & Row, 1979).

13 Cited in William Kittredge and Annick Smith (eds), *The Last Best Place: A Montana Anthology* (Helena: Montana Historical Society, 1991), p. 26.

14 W. H. Lewis (ed.), *The Letters of C. S. Lewis* (New York: Harcourt Brace Jovanovich, 1966), p. 247.

15 "On Living Without God", in *The Works of John Wesley*, 3rd edn (Peabody, MA: Hendrickson, 1986), vol. 7, p. 353.

16 *New Catholic Encyclopedia* (Washington, DC: Catholic University of America, 1967), vol. 5, p. 768.

17 Gerald A. McCool (ed.), *A Rahner Reader* (New York: Seabury Press, 1975), p. 218. See especially his selections in Chapter 10 on "Anonymous Christians" and "Christianity and non-Christian religions". Cf. Race 1983, Knitter 1985, D'Costa 1986.

18 In David Gill (ed.), *Gathered for Life: Official Report of the VI Assembly of the WCC* (Geneva: World Council of Churches, 1983), p. 40.

19 The "Baar Statement" is printed in full in S. Wesley Ariarajah, "Theological Perspectives in Plurality", *Current Dialogue*, June 1990, 2–7.

20 The report of the consultation, edited by Allan R. Brockway, is published as *The Meaning of Life: A Multifaith Consultation in Preparation for the Sixth Assembly of the World Council of Churches* (Geneva: World Council of Churches, 1983).

21 Dean Kleiman, "Immigrants Encountering Choice Between Friendship and Isolation", in the *New York Times*, 24 December 1982, cited by E. Allen Richardson at the outset of his superb book *Strangers in this Land* (New York: Pilgrim Press, 1988).

22 *Inessential Woman: Problems of Exclusion in Feminist Thought* (Boston, MA: Beacon Press, 1988), p. 182.

23 Ibid., p. 184.

24 "No Religion is an Island", in F. E. Talmadge (ed.), *Disputation and Dialogue: Readings in Jewish-Christian Encounters* (New York: KTAV Publishing, 1975), p. 345.
25 John B. Cobb, *Beyond Dialogue: Toward a Mutual Transformation of Christianity and Buddhism* (Philadelphia, PA: Fortress Press, 1982).
26 *The Faith of Other Men* (New York: New American Library, 1965), p. 92.

Chapter 3

A Muslim's Non-Reductive Religious Pluralism

Muhammad Legenhausen

Introduction

There are many varieties of pluralism. In what follows, I shall attempt to define what is meant by religious pluralism and discuss its several versions. To begin with, we may distinguish *reductive* from *non-reductive* varieties. The proponents of reductive forms of religious pluralism attempt to identify a common element among different religions on the basis of which the religions are successful in some specific way, whereas, according to non-reductive religious pluralism, God guides whomever He will,[1] not only by virtue of features common to several religions but also by their unique divine qualities. While reductive pluralism holds that what is good in any religion is what it has in common with other religions, non-reductive pluralism is the view that each religion has unique features through which God may guide people. I will argue that there are good reasons for scepticism about reductive religious pluralism, while non-reductive religious pluralism makes more sense, philosophically and theologically, especially given several important features of Islamic theology.

A Plurality of Pluralisms

The term "pluralism" was first used to signify a metaphysical doctrine by Christian Wolff (1679–1754), and later popularised by William James (1842–1910). A different but related sense of pluralism is *moral pluralism*. While metaphysical pluralists hold that there is an irreducible plurality of types of substance, truths, or original principles, "moral pluralists" hold that there is an irreducible plurality of independent moral values. The two sorts of pluralism, metaphysical and moral, are eloquently linked in the work of Isaiah Berlin (1909–97). Berlin defended moral pluralism throughout his long career. Political theorists use the term for systems in which a variety of ways of life are permitted to coexist or are encouraged. Perhaps the best place to look for a discussion of pluralism in this sense is in the more recent writings of the late John Rawls (1921–2002), particularly in his *Political Liberalism*. Rawls speaks of competing comprehensive systems of thought and value (for example, various religious systems, various theories of socialism, ethical humanism, and so on) whose differences can be expected to persist in democratic societies.[2]

Rawls then attempts to show that reasonable people who hold differing comprehensive views will develop an overlapping consensus with regard to basic procedural principles of justice. Finally, there is religious pluralism, or rather, there are religious pluralisms, for the label has been used for different and often confused claims. Some writers use the term "religious pluralism" for a theological view that allows salvation for the adherents of different religions and concedes some sort of validity to a plurality of religions. Many other writers, however, use the term in a political sense, for a position that advocates the acceptance of and respect for the followers of different religions. All too often, the different uses of the term are confused.[3]

We can give a rather abstract definition of religious pluralism by saying that it is a doctrine according to which some sort of favourable attribution is ascribed to a plurality of religions. This definition has the advantage of making it crystal clear that we can expect to find a wide variety of positions that could be covered by the term "religious pluralism". The variety is so wide that the claim that someone accepts religious pluralism in this sense is almost trivial.

In order to begin to put meat on the bones of this skeletal religious pluralism, two parameters must be specified: (1) the sort of favourable attribution to be ascribed, and (2) the scope of the plurality to which the favourable attribution is ascribed. There are all sorts of positive claims that can be made for the status of one or more religions. Religions are said to contribute to mental health, to facilitate social arrangements, to lead to salvation, to be true, to be ordained by God, to have a long and rich tradition, and so on. Some of the positive things said about religions make specific reference to their adherents, while other attributions apply to the doctrines, rituals, or historical features of religions, without making any claims about their followers. For example, with regard to adherents, it has been claimed that some religions provide a framework of beliefs and practices within which some of their followers have mystical experiences. A different sort of example is the claim that the adherents of different religions are entitled to certain rights, for example, rights of worship. With regard to the content of religions, it is said that some religions prescribe beautiful ceremonies; of some it is said that their creeds are true, and of some that the rules they impose are morally commendable.

One way of stopping short of pluralism is to claim that although each religion has some particular positive status, they do not have the status *equally*. For example, a Buddhist might hold that all the major religions of the world provide means to obtain peace of mind, but that the means provided by Buddhism are more efficient, or lead to a deeper sense of peace of mind, or bring quicker or longer lasting peace of mind. I don't know of a name that anyone has given for this sort of position, although many philosophers and theologians have held it. We might call it *degree pluralism*, but we should keep in mind that many modern defenders – as well as opponents – of religious pluralism would not call this a form of pluralism at all. They define pluralism in terms of a strict *equality* of status. Peter Byrne, for example, defines religious pluralism in terms of three equality conditions:

1　All major religious traditions are equal in respect of making common reference to a single transcendent, sacred reality.
2　All major religious traditions are equal in respect of offering some means or other to human salvation.
3　All major religious traditions are equal in their inability to provide a norm for interpreting the others, and offer limited, revisable accounts of the nature of the sacred.[4]

Byrne's position might be described as a kind of *equality pluralism*, as opposed to degree pluralism. Notice also that Byrne does not speak of the equality of religions, but of religious traditions. The difference can be crucial. For Muslims, religion, or *din*, is what God has revealed to guide us to Him. Religious traditions, however, include all sorts of things that humans have gathered in their attempts to follow religion. One might be an equality pluralist about religious traditions while taking a more exclusivist view about religions; that is, one could hold that God's guidance for us is to be found in a single religion, but that the religious traditions of humankind fall so far short of what God offers us that none of these traditions can be said to be any better than any of the others. On the other hand, one could take the reverse position and hold that although God has revealed several distinct forms of guidance for human beings, so that there are several true and divinely revealed religions, the followers of all but one of these religions have gone astray by adding and subtracting to and from divine guidance in their cumulative traditions, and that one religious tradition has remained faithful to divine guidance in a manner superior to the other major religious traditions. I do not intend to defend either of these positions, but the difference between them needs to be kept clear when we attempt to evaluate religious pluralism.

Most reasonable people will agree that various good things can be said about different religions and about different religious traditions, but they will differ about what good things can and cannot be said about them. This point is made by Professor Byrne: "We should be clear from the outset that pluralism is not as such committed to saying that all major religions are equal in every aspect of cognitive endeavour" (Byrne 1995: 5). In his opinion, what is required by religious pluralism is the tripartite equality claim mentioned above, while relative superiority in other respects may be allowed. Other advocates of religious pluralism have defined their versions of pluralism with regard to other features. John Hick, for example, places considerably more emphasis than Byrne on the moral function of religion,[5] while Frithjof Schuon contends that the transcendental unity of religions is to be found in their esoteric dimensions (Schuon 1953).

In order to avoid any confusion, at least the following seven sorts of pluralism should be distinguished. Other dimensions of religious pluralism could also be defined, but the following seem more pertinent to contemporary discussions.

1. *Soteriological religious pluralism* is defined in terms of salvation. According to an "equality soteriological pluralist", a plurality of religions may be considered equally effective in guiding people to salvation. A "degree

pluralist" would hold that people may be guided to salvation through a plurality of religions, although some ways will be more effective than others, either by providing guidance that is easier to follow, or that leads to a higher degree of salvation, or that is more suitable to guide a greater number of people to salvation.

2. *Normative religious pluralism* pertains to how adherents are to treat the followers of religions other than their own. An "equality pluralist" in this regard would claim that there should be no difference at all in one's behaviour toward persons of different religious beliefs. If carried out strictly, this would prevent any sort of participation in a particular religious community, for such participation requires a special sort of cooperation based on religious affiliation. The opposite extreme from equality pluralism would be the view that seems to have been held, unfortunately, by some Muslims as well as Christians, that one has no obligations whatsoever toward those who are not of one's own faith, that their blood is permitted to be shed and their property taken. More reasonable would be the view that we are bound by certain obligations toward all human beings, although we may have additional special obligations to our co-religionists.[6] One might consider Islam to prescribe a sort of normative degree pluralism by issuing duties owed to human beings as such, additional duties owed to the "Peoples of the Book", and further duties owed to other Muslims.

Notice that despite the historical facts linking exclusivist views on salvation with intolerance, *soteriological pluralism* and *normative pluralism* are logically independent. Various forms of normative religious pluralism have been the focus of attention of a number of writers, some of whom use the term "religious pluralism" exclusively for various forms of normative religious pluralism. For example, Françoise Champion understands religious pluralism to be a political principle, and describes how it has gained currency as such in France over the last fifteen or twenty years among political analysts and sociologists. She distinguishes two main types of (what I would call) *normative religious pluralism*, which she terms *emancipatory pluralism* and *identity-based pluralism*. Emancipatory pluralism is the claim that the adherents of different religions should be granted equal individual rights. Identity-based pluralism is an attempt to go beyond the liberalism of emancipatory pluralism by recognising an equality of group rights, as has been suggested by some communitarian thinkers (Champion 1999).

3. *Epistemological religious pluralism* is the view that all the major religious creeds are equally justified according to some proposed criteria of epistemo-logical justification or warrant (see Hick 1997). This way of putting the matter focuses on the beliefs regardless of who holds them. We could call this *epistemological belief pluralism* as opposed to *epistemological agent pluralism*, which would deny that the followers of any particular religion had any epistemological advantage in their beliefs over the followers of any other religion. Of course, this would be an *equality pluralism*, which means that we should regard the followers of all the major religions as epistemic peers. An epistemological *degree pluralist* would hold that the adherents of several religions may differ to some degree in being justified in holding their beliefs,

but that these differences are not sufficient for only one group to be justified and the rest unjustified. Again, this could be defined as a *belief pluralism* or as an *agent pluralism*. It would be reasonable to expect to find differences in degree of average intelligence among the followers of different religions. The issue becomes more contentious when we consider *belief pluralism*. Some religious beliefs seem to be intrinsically harder to justify than others. Perhaps every religion has its difficult beliefs and easy beliefs, and perhaps they balance out in the end. But it would not be unreasonable to suspect that there could well be differences on the whole in the justifiability of different creeds.

4. *Alethic religious pluralism* is about the truth of beliefs rather than their justification. Unlike epistemological pluralism, there is no division here between *belief pluralism* and *agent pluralism*. An *equality pluralism* here would be the position that all the major religions are equally true. This position could be interpreted in a number of different ways. It would not make much sense to say that all the statements in the creeds of every major religion are equally true, because they contradict one another. Of course, one could adopt a relativist position on truth, but that seems a heavy price to pay. Another way to accept contradictory religious claims would be to adopt what logicians call *dialetheism*, the view that some propositions are both true and false.[7] Although *dialetheism* seems to be accepted by the great Sufi theoretician Ibn 'Arabi (Chittick 1983: 66, 112–16, 324), it does not seem a promising way to resolve interreligious contradictions. The ordinary way to be an equality pluralist about truth is to claim that the same amount of truth is to be found in the creeds of every religion. The obvious problem here is that we have no way to measure relative amounts of truth. We cannot just add up the beliefs and see how many on each list turn out to be true.

5. Religions are not theories, nor can they be reduced to their creeds. They also have a practical side. The practical aspect of religion can give rise to two sorts of pluralism. First, one might claim that the major religions counsel equally noble moralities, either with regard to the values they instil, the obligations they place upon their adherents, or the virtues they encourage. Let us call this *ethical religious pluralism*. Like epistemological pluralism, ethical pluralism may take the form of an *agent pluralism* or a *precept pluralism*. Agent ethical pluralism holds that the adherents of no particular religion are morally superior to those of any other. Precept pluralism is the claim that the moral precepts taught by the major faith traditions are equally right. Once again, this sort of pluralism can be formulated as an equality pluralism or a degree pluralism. There are two main approaches to ethical precept equality pluralism. One way is to accept a version of moral relativism. Each religion's morality is excellent by its own lights, and there is no absolute position from which one could be said to be better than any other. The other way, which is more commonly proposed, is to claim that the fundamental moral principles of all the major religions boil down to some common set of moral principles, such as the Golden Rule, and that the particular differences in moral systems are unimportant.

6. The second sort of pluralism that arises in consideration of the practical aspect of religion pertains to specifically religious obligations instead of moral

obligations. Is it possible to fulfil one's religious obligations equally through adherence to any of a plurality of religions? Those who reject *deontological religious pluralism* would give a negative answer. They hold that God has commanded all of humankind at the present time to accept a specific religion. Choice of religion is not a matter of personal preference, but of obedience to divine prescription. Those who defend religious pluralism usually take religious choice to be a matter of personal preference because of the normative pluralistic claim that no one should impose any religion on anyone. However, normative and deontological pluralism should not be confused. One may endorse normative pluralism while denying deontological pluralism, that is, one may affirm that people should make their religious commitments in accord with their own personal consciences, and reject the notion that whatever they decide is in accord with the commands given by God through revelation. Indeed, I will argue that this sort of position is more consistent with a sound Islamic theology than a blanket acceptance of pluralism.

7. The sort of pluralism advanced by writers such as Ramakrishna (1834–86), Madame Blavatsky (1831–91), René Guénon (1886–1951) and Frithjof Schuon (1907–98) could be called *hermetic religious pluralism*. According to this theory, despite their exoteric differences, all the major religions share a common esoteric core. Although the thesis of hermetic pluralism is characteristically left rather vague, it is generally presented as the claim that the major religions lead to the same goal, which is a perennial wisdom comprising various metaphysical principles. A hermetic pluralist could claim that all the major religions are equally effective means for reaching this knowledge, or merely that the ultimate wisdom is the same, or that some essential portion of it is common to the esoteric traditions of the major religions.

Historical Background

Historically speaking, religious pluralism emerged as a theological position defended as such among Christian thinkers only in the twentieth century. Prior to that there were thinkers of various religious persuasions who advocated something that today we might call religious pluralism, at least in the form of a degree pluralism, but modern religious pluralism arose specifically in reaction to widespread Christian views about salvation.

According to the traditional teachings of the Roman Catholic Church, it was held that there is "no salvation outside the Church". Since those outside the church included unbaptised infants and the Old Testament prophets in addition to those considered damned, the church taught that at the end of time the souls of such innocents would enter the church and be saved. In this way it was maintained that there were absolutely no exceptions to the doctrine that only members of the Catholic Church could be saved. This explains the severity of excommunication, which is a form of censure by which the church announces that a person who has committed a particularly grievous offence, such as heresy or apostasy, is not permitted to take part in the sacraments and is excluded from the church. The most severe form of excommunication (officially dropped by the church after the Second Vatican Council), in which a person was declared anathema, was traditionally announced in a ceremony in which a bishop, wearing violet vestments, would recite a formula concluding with these words:

> We separate him, together with his accomplices and abettors, from the precious body and blood of the Lord and from the society of all Christians; we exclude him from our holy mother the church in heaven and on earth; we declare him excommunicate and anathema; we judge him damned, with the devil and his angels and all the reprobate, to eternal fire until he shall recover himself from the toils of the devil and return to amendment and to penitence.[8]

Excommunication was carried over from Catholicism into many Protestant denominations, although some preferred to speak of "church discipline" instead of excommunication. In any case, the result of Christian sectarianism was the widespread belief that those of all sects other than one's own were destined for hell. Often the belief that a person was destined for eternal punishment was taken as license for this worldly persecution. The church's Office of the Inquisition would hand over those it found guilty of heresy to the secular authorities to be tortured and executed. It was the Enlightenment and the spread of political liberalism rather than any change in theology that finally brought these practices to an end.

A major force opposed to the view that Christians not of one's sect are damned came in the form of the ecumenical movement. This movement grew out of Protestant missionary activity. In 1910 a number of Protestant missionary societies held a conference in Edinburgh to discuss common goals and overcome sectarian antagonism in the propagation of Christianity. This eventually led to the formation of the World Council of Churches in 1948. The Roman Catholic Church took major steps toward ecumenism at the Second Vatican Council (1962–65). Not only was there an attempt at reconciliation with Protestants, but a more tolerant attitude toward the adherents of non-Christian faiths was also encouraged. Reconciliation has not been quick. It was only in October 1999 that in Augsburg, Germany, representatives of the Lutheran World Federation and the Vatican signed a statement lifting the mutual condemnations of the sixteenth century.[9] Likewise, a respect for non-Christian faiths was advocated among Protestants through the Commission of Appraisal appointed by the Laymen's Foreign Missionary Inquiry in 1932. The report of this commission, chaired by William Ernest Hocking, was seen as unacceptably liberal by conservative Christians, and Hocking defended it from charges of relativism and syncretism.[10]

The sort of religious pluralism that emerged from the ecumenical movement has tended to be a degree pluralism. One religious tradition is generally taken to have an advantage over the others with regard to the truth of its creed, the morality of its precepts, and its efficacy in guiding to salvation. However, the ecumenical thinkers allow that those not of their own sect may attain salvation, lead moral lives, and understand the truth, at least partially. Sometimes this sort of ecumenical attitude toward other religions is called *inclusivism*. The focus of inclusivism is on salvation. Inclusivism is a form of reductive pluralism as defined above, because it holds that all who are saved through any religion are saved by virtue of an element common to them. Inclusivism is typically a degree pluralism because it holds that this common element is found in its best or purest form in a single religion.

John Hick, whose entire career has been devoted to a theological defence of religious pluralism, admits that his own pluralistic theology grew out of the ecumenical spirit of inclusivism, as taught by the Jesuit Karl Rahner (1904–84) (Hick 1985: 34). Hick moves beyond Rahner's inclusivism by approaching an equality pluralism rather than a degree pluralism, and by insisting that it is by virtue of moral guidance common to all the major religious traditions that the religions are vehicles of salvation. Hick's pluralism also shares various features in common with the proponents of hermetic pluralism, since he holds that religious differences are like the masks of an ineffable Reality.

Hermetic religious pluralism was thrust into the spotlight of theological discussion by the World's Parliament of Religions held in Chicago in 1893, and promoted by Theosophists, Swedenborgians, and Transcendentalists. The Theosophists, in particular, advocated a much more radical form of hermetic religious pluralism than that which grew out of the ecumenical movement. The most articulate spokesperson for hermetic religious pluralism today is Seyyed Hossein Nasr, who would call himself a traditionalist.[11]

A Critique of Reductive Religious Pluralism

In this section I shall briefly offer a critique of the pluralism advocated by John Hick.[12] In the following section I will sketch out a non-reductive religious pluralism that seems to be on a sounder footing, both philosophically and theologically.

Hick attempts to model the rationality of religious belief on that of perceptual belief. Although it is generally agreed that perceptual beliefs are supported by our sensory experiences, there is much disagreement about what religious beliefs can or should be adopted on the basis of religious experience. Aside from this problem, commentators have expressed dissatisfaction with the ineffability of the Ultimate Reality in Hick's theory. "If we are left with nothing to be said about God or the Ultimate as it is in itself", it is argued, "our religious belief more closely approximates unbelief and becomes relatively indistinguishable from atheism" (Peterson et al. 1991: 227).

Another problem with Hick's religious pluralism has to do with the fact that religions are more than collections of doctrines. Religions have important practical dimensions, not only because of the moral codes they promote, but also because of their ritual and aesthetic dimensions. Even if the doctrinal conflicts among religions could be reconciled along the lines suggested by Hick, the practical conflicts would remain. Of course, the practical demands of a religion with a strong juridical element, like Judaism, are integrated with its doctrinal elements. The force of Jewish law derives from its source in God mediated by the prophets. To the extent that the characterisation of God presented to Jews through their prophets is considered a merely human product, the force of Jewish law is weakened. The difference between being circumcised and uncircumcised becomes a mere cultural difference. Ritual and sacrament are able to lift the believer from the mundane world to a confrontation with the Ultimate because they are special; because the Ultimate, or the representative of the Ultimate, has ordained them. While this is compatible with there being a variety of ritual ways ordained by God, the replacement of particular beliefs about the Ultimate by the notion that particular beliefs and practices are mere cultural products by means of which one approaches an ineffable Reality, reduces the specifically religious imperative. If the Jewish law is a cultural expression of God's will in no way superior to the absence of such law in Christianity, then why bother with it?

In place of the Christian doctrine of salvation, Hick formulated a broader, more abstract understanding according to which salvation is simply the human transformation that takes place when a person turns from a life of self-centeredness to a life centred on the Ultimate Reality, regardless of whether this ultimate reality is called God, Brahman, Nirvana, or the Tao. This left little place for the special role given to Christ and the Incarnation in Christian dogma. Christ is just one vehicle among many by means of which the personal spiritual transformation may be realised. Hick did not shy away from this conclusion. Indeed, perhaps his most controversial work in Christian theological circles has been the collection of essays he edited in 1977 under the title, *The Myth of God Incarnate*.[13] But Hick does not really deny the doctrine of the Incarnation, rather he reinterprets it in accordance with the theory that a person may be considered to be divine, or an incarnation of Divinity, to the extent that the person lives in accord with the Divine will. To be redeemed in Christ then comes to mean that it is through Christ in his exemplary life that one finds the way to personal transformation from selfishness to a focus on Transcendent Reality.

Hick's religious pluralism is the advocacy of doctrinal synthesis. It will not allow for ultimate differences in religious belief. No matter how strenuously the Hindu or Buddhist denies the personal nature of Ultimate Reality, and no matter how fervently the Christian asserts it, Hick would claim that there is no real conflict. Each merely expresses features of his or her own avenue to the Ultimate. This fails to do justice to the lived differences and conflicts among the adherents of the world's religions. While religious pluralism is advertised as a theology of tolerance, it turns out to be intolerant of serious religious differences.

According to liberal political theory, there is a sharp distinction between the public and private realms. Essentially private individuals posit a public realm through the social contract in order to satisfy mutual interests. Since society includes those with differing religious ideas, religion is to be excluded from the public realm. Secularism is a corollary of political liberalism. Differences in religious belief are treated as aesthetic differences, or differences in taste. The social dimension of religion is subordinated to the personal. This attitude toward religion is also reflected in the philosophy of religious pluralism advocated by Hick, because he sees differences in religion as cultural differences in the expression of belief. All the religions involve a turning of the individual from self-centeredness to Reality-centeredness, and the differences between the ways in which this is done in the various religions are non-essential, like matters of personal taste. According to reductive pluralism, preference for the Buddhist, Islamic, or Jewish ways is not to be decided by rational deliberation, for it is simply a matter of feeling, largely determined by one's cultural training. As a result of such a view, reductive pluralists, like liberals, will underrate the social dimensions of religion. The specifically religious is excluded from public discourse by the liberal because of the lack of mutual interest, and by the reductive pluralist because the specifically religious can have no cognitive import, since it is merely an aspect of personal preference.

Liberalism and reductive religious pluralism both emphasise faith over practice in religion. The fact that no one should be forced to espouse a given creed is taken by liberals as a definitive statement of religious freedom. The use of the coercive force of the state to impose laws at odds with religious codes, for example, the illegality of Mormon polygamy, is not considered to impinge on religious freedom, for what is restricted is practice, not belief. Pluralism also emphasises faith over practice in its very conception of the problem of religious diversity as one to be solved by an ultimate reconciliation of beliefs.

Liberalism and reductive pluralism both present themselves in the guise of neutrality whereas in fact they both exclude various religious systems of belief and practice. In some cases we may applaud the exclusions. No one should object to the fact that religions in which human sacrifice is a central part are stifled in liberal societies. However, while Hick is willing to allow for a hidden compatibility among a wide variety of beliefs, exclusivist beliefs themselves are to be rejected rather than reinterpreted. Reductive pluralism dismisses the exclusivist claims of any religion as non-essential, no matter how important they may be in that religion's own tradition.

As we have seen, liberalism and reductive religious pluralism both discriminate against religious views in which there is a strong emphasis on the practical social dimension of religion. This line of criticism has been levelled against Hick's pluralism by Ninian Smart,[14] who points out that the differences among religions in truth-claims are at least matched in importance by differences in practice-claims. A similar critique of the religious pluralism of W. C. Smith has been presented by Ali Quli Qarai,[15] who argues that religion has been understood as law no less than as faith in most of the major religious traditions of the world. Even if an ultimate resolution of truth-claims were a plausible suggestion, this would not resolve the conflict of practice-claims. What is distinctive and important about any given religion is not only its particular system of belief but also its rituals, ethical ideals, and laws. If a religion is valuable and worth preserving, much of its value would appear to stem from its practical side. A freedom of religion limited to freedom to believe as one chooses, but not necessarily to practise the ordinances of one's faith, would result in the devaluation of religion.

A number of recent critics, whose views are presented and criticised by Peter Donovan (1993: 217–29), have taken note of the similarity between religious pluralism and political liberalism. Both involve compromise, accommodation, and the abandonment of tradition. Some conservative Christian thinkers contend that pluralism must be rejected because it threatens to undermine the doctrines of the Trinity and the Incarnation. As political liberalism undermines the political power of the Church, so religious pluralism undermines its dogmas. Jürgen Moltmann likens pluralism in religion to the consumerism of Western society, and accuses it of a "repressive tolerance", which allows everything a subjective possibility but is sceptical about any objective reality being adequately mediated by religious symbols.[16]

Many of the critics about whom Donovan reports find common cause with post-modernistic critiques of liberalism and the Enlightenment. Donovan finds it ironic "to see the descendants of Calvin and of the Inquisition joining forces with the disciples of Nietzsche to give lessons on tolerance to the children of the Enlightenment" (1993: 219), and he observes that despite their common cause in attacking liberalism, the conservative Christian and the post-modernist are fundamentally opposed on epistemological issues, with the post-modernist rejecting the realism of the conservative, while it is precisely because of his theological realism that the conservative cannot accept liberal religious pluralism.

Donovan himself seeks to defend some form of religious pluralism and liberalism, but only in the sense of respect for differences of belief, which he calls epistemic liberalism in contrast to the ideological liberalism of modernists who seek to bring the beliefs and practices of others into line with a secular, scientistic, and humanistic world-view to form a uniform global culture. The culture of materialistic consumerism and extreme individualism associated with ideological liberalism threatens to destroy the Christian culture out of which it emerged, a culture that often seems to have been taken for granted by advocates of liberalism themselves, at least prior to the second half of the twentieth century. Although political liberalism arose out of an attempt to protect Christian culture from destroying itself through sectarian strife, the social changes that are justified by contemporary ideological liberalism are no less destructive, particularly the weakening of traditional familial relationships.

The Christian response to the onslaught of ideological liberalism and its attendant social changes has been divided between the resistance and accommodation characteristic of conservative and liberal Christianity respectively. In this conflict, the religious pluralism advocated by John Hick, W. C. Smith and others provides a theological basis for ideological liberalism. Hick claims that on the basis of the common ethical ideals of the great traditions, beliefs may be discredited if they run contrary to the dominant ethical current, such as the Jewish doctrine of "the chosen people" (Donovan 1993: 339). Indeed, although Hick is willing to open the gates of heaven to the heathen, this does not mean that he is unwilling to pass moral judgement on religions. In fact, Hick argues that since reason cannot provide any useful criterion for grading religions, the standard against which they are to be measured is moral, although even here the great religious traditions of the world are so rich and varied that they cannot be judged as totalities.

How do we weigh the savage aspects of life in some Eastern and Middle Eastern countries – the bloody massacres at the time of the partition of India, the cutting off of a thief's hands under Islamic law – against the Christian persecution of the Jews throughout the ages and above all in our own century? (Hick 1985: 85). It is clear from Hick's query that, while religious traditions cannot be easily graded, this does not mean that particular elements and practices are not to be judged. And what are the standards to be used for such judgements? Hick's answer is clear. His preferred moral response to the Ultimate Reality is modern liberalism. He does not mean to claim that Christianity is preferable to other religions because of its liberalism, but rather he invites all to moral approbation under the wide umbrella of religious pluralism to the extent that they are willing to participate in the liberal agenda, about which Hick writes:

These modern liberal ideas have indeed first emerged in the West; but they are essentially secular ideas, which have been and are as much opposed as supported within the Christian churches. Contemporary Marxist, humanist and feminist critiques of economic, racial and sexual oppression have become common currency in Western liberal thinking, and have evoked their echoes in liberation and black and feminist theologies. But it would be erroneous to conclude, from the fact that these ideas have affected Western Christianity first among the religions, that Christianity has a proprietary interest in them. Our contemporary Western liberal-democratic, politically, racially and sexually liberated form of Christianity represents a creative synthesis of the Christian tradition with secular liberalism; and analogous syntheses are beginning to emerge within the other traditions.

(1985: 86–7)

Muslims will have no quarrel with the liberal's rejection of racism, but from the standpoint of Islamic morals (and for that matter, traditional Christian morals, as well), "sexual liberation" is a euphemism for licentiousness together with its public acceptance, which has profound social consequences. While the contemporary Western liberal assimilates condemnation of homosexual behaviour to racism, the contemporary Muslim considers any sort of sex out of wedlock, like racism, to be sinful.

Hick's willingness to use his liberal standards to condemn the application of the *shari'ah* is also clearly stated:

But, whilst the enshrining of detailed seventh-century Arabian laws as permanent divine commands for Islamic societies has hindered the development of more humane and sophisticated penal systems, fortunately it has not prevented many modern Islamic states from finding ways to depart in practice from the full rigour of the traditional Shariah. It has made penal advances difficult but happily not impossible.

(1989: 336)

We can summarise the criticisms of Hick's religious pluralism as follows. First, it advertises itself as the toleration of different faith traditions while in fact it prescribes the mutilation of these traditions in order to eliminate the ultimate differences among them. Second, it considers the apparent conflicts among religious traditions to be doctrinal rather than practical, thus ignoring the importance of religious law and community. Third, by diminishing the importance of doctrinal differences, it weakens the prescriptive force of religious law. Fourth, it dismisses the use of reason as a means to advance religious understanding and settle disputes, despite the fact that such rational argumentation has been prominent in the theological or scholarly traditions of all the major world religions. Fifth, it misconstrues mysticism as a means of obtaining personal religious experiences on the basis of which beliefs may be justified. Sixth, it presupposes the correctness of the modern ethos of political liberalism, despite the fact that this, too, is inconsistent with the moral traditions of the world religions as they have been understood for centuries.

On the other hand, it is part of the appeal of Hick's programme that it does promise some form of reconciliation, some attenuation of the conflicts among religious believers which cause so much suffering in the world today, even as they have for centuries past. It would seem that an ideal approach to the problem posed by the variety of religious faiths would be one that recognised and allowed for ultimately irreconcilable differences in practice as well as theory, while at the same time providing motivation for tolerance. I believe that valuable suggestions for such an approach to the world's religions can be found within the Islamic tradition, which I shall dub *non-reductive religious pluralism*. Non-reductive pluralism is able to avoid the objections raised against liberal or reductive pluralism while maintaining an attitude of tolerance and rejecting prejudice.

In order to develop a non-reductive pluralism, it will be helpful to reflect why the sort of pluralism advocated by Hick might be expected to win little support among Muslims, and why it has won the support of an important, if small, group of Christians. The first difficulty has already been mentioned: Islam, like Judaism, features a legalistic form of piety. Its aspirations are social. No matter how miserably we fail, Muslims aspire to build a society founded on the example of the Prophet's just governance in accordance with Divine law. This aspiration cannot be sustained if the *shari'ah* is nothing more than a by-product of early medieval Arabia's cultural response to its Prophet's confrontation with Reality. In terms of the Christian experience, however, in which legalistic forms of piety are viewed at best with suspicion, if not condemned as outright Pharisaic hypocrisy, the idea that ritual laws and taboos are human constructs rather than Divine ordinances is much more likely to be welcomed. Another difficulty is that its relationship to other religions is a matter treated fairly extensively within the *shari'ah* itself, and even in the Qur'an. Pre-Islamic paganism cannot be viewed as simply another way in which we relate ourselves to Ultimate Reality under the pretext that polytheism and monotheism are merely conceptually different approaches to what is inconceivable. This aspect of Hick's pluralism seems to be what is most repugnant to many Christian thinkers, as well as Muslims. Monotheism is inherently iconoclastic. If monotheism and polytheism are just two ways to the Ultimate, how can we justify Abraham's breaking of the idols? Was his message really nothing more than that the worship of idols had become inappropriate in his time and locale? A non-reductive pluralism should respect the absolute claims of monotheism.

According to traditional Christian thinking, salvation is only possible through belief in Jesus Christ as Lord, and it is through this faith that one participates in the redemptive sacrifice of the Son of God. True belief is a necessary condition for salvation. Christians who are unwilling to go as far as Hick in their acceptance of non-believers, yet who reject the dogmatic assertion of their damnation, have found a third alternative in Karl Rahner's concept of anonymous Christians mentioned above. According to this idea, non-Christians who lead good lives, and about whom it seems monstrous to claim that they must be damned, may be said to be Christians even though they do not recognise this themselves. Rahner goes on to assert that if such people were properly exposed to the true teachings of Christ, they would abandon their former beliefs and become official Christians. Being an anonymous Christian is rather like holding an honorary degree from a university: despite lack of training at the school, one's achievements are recognised by the university and the degree is awarded. Hick has argued that this view is unsatisfactory for a number of reasons. It is patronising. It fails to recognise the positive role a non-Christian faith may have in turning one from self-centeredness toward the Ultimate. It also substantially weakens the meaning of salvation through faith in the death and resurrection of Christ.

For anyone who is not a Christian, Hick's solution is not satisfactory. What is needed is a religious pluralism in which the significant differences among religions are appreciated, and the different ways toward human perfection and ultimate felicity are recognised, and yet the strength of the claims of each religion are not diluted by any kind of relativism. This is the promise of the non-reductive religious pluralism of Islam proposed below.

The Non-Reductive Religious Pluralism of Islam

When we consider how a non-reductive religious pluralism might be formulated in the context of Islam, we must keep in mind that the issue of religious pluralism arises in Christianity as a reaction to specifically Christian doctrines about salvation: that it is only through Christianity that one can benefit from the Redemption and gain salvation. A similar exclusivist doctrine can be found in some interpretations of the Jewish claim to be "the chosen people". These doctrines are thoroughly condemned in the Qur'an:

> And they say none shall enter paradise unless he is a Jew or a Christian, these are their vain wishes. Say, "Bring your proof if you are truthful." Yes! Whosoever submits himself to Allah and he is a doer of good, for him there shall be his reward with his Lord, on such shall be no fear nor shall they grieve.
>
> (2:110–11)

Religious pluralism emerges in Christianity in response to the attitude so eloquently condemned in the verses cited above. According to traditional Christian teaching, there is no way to salvation aside from the redemption offered by Christ, and even the great prophets, peace be with them, must wait in limbo until the resurrection, after which Christ must come to release them! Those Christian theologians who have opposed this line of thought, and have accepted the possibility of salvation for non-Christians, have claimed that the saving faith either includes the unconscious acceptance of Christianity or is the common heritage of the world's major religious traditions. Despite their differences, there is a common presumption shared by the various Christian parties to the dispute on pluralism. For Hick and Rahner, as well as the dogmatist, correct faith is necessary for salvation. In order to widen the opening of the gates of heaven, Rahner extends the notion of correct faith to those who live as if they were Christians and who would accept Christianity if properly exposed to it, while Hick goes further to deny that the apparent differences among the world's faiths are irreconcilable. Hick's ultimate reconciliation is what makes apparently different faiths correct. What Hick does is to loosen the condition of correct belief so that it is reduced to the common factor in all the world's religions, however abstract this may be; nevertheless, it remains as much a part of Hick's doctrine as Luther's that there can be no salvation without correct faith, even if the correct faith according to Hick is something of a least common denominator.

In order to understand how to approach the problem of religious pluralism in the context of Islam, the two issues of correct faith and salvation need to be clearly distinguished. According to Islam, the correct religion ordained by God is that revealed to the last of His chosen prophets, Muhammad (s); this and no other religion is required by Allah of all mankind. In this sense, Islam is exclusivist. However, at various times prior to His final revelation, God ordained other religions by means of His prophets ('a). So, the reason why the religion brought by Moses ('a) is not acceptable today is not that what Moses taught was wrong or incompatible with the teachings brought by Muhammad (s), for they taught basically the same things, but because God has ordained the latter teachings for this era. The previous teachings were not incorrect, and they were sufficient to guide the people for whom they were revealed to salvation. Although some scholars seek to minimise the importance of this fact by appealing to *riwayat* (narrations) according to which the differences among the revealed religions amount to no more than the details of ritual practice, such as how many prostrations occur in various prayers, the number of days on which fasting is prescribed, and the like, there can be no denying that different paths can lead to God, and in different circumstances have been ordained by Him.

All of the divinely revealed religions are called Islam in the general sense of complete submission to the commands of Allah; while Islam is used in a specific sense to refer to the final version of Islam (in the general sense) brought by Muhammad (s). The difference between general and specific Islam gives rise to a number of interesting questions. How much variation can there be in the varieties of general Islam? Could God have ordained a version of general Islam for a people so different from us that we would not recognise it as such? Why did God ordain different versions of general Islam? The exact answers to these questions are with God alone.[17] But in the present age, general Islam implies specific Islam, and this must be understood if one is not to fall into error about the position of Islam with respect to religious diversity.

It is because of the demand that Muhammad (s) be recognised as the Seal of the Prophets (s) that the reductive pluralists' solution to the problem of religious diversity cannot be accepted. To accept only some of the prophets ('a) to the exclusion of others, particularly Muhammad (s), with the excuse that it makes no difference because all the religions are ultimately saying the same thing, is to fail to heed the divine call:

> Verily those who deny God and His apostles and desire that they differentiate between God and His apostles and say "We believe in some and we deny, some," and intend to take a course between this [and that], these are the infidels, truly, and We have prepared for the infidels a disgraceful torment.
>
> (Qur'an, 4:150–51)

According to reductive religious pluralism, there can be no better reason for adopting one religion rather than another than cultural affinity. As a result, the importance of the divine law is undermined. In the context of Islam, on the other hand, the *shari'ah* brought by God's final chosen Apostle (s) is understood as the perfection of all previously ordained ways. The divine call to follow the law of Islam is extended to all humanity, not merely to those of a specific cultural setting: "And We did not send you but to all people as a bearer of good tidings and as a warner, but most people do not know" (Qur'an 34:28).

With regard to the question of the correctness of faith, the position of Islam is clear. At various times in human history different faiths and laws were decreed by Allah. At present, however, there is but one divinely ordained religion, Muhammadan Islam, which requires belief in God's oneness (*tawhid*), prophecy (*nubbuwah*), and the Resurrection (*ma'ad*). As God says, "O you who believe! Believe in Allah and His Apostle and the Book which He has sent down to His Apostle and the Book which He sent down before; and whoever decries Allah and His angels and His books and His apostles and the Last Day has indeed strayed off, far away" (Qur'an, 4:136).

In sum, reductive pluralism is incompatible with Islam because it does not require us to accept all of the prophets ('a) and to obey the divine prescriptions given through God's last chosen messenger (s). Reductive religious pluralism presents itself as an opening-up toward other traditions, while from the standpoint of Islam, it is an attempt to open the way to *kufr,* a covering of one's eyes and ears to the truth of God's final revelation and its practical implications.

The solution proposed by Hick to this conflict is garbed in the euphemism "creative doctrinal development" (1985: 50). The patronising tone in the following passage is typical of the liberal mentality:

Islam may be expected to go through essentially the same traumas as Christianity in its encounter both with modern science and with the emerging ecumenical outlook; only whereas the Christian trauma has been spread over a century or more, Islam is having to adjust in a single generation to an already formed modern culture. It is to be hoped that the Muslim world will eventually find its own Qur'anic way of combining modern knowledge with its faith in the Transcendent and its commitment to a morality of human community. And we may further hope that this development will also include an increased recognition of the ecumenical point of view that has already been so powerfully expressed within the Sufi strand of Islam.

(Hick 1989: 378)

The final remark about "the Sufi strand of Islam" requires a discussion more detailed than that to be offered here. But if Hick is under the impression that his reductive religious pluralism can find support in true *tasawwuf* or *'irfan*, a fairly powerful argument can be given that he is mistaken. While there may be some degenerate Sufi Orders, or *turuq,* willing to play the role assigned for them by Hick, and there are orders in the West into which non-Muslims have been initiated, the vast majority of the *'urafa'*, or gnostics, of Islam have required strict observance of the *shari'ah* prior to initiation into spiritual wayfaring (*sayr wa suluk*). Hick is fond of citing the following couplet of Shaykh Jalal al-Din Rumi: "The lamps are different, but the Light is the same."[18] But this is what the Qur'an also affirms: "Verily We sent down the Torah in which there is guidance and light ... (5:44). And We caused Jesus son of Mary to follow in their footsteps confirming the Torah which was before him and We gave him the Evangel in which was guidance and light ... " (5:46).

The conclusion reached in the Qur'an is not that, because all religions have divine light, it makes no difference which of them we follow, nor that religious choice is a matter of ethnicity. It is not as though we are presented with different lamps from which we are to choose in accordance with our own taste, background, and the quality of our personal experiences; rather God presents the lamps to humanity in succession, and it is our responsibility to follow what God has assigned for us in the present age.

Rumi was by no means a reductive religious pluralist of the sort Hick makes him out to be. Sufis have sought to explain religious differences by distinguishing between the exterior (*zahir*) and the interior (*batin*) aspects of religion. The differences among them are merely external. However, the vast majority of Sufis have affirmed the duty to follow the prescriptions of the law of Islam with the slogan: no *tariqah* without *shari'ah*. There is no way to the interior except through the exterior, and the exterior required in the current age is that of Islam: "Just as a thing fails if it lacks a kernel, so too it fails without a skin. If you sow a seed in the earth without its husk, it fails to germinate, whereas if you bury it in the earth with its husk, it does germinate and becomes a great tree" (Rumi 1972: 31).

Nevertheless, a theme commonly found in the Sufi poets such as 'Attar, Rumi and Hafiz is the expression of affinity toward Christianity or Zoroastrianism. This might lead some to the mistaken conclusion that these poets considered the differences between Islam and the other religions to be insignificant. What is really to be found in such expressions is the condemnation of the display of the outward signs of affiliation to Islam without any inward faith. It would be better to have nominal affiliation to an incorrect creed, but to believe sincerely in it and to follow the guidance in it for spiritual advancement, than to be a hypocrite who outwardly professes Islam while inwardly worshipping idols.

If we are to compare different forms of *kufr*, or unbelief, surely that of the hypocrite is worse than that of the sincere Zoroastrian. The outward denial of orthodoxy found in Hafiz (and even Imam Khomeini), for example, staining the prayer mat with wine or consulting the Magi (*pir-e moghan*), becomes a means of indicating the interior dimension of religion and denying hypocrisy, but unless the hyperbole is understood in this symbolism, it will appear as apostasy. Hypocrisy occurs with the outward affirmation of Islam and the inward denial. Imam Khomeini, following the example of Hafiz, wishes to emphasise the opposite of hypocrisy, namely sincere belief in Islam, so he exaggerates by invoking the opposite extreme, the outward denial of Islam with its inward affirmation; in this way *kufr* becomes a symbol for true faith!

> Kiss the hand of the shaykh who has pronounced me a disbeliever.
> Congratulate the guard who has led me away in chains.
> I am going into solitary retreat from now on by the door of the Magus.[19]

The great Sufi theoretician Ibn 'Arabi taught that the fact that God's truth can find expression in different, even apparently conflicting, religions does not mean that people are free to choose whatever religion suits their fancy. Ibn 'Arabi himself asserts that it is incumbent upon people in the present age to follow the *shari'ah* brought by Muhammad (s),[20] and it is in this sense that all previously revealed religions become invalid (*batil*) with the revelation of the Qur'an. This does not mean that they become false, but that it becomes obligatory to follow the *shari'ah* of specific Islam rather than that of a previous revealed religion. In this sense all previously decreed systems of religious law may be discarded, not because they are worthless, but because whatever is needed from them has been incorporated into the final revelation. He puts it as follows:

> All the revealed religions (*shara'i'*) are lights. Among these religions, the revealed religion of Muhammad is like the light of the sun among the lights of the stars. When the sun appears, the lights of the stars are hidden, and their lights are included in the light of the sun. Their being hidden is like the abrogation of the other revealed religions: that takes place through Muhammad's revealed religion. Nevertheless, they do in fact exist, just as the existence of the light of the stars is actualised. This explains why we have been required in our all-inclusive religion to have faith in the truth of all the messengers and all the revealed religions. They are not rendered null (*batin*) by abrogation – that is the opinion of the ignorant.[21]

The difference between the Sufis and the theologians on the diversity of religions is one of emphasis more than explicit doctrine. The Sufis emphasise the inner unity of the revealed religions while the theologians emphasise the outward superiority of Islam, but there is no real difference on either point.

The theologians admit that the previous revealed religions contain light and guidance, for this is explicitly stated in the Qur'an. The fact that in the present age it is only the Islam revealed to Muhammad (s) that is valid and whose law is obligatory is also accepted by the Sufis. Both groups hold that the previously revealed religions, including the Christianity brought by Jesus ('a), do not contain any doctrinal differences from Islam, but the Sufi is more willing than the theologian to look for insights contained in the other religions, despite what is considered by both the theologian and the Sufi to be the accretion of doctrinal error, to the precise extent that the primary concern of the Sufi is spiritual insight rather than doctrine. Because of his attention to the inward dimension, the gnostic ('arif) is also willing to allow for greater variance in outward diversity as expressions of a single Truth than those whose major preoccupation is doctrinal and ritual detail. In any case, both groups hold that Islam brings to perfection all that was contained in the previously revealed religions, and is the sole religion prescribed by God for the present age until the end of time. However, the 'arif is willing to give poetic expression to his faith and to the rejection of hypocrisy through the symbols of the other religions, including idol worship, as in the following lines from Baba Tahir and Imam Khomeini, respectively:

> Synagogue, Ka'abah, idol-temple, monastery,
> none are known to be empty of the sweetheart.[22]

> At the door of the tavern,
> temple, mosque and monastery,
> I have fallen in prostration,
> as though You had glanced upon me.[23]

Another line of thought about the diversity of religions is to be found in the tradition of Islamic philosophy. After explaining that the common people whom the prophets ('a) sought to guide are not capable of appreciating philosophical wisdom, al-Farabi writes: "These things are thus allegorised for every nation or people in terms familiar to them, and it is possible that what is familiar to one people is foreign to another."[24] In al-Farabi's view, which is to a great extent accepted by Ibn Sina, the religions all express a single philosophical truth in different symbols, and through these symbols, they serve to organise society and lead humanity to felicity. Furthermore, each great religion contains, in its corpus of revelations, "sufficient glimpses of pure truth to lead the elect seekers of truth to pursue this truth itself and to be able to allegorically interpret the rest of the symbols".[25] According to al-Farabi, the spiritual content and background of all religion is identical, since this is universal, but it is equally true that the symbols employed by the religions are not at the same level. Therefore some religions are "nearer to the truth than others, some are more adequate than others in leading humanity to the higher truth, some, again, are more effective than others in gaining the belief of people and becoming the directive force of their lives. Indeed there are religions whose symbolisms are positively harmful."[26]

Like the Sufi position on the diversity of religions, nothing in the position of the philosophers contradicts the idea emphasised by the theologians that in the present age the sole religion prescribed by God for humankind is Islam, that the previously revealed religions have become corrupted, that the beliefs associated with them differ from what was revealed to their prophets, and that Islam is the culmination of all previously revealed religions. Where the Sufis and the philosophers differ is on how to understand the interior (*batin*) of the revealed religions, whether through spiritual unveilings or through philosophical reasoning. What is notably absent is the sort of view advocated by reductive religious pluralism, according to which religions are validated by personal religious experience: that since all religions express a single interior truth, it makes no difference which is followed, and that the common truth of the world's religions in their contemporary forms are sufficient as guides to ultimate felicity. None of these essential elements of reductive religious pluralism would be acceptable within the theological, mystical, or philosophical traditions of Islam.

The view elaborated may seem to be exclusivist, because of the claim of the superiority of Islam among the religions of the world; however, it is in fact a degree pluralism that admits that a plurality of religious traditions contain divine light and truth, that it is the responsibility of true believers to treat the followers of other traditions with acceptance and respect, and that the followers of other traditions may find the way to salvation through their own faiths by the grace of God.

Conclusion

One of the major motivations for liberal Christian religious pluralists was to provide the theological groundwork for better relations between Christians and non-Christians. Instead of viewing the non-Christian with contempt as damned, he or she is seen by the Christian pluralist as in essential agreement with Christianity, for all the major religions are held to differ only in their external aspects. Differences in religion are to be understood on the model of ethnic differences, and relations among the participants in different faith traditions are presumed to take shape within the framework of the liberal state, which proclaims complete religious neutrality.

In Islamic thought, on the contrary, religious differences are not seen as a matter of personal preference, but as expressions of communal loyalty grounded in spiritual insight and critical evaluation. Those who choose a religion other than Islam are making a mistake, either sinfully or excusably. Since there is no way for us to tell whether or not the mistake is excusable, where good relations with non-Muslims are possible without condoning injustice, the presumption of an honest mistake is morally incumbent upon us.

In Christianity, especially in Protestant Christianity, there is a strong link between salvation and true belief, because it is through faith that one participates in the Redemption, which alone is believed to afford salvation. This link between true belief and salvation survives among Christian proposals for religious pluralism, like those of Wilfred Cantwell Smith and John Hick, in the idea that ultimately the variety of religious beliefs is a matter of surface differences over a fundamentally single faith, which may not even be expressible in human language. If one denies the doctrine of Redemption, and with it the link between faith and salvation which features so prominently in Christian thought, the obvious alternative, at least obvious in a Christian context, is the idea that faith is to be purchased through good works, an idea emphatically denounced by Luther and by the majority of Christian theologians, including Catholics, after him.

The Islamic tradition appears to offer another approach to the problem. Muslims, like Christians, reject the idea that good works alone are sufficient for salvation. It is not difficult to find Muslim expressions of the idea that there is nothing one can do through one's own efforts to make oneself worthy of salvation without the grace of God. This is a theme which runs throughout Imam Zayn al-'Abidin's *Sahifat al-sajjadiyyah*.[27] Good works without faith appear ungrounded, for faith provides the cognitive framework in which the final good is to be understood and intentions to do good works are to be formed, and it is through such orientation and intentions that God draws His servants toward Him by His Mercy. But faith is more than the mere acceptance of a list of doctrines, it is a spiritual readiness to travel the way toward Allah and wholehearted submission to His will. In Islam, salvation is seen in terms of the movement of the soul toward God, a movement that is explained in terms of the acquirement of the Divine attributes, and whose aim is a beatific encounter with Divinity. To achieve this, God demands faith and good works, and in the present age, this means the acceptance and practice of Islam as revealed to the last of His chosen messengers (s). Ultimately, however, it is neither by faith nor good works that humankind is saved, but by the grace of God.

An Islamic non-reductive pluralism may be contrasted with Hick's pluralism and Rahner's inclusivism in terms of the place of ignorance in the three views. In Hick's view, every major creed, no matter how different, expresses an ultimately single faith. That ultimate faith may not be expressible in human language, so there is a sense in which believers are ignorant of what they really believe. In Rahner's view, Christians know what they believe and it is only others who may be ignorant of their latent Christian belief. According to the non-reductive view, no attempt is made to reinterpret apparently conflicting beliefs to reveal some hidden agreement. Instead of positing ignorance about what we believe, we are to admit our ignorance of how God may guide the sincere, and what beliefs are the results of a sincere quest for the truth. The identities of all the prophets are not known, and in the most famous *hadith* about the number of the prophets, Abu Dharr reports that the Prophet (s) told him there were 124 000 prophets ('a). Corrupted forms of the teachings of these prophets may survive in any number of the variety of the world's religions and cultural legacies. The admission of ignorance in this matter is an expression of humility before the judgement of Allah; such humility has featured prominently in the Islamic tradition, and it may provide a basis for an Islamic form of a non-reductive religious pluralism. After mentioning some of the good people who will be saved and the hypocrites who will receive a double chastisement, the Qur'an mentions that there are others who must await the command of God. Until then, we cannot say whether they will be rewarded or punished: "And others must await the command of Allah, whether We will chastise them or whether He will turn to them. And Allah is all Knowing, all Wise" (9:106).[28]

John Hick's religious pluralism is to be lauded as a great improvement over its exclusivist and inclusivist predecessors in Christian theology, and Muslims will be impressed by the fact that the denial of the traditional Christian dogma of the Incarnation brings Hick's theology much closer to Islamic doctrine. Nevertheless, Hick's reductive pluralism hides a set of moral and political values that are at odds with Islam not only because of the detail of the judgements they inform, but, even more significantly, because of where they set their standards. Islam teaches that we are to look to the Qur'an and the teachings of the Prophet (s) to find guidance in politics and morals, while Hick would have us turn to the worldly currents of modern thought, which are more often than not decidedly opposed to Islam. And although a severe punishment awaits the enemies of Islam, as for those who honestly accept an invalid creed, it must be admitted that this invalid creed itself may be the vehicle through which God extends to them His grace and leads them to salvation. What is truly of value in Hick's religious pluralism is a tolerance that can be found more completely, in a sense, within the Islamic tradition, and may be formulated along the lines suggested above as a non-reductive religious pluralism.

Notes

1 "Their guidance is not your responsibility; but Allah guides whomsoever He will" (Qur'an, 2:272).
2 John Rawls, *Political Liberalism* (New York: Columbia University Press, 1993), 36–7.
3 For an overview of definitions gleaned by surfing the internet, see B. A. Robinson, "Quotations Showing Various Definitions of the Term 'Religious Pluralism,'" <http://www.religioustolerance.org/rel_plur1.htm>.
4 See Byrne 1995: 12. I have changed the wording of the third clause to stress the equality condition.
5 The definitive statement of Hick's view is spelled out in his *An Interpretation of Religion* (1989).
6 See the entry by Diane Jeske, "Special Obligations", in *The Stanford Encyclopedia of Philosophy*, ed. Edward N. Zalta (Winter 2002), <http://plato.stanford.edu/archives/win2002/entries/special-obligations>.
7 Graham Priest, "Dialetheism", *The Stanford Encyclopedia of Philosophy* (Winter 1998) <http://plato.stanford.edu/archives/win1998/entries/dialetheism>.
8 Notice the contradiction in condemning someone to never-ending torment that ends with penitence.
9 See Edgar Trexler, "God Smiles on Augsburg", *The Lutheran*, <http://www.thelutheran.org/9912/page42.html>.

10 See Eric Sharpe, "Dialogue of Religions", in *The Encyclopedia of Religion*, ed. Mircea Eliade (New York: Macmillan, 1987); and William Ernest Hocking, *Living Religions and a World of Faith* (New York: Macmillan, 1940).

11 For more on Traditionalism and a criticism of the hermetic pluralism of Dr Nasr, see Hajj Muhammad Legenhausen, "Why I Am Not a Traditionalist", *Religio-Scope* (2002), <http://www.religioscope.com/pdf/esotrad/legenhausen.pdf>.

12 The topic of religious pluralism is discussed in almost all of Hick's major works. In response to Hick and Knitter (eds), *The Myth of Christian Uniqueness* (1987), there is D'Costa 1990. See also Rouner 1984 and Hamnett 1990.

13 See Hick 1993. On the controversy provoked by this book, see Hick 1985, opening essay.

14 Ninian Smart, "Truth and Religions," in Steven M. Calm and David Shatz (eds), *Contemporary Philosophy of Religion* (New York: Oxford University Press, 1982), pp. 291–300.

15 See his lengthy review of Wilfred Cantwell Smith's *The Meaning and End of Religion* (New York: Harper & Row, 1978) in *Al-Tawhid*, vol. 3, no. 3: 163–89, concluded in vol. 3, no. 4: 154–96.

16 Donovan (1993: 218) here reports on the views of Moltmann expressed in his contribution to D'Costa 1990.

17 The question of religious diversity is discussed by Ibn 'Arabi, in Chapter 48 of the *Futuhat*, in which he explains that religious diversity is the product of the diversity in the divine relationships. Cf. Chittick: 1994: 155–60. In the text here "(s)" is short-hand for "*salla Allahu 'alayhi wa sallam*", "Peace and blessings be upon him". It is customary to say this whenever the Prophet's name is mentioned. When a prophet such as Moses is mentioned, one says, "*'alayhi as-salam*", "Peace be upon him", indicated by "('a)".

18 Hick 1989: 233; Hick 1985: 108; cf. Nicholson's edition of the *Mathnawi*, Book III, v. 1259.

19 From *Sabu-ye 'Ishq*, translated as *A Jug of Love: Eight Ghazals of Imam Khomeini*, trans. Muhammad Legenhausen and 'Azim Sarvdalir (Tehran: Islamic Thought Foundation, 1994).

20 *Futuhat*, III, 311.23, in Chittick 1994: 155.

21 *Futuhat*, III, 153.12, see Chittick 1994: 125.

22 From the *Divan of Baba Tahir*, trans. Muhammad Legenhausen and 'Azim Sarvdalir.

23 From *Sabu-ye 'Ishq*, trans. Legenhausen and Sarvdalir.

24 From his *Siyasat*, cited and translated by Fazlur Ralunan in his *Prophecy in Islam* (London: George Allen & Unwin, 1958), p. 40.

25 Ibid., p. 40.

26 Ibid., p. 41. A view similar to al-Farabi's is endorsed by Ibn Sina in his *Risalah al-Ahawiyyah*.

27 Trans. William Chittick (London: Mohammadi Trust, 1989).

28 See the discussion of this *ayah* and related *ahadith* in 'Allamah Tabataba'i's *Al-Mizan*; cf. Qur'an, 5: 118; 33: 24.

PART TWO

ISLAM AND THE WEST: CLASH OR DIALOGUE?

Our loyalties must become ecumenical rather than sectional. Every nation must now develop an overriding loyalty to mankind as a whole in order to preserve the best in their individual societies.

Martin Luther King

By relegating the civilisations of five-sixth of humanity to some obscure corner of history, the centres of power in the West have revealed their true colours. They are not interested in a multi-civilisational world that is based upon justice, equality and respect for diversity.

Chandra Muzaffar

Four commandments of the global ethic: Have respect for life! Deal honestly and fairly! Speak and act truthfully! Respect and love one another!

Hans Küng

What is hateful to you do not do to your fellow; that is the whole of the Torah, all the rest is commentary.

Rabbi Hillel

Chapter 4

Islam and the West: Clash of Civilisations?[1]

Francis Robinson

In 1993 the journal *Foreign Affairs* (vol. 72, no. 3) published an article entitled "Clash of Civilizations" by Samuel Huntington, Harvard Professor, former Director of Security Planning for the National Security Council, and President of the American Political Science Association. By 1996 Huntington had developed his article into a book, and it was published under the title *The Clash of Civilizations and the Remaking of World Order*. The argument was that in a post-Cold War world, the crucial distinctions between people were not primarily ideological or economic, but cultural. World politics was being reconfigured along cultural lines, with new patterns of conflict and cooperation replacing those of the Cold War. The hot spots in world politics were on the fault-lines between civilisations: Bosnia, Chechnya, West Asia, Tibet, Sri Lanka, and others. The civilisation with a particularly large number of hot spots was Islam. It had bloody borders and represented the greatest danger to world peace.

The argument has influenced, indeed, helped to frame the debate about the future world order to an extent which distresses even Huntington himself. It has not been well-received amongst professional scholars of Islam, who have objected to the way in which it has assisted in demonising Muslims and to the way in which, by generalising about Muslims, it has brushed over the many differences of economic and political status, outlook, and understanding which the Muslim world embraces. Huntington's argument has been assessed by several scholars, so it needs no further elaboration here.[2] However, the events of September 11 and the widespread realisation of the existence and purposes of Usama bin Ladin and his al-Qa'ida organisation have created a new dimension by which to examine this thesis.

First it is necessary to summarise the historical, particularly Islamic, background to the events of September 11 and the great change in power relationships between Muslim peoples and the West over the past two hundred years. For a thousand years, for much of the period from the eighth to the eighteenth century, the leading civilisation on the planet in terms of spread and creativity was Islam. It was formed in the seventh century when Arab tribesmen, bearing the prophecy of Muhammad, burst out of the Arabian Peninsula. Within a decade they defeated the armies of two rival empires to the north, those of Christian Byzantium and Sassanian Iran. A great new cultural and economic nexus came to be developed which was able to draw on the knowledge and commodities of lands from China and India in the East to Spain and Africa in the West, as well as those of the West Asian lands in which it was based. This new civilisation commanded a substantial slice of the world's area of cities and settled agriculture. In this region there was shared language of religion and the law. Men could travel and do business within a common framework of assumptions. In its high cultures they could express themselves in symbols to which all could respond. Arguably it is the first world system, the one which preceded that of Immanuel Wallerstein.[3] The first notable centres were found in the Arab worlds of Damascus, Baghdad, Cordoba, and Cairo from the eighth to the twelfth centuries, the second in the Turco-Iranian worlds of Istanbul, Isfahan, Bukhara, Samarqand, and Delhi from the fourteenth to the seventeenth centuries. There were great achievements in scholarship and science, in poetry and prose, and in the arts of the book, building, and spiritual insight, which are precious legacies to all humankind. For about half of what is termed the Christian era, Muslims could regard themselves as marching at the forefront of human progress. Over the same period, the odd crusade or loss of Spain aside, they could regard the community of believers created by God's revelation to humankind through the Prophet Muhammad as walking hand in hand with power.

Over the past two hundred years the Islamic world system has been overwhelmed by forces from the West, forces driven by capitalism, powered by the Industrial Revolution, and civilised, after a fashion, by the Enlightenment. The symbolic moment, when the leader's standard overtly passed to the West, was Napoleon's invasion of Egypt in 1798. From this moment Western armies and Western capital overran the lands of the Muslims: the British took India; the British and Dutch, South East Asia; the British, French, Germans, and Italians, North, East and West Africa; the Russians swamped Central Asia, and the British and French carved up West Asia between them. By the 1920s Afghanistan, Iran, Turkey, Central Arabia, and the Yemen were the only Muslim countries free from Western control, and even some of these were subject to influence. The caliphate, the symbolic leadership for the community of believers, which reached back to the Prophet, had been abolished. For a moment it was feared that the holy places of Islam – Mecca and Medina – might fall into the hands of the infidel. The community of believers, which for so many centuries had walked hand in hand with power, had good reason to believe that history – if not God – had deserted it.

For the remainder of the twentieth century matters did not seem a great deal better. Certainly, from the emergence of modern Turkey in the early 1920s to that of the Muslim republics of the former Soviet Union in the 1990s, we could talk of a steady decolonisation of the Muslim world – at least in the formal sense. But for many this has seemed a Pyrrhic victory. More often than not they have found Western rule replaced by that of Muslims with secular Western values, while Western capital and Western culture have come to be even more corrosive of their customs and their standards than before. This challenge has elicited from many Muslims the assertion of an Islamic, and for some a totalitarian Islamic, future for their people. Such views have not been shared by all Muslims but have come to be shared by enough of them to represent a significant threat to the secular leaders of their societies, and on occasion, as in the revolution in Iran, to drive their upholders to power. These Muslims, who are popularly known as "fundamentalist" in the West, are more appropriately known as "Islamists". I shall elaborate on these "Islamists" when I address the significance of the Islamic revival. For the moment it is enough to note that they represent the major opposition to the leadership of Muslim states, many of which have relations of greater or less strength with the USA, among them Saudi Arabia, Pakistan, Algeria, Tunisia, Turkey, Egypt, Jordan, Kuwait, and also of course, the Palestinian Authority. In this situation, lack of fairness or evenhandedness on the part of non-Muslim states is an irritant which helps to radicalise Muslim populations not just in the states concerned but also across the Muslim world. There are the problems of Muslim minorities in the Balkans and the resistance of the people of Chechnya to Russian military might. Indian Muslims experienced a sense of threat as they were first demonised by Hindu revivalism and then, in 1992, saw the Emperor Babur's Mosque torn down by Hindu revivalists. The Muslim majority in Kashmir have been oppressed by India's martial rule, while the peoples of Iraq suffered on account of their rogue regime. The Muslim and Christian peoples of Palestine have experienced the greatest injustice during these past fifty years and more. These are all complicated issues, but from the point of view of many Muslims in the streets and bazaars of Muslim towns and cities across the world they represent symbols of injustice and oppression. They represent a world order in which Muslims are victims. They constitute a world order in which Muslims must organise to resist.

There are three significant developments that accompanied the transformation of the Muslim position in the world in the nineteenth and twentieth centuries. They form strands in the long-term background to the events of September 11. First, Muslim peoples have long suffered a range of feelings from a tremendous sense of loss through to a deep bitterness and rage at their powerlessness in the face of the West. This was particularly strong in the Indo-Pakistan subcontinent, now the home of over 350 million Muslims, originally because of the speed with which the Mughal Empire lost power in the eighteenth century. Then it grew because of the new competition for power this brought with rival peoples, and finally because this was the area of the Muslim world most heavily exposed to rule from the West. This was expressed in the most powerful artistic form of culture: poetry.

The eighteenth and nineteenth-century poetic genre of Shahr Ashob mourned the passing of great cities, of great centres of Muslim civilisation. One of the greatest works of the nineteenth century, the *Musaddas* or Elegy of Altaf Husain Hali, is entitled *The Flow and Ebb of Islam*.[4] This was a great set-piece poem on the rise and decline of Islam and its causes. It was highly popular and came to be used almost as a national anthem for the Pakistan movement. It would be recited at the opening of political meetings and have everyone in tears as they contemplated the fate of Islamic civilisation:

> When autumn has set in over the garden,
> Why speak of the springtime of flowers?

> When shadows of adversity hang over the present,
> Why harp on the pomp and glory of the past?
> Yes, these are things to forget; but how can you with
> The dawn forget the scene of the night before?
> The assembly has just dispersed;
> The smoke is still rising from the burnt candle;
> The footprints on the sands of India still say
> A graceful caravan has passed this way.[5]

Of course there was admiration for the achievement of Europe, even if of a despairing kind. The secretary of the Moroccan envoy to France in 1846, after watching a review of French troops, wrote:

> So it went on until all had passed leaving our hearts consumed with fire for what we had seen of their overwhelming power and mastery ... In comparison with the weakness of Islam ... how confident they are, how impressive their state of readiness, how competent they are in matters of state, how firm their laws, how capable in war.[6]

But as Western power enveloped the Muslim world, there was growing protest against the West. From 1926 to 1957 Husain Ahmad Madani was principal of the great reformist school of Deoband, whose organisation and influence in Pakistan was to create the network of *madrassas* in which the Taliban were bred. "The British and the European nations do not consider Asians and Africans as human beings, and thus deny them human rights," he asserted in his autobiography written after his internment in Malta during World War I. "The British are the worst enemies of Islam and the Muslims on the earth."[7]

Muhammad Iqbal, a man who intellectually owed much to the West, accepted a knighthood from the British, and was the poet-philosopher behind the concept of Pakistan – a Muslim modernist, in no way radical; yet in his *Persian Psalms*, published in 1927, he declared:

> Against Europe I protest,
> And the attraction of the West.
> Woe for Europe and her charm,
> Swift to capture and disarm!
> Europe's hordes with flame and fire
> Desolate the world entire.[8]

The rejection of Europe, or by now the West in general, both as a destructive force and a false model of progress, was a theme of many of the leading ideologues who prepared the way for the Iranian revolution. "Come friends," said Ali Shariati in the 1960s, "let us abandon Europe; let us cease this nauseating apish imitation of Europe. Let us leave behind this Europe that always speaks of humanity, but destroys human beings wherever it finds them."[9] By this time, as the USA replaced Europe in the demonology of the Islamic world, it became the focus of bitterness and resentment, which was all the greater because it affected the lives of supposedly free peoples. Ayatollah Khomeini's howl of rage, when in 1964 the Iranian Parliament granted US citizens extraterritorial rights in Iran in exchange for a $200m loan, spoke for all Muslims who had felt powerless in the face of a bullying West, from the bombardment of Alexandria in 1882 to the plight of the Palestinians in the present crisis: "They have reduced the Iranian people to a level lower than that of an American dog."[10]

Such feelings were no less strongly held in the Arab world. Here a key focus was the Crusades, which Carole Hillenbrand explores in the epilogue to her brilliant book *The Crusades: Islamic Perspectives*. They permeate, she declares, "many aspects of modern life in the Arab and wider Muslim world",[11] where they have left psychological scars. They frequently referred to the Crusades and drew parallels as they felt the weight of European colonialism. The myth of Saladin, or more correctly Salahuddin, as the great leader of resistance to the West and his victory over the Crusaders at Hattin was a central theme in the Palestinian struggle under the British Mandate. Indeed, the Israeli state has come to be seen as a modern version of the Latin Kingdom of Jerusalem, which was established by what Sayyid Qutb, the leader of the second phase of the Muslim Brotherhood, called "the Crusader spirit which runs in the blood of all Westerners".[12] In his pronouncements Usama bin Ladin, along with his fellow Islamist leaders, conjured up this spirit of the Crusaders in Arab and Muslim minds. In a *fatwah* of 20 February 1998 he proclaimed the formation of a "world front for Jihad against Jews and Crusaders": "the rule to kill Americans and their allies – civilians and military – is an individual duty for any Muslim ... to liberate the al-Aqsa Mosque [in Jerusalem] and the Holy Mosque [in Mecca] from their grip, and in order for their armies to move out of all the lands of Islam, defeated and unable to threaten any Muslim" (Bodansky 1999: 226–7). Bin Ladin belongs to a long tradition of protest against Western power in Muslim lands, though in this case his words have been followed by action.

The second development is that of an increasingly active pan-Islamic consciousness in the Muslim world since 1800. There are reasons for this pan-Islamic sentiment which derive from Islam itself. Muslims believe that theirs is a community, an *ummah*, created by God's revelation to man through Muhammad. Moreover, that revelation tells them that they are the best community produced for mankind. They believe that it is an especial blessing to belong to this community. The brotherhood of all those who belong to the community, in total equality before God, is a strong concept which is widely celebrated from the *salam* in communal prayer through to the shared experience of the pilgrimage to Mecca. A concern to cherish and sustain the community against all forms of divisiveness is the underlying spirit of the *shari'ah*, the holy law.

The classical traditions of biography, moreover, were always designed to show the role of individuals, first in sustaining and enriching the community in their time and second in transmitting that precious knowledge to future generations as continuing manifestations of the community. There is a special magic in the community as expressed by Muhammad Iqbal, writing at a time when it was threatened by the growth of nationalism. In his *Secrets of Selflessness*, published in 1918, he declared:

> Our essence is not bound to any place;
> The vigour of our wine is not contained
> In any bowl; Chinese and Indian
> Alike the shard that constitutes our jar,
> Turkish and Syrian alike the clay
> Forming our body; neither is our heart
> Of India, or Syria, or Rum,
> Nor any fatherland do we profess
> Except Islam.

But twentieth-century realities were destroying this charismatic community:

> Now brotherhood has been so cut to shreds
> That in the stead of community
> The country has been given pride of place
> In men's allegiance and constructive work;
> The country is the darling of their hearts
> And wide humanity is whittled down
> Into dismembered tribes.[13]

Muhammad Iqbal, however, need not have been quite so concerned. The community was being re-created in a very special way in the age of the modern nation state, using basic religious building blocks. One pillar has been the great increase in the numbers of those performing the pilgrimage to Mecca in the nineteenth and twentieth centuries – from under one million in the 1920s to over ten million in the 1970s. Growing wealth and the great improvements in transport by land, sea, and air have facilitated this community-affirming ritual. But most important has been the growth of global news and communications systems, from the expansion of the press in the mid-nineteenth century to the development of global radio and television in the second half of the twentieth. The press flourished in British India as West Asia came under European domination from the 1870s: when Russia and the Ottoman Empire went to war in the late 1870s, when the British invaded Egypt in 1882, and when the Ottoman Empire began to decline, from 1911 to 1924.[14] Such was the fervour and excitement that many Muslims came to dream about the wider Islamic world. Muslims adopted headgear and other forms of dress to indicate their identification with West Asia. For the same purpose they stopped giving their children names from regional languages in favour of classical Islamic ones. Their writings revealed how they identified with Muslims of other countries.

During the second half of the twentieth century this process has intensified, with an especial focus on Iran, Iraq, and Palestine. Some of the crowds that have protested against allied action in Afghanistan or Israeli action in the West Bank will have been organised, but large numbers will have protested spontaneously out of fellow feeling for their Muslim brothers. What this strong sense of community, of Islamic brotherhood, means is that, although there are many differences and distinctions amongst Muslims, there is a level at which they will unite, especially when confronted by bullying, interference, or invasion from outside. This is reflected in the local press throughout the Muslim world and among people talking on buses and trains, in bazaars and villages. Of course, power players in the Muslim world have from time to time tried to hijack this sentiment for their own purposes, as the Ottoman Empire did with its pan-Islamic policies in the late nineteenth century, as Saudi Arabia has tried to do through their Islamic Conference Organisation and the Muslim World League from the 1960s, and as Usama bin Ladin did during 2001, harnessing global communications technology to his cause with no little skill.

The third development, and in many ways the most important, has been the worldwide movement of Islamic revivalism, which from the eighteenth century has been expressed in many different ways through differing social, economic, cultural, and political circumstances. It is important to recognise that this movement has profound Islamic roots and precedes the assertion of Western power in the Muslim world. From the nineteenth century onwards the movement has interacted powerfully with the Western presence and is in varying ways shaped by it. All the Islamic organisations that have gained attention through the events of September 11 have their roots in this revival and this reaction. The fundamental concern of this extraordinary movement has been the renewal of Islamic society from within and not an assault on outside forces, an internal struggle or *jihad*, not an external one.

At the heart of this Muslim revival lay a return to first principles. In the spread of Islam from West Africa to China and South East Asia too many concessions had been made to local religious practice, which compromised the monotheism of God's message to humanity through Muhammad. It was necessary to go back to first principles, to abandon much of the medieval superstructure of learning and concentrate on the Qur'an and the traditions of the Prophet, to try to recreate the perfection of the Prophet's community in the oasis of Medina. At the same time, there was an attack on all ideas about the intercession of God in the affairs of mankind, as represented by the shrines of saints. From the late eighteenth century, the concept that man alone was responsible for his salvation, indeed that he must act on earth to achieve it, steadily spread to many parts of the Muslim world. This, as is the case with the Protestant Reformation in Christianity, has released vast amounts of energy. It represents a shift in emphasis in the forms of Muslim piety from an other-worldly to a this-worldly Islam.[15]

There are three manifestations of this worldwide Islamic movement which link directly to the present. The first is the Wahhabi movement of Arabia. This was the creation of an eighteenth-century scholar Muhammad ibn Abd al-Wahhab, who preached a return to the Qur'an and the traditions and removal of all religious practices suggesting God's intercession. His preaching is the *locus classicus* of the Islamic revival and the name Wahhabi is given to similar forms of Islamic purism down to the present. The message of this scholar, however, would not have made much impact had he not teamed up in 1744 with a petty chieftain of Central Arabia, Muhammad ibn Saud. His message and Saud's ambitions proved an explosive mixture. They underlay the creation of the first Saudi empire, which was brought down by the armies of Ibrahim Pasha of Egypt in 1818. They subsequently inspired the creation of the second Saudi empire, the Kingdom of Saudi Arabia, which emerged in the 1920s.

This Saudi state became the corporate venture of the Saudi family, dependent on the legitimisation of Wahhabi '*ulama* that we know today. There has developed a constant and increasingly abrasive tension between the family and state interests of the Saudi family and the concerns of the Wahhabi '*ulama* to promote their Islamic understanding and to assert their authority. This situation has been exacerbated both by the Western life-style and corruption of many members of the royal family and by the state's close association with the USA. The presence of large numbers of Westerners in Saudi Arabia since the Gulf War of 1991 has made matters much worse. Other important factors are the growing Saudi middle class, which has no representation, and a growing population without jobs. As the median age in Saudi Arabia is 19.7, the situation will worsen, and the annual per capita income has fallen from $28 000 in the early 1980s to $7 000 today.

The Saudi regime could not afford to permit the USA to use the Prince Sultan airbase during the 2001 campaign in Afghanistan. It should be no surprise that the Saudis should have tried to gain Islamic credentials by supporting Hamas, the Palestinian Islamist organisation, or the Jama-at-i Islami of Pakistan, the Islamic Salvation Front of Algeria, or the Muslim Brotherhood of Egypt. Nearly half of the hijackers of September 11 were of Saudi origin, and one of the stated objectives of Usama bin Ladin, that Saudi citizen banished from his country, was the overthrow of the current Saudi regime.

The second manifestation of the Islamic revival connected with the present is the emergence of "reformist Islam" in South Asia in the nineteenth century. This is a movement whose ideas and organisation can be linked directly through time to the Taliban. At the heart of South Asia's "reformist Islam" was the Deoband *madrassa*, founded in 1867 and called by some the most important traditional Muslim university in the world after Egypt's al-Azhar. Deobandis were tackling the problem of how to sustain an Islamic society under British rule. They debated how to sustain Islam in the relatively novel situation in which they did not have, and would not wish to have, state support. The individual human conscience in search of salvation, knowing how to act properly as a Muslim, was to be the driving force sustaining a Muslim society. They embarked on a concerted effort to translate the Qur'an and other key texts into Indian languages. For the first time in the Muslim world the printing press was harnessed seriously and with enormous vigour to make these texts as widely available as possible. Schools were set up on the Deoband model: by 1967 there were said to be over 8000 worldwide, all supported by private subscription. This movement has come to be seen as a form of "Islamic Protestantism" in which Muslims without power developed their Muslim community by themselves. It was a self-sufficient form of Islam that could operate outside the colonial state, indeed, outside any state at all.[16]

The reformist Muslims, the Deobandis, largely opposed the creation of Pakistan – they did not need a Muslim state to create their Islamic world. Once it was created, they carried forward their message both in Pakistan and Afghanistan, where they had long-established *madrassas*. By the 1980s and 1990s hundreds of Deobandi *madrassas* had been established in Pakistan.

From at least the 1970s they were assisted from outside by funds, in particular from the Persian Gulf States and Saudi Arabia, and also by revenue remitted by Pakistanis working in the Gulf. The process was assisted, too, by the Islamic government of General Zia ul-Haq and by a Sunni Muslim urban elite concerned to consolidate its hold over the many Pakistanis who were moving from the countryside to the towns. Given their long-term connections with Afghanistan, it was natural after the Soviet invasion of 1979 that the Deobandi *madrassas* should perform a major role in assisting the large numbers of refugees who fled to Pakistan. Thus began the militarisation of the *madrassas* as the Afghans, but also Pakistanis and Arabs, fought their *jihad* against the Russians.

Once the Russians had been defeated, it was but a short step from this to the next stage: Pakistan's Inter-Services Intelligence agency used the students from these *madrassas*, the Taliban, to create a favourable regime in Afghanistan and to give Pakistan the strategic depth to the North-West that it had long sought. The Taliban were armed and trained, and in 1994 they invaded Afghanistan; by 1997 Pakistan recognised the Taliban as the rulers of Afghanistan.[17] The irony is that the Taliban, the heirs of a revivalist movement designed specifically to fashion an Islamic society which could exist without state power, should have been the very first group of Sunni Muslim *'ulama* to achieve total and unfettered control of a state – or at least the shattered remains of what was the Afghan state. Pakistan has been forced to assist in the destruction of the monster it helped to create, as it is now being pressed to curb the guerrilla groups whose action it has supported in Kashmir. These are not actions which it will be easy for the Jamiat ul-Ulama-i Islam (the Deobandi party in Pakistani politics) and its sympathisers to forgive.

The third aspect of the great Islamic movement of revival and reform which reaches into the present is the ideology and organisation of Islamism. Islamists are very much a twentieth-century phenomenon. They find the solutions of the reformers to the challenges of the West and modernity unsatisfactory because, by and large, they ignored modernity and dodged the issue of power. The responses of Muslim modernists, many of whom led nationalist movements, were no less satisfactory. Certainly they understood the issue of power, but in engaging with the West they were deemed to be willing to sacrifice too much that was essential to Islam and Muslim culture. Islamists saw the real danger as Western civilisation itself. Their real enemies were the secular or modernist elites in Muslim societies who collaborated with Western political, economic, and cultural forces, and enabled Western influence to flourish in their societies. Their prime aim was to take power themselves so that their societies could be sealed off from these corrupting influences. They would then be able to introduce their Islamic system in which the Qur'an and the *shari'ah* were sufficient for all human purposes. This was a system to match capitalism or socialism; it envisaged the Islamisation of economics, knowledge, and so on – it was an ideology.

The founders of the Islamist trajectory in Islamic revivalism were Maulana Mawdudi of India and Pakistan (1903–79), whose organisation was the Jama-at-i Islami, and Hasan al-Banna of Egypt, assassinated in 1949, who founded the Muslim Brotherhood. From the 1970s Islamist organisations had spread widely in the Muslim world. Among the more notable organisations were the Islamic Salvation Front of Algeria, Hamas of Palestine, and the Rifa Party of Turkey. Amongst their notable successes were the dramatic assassination in 1981 of Anwar Sadat, President of Egypt, the steady Islamisation of the Pakistani constitution and law, and, of course, the Iranian Revolution.

It is important to understand that Islamism is in its way a profoundly "modern" movement, concerned to chart an Islamically-based path of progress for Muslim societies. While concerned to resist the West, its leaders have been influenced by Western knowledge. Sayyid Qutb who took over the leadership of the Muslim Brotherhood from Hasan al-Banna was much influenced by the French fascist thinker, Alexis Carrell, and a visit to the USA. Ali Shariati, ideologue of the Iranian Revolution, was much influenced by Sartre, Fanon, and Louis Massignon. Erbakan, the leading Turkish Islamist politician was an engineer. Bazargan and Bani-Sadr, early leaders of the Iranian Revolution were an engineer and an economist. The followers of Islamist movements are the displaced. More often than not they have moved from countryside to city and look for medical, educational, and psychological support, often in areas where the state is failing. Anthropological studies have shown that Islamism and its organisations often provide the means by which both men and women can come to participate in the modern economy and state.

Classically, the prime concern of Islamist groups has always been to effect change in their own societies, to seize power if possible. The one exception to this rule has been a concern from the beginning with the fate of Palestine. However, we are told that Usama bin Ladin's al-Qa'ida network contains members of former Islamist groups and is in contact with Islamist groups throughout the world. This network, moreover, seems to have been that which from the early 1990s has consistently waged war on US targets in West Asia and the USA itself. We need to know why this change has taken place. Is there, for instance, a new strand of Islamism which sees the struggle for power in Pakistan, Saudi Arabia, and Egypt as one which can only be won by assaults on the USA? Or are we dealing with the personal vendetta of an evil genius brilliantly able to make the anger and hunger for justice in the Islamic world serve his purpose?

How far, then, does this scenario represent the makings of a clash of civilisations, of Islam and the West? It is possible to portray the fourteen hundred years of interaction between the Islamic world and the West as a clash of civilisations, of world-views. We can refer to our Crusades against Islam in West Asia and in Spain, or the annual Ottoman campaign in Europe, which took the form of holy war. We can be blinded by the legacy of hundreds of years of polemic against Islam just as Muslims belittled European civilisation until the nineteenth century. But, alternatively, we could, as more and more scholars are doing today, note how much through history Christian and Islamic civilisations have fruitfully interacted and played a part in shaping each other.[18]

The roots of Islamic civilisation lie in the monotheistic and Hellenistic traditions of the Eastern Roman Empire. Indeed, its universalism is directly derived from the political and religious universalism of Constantine's Byzantine Empire. Medieval Europe was hugely enriched by the Arab-Muslim knowledge that was transmitted through Italy and Spain. Down to the nineteenth century Europeans measured themselves in various ways against the world of Islam. During the nineteenth and twentieth centuries, as we have seen, the Muslim world came to be shaped by Europe. And now, of course, Muslims play their part in shaping the West, both from within and from without. These two worlds, Christian and Muslim, have shared much and have much more to share. In a most important statement the Second Vatican Council asked Christians to reflect on what they shared with Muslims:

> The Church also regards Muslims with esteem. They adore the one God, living and subsisting in Himself, merciful and all-powerful, the Creator of heaven and earth, who has spoken to men; they take pains to submit wholeheartedly to even His inscrutable decrees, just as Abraham with whom the faith of Islam takes pleasure in linking itself submitted to God. Though they do not acknowledge Jesus as God, they revere him as a prophet. They also honour Mary, His virgin Mother; at times they even call on her with devotion. In addition they await the Day of Judgement when God will render their desserts to all those who have been raised up from the dead. Finally, they value moral life and worship God especially through prayer, almsgiving and fasting.[19]

Arguably, if there is a clash of civilisations, it is between those who believe in God and those who do not. Do the howls of rage and protest at the dominance of the West speak for all Muslims? No. Throughout the period of Western dominance in the world, there have been Muslims who have felt that Western power and dominance was not a cause for complaint but a call to constructive action. Western power and dominance was based on knowledge from which they should benefit. This goes as much for leading figures such as Sir Sayyed Ahmed Khan, the creator of Islamic modernism, or Mustafa Kamal Atatürk, who gave modern Turkey such distinctive direction, as it does for the tens of thousands of Muslims every year who come to the West to be educated in its universities. These expressions of protest, moreover, stem less from an intrinsic hatred of the West than from the impact of the West on Muslim societies. Often it is part of a discourse within Muslim societies about how they should progress, a discourse in which Western influence is felt to be a constraint. It is worth reflecting on the sense of self-confidence that Iran has gained from its revolution, a revolution which has allowed it to chart its own destiny. "What has your revolution achieved? What has it given the Iranian people who are suffering from the ravages of war? " a journalist asked an Iranian leader in 1989, as ten years of the revolution were celebrated. He replied: "We have given the Iranian people a sense of self-respect and dignity. Now Iranians in Tehran, and not in Washington or in London, make decisions about the destiny of Iran."[20]

In considering the clash of civilisations, how much weight should we give to pan-Islamic consciousness, to Islamic solidarity? Traditionally, Islamic solidarity has tended to founder on the other affinities which bind groups of Muslims: the differences between major ethnic groups – Arabs, Persians, Turks, South Asians, and so on. There are the subnational affinities which bedevil the politics of many states: Kurds, Berbers, Azeris; the differences between the Punjabis and the rest in Pakistan, those between the Pathans and the rest in Afghanistan. We have the great religious distinctions between Shi'ah and Sunni. There are the often bitter sectarian distinctions generated by the process of Islamic revival on the Indian subcontinent: Deobandi, Barelvi, Ahl-i Hadith, Ahl-i Quran, Ahmadi, Jamaat-i Islami, Tablighi Jamaati, and others. Then on top of this there are the often-competing interests of Muslim states. For a moment, iconic issues such as Palestine can bring Muslims together, but in the long term solidarity is always likely to be broken by local affinity, local antagonism, state interest, and the mundane (Fuller and Lesser 1995: 109–36).

What weight should we give to the issue of Islamism? Islamist parties form the chief opposition to current governments in many Muslim states. Moreover, given the weakness of these states, given their economic problems, and in particular given their age structures – most Muslim societies are experiencing, or about to experience, massive youth bulges (the Muslim population of the world which was 18 per cent in 1980 is due to become 30 per cent by 2025)[21] – it is likely that a number of Islamist parties will come to power. Will the accession to power of parties, which more often than not see Western civilisation as the enemy, bring us closer to a clash of civilisations? Certainly, in the first flush of victory we might expect some hardening of attitudes towards Israel, a revision of oil policy, or a withdrawal of support for UN resolutions supporting interventionist policies. However, as Anthony Parsons, HM Ambassador to Iran at the time of the revolution, always used to maintain, and Fred Halliday does now, these regimes will be swiftly constrained by the political economies of their societies and by the geopolitics of their environment. It is remarkable how increasingly pragmatic the revolutionary regime in Iran has become, whether it be over allied intervention in Afghanistan, sending its students to Europe, or talking to the "Great Satan" itself. Deputy Foreign Minister Kharazi had to resign in April 2002, not because he was talking to the USA, but because he revealed the fact in public.

The final issue is whether Usama bin Ladin's al-Qa'ida represents a new strand of Islamism which has broader objectives. By his own account, it does. He is no longer concerned just to take power in Muslim societies but to wage war on Western hegemony. In his book *America and the Third World War*, for instance, which became available in 1999, he calls on the entire Muslim world to rise up against the existing world order to fight for their rights to live as Muslims, rights he says, which are being trampled on by the West's intentional spreading of Westernisation (Bodansky 1999: 388). In bin Ladin we have a Muslim who sees the current situation in terms of a clash of civilisations, and who has created a global terrorist network to resist Western hegemony. In addressing this threat, it will not be enough to focus on the terrorist network itself, the West must address and be seen to be addressing, the many issues of injustice from Palestine onwards which drive young Muslims into the bin Ladin camp. The prize is Muslim public opinion, that third of the world's population by 2025. If we act so as to alienate, or sustain the existing alienation of, that public opinion, which is what seems to be happening at the moment, we might just begin to have a real clash of civilisations.

Notes

1   Essay based on a lecture delivered at the Royal Society for Asian Affairs on 5 June 2002, published in their journal *Asian Affairs*, vol. 33, part 3 (October 2002), pp. 307–20, <www.tandf.co.uk/journals/> and reproduced here with permission.
2   See the critique of Huntington in Fuller and Lesser (1995), and Halliday (2002).
3   Immanuel Wallerstein, *The Modern World System*, vol. 1–3 (New York: Academic Press, 1974–89).
4   For a translation and commentary on this most influential work on the lives of Urdu-speaking Muslims in South Asia, see Christopher Shackle and Javed Majeed, *Hali's Musaddas: the Flow and Ebb of Islam* (Delhi: Oxford University Press, 1997).
5   Gail Minault (trans.), "Urdu Political Poetry during the Khilafat Movement", *Modern Asian Studies*, vol. 8, no. 4 (1974), 459–71.
6   Susan G. Miller (trans. and ed.), *Disorienting Encounters: Travels of a Moroccan Scholar in France in 1845–1846: The Voyage of Muhammad As-Saffar* (Berkeley: University of California Press, 1992), pp. 193–4.
7   Quoted in R. Malik, "Mawlana Husayn Ahmad Madani and Jami-yat 'Ulama-i Hindi, 1920–1957: Status of Islam and Muslims in India", PhD thesis (University of Toronto, 1995), pp. 44–5.
8   A. J. Arberry (trans.), *Persian Psalms (Zabur-i Ajam) ... from the Persian of the late Sir Muhammad Iqbal* (Karachi, 1968).
9   Quoted in Hamid Algar's introduction to H. Algar (trans.), *On the Sociology of Islam: Lectures by Ali Shari'ati* (Berkeley, CA: Mizan Press, 1979), p. 23.
10 Hamid Algar (trans.), *Islam and Revolution: Writings and Declarations of Imam Khomeini* (Berkeley, CA: Mizan Press, 1981), p. 182.
11 *The Crusades: Islamic Perspectives* (Edinburgh: Edinburgh University Press, 1999), p. 590.
12 Ibid., p. 602.
13 William Theodore de Bary (ed.), *Sources of Indian Tradition: From the Beginning to 1800* (New York: 1958), p. 756.
14 Francis Robinson, "Islam and the Impact of Print in South Asia", in F. Robinson, *Islam and Muslim History in South Asia* (Delhi: Oxford University Press, 2000), pp. 66–104.
15 For a sketch of the development of this process, see Francis Robinson, *Atlas of the Islamic World since 1500* (Oxford: Oxford University Press, 1982), pp.110–75; and for its impact on the individual, see Francis Robinson, "Religious Change and the Self in Muslim South Asia since 1800", *South Asia*, vol. 22 (Special Issue, 1999), 13–27.
16 For an authoritative analysis of the Deobandi movement, see B. D. Metcalf, *Islamic Revival in British India: Deoband, 1860–1900* (Princeton, NJ: Princeton University Press, 1982).
17 For the growth of *madrassas* and their significance in Pakistan, see M. Q. Zaman, "Sectarianism in Pakistan: The Radicalization of Shi'i and Sunni Identities", *Modern Asian Studies*, vol. 32, no. 3 (1998), 689–716, and S. V. R. Nasr, "The Rise of Sunni Militancy in Pakistan: The Changing Role of Islamism and the Ulama in Society and Politics", *Modern Asian Studies*, vol. 34, no. 1 (2000), 139–80; and for the relationship between the Taliban and the *madrassas*, see Rashid 2000.
18 Francis Robinson, "The Muslim and the Christian Worlds: Shapers of Each Other", in F. Robinson, *Islam and Muslim History*, pp. 28–43.
19 *Nostra Aetate*, proclaimed by Pope Paul VI on 28 October 1965.
20 M. Hussain, "Roots of anti-Americanism", *Herald*, October 2001, 50–54.
21 See Huntington 1996: 102–21.

Chapter 5

Of Saints and Sufis in the Near East: Past and Present

William Dalrymple

In the spring of the year 587 AD, had you been sitting on a bluff of rock overlooking Bethlehem, you would have been able to see two figures setting off, staff in hand, from the gates of the great desert monastery of St Theodosius. The two figures – an old grey-bearded monk accompanied by a tall, upright perhaps slightly stern younger companion – would have headed south-east through the wastes of Judea, towards the then fabulously rich port-metropolis of Gaza.

It was the start of an extraordinary forty-year journey that would take John Moschos and his pupil Sophronius the Sophist in an arc across the entire Eastern Byzantine world, from the shores of the Bosphorus, through Cappadocia, to the sand dunes of desert Egypt. Now, unlike the wonderful serais built by the Ottomans, Byzantine caravanserais were rough places and the provincial Greek aristocracy did not enjoy entertaining: as the Byzantine writer Cecaumenus put it "houseparties are a mistake, for guests merely criticise your housekeeping and attempt to seduce your wife."

So everywhere they went, the two travellers stayed in some of the thousands of monasteries, caves, and hermitages which then littered the Middle East from Egypt to Cappadocia, the sheer numbers of which are often forgotten. By the early fifth century, some seven hundred monasteries filled the area between Jerusalem and Upper Egypt alone; indeed, they flourished to such an extent that travellers reported that the population of the desert now equalled that of the towns. "The number of monks is past counting," wrote the Italian pilgrim Rufinus of Aquilea in the fourth century. "There are so many of them that an earthly emperor could not assemble so large an army. There is no town or village in this part of the world which is not surrounded by hermitages as if by walls; while other monks live in desert caves or in even more remote places." This fashion of monasteries soon spread north, first into Syria, then to Anatolia. By the sixth century the wildernesses of Anatolia – and especially Cappadocia – had also become packed with monks.

As well as the monks there were also countless cave-dwelling hermits and great herds of "grazers", nomadic ascetics who, according to the older of the two travellers, John Moschos, "wander in the desert as if they were wild animals: like birds they fly about the hills; they forage like goats. Their daily round is inflexible, always predictable, for they feed on roots, the natural products of the earth." In that period those monasteries in Cappadocia would once not have been exceptional in their density; they are exceptional merely in that being carved out of solid rock they have survived.

In every monastery that they visited the two travellers, John and Sophronius, dined with the monks and ascetics. In each abbey, Moschos jotted down onto papyrus accounts that he heard of the sayings of the stylites and Desert Fathers, the sages and mystics of the Byzantine East, before this world, that was clearly on the verge of collapse, finally disappeared for ever. Later, exiled in Constantinople, Moschos wrote an account of his travels; entitled *The Leimonarion*, or *The Spiritual Meadow*, his book received an enthusiastic reception in monasteries across the Byzantine Empire. Within a generation or two, it had been translated into Latin, Georgian, Armenian, Arabic, and a variety of Slavonic languages.

Part of the reason for the book's success, and the reason why Moschos is still a pleasure to read, is that he has a wonderfully wicked sense of humour, and there is an endearing lightness of touch evident in the stories he tells of the monks he encountered on his travels. One typical tale concerns a novice from Antinoe in Upper Egypt "who," according to Moschos "was very careless with his own soul. When the novice dies, his teacher is worried that he might have been sent to hell for his sins, so he prays that it might be revealed what has happened to his pupil's soul. Eventually the teacher goes into a trance, and sees a river of fire with the novice submerged in it up to his neck. The teacher is horrified, but the novice turns to him saying, 'I thank God, oh my teacher, that there is relief for my head. Thanks to your prayers I am standing on the head of a bishop.' ".

However, the real fascination of John Moschos's writing for us today is that it brings to life, as no other source, the daily life of the Desert Fathers who lived in the hermitages and monasteries in Cappadocia, and the stories in *The Spiritual Meadow* form a detailed picture of one of the strangest periods in Turkey's history. Today, of course, it seems almost inexplicable that so many people – many of them highly educated and cosmopolitan – from across the width of the civilised Byzantine world would give up everything and travel for thousands of miles to live a life of extreme hardship in the discomfort of the desert; yet to the Byzantine mind, nothing could have been more logical. In one of Moschos's stories, a stranger visits the renowned holy man, Abba Olympios, in his monastery in the heat of Anatolia. "How can you stay in this place with its burning heat and so many insects?" he asks. The holy man gives a simple answer: "I put up with the stings of the insects to escape from what scripture calls 'the stings that never cease'. Likewise, I endure the burning heat for fear of the eternal fire. The one is temporary, but of the other there is no end."

Yet this was not the whole story. While Moschos never underestimates the hardship involved in living the life of the Desert Fathers, he is also well aware of its joys. Indeed one of the principal themes of his writing is that by living their life in utter simplicity and holiness, the monks of Anatolia were returning to the conditions of the Garden of Eden, in harmony both with the natural world and its Creator. The close relationship of beasts and saints was in fact a constant theme in monastic literature: the early Coptic *Life* of St Pachomius, for example, tells how the saint summoned crocodiles to ferry him across the Nile rather as today one might call a cab from a taxi rank.

Now the monastic world described by John Moschos, of which Cappadocia was an important part, was a very different scene from the settled world of the medieval Western cloister with which most of us are familiar; it was a place where oracle-like stylites settled the domestic disputes of Eastern Christendom from atop their pillars, where dendrites took literally Christ's instruction to behave like the birds of the air, and who therefore lived in trees and built little nests for themselves in the branches – and where other hermits walled themselves up in hermitages, suspended themselves in cages, and where one gentleman, named Baradatus, even sowed himself up in animal skins so that he would be baked alive in sweltering Syrian midsummer heat, a sort of Byzantine boil-in-the-bag monk.

It is easy to laugh at these strange Byzantine hermits, but it is well worth making the effort to try to understand them. By their ability to endure physical suffering, Byzantine holy men, such as Baradatus, were believed to be able to wear away the curtain that separated the visible world from the divine and, by reaching through, gain direct access to God, something that was thought to be impossible for the ordinary believer. For by mortifying the flesh, it was believed that the holy men became transformed: "If you will, you can become all flame," said Abba Joseph in one of the stories of the Desert Fathers, holding up his hand to show fingers which had "become like ten lamps of fire", radiant with the "uncreated light of divinity", the same form of divine illumination that is shown surrounding the great saints in icons. In this heightened state, the holy men who lived in these Cappadocian caves were believed to be able to act as intercessors for their followers at the distant court of heaven, and like the old pagan gods had the power to give children to barren women, to cure the sick, and to divine the future.

But perhaps the holy men's most important task was to fight demons. The world was believed by the Byzantines to be besieged by invisible agents of darkness, and to sin was not merely to err: it was to be overcome by these sinister forces. Demonic activity was a daily irritation and was believed to intrude on the most ordinary, domestic activities. Gregory the Great, for example, always used to recommend making the Sign of the Cross over a lettuce in case you accidently swallowed a demon that happened to be perched on its leaves. In much the same vein, John Moschos tells the story of a nunnery in south-west Turkey which was attacked by a troop of demons; as a result "five of the virgins conspired to run away from the monastery and find themselves husbands."

Like the Muslim *djinns* which superseded them, Byzantine demons lurked especially in old temples and remote hillsides. The *Life* of a Cappadocian holy man named Theodore of Sykeon tells how a group of farmers, digging into a mound of earth on a distant hillside, inadvertently released a great swarm of demons that took possession not only of them, but of their neighbours and their animals; only a holy man like Theodore was able to drive the evil spirits back into their lairs again and seal them in. Monks and holy men were thought of as "prize-fighters" against the devil's minions, and only with their help – and their amulets, relics, and remedies – could demons be fought or defeated. Across the Eastern Mediterranean the tradition still continues: to this day the remaining Christian monks – particularly those in Egypt – are believed to be powerful exorcists, a talent they share with their Islamic counterparts, the Muslim Sufi mystics.

For all their strangeness, there is a great deal in the period and in the ideals of the monks of Cappadocia that is still deeply attractive: the Great Orthodox monastic tradition which aims at the purification of the soul through the taming of the flesh, where the material world is pulled aside like a great heavy curtain to allow man's gaze to go straight to God. Moreover, the monasteries where this spiritual warfare took place were fortresses that preserved everything that had been salvaged from the wreck of classical civilisation, so preserving the learning of antiquity from extinction, until such a time as Islamic scholars would translate the Greek and Latin classics into Arabic and so pass them back to Europe via Sicily and Islamic Spain.

In 1994, I set off on a six-month journey, circling the Levant from Athos to the monasteries of southern Egypt, following very roughly in John Moschos's footsteps, to discover what was left of the world of the Desert Fathers that he so beautifully describes. To my surprise, despite all the changes that have taken place across the Middle East in the last fifteen hundred years, and thanks largely to the often forgotten tolerance of Islam to its Christian subjects, a surprising number of the monasteries visited by Moschos and Sophronius in the 570s still, just, survive. There are even some in Anatolia: less than 150 miles east of here, in the Tur Abdin, there survives a last group of Christian monasteries, where the monks – and the surrounding laity – still speak Aramaic, the language of Christ.

Like timeless islands of Byzantium, with their bells and black robes and candle-lit processions, the monasteries are still occupied by elderly monks whose heavily-whiskered faces mirror those of the frescoed saints on the monastery walls. The monk's vestments remain unchanged since Byzantine times; the same icons are painted in the same way. Today, sitting under a candle-lit Byzantine mosaic, listening to plain-chant still sung in the language of sixth-century Byzantium, it is still – just – possible to forget the intervening centuries and feel that the lifeline of tones and syllables, fears and hopes, linking us with the time of John Moschos and the Desert Fathers is still intact.

One of the reasons I wanted to make the journey is that in many places, this ancient Christian way of life is now threatened with extinction. In the Holy Land for example, Greek Orthodox monasteries built to hold two thousand monks often now contain only one single monk or nun. In Upper Egypt armed fundamentalists attack the Coptic monasteries with machine guns, and last year there were even stories of terrorists of the Gamaat al-Islamiyyah, or Muslim Brotherhood, crucifying Coptic peasants.

As Islam and Christianity are usually viewed as rival and even adversarial religions, I had expected on my journey in John Moschos's footsteps to encounter a record of a long succession of conflicts, and certainly there were a few places where this was the case. But to my surprise, what I saw was by and large a very much more intimate relationship between the two religions. For it is only when you travel in remote rural places in Christianity's Eastern homelands do you realise how closely the two religions are really connected, Islam growing directly out of what was then an entirely Christian environment, and to this day, embodying many aspects and practices of the early Christian world now lost in Christianity's modern Western-based incarnation.

When the early Byzantines were first confronted by the Prophet's armies, they assumed that Islam was merely a variant form of Christianity, and in some ways they were not so far wrong: Islam of course accepts much of the Old and New Testaments, obeys the Mosaic laws about circumcision and ablutions, and venerates both Jesus and the ancient Jewish prophets. The way the very first Muslims acted towards Christians – and particularly towards Christian holy men – is very significant in this respect. When Muhammad's successor Abu Bakr stood on the borders of Syria, he gave very specific instructions to his soldiers: "In the desert," he said, "you will find people who have secluded themselves in cells; let them alone, for they have secluded themselves for the sake of God." Likewise, when his successor 'Umar ibn al-Khattab went to Syria, he actually stayed with the Bishop of Ayla and went out of his way to meet the Christian holy men in the town. For many years Muslims and Christians used to pray side by side in the great churches of the Middle Eastern cities: in Damascus, for example, the great basilica of St John was used for worship by both Christians and Muslims; only fifty years later were Christians obliged to pray elsewhere and the building was formally converted into what is now known as the great Ummayad mosque.

Indeed, the greatest and most subtle theologian of the early Church, St John Damascene, was convinced that Islam was at root not a new religion, but instead a variation on a Judeo-Christian form. This perception is particularly remarkable as St John had grown up in the Ummayad Arab court of Damascus – the hub of the young Islamic world – where his father was chancellor, and he was an intimate boyhood friend of the future Caliph al-Yazid; the two boys' drinking bouts in the streets of Damascus were the subject of much horrified gossip in the streets of the new Islamic capital. Later, in his old age, John took the habit at the desert monastery of Mar Saba where he began work on his great masterpiece, a refutation of heresies entitled the *Fount of Knowledge*. The book contains an extremely precise and detailed critique of Islam, the first ever written by a Christian, which, intriguingly, John regarded as a form of Christianity and closely related to the heterodox Christian doctrine of Arianism and Nestorianism. After all, these doctrines, like Islam, took as their starting-point a similar position: that God could not become fully human without somehow compromising his divinity. This was a kinship of which both the Muslims and the Nestorians were aware. In 649 CE the Nestorian patriarch wrote: "These Arabs fight not against our Christian religion; nay, rather they defend our faith, they revere our priests and saints, and they make gifts to our churches and monasteries." At this stage of Islamic history, there were never any conversions by the sword, a myth much propagated in anti-Islamic literature.

The longer you spend in the Christian communities of the Middle East, the more you become aware of the extent to which Eastern Christian practice seemed to have formed the template for what were to become the basic conventions of Islam. The Muslim form of prayer, with its bowings and prostrations, appears to derive from the older Syrian Orthodox tradition that is still practised in pewless churches across the Levant. The architecture of the earliest minarets, which are square rather than round, unmistakably derive from the church towers of Byzantine Syria, while Ramadan, at first sight one of the most specific and distinctive of Islamic practices, is in fact nothing more than an Islamicisation of Lent, which in the Eastern Christian churches still involves a gruelling all-day fast.

Certainly if a monk from sixth-century Byzantium were to come back today, it is probable that he would find much more that was familiar in the practices and beliefs of a modern Muslim Sufi than he would with, say, a contemporary American Evangelical. Yet this simple truth has been lost by our tendency to think of Christianity as a thoroughly Western religion rather than the Oriental faith which by origin it actually is. Moreover, the modern tendency to demonise Islam in the West has led to an atmosphere where few in either camp are aware of, or indeed wish to be aware of, the profound kinship of Christianity and Islam.

In some traditional accounts of the cave churches of Cappadocia, emphasis is put on the degree to which these hidden caves allowed the local monks to hide from their Muslim enemies. But this view is now being challenged. Indeed, the degree to which the later monks in this region lived cheek by jowl with their Muslim neighbours is told in the paintings – if you look carefully enough. In the paintings of some of the rock churches, bands of Kufic ornament can be seen framing the images of the saints. Kufic borders also line the edges of robes, or enliven the surfaces of objects, like the shields of the soldiers guarding the tomb of Christ, or Salome's ewer at the Nativity. A new type of long narrow over-garment, with a frontal slit at the skirt, seems to have arrived via the current fashions of the Abbasid court in Baghdad. Moreover, the image of Christ in the west arm of Yilanli Kilise, in the valley of Peristrema, is not properly enthroned, according to the conventional Western iconography, but instead is seated cross-legged on the floor in the Arab manner.

Perhaps no branch of Islam shows so much Christian influence as Islamic mysticism or Sufism. For Sufism, with its holy men and visions, healings and miracles, its affinity with the desert, its emphasis on the mortification of the flesh, and the individual's personal search for union with God, has always borne remarkable similarities to the more mystical strands of Eastern Christianity, and many Muslim saints – such as the great Mevlana Rumi – worked to reconcile the two religions. Indeed, the very word Sufi seems to indicate a link with Christianity. For *suf* means wool, which was the characteristic clothing material of Eastern Christian monks, taken over by the early mystics of Islam. Other styles of dress adopted by the Sufis are also anticipated in pre-Islamic Christianity: the patchwork frock made from rags, and the use of the colour of mourning, black for the Christians, dark blue for the Muslims. Another interesting link – at the extreme edge of both Christian and Muslim asceticism – is the wearing of heavy chains. This was a practice first adopted by the Christian grazers whom I mentioned earlier, and which was later adopted by some Sufi sects. Through punishing the flesh, such exercises were believed by both groups of ascetics to induce visions and spiritual ectasy.

With this shared history, it is hardly surprising therefore that it is at Sufi shrines that today one finds Christians and Muslims coming into the closest religious contact. On my 1994 journey, as I was passing through Syria, I saw Christians coming to sacrifice a sheep at the shrine of a Muslim saint. This was in the ruins of the old Byzantine city of Cyrrhus, north-west of Aleppo, just over the Turkish border, not far from Antakya. I was told that a Syrian Orthodox girl, struck down by some apparently incurable sickness, had had a dream, telling her to visit the shrine of Nebi Uri at Cyrrhus. She had done so, spent the night in his shrine, and the next day had been healed. The sheep, which was covered with flowers and ribbons like the Old Testament scapegoat, was being slaughtered as an offering.

"We believe that if you are generous and give a good sheep to fulfil your vow," said the Sufi Shaykh who presided over the shrine, "then you will ride that sheep at the Day of Judgement. That sheep will carry you into Paradise."

"And the Christians believe this too?" I asked.

"There is no difference between ourselves and the Christians on this matter," said the Shaykh, "except that sometimes the Christians make the sign of Christ over the forehead of the person they want cured."

Again and again on my journey through the Levant, I came across this extraordinary Christian-Muslim syncretism, this porousness of faith, where the ideas, practices, and superstitions of one religion have trickled imperceptibly into another. But there was something else too. It wasn't just that in many places Christianity and Islam were still managing to coexist: seeing them together, and seeing the way the Eastern Christians practised their faith, brought home quite how closely the two faiths are really linked. Perhaps the most remarkable testament to this was what I saw was at Seidnaya, a Greek Orthodox convent in Syria, three hours' walk from Damascus. The monastery sits on a great crag of rock overlooking the orchards and olive groves of the Damascene plain, and at first sight, with its narrow windows and great rugged curtain walls, looks more like a Crusader castle than a convent.

According to legend, the monastery was founded in the early sixth century after the Byzantine Emperor Justinian chased a stag onto the top of the hill during a hunting expedition. Just as Justinian was about to draw his bow, the stag changed into the Virgin Mary, who commanded him to build a convent on the top of the rock. The site, she said, had previously been hallowed by Noah, who had planted a vine there after the flood.

Partly because of this vision, and partly because of the miracle-working powers of one of the convent's icons, said to have been painted by St Luke himself, the abbey quickly become a place of pilgrimage and to this day streams of Christian, Muslim, and Druze pilgrims trudge their way to Seidnaya from the mountains of Lebanon and the valleys of the Syrian *jebel*. In 1994, on my six-month journey, I went to spend a night within its walls.

By the time I arrived at the monastery gate, it was after eight o'clock on a dark and cold winter's night. Walking into an empty courtyard, my feet echoing on the flagstones, I wondered for a second where everyone had gone. Then I heard the distant sound of Orthodox chant drifting from the church and headed towards it.

Two nuns in black veils were chanting from a lectern, while a priest, hidden behind the iconostasis, echoed their chants in a deep reverberating bass. The only light came from a few flickering lamps suspended from the ceiling on gold chains. As the candle-light waxed and waned in the breeze, the highlights of the frescoes in the domes and semi-domes flashed momentarily into view, then disappeared again into the shadows.

When a friend of mine visited the convent thirty years ago, he said he witnessed a miracle: that he saw the face of the icon of Notre Dame de Seidnaya stream with tears. In the same church I too witnessed a miracle, or something that today would certainly be regarded as a miracle in almost any other country in the Middle East. For the congregation in the church consisted, not principally of Christians, but almost entirely of heavily bearded Muslim men and their shrouded wives. As the priest circled the altar with his thurible, filling the sanctuary with great clouds of incense, the men bobbed up and down on their prayer mats as if in the middle of Friday prayers in a great mosque. Their women, some dressed in full black chador, mouthed prayers from the shadows of the exo-narthex. A few, closely watching the Christian women, went up to the icons hanging from the pillars; they kissed them, then lit a candle, and placed it in the candelabra in front of the image. As I watched from the rear of the church, I could see the faces of the women reflected in the illuminated gilt of the icons.

Towards the end of the service, the priest circled the length of the church with his thurible, gently and almost apologetically stepping over the prostrate Muslims blocking his way. It was a truly extraordinary sight, Christians and Muslims praying. Yet this was, of course, the old way: the Eastern Christians and the Muslims have lived side by side for nearly one-and-a-half millennia and have only been able to do so due to a degree of mutual tolerance and shared customs unimaginable in the solidly Christian West.

The West, we sometimes like to think, is the home of freedom of thought and liberty of worship, and we forget how, as recently as the seventeenth century, Huguenot exiles escaping religious persecution in Europe would write admiringly of the policy of religious tolerance practised across the Islamic world: as M. de la Motraye put it, "there is no country on earth where the exercise of all Religions is more free and less subject to being troubled, than in Turkey." The same broad tolerance that had given homes to the hundreds of thousands of penniless Jews expelled by the bigoted Catholic kings from Spain and Portugal, protected the Eastern Christians in their ancient homelands – despite the Crusades and the almost continual hostility of the Christian West. Only in the twentieth century has that tolerance been replaced by a new hardening in Islamic attitudes; only recently has the syncretism and pluralism of Seidnaya become a precious rarity.

As vespers drew to a close, the pilgrims began to file quietly out, and I was left alone at the back of the church with my rucksack. As I was standing there, I was approached by a young nun. Sister Tecla had intelligent black eyes and a bold, confident gaze; she spoke fluent French with a slight Arabic accent. I remarked on the number of Muslims in the congregation and asked: was it at all unusual?

"The Muslims come here because they want babies," said the nun simply. "Our Lady has shown her power and blessed many of the Muslims. The people started to talk about her and now more Muslims come here than Christians. If they ask for her, she will be there."

As we were speaking, we were approached by a Muslim couple. The woman was veiled – only her nose and mouth were visible through the black wraps; her husband, a burly man who wore his beard without a moustache, looked remarkably like the wilder sort of Hizbollah commander featured in news bulletins from southern Lebanon. But whatever his politics, he carried in one hand a heavy tin of olive oil and in the other a large plastic basin full of fresh bread loaves, and he gave both to the nun, bowing his head as shyly as a schoolboy and retreating backwards in blushing embarrassment.

"They come in the evening," continued the nun. "They make vows and then the women spend the night. They sleep on a blanket in front of the holy icon of Our Lady. Sometimes the women eat the wick of a lamp that has burned in front of the image, or maybe drink the holy oil. Then, in the morning, they drink from the spring in the courtyard. Nine months later they have babies."

"And it works?"

"I have seen it with my own eyes," said Sister Tecla. "One Muslim woman had been waiting for a baby for twenty years. She was beyond the normal age of childbearing but someone told her about the Virgin of Seidnaya. She came here and spent two nights in front of the icon. She was so desperate she ate the wicks of nearly twenty lamps."

"What happened?"

"She came back the following year," said Sister Tecla, "with triplets."

The nun led me up the south aisle of the church, and down a corridor into the chapel which sheltered the icons. It was darker than the church, with no windows to admit even the faint light of the moon which had cast a silvery light over the altar during vespers. Here only the twinkling of a hundred lamps lit the interior, allowing us to avoid tripping over a pair of Muslims prostrated on their prayer carpets near the entrance. Sister Tecla kissed an icon of the warrior saints Sergius and Bacchus, then turned back to face me: "Sometimes the Muslims promise to christen a child born through the Mother of God's intervention. This happens less frequently than it used to, but of course we like it when it does. Others make their children Muslims, but when they are old enough, they bring them here to help us in some way, cleaning the church, or working in the kitchens."

Only one hundred years ago such syncretism was very common in Turkey too. Even today, there are still a few places where this syncretism still survives. In the Syrian Orthodox Monastery of Mar Gabriel near Mardin, less than 150 miles east of Seidnaya, I saw local Muslim villagers coming to pray at the shrine of the monastery's patron saint; indeed some take dust from the tomb to give both to their animals and children to keep them healthy during epidemics. More bizarrely still, Muslim women queue up with their Christian neighbours to drink water from the skull of a local saint named St John the Arab, something they believe will help barren women bear children.

Nor are such syncretisms just to be found in the rural outback of the far south-east: in Buyuk Ada, an island just off the coast of Istanbul, I saw similar activity at the Christian shrine of St George. Having walked up the path to the shrine, I marvelled at what I took to be thick white hibiscus blossom on the bushes near the summit. Only when I reached the top did I realise what they really were: on every bush, local Muslim pilgrims had tied strips of cloth – primitive fertility charms – to the branches. Some were quite elaborate: small cloth hammocks supporting stones, or pebbles, or small pinches of pine needles; others were tangled cat's cradles of threads, wrapped right around the bushes, as if packaged for the post.

Inside the shrine, it was just as remarkable. At some stage an unexplained fire had half-gutted the building, leaving charred rafters and singed window frames standing in the open air. But the rooms, though half-exposed and quite unrestored, were filled by a continuous trickle of supplicants. The two nationalities were praying side by side, the Greeks standing in front of the icon of the mounted saint, hands cupped in prayer, while the Turks lay prayer carpets on the floor and bent forward in the direction of Mecca. One veiled Muslim lady scraped with long nails at a tattered nineteenth-century fresco of the saint, then, with her fingertip touched a fragment of the paintwork to her tongue.

This essential kinship between the different religions of the book is something Muslim writers have been aware of for centuries. The thirteenth century Sufi Jalal al-Din Rumi, or the Maulana as he is known here in Turkey, was perhaps the greatest of all the mystical writers of Islam, and lived not far from here in Konya, at a time when its population was almost equally divided between Muslims, Christians, and Jews. When he was asked about the relationship between these three apparently incompatible religions, he replied with the following story:

> Once upon a time, in a far distant country somewhere north of Afghanistan, there was a city inhabited entirely by the blind. One day the news came that an elephant was passing outside the walls of the city.
>
> The citizens called a meeting and decided to send a delegation of three men outside the gates so that they could report back what an elephant was. In due course, the three men left the town and stumbled forwards until they eventually found the elephant. The three reached out, felt the animal with their hands, then they all headed back to town as quickly as they could to report what they had felt.
>
> The first man said: "An elephant is a marvellous creature! It is like a vast snake, but it can stand vertically upright in the air!" The second man was indignant at hearing this: "What nonsense!" he said. "This man is misleading you. I felt the elephant and what it most resembles is a pillar. It is firm and solid, and however hard you push against it, you could never knock it over." The third man shook his head and said: "Both these men are liars! I felt the elephant and it resembles a broad fan. It is wide and flat and leathery, and when you shake it, it wobbles around like the sail of a *dhow*." All three men stuck by their stories and for the rest of their lives refused to speak to each other. Each professed that they and only they knew the whole truth.

Now of course all three of the blind men had a measure of insight. The first man felt the trunk of the elephant, the second the leg, the third the ear. All had been granted part of the truth, but not one of them had begun to grasp the totality, or the greatness of the beast they had encountered. If only they had listened to one another and meditated on the different facets of the elephant, they might have grasped the true nature of the beast. But they were too proud and, instead, preferred to keep to their own half truths.

So it is with us. We see the Almighty one way, the Jews have a slightly different conception, and the Christians have a third. To us, all our different visions are irreconcilable. But what we forget is that before God we are like blind men stumbling around in total darkness ...

Chapter 6

Islam and the West:
Clash or Dialogue of Civilisations?[1]

Akbar S. Ahmed

Islam versus the West?

In the century just begun, how we organise our lives, view our own cultures, and interact with others will be shaped by the outcome of a struggle between two diametrically opposed ideas. These ideas are further separated, and the differences between them sharpened, by the process that has come to be called globalisation.[2] The first of these opposed ideas is the so-called "Clash of Civilisations", in which Muslims are invariably seen as the main opponents of the West. This Muslim–Western opposition is not a new idea.[3] In fact, it is a continuation of older ideas about Islam as a predatory civilisation threatening the West.[4]

The second and opposed idea is the "Dialogue of Civilisations", which was advocated by President Muhammad Khatami of Iran in the United Nations General Assembly in New York on 24 September 1998, with the support of the UN Secretary General Kofi Annan. President Khatami's statement made a dramatic impact because his country is associated in Western minds with "terrorism" and "extremism", although this idea too is not entirely new (Segesvary 2000, Picco 2001). World figures, including Pope John Paul II,[5] the Archbishop of Canterbury, George Carey, Nelson Mandela of South Africa, Prince Charles of Great Britain, and Bishop Desmond Tutu of South Africa have been involved in their own ways in precisely this kind of dialogue for many years. For people of good will or faith, the idea of dialogue lies at the heart of the human condition and the need to reach out.

The idea of dialogue was struck a deadly blow in America on 11 September 2001, when four hijacked planes killed thousands of innocent people and destroyed the lives of many more. Other global ideas lay buried in the rubble of the World Trade Centre in New York and in the smoking ruin of the Pentagon in Washington: that of triumphant globalisation as an irresistible, irreversible process, and the idea of America as an impregnable fortress.

On that extraordinary day, the President of the United States kept away from the capital, zigzagging across the country in Air Force One, escorted by F-16s and F-15s, only returning to take charge late in the day. The Stock Exchange closed after stocks and shares tumbled, all flights were suspended, emergency was declared in several states, and false alarms sent people scurrying for their lives. The scenes of panic on television would have seemed farfetched and unreal in a Hollywood film.

America began to recover quickly from the unprecedented carnage and mayhem; its native optimism began to reassert itself. The Stars and Stripes appeared everywhere and interfaith dialogue was heard across the land. President George W. Bush made a welcome visit to the Islamic Centre in Washington, DC. Dramatically, imperceptibly, the miasmic pall of uncertainty, of our lives being vulnerable and out of control, that hangs over much of the world now descended on Americans. People were aware that something had changed fundamentally.

The media created a sense of urgency, verging on hysteria. Anthrax cases, fires in the subway, even a tremor in California – everything was instinctively being blamed on the "terrorists". The news and discussions in the media were broadcast under the heading "America Under Attack". "Why do they hate us?" asked Americans. War was declared on "terrorists" and in early October the bombing of Afghanistan began. Muslim demonstrators protested in many parts of the world.

Wars are usually a consequence of the breakdown of communication between the protagonists. In this case it was a totally asymmetrical war in the most profound ways possible: the two different societies, one highly industrialized and world-dominating, the other still pre-industrial, impoverished and tribal, speaking different languages and living in different cultures. The only thing they had in common was the mutual incomprehension with which they viewed each other.

American commentators pointed to Iraq, Syria, and Iran as other "terrorist" states and potential targets. Pakistan, which had nurtured and supported the Taliban in Afghanistan, escaped the wrath of the United States by hastily ditching the Taliban and siding with Washington. Usama bin Ladin, in an extraordinary interview broadcast on American television,[6] argued that this was a war between Islam and the West. The main grievances he listed were the plight of the Palestinians and the people of Iraq; foreign, non-Muslim troops stationed in Saudi Arabia, and the oppression of Muslims by repressive Muslim regimes. The list struck a nerve in the mosques, shantytowns, and bazaars of the Muslim world. The idea of Islam as an enemy was gaining ground in the West in spite of Western leaders insisting that this was not true.

Commentators had associated Muslims with the September 11 attacks from the moment the news broke. Usama bin Ladin, who had threatened the United States with mass terror on several occasions, was widely believed to be the mastermind. If a Japanese cult had stepped forward and claimed responsibility, no one would have paid any heed. In the public mind Islam was to blame. Reports of the harassment of Muslims and attacks on mosques began to circulate. Girls wearing the *hijab*, or headscarf, were attacked and abused. Arabs and Pakistanis were killed; so was a Sikh, mistaken for a Muslim because of his beard and turban. The years of negative press, news of hijacking or hostage-taking or honour killings, reinforced by big-budget, mainstream Hollywood films like *True Lies, Executive Decision*, and *The Siege*, had conditioned the public to expect the worst from a civilisation widely viewed as "terrorist", "fundamentalist", and "fanatical". Immediately, unthinkingly, the explosions in Oklahoma City in 1995 were at first blamed on the Muslims. It was hard for the media to accept that a white Anglo-Saxon American man was responsible.

Muslims were not helping their case after 9/11. Muslim guilt seemed to be confirmed for Americans long before any concrete evidence came in, as they saw the jubilation in parts of the Muslim world where people distributed sweets and chanted slogans against America. Although these were very small groups, the insensitivity of the Muslim reaction rubbed salt into American wounds. Any doubts about taking a savage revenge were removed. Few recognised the humiliation, terror, and neurosis in Muslim society from the decades of emotional and physical violence that they had been subjected to, and fewer understood that many Muslims blamed America for their plight. The idea of Islam set on a collision course with America triumphed over any other ideas of global peace and dialogue.

Yet the actions of the hijackers had nothing to do with Islamic theology. The killing of innocent civilians is specifically forbidden in the Qur'an. Killing a single innocent individual is like killing all of humanity, warns the Holy Book (5:32). The actions of the hijackers may have had nothing to do with Islam, but the causes and consequences of their action will have everything to do with how and where Islam will be going in the twenty-first century.

What we will increasingly face in this century is the possibility of a few determined men hijacking the engine of a global religion and, by their actions, involving millions of people. What 9/11 illustrated was the ability of a few determined individuals to pull their entire civilisation, whether it agrees or does not agree with their thinking or actions, into a confrontation with other civilisations.

Now imagine the ultimate nightmare terrorist scenario: the destruction of the al-Aqsa mosque, situated on the Temple Mount in Jerusalem, the holy city for all three faiths, and the one city where the three faiths live side by side, with the potentiality for positive interfaith interaction and reconciliation. This mosque is the third most venerated shrine in Islam, associated with the origins of the faith and with the Prophet Muhammad's visionary ascent to the heavens, or *mi'raj*. If some trained and determined individuals were to blow up the mosque – as many have threatened to do for political and religious reasons – the action could trigger immediate world conflict. Islam could be set on a collision course with Judaism and Christianity. Perhaps it would not be "war" in the sense of military battles because governments do not respond in apocalyptic terms, but Muslims, whether living in the West or their own homelands, might be determined to take revenge by acts of violence. If such a catastrophe were to occur, few Muslims – however keen on dialogue – would want to be involved in looking for explanations. Emotions would be too powerful for rational thought. Dialogue and understanding would simply be ignored.

Yet the idea of a dialogue of civilisations is central to the Muslim perception of self. By knowing God as Compassionate and Merciful – the two most frequently repeated of the ninety-nine names of God – Muslims know they must embrace others, even those who may not belong to their community, religion, or nation. God tells us in the holy Qur'an to appreciate the variety He has created in human society: "And of His signs is the creation of the heavens and the earth, and the difference of your languages and colours" (30:22).

Global Theories

We must not consider this discussion as merely an academic exercise. The events of 9/11 have made it clear how urgent it is to understand Islam in our world. Just the span and scale of Muslim society warrant understanding. There are fifty-five Muslim states and Islam has over one billion followers. The urgency demands a two-way process: for Muslims to explain Islam to non-Muslims, and for non-Muslims to be responsive and make an effort to understand the Western mindset.

Yet Muslims appear to be reluctant to participate in dialogue. They seem to feel threatened by certain cultural and intellectual aspects of globalisation and so equate globalisation with Westernisation. In this, they echo many Western analysts who also equate the two. Indeed Anthony Giddens argues that modernity itself, the very engine driving globalisation, is a "Western project" (1990: 174). Thomas Friedman narrows globalisation down further to "Americanization" (2000: xix).

Although Muslims appear to be uncomfortable with globalisation, the idea and practice of globalisation are familiar to students of Muslim history. Islam's vision of the world is by definition global. Islamic history has had long periods in which we recognise elements of what we would today call globalisation: societies living within different ethnic, geographic, and political boundaries, but speaking a language understood throughout, enjoying a common cultural sensibility, and recognising the same over-arching ethos in the world-view (see Albert Hourani[7] and Marshall Hodgson[8] for just how much globalisation there once was in Islamic civilisation). A man could travel from Granada in Europe to the Maghreb, on to Cairo, then to the Arabian Peninsula, and from there to Baghdad across three continents, and still be in one familiar culture. Ibn Khaldun in the fourteenth century AD is just one such example.

Another aspect of that time can provide inspiration for those of us searching the past for examples of the dialogue of civilisations. The Jews, Christians, and Muslims living in Spain under Muslim rule until 1492 created a rich cultural synthesis, which resulted in literature, art, and architecture of high quality. The library in Cordoba in al-Andalus had more books than all the other libraries of Europe put together. There were long periods of religious and cultural harmony.[9] The influence of Muslim ideas, culture, art, and architecture on Europe was wide and deep. Key figures like Thomas Aquinas were influenced by Islamic thought. The Greeks were introduced to Europe via Muslim Spain and through the filter of Arabic.

Most people in the West are unaware of Europe's cultural and intellectual debt to Islam. Muslims take this indifference as a deliberate slight. It provides the background to why they view with suspicion developments in our time. It allows them to simplify global issues and interpret a series of recent developments, on the surface unconnected, as a well-laid plan by the West to humiliate and even subjugate them: the controversy raised by Salman Rushdie's *The Satanic Verses*, the collapse of the Bank of Commerce and Credit International (BCCI), the Gulf War, the rape and death camps of Bosnia, Kosovo, and Chechnya, and the continuing plight of the Palestinians and Kashmiris. In turn, critics accuse Muslims of human rights abuse in many countries, including Sudan, Afghanistan, and Pakistan. In Pakistan, in an extreme act of desperation, a bishop shot himself in protest at the treatment of his community.

In this milieu of suspicion even scholarly exercises, such as Samuel Huntington's essay, "The Clash of Civilisations?",[10] Francis Fukuyama's *The End of History and the Last Man* (1992), and Felipe Fernandez Armesto's *Millennium*,[11] are seen by Muslims as part of a global conspiracy against Islam, part of a "bludgeon-Islam-out-of-existence" school of thought. These theorists made an unexpected contribution to the discussion of Islam by underlining the role of religion in contemporary society: it is no longer possible to talk of globalisation only in terms of world trade and high finance. However, they have also allowed deeply rooted historical prejudices to resurface in discussion, at times, even giving them a degree of respectability.

In his influential essay, "The Clash of Civilisations?", Huntington argued that future conflicts would be based on religious culture, not on ideology or economic interests. Islam was singled out as a potential enemy civilisation in an argument that was as deterministic as it was simplistic. "Islam has bloody borders," concluded Huntington (p. 35). This dangerously deterministic argument takes us directly to a clash of civilisations. It carries the danger of becoming a self-fulfilling prophecy. Yet, as I shall explain in due course, the real cause of the turmoil is to be located *within* Islam.

Besides, the global strategic and security interests of the West are directly related to Muslim lands, and many Muslim nations are seen as important allies. Of the nine "pivotal states", identified in a recent article by Western experts, around which the United States forms its foreign policy, five were Muslim: Algeria, Turkey, Egypt, Pakistan, and Indonesia.[12] In addition, over twenty million Muslims are permanently settled in the West, and these tend to be ignored by the partisans of the "Clash" theory. The events of 9/11 have underlined their role as a bridge between the two civilisations. It is they who carry the potential to challenge the "Islam versus the West" dichotomy.

Then there are the serious efforts, at a global level, perhaps for the first time on this scale and frequency, of influential individuals advocating mutual understanding. The Pope's statements are one example. The Prince of Wales' initiative to bring better understanding between Islam and Western civilisation, which began with his celebrated lecture at Oxford in 1993 on "Islam and the West",[13] is another. The speech was widely reported in the Muslim world and struck a chord. The King of Saudi Arabia, one of the most powerful and inaccessible monarchs on earth, broke all protocol and drove to the Prince's hotel late at night to congratulate him when the Prince visited his country shortly after the lecture.

The Breakdown of Social Cohesion and the Crisis of Leadership

Ibn Khaldun, "one of the fathers of modern cultural history and social science",[14] highlighted the importance of the ruler and his duties to the ruled in this world so that both might aspire to and secure the next. The leader embodies both political and moral authority.[15] Ibn Khaldun's science of culture ultimately functions to illuminate the science of good governance. In our time, one of the major crises that face Muslim society – which influential contemporary Western thinkers like Huntington and Fukuyama have not discussed – is that of leadership.

On the surface there is a bewildering range of Muslim leadership: kings, military dictators, democrats and, as in Afghanistan at least until recently, young and inexperienced tribesmen, or religious students (which is the meaning of *Taliban*), running a country. The Taliban and their guest[16] from Saudi Arabia, Usama bin Ladin, symbolise a certain Muslim response to our time. In other countries, such as Algeria, Egypt, Pakistan, and Indonesia, Muslim leaders akin to the Taliban in thought and behaviour actively challenge government. The Iranians, themselves considered fanatics by some in the West, complain that the Taliban are so extreme that they are giving Islam a bad name. Clearly, ideas and styles of Muslim leadership are varied and hotly contested.

What then is going on in Muslim society? Defining these leaders is no longer a simple question of taxonomy but of examining what factors are responsible for their emergence and the changes taking place in society. The collapse of leadership is thus a symptom of the breakdown of society and is also a cause of the breakdown.

It is time to turn for assistance to Ibn Khaldun's most widely known theory, that of '*asabiyyah* or social cohesion, which is central to his definition of civilisation. Without social organisation, writes Ibn Khaldun, "the existence of human beings would be incomplete and God's desire to settle the world with human beings and to leave them as His representatives on earth would not materialize" (1967: 46). '*Asabiyyah* binds groups together through a common language, culture, and code of behaviour, and when there is conscious approximation of behaviour to an idea of the ideal, at different levels, family, clan, tribe, and kingdom or nation, society is whole. With '*asabiyyah*, society fulfils its primary purpose, which is to function with integrity and transmit its values and ideas to the next generation. '*Asabiyyah* is what traditional societies possess (the Arabic root has to do with the cohesiveness of the tribe), but which is broken down in urbanised society over a period of time.

Ibn Khaldun famously suggested that rural and tribal peoples come down from the mountains to urban areas and dominate them, and four generations on, as they absorb the manners and values of urban life, they lose their special quality of social cohesion and become effete and therefore vulnerable to fresher invasions from the hills (1967: 123–42). This cyclical, if over-simplified, pattern of rise and fall held for centuries up to the advent of European colonialism.[17] Even the disruptive force of European imperialism did not fully break the cycle.

Paradoxically, it is only after independence from the European colonial powers in the middle of the twentieth century, when Muslim societies should have become stronger and more cohesive, that Ibn Khaldun's cycle began to be seriously affected. It is now drying up at the source. Tribal and rural groups can no longer provide *'asabiyyah*, urban areas in any case are inimical to it: the result is loss of vigour and cohesion. Muslims everywhere voice their alarm at the breakdown of society. They know that something is going fundamentally wrong, but are not sure why.

Some Americans thought they had the answer. It came in response to the question Americans asked after 9/11, "Why do they hate us?" And because psychiatrists play such an important role in interpreting behaviour in American society, the answers were couched in terms of "envy", "jealousy", and "hatred". We will look elsewhere for the answers. We will examine the reasons why *'asabiyyah* is collapsing and the consequences of the collapse.

'Asabiyyah is breaking down in the Muslim world for the following reasons: massive urbanisation, a population explosion, large-scale migrations to the West, the growing gap between rich and poor, the widespread corruption and mismanagement of rulers, rampant materialism coupled with the low premium on scholarship, the crisis of identity, and – perhaps most significantly – new and often alien ideas and images, at once seductive and repellent, instantly communicated from the West, which challenge traditional values and customs. This process of breakdown is taking place when a large percentage of the population in the Muslim world is young, dangerously illiterate, mostly jobless, and therefore easily mobilised for radical change.[18]

It is easy to blame globalisation for the problems of our world. But *'asabiyyah* was damaged from the mid-twentieth century onwards as a direct result of political developments that split communities, shattered families, and caused the death of millions of people: the creation of Pakistan and Israel, the full-blown revolution in Iran, and civil wars in Algeria, Afghanistan, and parts of Central Asia.

Jahannum (hell), or Jail: The Dilemma of the Muslim Scholar

The crisis in Muslim societies is compounded by the absence of intellectual freedom: the scholars of Islam who can offer balanced advice and guidance are in disarray. Muslims believe that those who possess *'ilm*, or knowledge, can best explain what God desires from us on earth. So crucial is *'ilm* to understanding Islam that it is the second most used word in the Qur'an. The Prophet's *hadith*, or saying, that "The death of a scholar is the death of knowledge" emphasises the importance of scholarship.[19]

Unfortunately, the reality in the Muslim world is that scholars are silenced, humiliated, or chased out of their homes.[20] The implications for society are enormous. In the place of scholars advising, guiding, and criticising the rulers of the day, we have the sycophants and the secret services. The wisdom, compassion, and learning of the former risk being replaced by the paranoia and neurosis of the latter. And where do the scholars escape? To America or

Europe. Yet it is popular to blame the West, to blame others, for conspiracies.

With the scholars driven out, or under pressure to remain silent, it is not surprising that the Muslim world has such poor standards of education. Literacy figures are far from satisfactory, and for women they are alarming. As a result women in the Muslim world are deprived of their inheritance and their rights, and the men in their families tell them that this is Islam.

With the scholars silenced, who can provide objectivity within the Islamic tradition and resilience in times of change? Other kinds of religious scholars – like the Taliban – working in a different tradition, interpret Islam narrowly. Islam for them has become a tool of repression. Its brunt is felt by women and the minorities. Political tyranny also grows unchecked, as the real scholars are not at hand to comment and criticise. Professor AbdulHamid AbuSulayman, the President of the International Institute for Islamic Thought and based in America, summed up the crisis to me in personal conversation: "The Muslim scholar is caught between the ignorant Mullahs threatening him with *Jahannum* (hell) and the corrupt rulers threatening him with jail" (cf. AbuSulayman 1993).

The Challenge to Identity

The scale of the collapse of *'asabiyyah* and the power and speed of globalisation – and the two appear to be related – have challenged ideas of identity which define and shape Muslim society. Primary identities in society are based in kinship, place, or religion (Kottak 2000, Lewis 1998). Language sometimes reinforces identity in all three categories. In Iran, the Persian language is a source of pride for each and every category. In other countries, language expresses the barriers between the categories. In Pakistan, Urdu is the declared national language, Punjabi the language of the ethnic majority, and Arabic the language of religion. Invariably, linguistic tensions translate into ethnic and political clashes. Sometimes the divisions within religion into sects result in conflict and violence. The clashes between Shi'ites and Sunnis in Islam have formed a major historical theme in the Middle East. In South Asia the annual clashes still cost lives.

In the last century, of the three main sources of identity that defined an individual, ethnicity, nationalism, and religion, it was nationalism that was the dominant source of identity. The two world wars were fought on the basis of nationalism. With the emergence of Communism as a world force in the middle of the twentieth century and its aggressive hostility to religion, it appeared that religion, as a source of identity, would soon be irrelevant to most people.

With the processes of globalisation accelerating at the end of the last century, the situation changed. Ethnicity sometimes fused with religion, as in the Balkans. In other places ethnicity re-emerged with virulence, as in the war between Hutus and Tutsis in central Africa. Nationalism changed too, as national borders have melted for business people, specialists, and experts who cross the globe pursuing their economic, cultural, or political interests.

Hundreds of thousands of Asian workers in information technology, for example, have recently been welcomed by the USA and Europe. The poor, however, find borders as impenetrable as ever.

With the rise of migration, nationalism and ethnicity became weaker. Religion, on the other hand, can be transported and can flourish anywhere in the world, given the right circumstances. We have the example of Islam, which began to make an impact in America at the turn of this century. Muslim political commentators feel that, although the Muslim vote is still small in terms of voter strength, it made a contribution to the election in 2000 by supporting George Bush against Al Gore in their tightly contested election battle.

Muslim leaders confirm these trends. The leaders of the first part of the twentieth century would be cast in nationalist terms leading "national" movements – for example, Mustafa Kemal Atatürk in Turkey, Muhammad 'Ali Jinnah in Pakistan, Sukarno of Indonesia, and Jamal 'Abd al-Nasir in Egypt. Later in the century, other kinds of leaders would be at the head of movements with a religious message not restricted to national borders: Ayatollah Ruhollah Khomeini is an example for one tradition in Islam; the Taliban are another. The nationalist leaders had national opponents – the Greeks for the Turks, and the Indians for the Pakistanis. The opponents of the religious leaders would be moral opponents – America became in Iran the Great Satan.

The tidal wave of religion, which engulfed national and ethnic identities, has yet to crest in the Muslim world. The tensions between the three sources of identity are acute. In some countries the old-fashioned nationalism left over from the past results in a ruthless suppression of other forms of identity. Iraq and Syria provide us examples of this. Countries like Pakistan exhibit severe tension between an emerging religious identity and a battered nationalist one. Ethnicity also remains an unresolved factor in Pakistan. The tensions are expressed through violence and political instability.

With the inherited colonial structures of administration, politics, and education disintegrating, and new ones yet to supplant them or even consolidate, with old identities being challenged, Muslim society is in a state of flux. '*Asabiyyah* is at its weakest in these societies. Central and South Asian states provide us with examples.

Paradoxically, it is in those parts of the Muslim world where there is the unifying factor of dynastic rule or language, as, for example, in the states of the Arabian Peninsula, that there is comparative stability. We say "paradoxically", because these states are seen as reactionary by those Muslims who want genuine democracy and stagnant by those who want an Islamic state based on the pristine principles of the early egalitarian Islamic order. Nonetheless, the unifying factors of dynasty and language sustain '*asabiyyah*, ensuring continuity and stability in times of global change.

Muslim Responses to the West

Some scholars have argued that there is a deliberate attempt to "exclude" Islam from the community of world civilisations, to make it a pariah. The Muslim response has been varied and includes mysticism, fatalism, activism, and rejection.[21] Perhaps the greatest model for dialogue still relevant is provided by the two great mystics Jalal al-Din Rumi and Ibn 'Arabi, whose works convey the essential unity of the divine vision in synagogue, church, and mosque.

We can discern two basic and diametrically opposed reactions to the present crisis: one is to advocate a policy of inclusion, as I have done throughout my academic career, in the hope of generating dialogue and understanding; the other is to promote a policy of exclusion, confrontation, and rejection, which is what militant Islamists such as the Taliban have sought to do.

My own personal case can serve as an example of the inclusivist approach. Projects such as the six-part BBC television series *Living Islam*[22] and the "Jinnah Quartet"[23] took over a decade to complete. These projects helped to change the negative climate around Islam, and they assisted in the start of serious interfaith dialogue between Jews, Christians, and Muslims. They also aroused controversy. This was understandable: they were not only changing images in the media, in itself a major challenge, but touching on central issues in society, such as leadership, the nature of the state, and the status of women and minorities. They stressed the compassionate and tolerant nature of Islam.

The reverse of this approach is that of the Taliban. To understand their narrow exclusivist version of Islam, it is necessary to study the *madrassas* or religious schools that produced them. These schools, which offer an alternative system of education that is cheaper, more accessible, and more "Islamic", remain largely unstudied (Rashid 2000). The syllabus of a typical *madrassa* is exclusively Islamic in content, based on the Qur'an and the Shari'ah, the corpus of Islamic law. That is how it should be for an Islamic school. But the Qur'an and the Sunnah of the Prophet – upon which the Shari'ah is based – repeatedly ask Muslims to acquire knowledge. One proverbial instance is "Seek knowledge, even unto China."[24] China then, in the seventh century, symbolised the furthest non–Muslim civilisation. It was a challenge to the imagination to even think of the journey.

There are no non-Muslim philosophers or historians on those *madrassa* syllabi – not even modern ones like Karl Marx or Max Weber. Even Muslim ones, such as Ibn Khaldun, who are thought to be too "scientific", are missing. The typical syllabus is reduced to what commentators call "political Islam": Islam as a vehicle for all-encompassing change, challenging not only the corrupt local elite but also the world order.

These *madrassas* laid the foundations for the populist militant Islamic leadership that would emerge in the 1990s. Mostly from poor, rural backgrounds, speaking only the local language, dressed traditionally with beards that assert their Islamic identity, these students became the warriors who formed the Taliban and went on to conquer Afghanistan. The word "Taliban" – from *talib* or student – entered the global vocabulary.

The battle of Afghanistan against the Soviets was won not on the playing fields of the Etons of the Muslim world but in the humble classrooms and courtyards of the *madrassa*. Its outcome challenged and changed the already shaky educational and political structures in the entire region. The impact of the Taliban frame of mind can be seen in Muslim groups from Los Angeles to Lahore. Living in the West is no guarantee of freedom from Taliban thinking. The US bombing campaign against the Taliban in late 2001 may have hammered them in Afghanistan, but did little to counter their influence elsewhere in the Muslim world.

Wherever they live, Muslims are aware of the injustices perpetrated by their rulers and the fact that some rely on the support of the West, and they are aware of the cultural invasion from the West, and the stereotypes of Muslims in the Western media, including many Hollywood films in which Muslims are shown as terrorists and fanatics. These are not art films, but mainstream "blockbusters" seen by millions. They influence public opinion. Such negative propaganda, coupled with what is seen as the indifference of the West to the outstanding political problems in the Muslim world, combine to create a focus on the West as the root cause of Muslim problems. We have lost our honour, the honour of our faith and traditions, and have no power to correct the wrongs of our own world, Muslims lament, blaming the West for this loss. From this perception to actively opposing the West as a form of *jihad* is one short step for groups like the Taliban.

The bitter anti-Western edge to the Taliban comes partly from their feeling that while they sacrificed their lives and land in fighting the Soviets as allies of the Americans, when the Soviet troops withdrew, the Americans left them and their devastated land in the lurch. They will remind you that those whom the West now calls "crazies" and "extremists" were once hailed as "freedom fighters". Their actions, such as the destruction of the priceless Buddhist statues, are partly motivated by a psychological compulsion to enrage and defy their critics.[25]

Although the Taliban-style leadership is "new" in the sense that it emerged in opposition to the more Westernised leaders in power after the First World War, in fact the division in Muslim leadership goes back to the nineteenth century. In 1857, after the great uprisings in India against British rule ("the Indian Mutiny"), two rival models of leadership began to emerge. Sir Sayyed Ahmed Khan, who created the Aligarh University on the model of Oxbridge, was a loyal servant of the Raj and wished to synthesise Islam and modernity. It was his example that inspired Iqbal, Jinnah, and the leaders of the Pakistan movement. In contrast, the founders of the *madrassa* at Deoband near Delhi fought the British during the uprisings, and their influential schools created networks throughout India and now influence groups like the Taliban. The schism in Muslim leadership, Usama at one end and Jinnah at the other of the spectrum, is thus rooted in the indigenous response to modernity and the threatening presence of Western imperialism.

We saw the interconnectedness of our world even before 9/11. In the aftermath of the attack on the USS *Cole* in Aden in October 2000, President Bill Clinton in Washington threatened Usama; the head of the Islamic party, the Jamiat ul-Ulama-i Islam (JUI), in Pakistan in turn threatened all US citizens in Pakistan, including the Ambassador, if Usama were harmed; Afghanistan was on high alert and Americans throughout the world were warned to be on their guard. Once again Islam had been pushed in a certain direction by those intent on confrontation.

Clinton and his Secretary of State, Madeleine Albright, had predicted that such events were a foretaste of things to come. But the response of the Muslim world will depend on the nature of Muslim leadership; whether the Usama model prevails, or that of Jinnah, and also, more importantly, on the nature of Western leadership. Whatever happens, the relationship between Islam and the West will play a major part in influencing the course of events in the twenty-first century.

Global Society in the Twenty-First Century

With Ibn Khaldun's cycle broken down – with the interpenetration of global religious cultures, with the emergence of the audio-visual media penetrating even the most remote areas, with the mounting clamour of those who see the signs of the apocalypse, with the scholars silenced, with the growing sense of despair at the poverty and inequality in many parts of the world that challenge the notion of a just God in heaven – we need to develop a post-Khaldunian paradigm, a new methodological framework to study global society in the twenty-first century.

The unexpected and unpredictable expressions of religious revivalism today would have surprised the philosophers and sociologists of the modern age. Certainly Nietzsche, who declared God dead,[26] and even Max Weber who saw the "Protestant ethic" as laying the foundations for a stable, safe, capitalist, and bureaucratic world, would have been surprised. God was back and it seemed with a vengeance; He was busy upsetting the very order that He was supposed to champion. Perhaps Marx would be the most surprised. Religion is no longer an "opiate" numbing people into docility; if one needs a drug metaphor, religion is more like "speed".

The "clash of civilisations" thesis, which remains influential in some circles, rests on the assumption that the wars of this new century will be fought along religious lines. It is therefore urgent to understand what factors are responsible for the emergence of religion.[27] However, we need to penetrate beneath the sensationalist nature of these theories and discover alternative ways of understanding society. We do not suggest that we accept each other's, or all, religions uncritically, but that we understand them in order to make sense of what is happening in global society.

Muslims are often attacked in the media for what is called "revivalism", but religious revivalism is taking place globally, in Judaism and Christianity, and in Hindu and Buddhist societies. The "rediscovery" of the divine is noted even in Western scientific and intellectual circles once dismissive of religion (Glynn 1999). We need to know how the different world civilisations view themselves and each other; we need to know about their vision of the coming time.

This raises our first set of questions: why is there a revival of religions, and how are people negotiating the idea of God or the divine? Is the revival a consequence of the impact of globalisation? Is the explanation to be found in the weakening of traditional structures – like the family and the nation state – as individuals look to religion to provide certainty in an uncertain world, continuity in a changing one? Is it an attempt to (re)create '*asabiyyah* in order to (re)build human civilisation? But can we apply Ibn Khaldun's theories to non-Muslim civilisations? Indeed, can they still be applied to Muslim societies?

A second set of questions that have a global resonance after 9/11 is: why is the understanding of the divine often distorted through the prism of violence? Why are people killing and raping in the name of the divine? No religion encourages violence of this kind, and yet we see examples throughout the world in the news every day. Why are people not able to focus on compassion and goodness as attributes of the divine? This failure has global implications for the so-called "clash of civilisations".

Third, we need to ask: what is to be done about it? Can there be genuine dialogue across religions and national boundaries to negate the idea of a clash of civilisations? How can this be implemented in a practical way, which will affect the thinking and behaviour of people?

These are questions that would not have occurred naturally to Ibn Khaldun. His was a Muslim world, admittedly disintegrating in one part but strong in others, and there was nothing but Islam on the horizon. For us, the dialogue of civilisation is a necessary precondition to global harmony. But dialogue by itself is no solution. There must be dialogue that leads to the understanding of other civilisations. For this, we must move beyond Islam and understand the religions with which it interacts: Judaism, Christianity, Hinduism, Sikhism, and Buddhism. Too many non-Muslims see Islam as caricature. With understanding comes sympathy and compassion towards those who do not belong to our group or community or religion. Scholars and thinkers who can transcend religious and national positions are crucial to the global debate.

Conclusion

What can be done to encourage dialogue? The first steps are to try to understand the world we live in and the way it is forming. In the short term, the prospects for a harmonious relationship between Islam and the West look uncertain, even pessimistic. In the longer term, a great deal will depend on whether those who encourage dialogue and understanding will succeed or not.

The common problems – which affect everyone regardless of race, nationality, or religion – in this shrinking world need to be identified to strengthen the idea of dialogue: drug and alcohol abuse, divorce, teenage violence and crime, racial prejudice, the problems of the aged and the poor, the growing sense of anarchy, rampant materialism, the sexual debasement of women and children, the depletion of our natural resources, and damage to the environment. On all these issues, many Muslims find support for taking a strong, enlightened position in Islam. This is the real Islamic *jihad* and, if it is properly harnessed and understood, it can provide fresh, sorely needed solutions to these global issues.

Muslims face an internal challenge. Reducing a sophisticated civilisation to simple rituals encourages simple answers: reaching for guns and explosives, for instance. For Muslims to confront the world with poise and confidence is to rediscover and begin to repair the mainsprings of Islamic civilisation. They need to rebuild an idea of Islam that includes justice, integrity, tolerance, and the quest for knowledge – the classic Islamic civilisation – not just the insistence on the rituals; not just the five pillars of Islam, but the entire building.

The West must put pressure on Muslim governments to "get their act together", to ensure justice and provide clean administration. It must send serious signals to the ordinary Muslim people that it does not consider Islam as the enemy. Serious and urgent rethinking is required by the scholars, policy planners and policy makers in the corridors of power – not only in Washington, London, Moscow, and Paris, but also in Cairo, Kabul, and Tehran.

We need to be thinking in terms of what Ibn Khaldun called "human civilisation" or, to use the contemporary phrase, globally. We may not like words such as postmodernism and globalisation, but only with the compassionate understanding of other civilisations, through the scholarship of inclusion, can we resolve some of the deleterious consequences of globalisation, such as the increasing gap between the rich and the poor and the growing sense of despair. This is the only way to check the tragic confrontation of the great faiths in the Balkans, the Middle East, and South Asia.

The events of 9/11 conveyed the urgency of the call for dialogue. The creative participation in the dialogue of civilisations, the committed search for global solutions to the global problems confronting human society, and the quest for a just and peaceful order will be the challenge human civilisation faces in the twenty-first century. Without dialogue, knowledge, and friendship, all of us will face a dangerous, violent, and uncertain future.

Notes

1 This paper is a fully re-edited version of an article that appeared in *The Middle East Journal*, vol. 56, no. 1 (Winter 2002), 1–26, based on Akbar Ahmed's inaugural lecture as holder of the Ibn Khaldun Chair of Islamic Studies, American University, Washington DC. This version of Dr Ahmed's paper is reproduced with the permission of the author and *The Middle East Journal*.

2 For different perspectives on globalisation, see Ahmed 1992, Bauman 1998, Braibanti 1999, Falk 1999, Izetbegovic 1994, Khatami 1998, Micklethwait and Wooldridge 2000, Mische and Merkling 2001. See also Lewis 1998 (historical), Friedman 2000 (journalist's perspective), Mittelman 2000 (political or economic), Giddens 2000 (sociological), and Kottak 2000 (anthropological). For an apocalyptic interpretation, see Halsell 1986 and 1999, Kaldor 1999, and Kaplan 1997.

3   The idea is contained in the simplistic division of the world into *dar al-Islam*, the Abode of Islam, and *dar al-harb*, the Abode of War. The concept can be traced to the origins of Islam. After the Prophet's migration to Medina, the town was declared *dar al-Islam*, while Mecca, whence he migrated, remained *dar al-harb*.

4   See Falk 2000, Izetbegovic 1994, Esposito 1992, Barber 1995, Fuller and Lesser 1995, and Halliday 1996.

5   See John Paul II, *Crossing the Threshold of Hope* (New York: Alfred A. Knopf, 1994).

6   An interview with Al-Jazeera television (Qatar), broadcast 7 October 2001, and rebroadcast regularly on CNN.

7   *A History of the Arab Peoples* (London: Faber & Faber, 1991).

8   M. G. S. Hodgson, *The Venture of Islam*, 3 vols (Chicago, IL: The University of Chicago Press, 1974).

9   Some scholars see the USA as having the potential to create a genuinely harmonious multi-religious and multi-cultural society; see Eck 2002 and Findley 2001.

10   *Foreign Affairs*, vol. 72, no. 3 (Summer 1993), later expanded into a book (Huntington 1996).

11   Felipe Fernandez Armesto, *Millennium: A History of the Last Thousand Years* (New York: Scribner, 1995).

12   Robert Chase et al., "Pivotal States and US Strategy", *Foreign Affairs*, vol. 75, no. 1 (January–February 1996).

13   Speech delivered at the Sheldonian Theatre, Oxford, on the occasion of the Prince of Wales' visit to the Oxford Centre for Islamic Studies, 27 October 1993; see Charles 1994.

14   Muhsin Mahdi, "Ibn Khaldun" in *International Encyclopedia of the Social Sciences*, ed. David L. Sills (New York: Macmillan, 1968), vol. 7, p. 56.

15   See Akbar S. Ahmed, *Jinnah, Pakistan and Islamic Identity: The Search for Saladin* (London: Routledge, 1997) and *The Quaid: Jinnah and the Story of Pakistan* (Karachi: Oxford University Press, 1997).

16   The reluctance of the Taliban to hand over Usama bin Ladin without firm evidence must be understood within the context of Pashtun ideas of hospitality and revenge, which are central to their code of honour, or *Pukhtunwali*.

17   Ibn Khaldun was studying society in the Western part of the Muslim world. But the Khaldunian cyclical pattern of rise and fall of dynasties is also applicable to Central and South Asia. Tribes from Central Asia invaded India and gave it seven dynasties, which ruled from Delhi, each one in turn becoming effete over the generations and giving way to those with stronger *'asabiyyah* from the north.

18   See *Human Development Report* (Oxford and New York: Oxford University Press, UN Development Program, 1995). Also see Shahid Javed Burki, "Population as an Asset", *Pakistan Link* (California), 10 August 2001. Burki makes the telling point that Pakistan has 72 million people under the age of 19, while the USA, with double the population, has 70 million.

19   This *hadith* is found in *Sahih al-Bukhari*, no. 6763, and *Sunan Darami*, no. 242.

20   The picture of Saad Eddin Ibrahim, the noted Egyptian scholar, on the cover of *The New York Times Magazine* (17 June 2001) behind bars and in a cage, was a powerful metaphor for Muslim scholarship in the world today. Like Anwar Ibrahim in Malaysia [released in 2004], this Egyptian professor is in jail, charged with embezzlement and spying for the West – standard charges across the two continents (though Anwar Ibrahim was also charged with homosexuality). For a detailed analysis of such persecuted scholars, see Deina Abdelkader, *Social Justice*

in Islam (Herndon, VA: International Institute of Islamic Thought, 2000); cf. Ahmed and Rosen 2001. There is another category of scholars on the run: writers such as Salman Rushdie of *Satanic Verses* fame, and Khalid Duran, author of *Children of Abraham: An Introduction to Islam for Jews* (Hoboken, NJ: The American Jewish Committee, 2001), both in hiding for fear of their lives. They form a distinct category as persons of Muslim origin deemed beyond the pale by most Muslims.

21   See the chapter "The Geo-Politics of Exclusion: The Case of Islam" in Falk 2000.
22   *Living Islam*, broadcast in 1993, was based on the accompanying book, *Living Islam* (1993).
23   The "Jinnah Quartet", based on the life of the founder of Pakistan, took me a decade to complete. It included a feature film, *Jinnah*; a documentary, *Mr. Jinnah: The Making of Pakistan*; an academic book, *Jinnah, Pakistan and Islamic Identity: The Search for Saladin*; and a graphic novel, *The Quaid: Jinnah and the Story of Pakistan*. The Quartet attempted to answer the question: Do Muslims have leaders who care for human rights, women's rights, and minority rights? I believed Jinnah was one such leader and provided a relevant model.
24   This *hadith* is considered "weak" and unreliable, but it has become proverbial.
25   Blowing up the marvellous statues of the Buddha in Bamiyan in 2001, which had survived the ravages of past rulers, even Jinghiz Khan, enraged people who cared for the cultural legacy of civilisation. The refusal of the Taliban to heed the UNESCO delegation, or the pleas of the Dalai Lama and other leading Buddhists, was again an unmitigated global PR disaster for Islam.
26   When Friedrich Nietzsche, in *Twilight of the Idols* and *Beyond Good and Evil*, dubbed himself the Anti-Christ and preached the nobility of barbarism, he underestimated the power of ideas to direct political events: the Nazis were inspired by this poisonous philosophy.
27   As an indication of the interest in religion in 2001 alone, several popular journals like *Newsweek*, *Time Magazine*, and *US News and World Report* have featured cover stories on religion. Also see Armstrong 2000, Eck 2002, Johnston and Sampson 1994, Mische and Merkling 2001, Smith 2001, and Wuthnow 2001.

Chapter 7

The "Clash of Civilisations"?: Sense and Nonsense[1]

Fred Halliday

The "Clash of Civilisations", in Arabic "*saddam al-hadharat*", is both topical and complex, leading to a false generalisation, and is a topic that is bound to stir up a great deal of controversy. For this very reason, it should not lend itself to hasty conclusions. Any preliminary remarks on the subject are likely to provoke a heated debate about the West and the Middle East, or between the West and the Third World. Furthermore, everywhere in the world, events are changing fast and the debate is still raging. The discussion of this clash began in the early 1990s with the publication of Huntington's 1993 article. But 11 September 2001 has both accelerated and greatly embittered this discussion, in which too few hold to a centre position. The stakes have never been higher.

The central issue in this debate appears to be whether cultures can coexist, or need to clash. Huntington famously argues that they must conflict. If not civilisations then what?, he asks, starting from the premise that states must conflict. But the very assumptions that cultures are (a) distinct, and (b) clashing, entities need to be questioned. In regard to the first, the temporal, contingent, nature of our supposed identities and traditions needs to be emphasised: they have not been there for ages, nor are they the only reading of the past. Some elements of our culture that are presented as traditional are associated with aspects of the past that were not always so important but that one chooses to revive in the present. Take Britain for example. For years St George's Day, an English (but not a British) national feast-day, was no longer celebrated. It was made a Saint's Day in 1222, but that is a while ago. Yet nowadays one sees many people on 23 April displaying in their windows or on their cars a white flag with a red cross. Even candidates in the 1997 elections – John Major as well as Tony Blair – wore the St George's flower. The English maintain that this is part of their national heritage: but this is a case of the *re-emergence* of a so-called traditional element that has become a more potent cultural symbol in the contemporary context. The prominence of this symbol is connected with current problems of identity and integration: the identity of the English *vis-à-vis* immigrants, the contested integration of Britain in the European Union, new tensions with Scotland, and, of course, football nationalism.

However, not everything that is presented as traditional, or ancient, is even historic at all: one can even invent, or reinvent the past. Take for example the kilt, a symbol of Scottish nationalism in British culture. This garment is in fact an invention that only dates from the beginning of the nineteenth century. Modern identity politics and a cult of "heritage" have made it a cultural or ancestral symbol. One therefore has to study how traditions come about. Some are selected and revived, some invented. They are also always changing: despite all the talk of a clash of civilisations, one must admit that the major cultural forms that make a society, languages, musical forms, food, and the criteria of identity, are not as permanent or static as we believe.[2]

The state plays a central role in defining culture: here again it is not a "given". In some Arab countries we may observe how a pre-Islamic past and its symbols have been revived for modern political purposes. When Yemen was in conflict with Saudi Arabia in the 1980s and 1990s, the Yemeni president used to begin his speeches with the words, *Ya abna Saba* ("O sons of Sheba!", in reference to the ancient Yemeni Kingdom of that name and its legendary queen). When Saddam Hussein wanted to portray himself as an Iraqi rather than an Arab ruler, he used to invoke the memory of Hammurrabi, the ancient king of Mesopotamia. When Anwar Sadat wanted to change Egypt's political alignments, he used the expression "the sons of the Nile" to distance his audience from the other Arabs. Egyptian traditions are not exclusively Islamic, so this does not necessarily create contradictions. In Tunisia the pre-Islamic past also plays a role: references are made to both Hannibal and Amilcar, heroes of the Phoenician or Punic period, before the Roman destruction of Carthage. This change in cultures and in how the past is defined is a necessary part of the development of the modern world and is evident in every country, from the USA to Qatar.

We can now examine the problem of the "Clash of Civilisations", and ask, first of all, what it means. We can do this within the framework of international relations and, in particular, inter-state relations. First of all, one observes, nearly everywhere in the world, a revival of nationalism as a source of influence on foreign policies and social conflicts, whether in the former Yugoslavia, in the countries of the former Soviet Union, or in India. In Western Europe there are nationalist movements in several parts of Spain, in Belgium, Scotland, and Wales; and the United Kingdom has still not entirely resolved its conflict with Northern Ireland. The UK, at state and popular level, will probably never settle its relationship to continental Europe, and to the EU in particular. One finds that in the USA, Germany, and in Russia, where they cannot be sure which of three possible words is the correct one for "Russian",[3] people are once again troubled by questions of identity in political as well as cultural form: what and where are our roots? What are our traditions? Where does our community stop? This debate takes a particular form in countries with high immigration, such as France, Germany, and the USA, where the social integration of migrants is a problem, but it is also perceptible elsewhere.

In the Middle East, we have all witnessed, either as Arab participants or European observers, the great debate about Arab identity. Every day one reads articles on this subject in the newspapers. Thirty years ago this debate was formulated, more or less, in established secular terms: Arabs were classified as nationalists, Baathists, Marxists, and parties struggling for real independence or "national liberation" – that which exists after official independence.

Gradually, and above all under the traumatic impact of the 1967 defeat of the Arab world by Israel, we have seen a renewal of interest in the past, or, to be more precise, in cultural heritage, what the Arabs call both national and religious *turath*: this heritage may be traced back to a selective definition of Islam, in *salafi* or "ancestral" terms, or to ancient history, whether to the time of the Pharoahs in Egypt, of the Sabaeans and Himyaris in Yemen, or of the Carthaginians in Tunisia.

Despite proclaimed, and real, shared Arab and Islamic values, there is also a different version of the past corresponding to each Arab country. At the same time the shaping of Arab identity is also not exclusively Islamic because Christians and others have played their part and religion is not the only relevant factor, as was pointed out during the 1950s and 1960s by Michel Aflaq in Syria and Anwar Abdel Malek in Egypt.

A generation or two ago the state emphasised "modernisation", an aspiration to a shared, globally defined, goal. Today all countries of the Middle East and the Levant – Iran, Iraq, and Turkey – are concerned about their cultural heritage. Necmettin Erbakan, the first non-secular prime minister of Turkey since the establishment of the republic in 1923, used to speak at length about the defence of culture and morality. Some Muslims may opt for a form of return to "ancestral" values, for Sunnis *salafism* or the Caliphate, or a religious movement that proposes returning to a past that is inevitably, to a large extent, reconstructed, as is the case with the Shi'ite goal of *velayat-i faqih*. But the past is not a fixed recipe. Here again it is the present that defines the past: secular nationalism and religious fundamentalism each have to find their own way. This phenomenon is not confined to the Arab world; one finds the same thing in India with the reformulation of Hinduism as a legitimation of modern politics. Political movements based on religion have re-emerged in Israel, in Europe, and in the USA. Thus the old secular and modernist concept of politics and social life is facing a crisis: it does not sufficiently take into consideration the rediscovery of the past, and seems to cede ground to this retrospective discourse.

There is another equally important problem with regard to culture itself. When one speaks about secular nationalism, one has to distinguish between economic and political nationalism, on the one hand, and cultural nationalism, on the other. The latter has grown not only as a result of the colonial experience, and the impact of colonialism on colonised peoples, but also as a result of the globalisation of the mass media and international communications, and to the inexorable spread of a world economy. All these factors have contributed to the destruction of local cultures, regional literary traditions, family structures, traditional relations between the sexes, even cuisines, as well as of local economies.

In the cultural sphere, critical discourse about globalisation has recently emerged, claiming a future for the national culture that will represent a "genuine" facet of its national identity and independence, which is much more important nowadays than it was thirty or forty years ago. This leads to hostile reactions to the invasive cultures of other countries, to the symbols of colonialism and cultural influence, such as Coca-Cola and McDonald's.[4] In my opinion, this often very negative perception, a cult of nativism and obscurantism, is partially responsible for a rupture in the dialogue between people of different countries.

In 1997, I had the opportunity to visit an Arab country that I did not hitherto know, Saudi Arabia. What struck me the most were the bookshops. They are huge and well stocked; one finds books there on every imaginable subject, except on Saudi Arabia. Yet there were also disturbing features. One section of the bookshop I visited was devoted to "Activities of Imperialist Espionage", which is perhaps not surprising, but nearby, next to this one and another section entitled "*mu'amarat*" ("conspiracies"), was a section on "*al-istishraq*" (Orientalism). It was, in effect, a section reserved for people who try to write about the Arab world, who want to learn the Arabic script and language to enable them to converse with Arabs, and who, unfortunately, are said to be involved in plans of cultural infiltration. In other words, this section was about people like me. During that visit, I saw, on Saudi television, the report of a conference on the role of Middle Eastern specialists as spies. One interviewer asked me about this: "Why do you want to study our country and our culture?" "What is your ulterior motive?" These questions were always implicit, and I got the impression that they reflected an attitude that was quite widespread among Saudi, Lebanese, and other Arab colleagues who were attending the colloquium to which I had been invited. Such an attitude is not new, but it seemed more pronounced than before. It really shocked me: to intellectuals of my generation, reared in the internationalist atmosphere of the 1960s, interest in other peoples, their languages, cultures, histories, is something positive, culturally and politically. No more, it seems.

Much contemporary discussion of the "Clash of Civilisations" is because of a book about which everyone is talking and which some have even read, published in 1996: *The Clash of Civilisations,* by Samuel Huntington. Huntington is an intelligent man, so his ideas cannot be lightly dismissed. The central thesis of his book is not about culture, but about international relations, and is as follows: we live in a world where there are always inter-state conflicts. He therefore takes it as axiomatic that there have always been conflicts between states for economic, military, or strategic reasons, all other causes of dispute having been eliminated. In the future, the main cause and definition of any conflict will be expressed in terms of culture and civilisation, the latter being itself a form of large-scale culture. Their role is residual, as stimulator of conflict, not causative, that is, it is because states always clash, not because cultures are inherently antagonistic. Nowadays, we have in the world seven or eight major cultures: European, American, Latin American, African, Japanese, Confucian (or Chinese), and Muslim. According to Huntington, therefore, the great conflicts of the twenty-first century will be confrontations between different civilisations. In sum, on the one hand, other causes of conflict, those of 1870–1991, such as colonialism, communism, and the Cold War, are no longer valid; on the other hand, one can already cite many examples of conflicts based on culture: conflicts over immigration in Europe and the USA, and ethnic conflicts as in Rwanda, the Caucasus, and the former Yugoslavia.

There is another premise of Huntington's argument, one that helps to set it in context; it is not that of Islam or global civilisations, but of the debate on multiculturalism in the USA. As in his more recent work, he argues that Western countries must defend themselves against cultural globalisation and against the decline of their culture. They must defend their own culture, abandon "multiculturalism", and pursue a policy of cultural integration, which concentrates on the assimilation of immigrants into the core values of the host society. Huntington is not primarily concerned with the Muslim world, about which he knows little. He is above all concerned with China and Japan, their cultural *and* economic challenge. He believes that while other countries have great faith in the importance of their culture, civilisation in the West is weakening because it has lost this faith. He asserts that in order to survive in tomorrow's world, Americans ought to do what others are doing: support their own core culture while, at the same time, accept a global pluralism of values, including on human rights, and hence reject universalism, as a fact of life.

Huntington's conclusion is therefore striking: the United States and Western countries ought to abandon not only global policies in defence of "universal" values such as rights, but also any sense of responsibility for other countries and any policy of intervention in the interests of maintaining international peace. They ought to accept the division of the world into six or seven civilisational blocs and leave others to do what they want. It is not for them to tell others what to do, and it is no use imposing their values on others. It is a position that reflects great confidence in so-called Western or American values, while at the same time advocating a renunciation of those international and universal claims that have been a central feature of American foreign policy at least since the Second World War. Huntington insists that we must keep our own interests in mind and leave others to do as they please. It has to be acknowledged that this is a rather pessimistic argument if it is applied to international politics. For Western societies, this means a rejection of global planning and aspirations to stronger global governance and also an assault on universalism, international institutions, and the United Nations, which the author does not consider to be of any importance.

As his later work on the politics of culture in the USA has shown, Huntington's ideas did not originate in the analysis of international politics, despite the examples he gives, but in the internal problems of the United States, and in particular as a critique of multiculturalism and immigration, particularly from Mexico. If one accepts his conclusions, the world will divide itself naturally into these large civilisational blocs. Many people, including myself, have criticised Huntington, but there are some who are ready to go along with him. In China, Japan, and India the new, more assertive, nationalists are happy with the idea that the influence of the Americans will disappear and that they can do what they want. One also has the impression that one segment of the Muslim world, namely the fundamentalist branch, is pleased with some aspects of this theory, although it rejects others, such as his attribution of blame to the Muslim world for contemporary conflicts. Moreover, as befits a proponent of ideas, his analysis may have consequences

– this is what sociologists call "reflexivity". Even though it is easy to criticise Huntington, and to show he is historically and conceptually confused, his vision *may* therefore come true: it has to be recognised that numerous political myths, which have been disseminated in the course of time, have ended up acquiring a force of their own, anti-Semitism, and indeed nationalism, being examples of this. The debate is far from closed. It is our duty not merely to analyse the myths that are created and exploited by political and social forces in international society but also to explain the factors that produce them. Such analysis may, and I stress only may, have a therapeutic impact.

Huntington is not alone. He has his European counterparts. A parallel argument is that of the French writer Alain Minc, in his *Le Nouveau Moyen-Âge*, who says that since the fall of communism we have entered a new medieval era, where international anarchy rules, where values vary from country to country, and where each tribe does what it wants. He believes that we must refute all world-views – whether they are Communist, Islamist, nationalist, or cultural – that reject the possibility of global dialogue on the grounds that, civilisations being what they are, conflict is inevitable.

This leads us to the conclusion that if we wish to avoid becoming entrapped in the framework of the "Clash of Civilisations", we have to produce a counter-argument and create a new form of discussion. Several questions need to be asked about Huntington's thesis. First of all, is his "Clash", insofar as it exists, so new? There have been conflicts between Christians and Muslims for over a thousand years. Moreover, similar ideas about cultural conflict are found in European colonial literature. Since the end of European colonialism in the 1940s, we have only started speaking again about conflicts between civilisations after the fall of Communism and following the economic success of Asian countries such as Japan, South Korea, and Singapore. It used to be said that the latter were successful because the people worked hard.

The cultural explanation has therefore been with us for a long time. Culture plays an important role in the life of every society and contributes to its economic, social, military, or political success. But culture is always associated with other factors: culture in itself does not explain anything. The uses of language, history, symbol are determined not by these cultural elements themselves, but by social and political actors. We live in a world where there is much discussion about culture and cultural symbols as part of "tradition", yet, on closer examination, this use of symbols is not determined by the past. It is linked to a contemporary need: one selects what one wishes from the past in order to justify what we are now doing. When we speak today about cultures and civilisations in the modern world, we are not talking about facts or concrete objects like mountains, seas, and natural resources, or even national territories. Cultures are constructed all the time. This involves choice, and change. To take the example of language: all of us are heirs to the linguistic treasures of the past, but what we do with this legacy, with these definitions and grammatical rules, is our responsibility and proof of our choice, or opportunism. Consider, for example, the most tragic of all conflicts in the Middle East, the 1980–88 war between Iran and Iraq. On the one side, Saddam Hussein would speak about al-Qadisiyyah, a seventh-century battle in which the Persians were defeated by the Arab Muslims, and would call Khomeini *Magus*, a Zoroastrian priest. On the other side, the Iranians called Saddam Hussein *Yazid*, a seventh-century anti-Shi'ite tyrant. But does this demonstrate the importance of the past, or rather the exploitation of the past by two sides in a very bloody war?

Take another subsidiary question with which you will all be very familiar: is Islam compatible with nationalism? We do not have one reply but several. We may say, on the basis of numerous religious texts and traditions, that the religion of Islam does not tolerate divisions, frontiers or barriers, between nations. Mecca is one of the world's great cosmopolitan cities. On the other hand, one finds quotations such as the saying of the Prophet Muhammad: "To love one's country is an aspect of one's faith" – "*Hubb al-watan min al-iman.*" One could carry out the same exercise with Christian texts and assert that religion and nationalism are contradictory or else compatible, depending upon one's own political opinion.

There need not be any contradiction between nationalism and Islam. There are over fifty Muslim countries that have bilateral, not Islamo-multilateral, trade relations with Europe. Each pursues its own *national* interest, and espouses its own *nationalism*. There are inevitably conflicts or disputes with the non-Muslim world. On the other hand, there are conflicts between Muslims in certain states or societies, and some rulers of Muslim countries who have very poor relations with other Muslim countries (for example, Iran and Azerbaijan). These intra-Muslim conflicts can be explained without recourse to civilisations or religions. In South East Asia, the greatest tension is also intra-cultural, that which exists between China and Japan, both Asian countries with Confucian traditions. It is there that in the 1880s and 1890s the wars leading to the First World War began and where now the arms race is most worrying for the world. The greatest conflicts of the twentieth century were between (Christian) states in Europe. To take another example where choice is central: among the Palestinians there is a lively debate on whether or not there should be reconciliation with Israel. Some reject it, saying that the Israelis are infidels (*kuffar*). Others recall that the Prophet Muhammad accepted an armistice with his enemies and even, on one occasion, with the Jews. The answer is given by contemporary choice: the past does not necessarily justify the present. Several years ago, I was invited to the University of Peking by the Department of International Relations, and I had the opportunity to meet a group of Chinese academics. I asked them what was their programme of research. They replied that it was about developing theories of international relations based on Confucianism. I had no doubt that they reached those conclusions that suited their own interests, emphasising the defence of their national territory, economic growth, and above all everything that was required to place their country in a global context.

Culture does not, therefore, explain everything: indeed in international relations it may explain very little. Think of Saddam Hussein: he was never an Islamic militant, he founded a secularist regime, he suppressed Islamic opposition, and his speeches were inspired by nationalism, not religion. The foreign policy of the Islamic Republic of Iran is supposedly elaborated on the basis of religion, but the country nevertheless maintains good relations with an often anti-Muslim India and supports the Chinese government, which is engaged in a conflict with Uighur Muslims in Sinkiang. On the border of Iran there is a dispute between Armenian Christians and Azerbaijani Shi'ites over the region of Karabakh. Iran supports the Armenians because its strategic rival Turkey supports the Azerbaijanis. Where, in these cases, is the clash of civilisations?

Similarly, one should be careful about citing as proof of any "Clash of Civilisations" the example of former Yugoslavia. Nowadays it is said that, until its breakup in 1992, Yugoslavia was made up of three communities that always hated one another: Serbs (Orthodox), Croatians (Catholic), and Bosnians (Muslim). That is not true. Formerly, Yugoslavia was one of the most successful of states marriages, where people in the three communities all spoke the same language, Serb-Croat, whereas now, in a preposterous linguistic charade, each community claims to speak its own language. Many people have explained the crisis in Yugoslavia by means of facts that are not based on the theory of a Clash of Civilisations, and they are right to do so. The wars of the 1990s were the result, not of cultural fault-lines, but of competition between post-communist élites, who used, exaggerated, and invented cultural differences. Yugoslavia is more a case of a clash of thieves and racketeers – with Milosevic, Tujman, and Izetbegovic in the lead.

There is a further historical elision invoked here. When speaking about cultures and civilisations, Huntington and his disciples talk about "Civilisations" as if they are distinct boxes, that is, not only, as discussed, that they are monolithic, or univocal and unitary, but that they have been separated historically and now confront one another. These divisions are often artificial, retrospective drawings of a line. For example, where does Christianity come from? It does not come from Europe, but from the Middle East. So does much of our vocabulary. We are now constructing a divided world, with frontiers demarcated as on a map. But civilisations cannot be carved up in this way. Take Japanese culture. It is distinctive, but it incorporates Indian, Chinese, and, more recently, American elements. These influences cannot be separated. No culture is a free-standing tree. Now people say that the world is divided into different cultures that are incapable of communicating with one another, but for hundreds of years Islam and Christianity have exchanged ideas and symbols, and have traded. Many names for textiles or food are taken from cities of the Middle East – damask (Damascus), muslin (*mawsil* or Mosul), gauze (*jazz* or Gaza), mocha (*mukha* or Mocha in Yemen), tangerine (Tangiers), to name but some. It was the same with Iran and Iraq: they interacted more than they fought. The Arab, but strongly Persian-influenced, *One Thousand and One Nights*, in literary terms a rather mediocre set of stories, is not only itself a cultural hybrid but had a great influence on European literature.

In every culture, every language, every religion, there are no blocs – diversity exists, offering different ways of defining a political, social, or cultural system, and a system of moral values, and external influences are incorporated. If one speaks of human rights, one has initially to consider three systems that appear separate: the Western, the Oriental, and the Islamic. But this is misleading. One can discern different attitudes with regard to the importance of human rights *within* any given political system while at the same time much of the substance is shared between them. In every culture torture and murder are crimes.

At this point, it is possible to demand that the discussion get "real", quitting a world of culturalist fantasy, and reified but historically inaccurate "Clashes", and looking coldly at what is involved in international relations. To be clear, most, if not all, international disputes do not involve a Clash of Civilisations, but are, on the contrary, each situated *within* the framework of *one* civilisation, each claiming that its definition is the best and accusing the other of engaging in cultural imperialism, "capitulation" to the West, and so forth. States tend to define their own culture for reasons of their own, thereby denying their own diversity: it is this, the drive for a monolithic definition, which explains much cultural nationalism. An example of this is Iran after the revolution in 1979, where in April 1980 a "Cultural Revolution" was launched. Khomeini said he wanted to eradicate all Western influences that were considered imperialist, but this was only part of his goal. What do you think happened? Khomeini destroyed a large amount of *Iranian* culture: women's songs, Persian literature, and poets such as Hafiz and Omar Khayyam, who celebrated the joys of love and wine, were all part of the Iranian heritage. Their suppression was justified as a return to a so-called "authentic" but actually selective and authoritarian culture. We should therefore always distrust politicians whose cultural horizons are limited or supposedly authoritative: we should not exclude or overlook the diversity that exists at the heart of every culture, and is a recurrent, necessary, part of their vitality.

To conclude with three observations. First, as the literary critic Raymond Williams in his *Keywords* observed: the word "culture" is one of the most complex words in the language of politics. It may refer to the higher or noble arts, such as music, literature, or opera; and it may allude to the customs and habits of people in a more general way, from a sociological or anthropological perspective. We also have something which is, quite reasonably, referred to as "political culture", the values underlying national political life. When one speaks of a Clash of Civilisations, all three senses of the word, at least, come into play. There is a struggle to propagate a high culture, and, at the same time, a cultural struggle in the anthropological, popular and everyday, sense. In our own society, we are all heirs to a mixed culture, whether one is speaking in terms of literature, gastronomy, religion, or ethics. All of this, and more, is fought out within a set of public, national values and discourses. We cannot deny the influence of the past and the heritage of a refined culture: we cannot say that we have no culture, rejecting Mutanabbi, Shakespeare, or Cervantes. But we are free to judge our past and our heritage, and to select how we wish to use them. Similarly we can use, adjust, or reject elements in our political culture. This can be done by writing, by making speeches, and by introducing political reforms: our freedom is not complete, but it is sufficient. We should use it, to celebrate what we know to be rich in our own culture, to celebrate its diversity, and to be open to other cultures.

There is no single message here. Whether we are speaking of England or Tunisia, every country can draw lessons from one side or the other in the contemporary debate that is raging over its own culture, and its own economic and political system: but choice is possible because, in a very real sense, the past does not determine the present. In England there has recently been a debate about the monarchy, which would have been unthinkable thirty years ago. Monarchies may adjust to the world, but this will happen in a very different context from that which existed a generation ago. It is a topic of discussion that is political in nature, and in every country one will find a similar debate about whether to accept or reject some aspect of the political and cultural heritage.

To illustrate this issue of diversity and choice with regard to the most canonical of English forms, literature, in academic terms normally denoted, in a symptomatic elision, as "English", I was recently on holiday in the south of the country, in two of the most peaceful and least industrially developed counties: Hampshire and Dorset. Jane Austen, who described the large country estates and the quiet countryside of the 1800s, is the most celebrated writer to come from Hampshire. Not far from there, Dorset's best-known author is Thomas Hardy, who in the 1890s was deeply troubled by the problems of the farm labourers and the harsh conditions of life, and whose style is realistic. It is paradoxical that two counties so close geographically and in other ways so similar have produced two completely different, each in their own way genuine, authors, and two contrasting versions of the English heritage.

My second conclusion is that the modern world forces us to rethink what we understand by a political or religious culture. In Ireland today, as in Israel, there is a movement, termed "revisionist", in favour of the rewriting of history. Yet history is *always* revisionist because from history one obtains new evidence and acquires new perspectives. The discourse of the Moderns versus the discourse of the Ancients is inexorable, not transient. This does not mean that our present definitions are false, but they will probably be modified and reassessed by future generations.

It is possible to reconcile the defence of a specific culture and a specific past with universalist commitments and obligations. This means that one should link the defence of a nation's cultural values not only with certain universal principles, such as those defined in the Charter and subsequent conventions of the United Nations, but also with a commitment in favour of dialogue, open not stage-managed, and an opening-up of discussions between people of different nations and civilisations. Here, above all, I would reject, on the one hand, the arguments of those Arab writers who are hostile to Orientalism, that is, to Western attempts to study and understand the Middle East, and, on the other hand, the position of Samuel Huntington who, by an apparently different course, reaches more or less the same conclusion, of blocs in conflict that are mutually unintelligible or incommensurate.

To say that we live in a world in which many cultures are homogeneous is true insofar as it denotes an aspiration for each to have some core, shared, values, like rules of grammar and meaning in a language. Diversity nonetheless exists in the world, and diversity with regard to the past offers the possibility of discussing, listening, assessing what is important in different countries. Despite some scepticism about the sincerity and open-mindedness of some of those involved, I would stress the possibility of establishing a dialogue on the basis of universalist principles. This will necessarily be unfinished, but it can always continue and develop. The alternative is, at best, some very boring, set-piece, conferences, at worst political paralysis, fear and, at some point down the road, the bullet, the knife, the jail, or worse. Both within cultures and between cultures, we should accept, indeed celebrate, diversity, instead of regarding it as a source of rivalry and conflict. We should recognise, and when possible promote, discussion, borrowing and hybridity. As the Prophet Muhammad is quoted as saying: *"ikhtilaf ummati rahmah"* – "The diversity of my people is a blessing." This sage *hadith* is a far cry from the incendiary banalities of Professor Samuel Huntington.

Notes

1   This article is based on a translation of a lecture given in Tunis, in 1997, to the Association des Études Internationales. The French text was published in their journal, *Études Internationales*, in 1998. The translation has been updated and completely rewritten by the author.
2   See the famous, and most stimulating, book published in 1984: *The Invention of Tradition* (Cambridge University Press), eds Eric Hobsbawm and Terence Ranger.
3   *russkii, russiski, rossayn.*
4   In the Middle East much is made of "cultural aggression", in Arabic *al-hujum al-thaqafi.*

Chapter 8

The Dignity of Difference: Avoiding the Clash of Civilisations[1]

Jonathan Sacks

Religion has become a decisive force in the contemporary world, and it is crucial that it be a force for good – for conflict resolution, not conflict creation. If religion is not part of the solution, then it will surely be part of the problem. I would like therefore to put forward a simple but radical idea. I want to offer a new reading, or, more precisely, a new listening, to some very ancient texts. I do so because our situation in the twenty-first century, post-September 11, is new, in three ways.

First, religion has returned, counter-intuitively, against all expectation, in many parts of the world, as a powerful, even shaping, force.

Second, the presence of religion has been particularly acute in conflict zones such as Bosnia, Kosovo, Chechnya, Kashmir and the rest of India and Pakistan, Northern Ireland, the Middle East, sub-Saharan Africa, and parts of Asia.

Third, religion is often at the heart of conflict. It has been said that in the Balkans, among Catholic Croats, Orthodox Serbs, and Muslims, all three speak the same language and share the same race; the only thing that divides them is religion.

Religion is often the fault-line along which the sides divide. The reason for this is simple. Whereas the twentieth century was dominated by the politics of ideology, the twenty-first century will be dominated by the politics of identity. The three great Western institutions of modernity – science, economics, and politics – are more procedural than substantive, answering questions of "What?" and "How?" but not "Who?" and "Why?" Therefore when politics turns from ideology to identity, people inevitably turn to religion, the great repository of human wisdom on the questions "Who am I?" and "Of what narrative am I a part?"

When any system gives precedence to identity, it does so by defining an "us", in contradistinction to a "them". Identity divides, whether Catholics and Protestants in Northern Ireland, Jews and Muslims in the Middle East, or Muslims and Hindus in India. In the past, this was a less acute issue, because for most of history, most people lived in fairly constant proximity to people with whom they shared an identity, a faith, a way of life. Today, whether through travel, television, the Internet, or the sheer diversity of our multi-ethnic and multi-faith societies, we live in the conscious presence of difference. Societies that have lived with this difference for a long time have

131

learned to cope with it, but for societies for whom this is new, it presents great difficulty.

This would not necessarily be problematic. After the great wars of religion that came in the wake of the Reformation, this was resolved in Europe in the seventeenth century by the fact that diverse religious populations were subject to overarching state governments with the power to contain conflict. It was then that nation states arose, along with the somewhat different approaches of Britain and America: John Locke and the doctrine of toleration, and Thomas Jefferson and the separation of church and state. The British and American ways of resolving conflict were different but both effective at permitting a plurality of religious groups to live together within a state of civil peace.

What has changed today is the sheer capacity of relatively small, subnational groups – through global communications, porous national borders, and the sheer power of weapons of mass destruction – to create havoc and disruption on a large scale. In the twenty-first century we obviously need physical defence against terror, but also a new religious paradigm equal to the challenge of living in the conscious presence of difference. What might that paradigm be?

In the dawn of civilisation, the first human response to difference was tribalism: my tribe against yours, my nation against yours, and my god against yours. In this pre-monotheistic world, gods were local. They belonged to a particular place and had "local jurisdiction", watching over the destinies of particular people. So the Mesopotamians had Marduk and the Moabites Chamosh, the Egyptians their pantheon and the ancient Greeks theirs. The tribal, polytheistic world was a world of conflict and war. In some respects that world lasted in Europe until 1914, under the name of nationalism. In 1914 young men – Rupert Brooke and First World War poets throughout Europe – were actually eager to go to war, restless for it, before they saw carnage on a massive scale. It took two world wars and 100 million deaths to cure us of that temptation.

However, for almost 2500 years, in Western civilisation, there was an alternative to tribalism, offered by one of the great philosophers of all time: Plato. I am going to call this "universalism". My thesis will be that universalism is also inadequate to our human condition. What Plato argued in *The Republic* is that this world of the senses, of things we can see and hear and feel, the world of particular things, isn't the source of knowledge or truth or reality. How is one to understand what a tree is, if trees are always changing from day to day and there are so many different kinds of them? How can one define a table if tables come in all shapes and sizes – big, small, old, new, wood, other materials? How does one understand reality in this world of messy particulars? Plato said that all these particulars are just shadows on a wall. What is real is the world of forms and ideas: the idea of a table, the form of a tree. Those are the things that are universal. Truth is the move from particularity to universality. Truth is the same for everyone, everywhere, at all times. Whatever is local, particular, and unique is insubstantial, even illusory.

This is a dangerous idea, because it suggests that all differences lead to tribalism and then to war, and that the best alternative therefore is to eliminate differences and impose on the world a single, universal truth. If this is true, then when you and I disagree, if I am right, you are wrong. If I care about truth, I must convert you from your error. If I can't convert you, maybe I can conquer you. And if I can't conquer you, then maybe I have to kill you, in the name of that truth. From this flows the blood of human sacrifice through the ages.

September 11 happened when two universal civilisations – global capitalism and medieval Islam – met and clashed. When universal civilisations meet and clash, the world shakes and lives are lost. Is there an alternative, not only to tribalism, which we all know is a danger, but also to universalism?

Let us read the Bible again and hear in it a message that is both simple and profound and, I believe, an important one for our time. We will start with what the Bible is about: one man, Abraham, and one woman, Sarah, who have children and become a family and then in turn a tribe, a collection of tribes, a nation, a particular people, and a people of the covenant.

What is striking is that the Bible doesn't begin with that story. For the first eleven chapters, it tells the universal story of humanity: Adam and Eve, Cain and Abel, Noah and the flood, Babel and the builders, universal archetypes living in a global culture. In the opening words of Genesis 11, "The whole world was of one language and shared speech." Then in Genesis 12, God's call to Abraham, the Bible moves to the particular. This exactly inverts Plato's order. Plato begins with the particular and then aspires to the universal. The Bible begins with the universal and then aspires to the particular. That is the opposite direction. It makes the Bible the great counter-Platonic narrative in Western civilisation.

The Bible begins with two universal, fundamental statements. First, in Genesis 1, "Let us make man in our image, in our likeness." In the ancient world it was not unknown for human beings to be in the image of God: that's what Mesopotamian kings and the Egyptian pharaoh were. The Bible was revolutionary for saying that every human being is in the image of God.

The second epic statement is in Genesis 9, the covenant with Noah, the first covenant with all humankind, the first statement that God asks all humanity to construct societies based on the rule of law, the sovereignty of justice, and the non-negotiable dignity of human life.

It is surely those two passages that inspire the words "We hold these truths to be self-evident, that all men are created equal, that they are endowed by their Creator with certain unalienable Rights … ." The irony is that these truths are anything but self-evident. Plato or Aristotle wouldn't know what the words meant. Plato believed profoundly that human beings are created unequal, and Aristotle believed that some people are born to be free, other to be slaves.

These words are self-evident only in a culture saturated in the universal vision of the Bible. However, that vision is only the foundation. From then on, starting with Babel and the confusion of languages and God's call to Abraham, the Bible moves from the universal to the particular, from all humankind to one family. The Hebrew Bible is the first document in civilisation to proclaim monotheism, that God is not only the God of this people and that place but of all people and every place. Why then does the Bible deliver an anti-Platonic, particularistic message from Genesis 12 onwards? The paradox is that the God of Abraham is the God of all humankind, but the faith of Abraham is not the faith of all humankind.

In the Bible you don't have to be Jewish to be a man or woman of God. Melchizedek, Abraham's contemporary, was not a member of the covenantal family, but the Bible calls him "a priest of God Most High". Moses' father-in-law, Jethro, a Midianite, gives Israel its first system of governance. And one of the most courageous heroines of the Exodus – the one who gives Moses his name and rescues him – is an Egyptian princess. We call her *Batya* or *Bithiah*, the Daughter of God.

Melchizedek, Jethro, and Pharaoh's daughter are not part of the Abrahamic covenant, yet God is with them and they are with God. As the rabbis put it two thousand years ago, "The righteous of every faith, of every nation, have a share in the world to come." Why, if God is the God of all humanity, is there not one faith, one truth, one way for all humanity?

My reading is this: that after the collapse of Babel, the first global project, God calls on one person, Abraham, one woman, Sarah, and says "Be different." In fact, the word "holy" in the Hebrew Bible, *kadosh*, actually means "different, distinctive, set apart". Why did God tell Abraham and Sarah to be different? To teach all of us the dignity of difference. That God is to be found in someone who is different from us. As the great rabbis observed some 1800 years ago, when a human being makes many coins in the same mint, they all come out the same. God makes every human being in the same mint, in the same image, His own, and yet we all come out differently. The religious challenge is to find God's image in someone who is not in our image, in someone whose colour is different, whose culture is different, who speaks a different language, tells a different story, and worships God in a different way.

This is a paradigm shift in understanding monotheism. And we are in a position to hear this message in a way that perhaps previous generations were not. Because we have now acquired a general understanding of the world that is significantly different from that of our ancestors. I will give just two instances of this among many: one from the world of natural science and one from economics.

The first is from biology. There was a time in the European Enlightenment when it was thought that all of nature was one giant machine with many interlocking parts, all harmonised in the service of mankind. We now know that nature is quite different, that its real miracle is its diversity. Nature is a complex ecology in which every animal, plant, bird, every single species has its own part to play and the whole has its own independent integrity.

We know even more than this thanks to the discovery of DNA and our decoding of the genome. Science writer Matt Ridley points out that the three-letter words of the genetic code are the same in every creature. "CGA means arginine, GCG means alanine, in bats, in beetles, in bacteria. Wherever you go in the world, whatever animal, plant, bug, or blob you look at, if it is alive, it will use the same dictionary and know the same code. All life is one." The genetic code, bar a few tiny local aberrations, is the same in every creature. We all use exactly the same language. This means that there was only one creation, one single event when life was born. This is what the Bible is hinting at. The real miracle of this created world is not the Platonic form of the leaf, it's the 250 000 different kinds of leaf there are. It's not the idea of a bird, but the 9000 species that exist. It is not a universal language; it is the 6000 languages actually spoken. The miracle is that unity creates diversity, that unity up there creates diversity down here.

One can look at the same phenomenon from the perspective of economics. We are all different, and each of us has certain skills and lacks others. What I lack, you have, and what you lack, I have. Because we are all different we specialise, we trade, and we all gain. The economist David Ricardo put forward a fascinating proposition, the Law of Comparative Advantage, in the early nineteenth century. This says that if you are better at making axe-heads than fishing, and I am better at fishing than making axe-heads, we gain by trade even if you're better than me at both fishing and making axe-heads. You can be better than me at everything, and yet we still benefit if you specialise at what you're best at and I specialise at what I'm best at. The law of comparative advantage tells us that every one of us has something unique to contribute, and by contributing we benefit not only ourselves but other people as well.

In the market economy throughout all of history, differences between cultures and nations have led to one of two possible consequences. When different nations meet, they either make war or they trade. The difference is that from war at the very least one side loses, and in the long run, both sides lose. From trade, both sides gain. When we value difference the way the market values difference, we create a non-zero-sum scenario of human interaction. We turn the narrative of tragedy, of war, into a script of hope.

So whether we look at biology or economics, difference is the precondition of the complex ecology in which we live. And by turning to the Bible we arrive at a new paradigm, one that is neither universalism nor tribalism, but a third option, which I call the dignity of difference. This option values our shared humanity as the image of God, and creates that shared humanity in terms like the American Declaration of Independence or the UN Universal Declaration of Human Rights. But it also values our differences, just as loving parents love all their children not for what makes them the same but for what makes each of them unique. That is what the Bible means when it calls God a parent.

This religious paradigm can be mapped onto the political map of the twenty-first century. With the end of the Cold War, there were two famous scenarios about where the world would go: Francis Fukuyama's *The End of History* (1992) and Samuel Huntington's *Clash of Civilizations and the Remaking of World Order* (1996).

Fukuyama envisaged an eventual, gradual spread first of global capitalism, then of liberal democracy, with the result being a new universalism, a single culture that would embrace the world.

Huntington saw something quite different. He saw that modernisation did not mean Westernisation, that the spread of global capitalism would run up against counter-movements, the resurgence of older and deeper loyalties, a clash of cultures, or what he called civilisations – in short, a new tribalism.

And to a considerable extent, that is where we are. Even as the global economy binds us ever more closely together, spreading a universal culture across the world – what Benjamin Barber calls "McWorld" – civilisations and religious differences are forcing us ever more angrily and dangerously apart. That is what you get when the only two scenarios you have are tribalism and universalism.

There is no instant solution, but there is a responsibility that rests with us all, particularly with religious leaders, to envision a different and more gracious future. As noted earlier, faced with intense religious conflict and persecution, John Locke and Thomas Jefferson devised their particular versions of how different religious groups might live together peaceably. These two leaps of the imagination provided, each in their own way, bridges over the abyss of confrontation across which future generations could walk to a better world.

I have gone rather further than Locke's doctrine of toleration or the American doctrine of separation of church and state because these no longer suffice for a situation of global conflict without global governance. I have made my case on secular grounds, but note that the secular terms of today – pluralism, liberalism – will never persuade a deeply passionate, indeed fanatically passionate religious believer to subscribe to them, because they are secular ideas. I have therefore given a religious idea, based on the story of Abraham, from which all three great monotheisms – Judaism, Christianity, and Islam – descend. A message of the dignity of difference can be found that is religious and profoundly healing. That is the real miracle of monotheism: not that there is one God and therefore one truth, one faith, one way, but that unity above creates diversity here on earth.

Nothing has proved harder in civilisation than seeing God or good or dignity in those unlike ourselves. There are surely many ways of arriving at that generosity of spirit, and each faith may need to find its own way. I propose that the truth at the heart of monotheism is that God is greater than religion, that He is only partially comprehended by any one faith. He is my God, but he is also your God. That is not to say that there are many gods: that is polytheism. And it is not to say that God endorses every act done in His name: a God of yours and mine must be a God of justice standing above both of us, teaching us to make space for one another, to hear one another's claims, and to resolve them equitably. Only such a God would be truly transcendent. Only such a God could teach humankind to make peace other than by conquest or conversion and as something nobler than practical necessity.

What would such a faith be like? It would be like being secure in my own home and yet moved by the beauty of a foreign place knowing that while it is not my home, it is still part of the glory of the world that is ours. It would be knowing that we are sentences in the story of our people but that there are other stories, each written by God out of the letters of lives bound together in community. Those who are confident of their faith are not threatened but enlarged by the different faiths of others. In the midst of our multiple insecurities, we need now the confidence to recognise the irreducible, glorious dignity of difference.

Note

1 The Templeton Lecture on Religion and World Affairs for 2002, reproduced with the author's permission from the journal *Interreligious Insight*, vol. 2, no. 3 (July 2004), 35–42.

Chapter 9

Conservative Ecumenism: Politically Incorrect Meditations on Islam and the West

Antony T. Sullivan

Overview

These are not propitious times to attempt to comment objectively on relations between Islam and the West.[1] In the United States, Islam has come to be widely identified with terrorism and frequently is assumed to constitute a surrogate, perhaps in tandem with Confucian China, for the late USSR as an exigent geostrategic threat. In the Muslim world, a small minority of extremists disfigure the third of the three monotheistic revelations by invoking putative religious sanctions for actions that are baldly criminal. Terrorism by individuals who call themselves Muslims constitutes first and foremost a direct attack on the tolerance, compassion, and mercy that historically have characterised Islam both as creed and practice.[2] However, extremism is not limited to the Arab Middle East, or indeed to the Muslim world. In fact, it may well be that since 11 September 2001, it is in the United States itself where ideological extremism may have become most obvious, and where obstacles to understanding between civilisations have now assumed their most intimidating forms.

In recent years, a powerful political alliance has emerged between Southern Baptist and other Christian fundamentalists on the one hand, and former Cold Warriors and neo-conservatives on the other. For theological reasons in the first case[3] and ideological and geostrategic reasons in the second, a view of Islam is now promoted in the United States that bears little resemblance to the faith as it is understood by the enormous majority of the world's Muslims. One consequence of this new reality is that those few American conservatives and cultural traditionalists committed to interfaith understanding and cooperation among civilisations face unprecedented difficulties in their labours. In this chapter, an argument will be made that Islam should be analysed within a radically different framework from that commonly adopted by many "Christian" websites and radio broadcasts, and by such neo-conservative organs of opinion as the *Wall Street Journal*, the *Weekly Standard*, and *National Review*.

But the problem is not restricted to an inaccurate understanding of what Islam is and what it advocates. Today, there exists in the United States – and

139

especially in conservative circles – widespread amnesia concerning what conservatism itself once was, and near total incomprehension of how traditional American conservatism has been transformed into a radical and aggressively interventionist Wilsonianism. This second misunderstanding may be fully as important as the first. The essay at hand gives substantial attention to both misunderstandings of Islam, on the one hand, and culturally traditionalist conservative dissent from American foreign policy, on the other.

In fact, the hard reality now is that, in both the West and the Muslim world, religions and civilisations have become increasingly reified.[4] Before 9/11, little effort was being devoted to acquiring understanding of supposedly homogeneous and inimical "Others". But the situation now is immeasurably worse. Wholesale vituperation of Islam and Arabs now seems the order of the day, and explanations or analyses are all too often dismissed as apologies. Nevertheless, the truth remains that unless Christians and Muslims begin to hear each other when they whisper prayers to their common God, they indeed are likely to meet on ever more battlefields around the world. Clearly, there is now a need to rethink the stereotypes that today are pushing the children of Abraham ever more widely apart.[5]

In addition to proposing new paradigms for both Westerners and Muslims to employ in thinking about Islam, this essay focuses on the reinterpretation or revival of such key Islamic concepts as *jihad* and *hirabah* that is now exemplified by an increasing number of Muslim intellectuals. It also makes the point that Jihad, as currently propagated by assorted Islamist extremist groups, is simply illegal according to traditional Islamic criteria. In addition, this chapter discusses one conservative ecumenical initiative now under way that suggests the possibility of a better future for all of the children of Abraham. This initiative is intended to enable Western and Muslim cultural traditionalists to move deeper into the new century as companions rather than as enemies. Above all, the subtext of this essay is that every possible effort should be made to avoid a war of civilisations, in the interests of all mankind.[6]

Mediterranean Commonalities

Muslims understand their faith as pure and unadulterated Abrahamic monotheism, purged of the textual deformations and theological misunderstandings that they believe have compromised Judaism and Christianity. For some years after he began his mission in 610 CE, the prophet Muhammad had no idea that he would in fact establish a new and separate Abrahamic monotheism. Rather, he understood his charge to be the same as that given to the many prophets who had come before him. Muhammad originally conceived his mission to be that very ancient, Semitic one of calling upon a fallen humankind to repent, and discover the love and mercy of what in Arabic is al-Lah, the one and only God.

Christianity and Islam share a vast reservoir of faith. Revelations to Muhammad included important portions of Christian scripture that were duly incorporated into the Qur'an. The specific vehicle for revelation to Muhammad was the Archangel Gabriel. In fact, Gabriel is the messenger through whom Muslims believe that God spoke to all of His prophets, from Abraham to Jesus Christ. Concerning Jesus, the Qur'an states that he is "worthy of regard in this world and the hereafter, and is one of those drawn nigh to God" (3:44). Concerning the crucifixion, it says: "O Jesus! I will cause you to die and exalt you in my presence and clear you of those who disbelieve and make those who follow you above those who disbelieve to the Day of Resurrection" (3:54). The Virgin Mary is also a major figure in the Qur'an, and is depicted as the God-touched mother of one of the very greatest of the prophets. Examples of this sort could be multiplied. For present purposes, it is sufficient to summarise the religious similarities between Christianity and Islam by citing the remarks of Imam Muhammad Abd al-Raouf: Muslims believe in the "Christian Gospel, the Christian Prophet [Jesus Christ], his twelve Apostles, his mother's purity, and his miraculous birth ... Above all, [they] share a belief in ... [a] common God." Most bluntly put, without Judaism and Christianity having preceded it, Islam as revealed and practised would simply be inconceivable.

It may be especially important for Westerners to understand that the Qur'an specifically forbids any imposition of Islam on non-Muslims by force.[7] The Qur'an endorses free will, as represented by the freedom it accords each individual to choose whether to believe or not to believe. On the subject of religious tolerance, the Qur'an is categorical: "There shall be no compulsion," it states, "in matters of faith" (2:256). "The truth is from your Lord," the Qur'an states, "so let him who pleases believe; and let him who pleases disbelieve" (18:29). The Qur'an states elsewhere: "Say: O Mankind! Indeed there has come to you the truth from your Lord. Whosoever, therefore, chooses to follow the Right Path, follows it but for his own good, and whosoever chooses to go astray, goes astray but to his own hurt" (10:108). To the degree to which Muslims or self-proclaimed Islamic regimes have in fact violated such injunctions prescribing tolerance and religious pluralism, they have grossly transgressed against the most fundamental tenets of Islam itself.[8]

One should always remember that Islam was revealed and first adopted within the same Semitic ethos and general geographic location as were Judaism and Christianity. Like them, Islam was born not far from the Mediterranean and, like the prior Abrahamic revelations, has been profoundly shaped over 1400 years by its interactions with the other monotheistic faiths that ring that sea. Islam should be understood religiously, and Arab Islam culturally, as part of the same Mediterranean ecumene that has also profoundly shaped Judaism and Christianity.[9] The "West" (despite current headlines) does not stop at the Bosphorus,[10] but in fact at the Indus.

It is worthy of note that both China and India consider the West to constitute one civilisational block derived from three constituent parts: Byzantium, Europe, and the world of Mediterranean Islam. For the very different civilisations located to its east, Western civilisation is most emphatically not made up only of Europe and North America but consists also of both Arab Christianity and the Arab Muslim world. The distinguished Roman Catholic historian and economist Leonard Liggio has amplified this point:

When Islam arose, it adopted (especially in Syria) the Hellenistic culture which Byzantium and Europe were rejecting. Islam carried logic, philosophy and science beyond the Hellenistic legacy. [During the Middle Ages] Islam passed on the classical intellectual tradition to Europe ... Europe built on the shoulders of the Islamic part of that tradition. Similarly, Islam built on the capitalism and commerce of the Hellenistic tradition and for centuries was far ahead of Byzantium and Europe. Later, Islam was burdened by the domination of Ottoman rule. In a sense, Islam became like Byzantium – one large empire – rather than the European continuity of the Islamic tradition of many different political centres.[11]

I would suggest that the civilisation of the contemporary West might more accurately be designated as "Abrahamic" rather than "Judeo-Christian". The latter term excludes Islam from the values that Jews and Christians are presumed to share. In that sense, Judeo-Christian is not only inaccurate but may in fact contribute to polarisation between the West and a reinforcement of the stereotype of an alien and homogeneous Muslim enemy. The fact is that the term Judeo-Christian is a category invented and widely disseminated only during the past four decades. As late as the 1950s, the operative term for describing the heritage of the West was "Greco-Roman". Precisely how and why "Judeo-Christian" came to replace "Greco-Roman" is a story awaiting an author.[12] With more than 6 million Muslims now in the United States, as against 5.6 million Jews, and major immigrant Muslim communities in Western Europe, the time may be ripe to rethink how most accurately to describe civilisations and categorise the monotheistic faiths. Most important to keep clearly in mind is that Islam is today fully in and of the West, just as the West has become in and of Islam.

American Conservative Dissenters from the Ideology of Crusade: Peter Kreeft and Russell A. Kirk

In stark contrast to many Southern Baptists and evangelicals, Roman Catholic scholars such as Peter Kreeft and Russell Kirk have frequently adopted ecumenical positions sympathetic to Islam. Moreover, they have voiced powerful criticism of the now-ascendant foreign policy that Christian fundamentalists and neo-conservatives so strongly support. Serious attention to the thought of such cultural traditionalists concerning religion on the one hand, and American national security policy on the other, is long overdue.

In this age of the "war against terrorism", penetration of the spiritual nature of Islamic religiosity by Western non-Muslims is rare indeed. Such penetration by Western conservative thinkers is almost non-existent. One striking exception to this sad reality is *Ecumenical Jihad*, a truly excellent book by Professor Peter Kreeft of Boston College. In it, Kreeft presents an imaginary dialogue between himself in the role of a contemporary non-Muslim and misinformed Westerner, and the Prophet Muhammad. The exchange suggests that at least one Western Christian has finally succeeded in gaining access to the spiritual core of Islam.

The dialogue begins when a departing Buddha, with whom Kreeft had just completed a discussion, says, "This [next] man will teach you more about religion than Confucius or [I] ... He will teach you the heart and soul of all true religion." Kreeft confesses to being "shocked" by this, since the man who now appeared before him was clearly Muhammad. "So I asked [Muhammad]," Kreeft writes, "What is the heart and soul of all true religion?" And the answer "... came from [him] in a single word: Islam – surrender – and the peace that comes from surrender, the peace that the world cannot give, that comes only from total surrender to the will of God. This is the heart and soul of all true religion ... The only true first step is adoration, the bent knee and the bent spirit, surrender, Islam."

Muhammad goes on to utter a warning:

"You [Westerners] are not winning your world, you are not winning your Jihad, your spiritual warfare; your world is sliding down the road to Hell. Why? Why have you lost a century to the devil? [It is] because you prattle about yourselves and your freedoms and your rights and your self-fulfilment rather than forgetting yourself and adoring and obeying the Lord ... the child you must become again if you are to enter His Kingdom. The saying is His, not mine. I am only His prophet. He is the One than whom there is no other. *Laa ilaaha illa al-Lah.*"

And Muhammad then fell to his knees, Kreeft writes, "and bowed his back and prayed."

Kreeft continues:

The comfortably condescending cultural chauvinism with which I had always unconsciously viewed those holy Arabic words and that holy Arabic deed seemed to have suddenly died in me ... I wondered ... whether my world could ever be saved in any other way ... I suspected then that the explosive growth of Islam in our time might be due to a simpler cause than any sociologist had yet discovered: that God blesses obedience and faithfulness, especially when surrounded by unfaithful and disobedient cultures.

Meanwhile, Muhammad had more to say:

Muhammad: "The religion I taught my people was the simplest one in the world. There are times that call for complexity, and there are times that call for simplicity. Today is a time when 'simplistic' is the favourite sneer word of a decadent, arrogant, corrupt, and aggressively anti-God establishment. So what time do you think it is today?"
Kreeft: "I had nothing to say, so Muhammad answered his own question."
Muhammad: "It is time for a Jihad, a holy war, a spiritual war ... [I]t is time to wake up to the fact that, whether you like it or not, you are in the middle of one."
Kreeft: "But we are commanded to love our enemies, not to make war."
Muhammad: "We love our human enemies, we war against our spirit enemies."

Kreeft: "Aren't Muslims famous for confusing the two and fighting literal holy wars?"

Muhammad: "Some. About three per cent of Muslims in the world believe that Jihad means physical war, killing infidels. But the Qur'an makes it quite clear that this war is first within oneself and against one's own sins and infidelities."

Kreeft: "But your people, the Arabs, are world-famous for violence."

Muhammad: "Unlike your people in Northern Ireland, I suppose."

Kreeft: "But your whole history is full of ..."

Muhammad: "Crusades and inquisitions and forced conversions and anti-Semitism and religious wars?"

Kreeft: "I quickly realised that my 'argument' was going nowhere except to blow up in my face."

Thereupon Muhammad continued more gently:

Muhammad: "Let me try to explain. Islam and Jihad are intrinsically connected. For Islam means not only 'submission' but also 'peace,' the peace that the world cannot give, the peace that only God can give when we submit to Him. And this submission requires the inner Jihad, a war on our war against God. So we get the paradoxical result that peace (Islam) is attained only through war (Jihad). And this peace also leads to war, because the submission that is this peace requires us to obey God's will, and God's will for us is to become spiritual warriors against evil."[13]

These few pages should be considered required reading by Christian fundamentalists, neo-conservatives, and Washington policy makers alike. Kreeft's imaginary dialogue says more about the real nature of Islam as a faith than any number of academic or journalistic articles. Given the contemporary international situation, it is imperative that Kreeft's comprehension of the soul of Islam be disseminated as widely as possible both in the West and in the Muslim world.

Russell Kirk had little to say about Islam itself but a very great deal to say about what American conservatism is, or at least should be. The author of some thirty books[14] dealing with political philosophy, economics, history, and culture, as well as haunting ghost stories and tales of adventure, Kirk thought deeply about the meaning and importance of history. He understood the prescriptive claims of the past, and the unalterable nature of history as tragedy. Man's state, man's prospects, and man's fate were primary concerns for him throughout a professional career spanning almost half a century. And Kirk, like Kreeft, accorded to religion fundamental importance in explaining how the world works. "Culture (or civilisation)," Kirk never tired of reminding his interlocutors, "comes from the cult." As a practising Roman Catholic, Kirk was himself a vibrant exemplar of how religion must inform culture if society is to flourish. Kirk's sympathy for both religion and tradition may not have been unconnected with the open-mindedness of his posture toward the Arab and Islamic world.

For Kirk, conservatism[15] constituted the negation of ideology. Conservative politics, he believed, is always prudential politics, and prudential politics is the opposite of ideological politics. True conservatives, Kirk understood, regard politics as merely the art of the possible, while ideologues consider politics to be a "revolutionary instrument for transforming society and even transforming human nature" (1993: 1). Kirk pointedly remarks: "Ideologues ... [are] enemies [of] religion, tradition, custom, convention, prescription, and old constitutions ... In [their] march toward utopia, ideologue[s] [are] merciless" (1, 3). Indeed, Western ideologues have consistently attempted to "substitute secular goals and doctrines for religious goals and doctrines [in order to] overthrow present dominations so that the oppressed may be liberated" (5). In Kirk's opinion, ideologues have offered a formula that "promises mankind an earthly paradise but in cruel fact has created a series of terrestrial hells" (5).[16] What, then, are some of the specific aspects of conservatism that may serve as antidotes to the poison spread by ideologues of all sorts?

For Kirk, conservatives believe that there exists an "enduring moral order" (17). In other words, conservatives believe that human nature is a constant, and that moral truths are permanent. Moreover, they believe that the "inner order of the soul, and the outer order of the commonwealth" (17) are inseparably connected. For those who wish to establish and strengthen viable democratic systems, understanding this conservative conviction may be especially important. For Kirk and other conservatives, the "body social is a kind of spiritual corporation ... it may even be called a community of souls" (19). Therefore, human society and its political systems cannot be understood as mere machines, to be treated as machines are. In the case of democratic governance, this means that although technique (constitutions, separation of power, parliaments, and a formal rule of law) is essential, it can never be sufficient without a commonality of values to which such technique must be grafted.

Above all, prudence must pervade the polity. "Any public measure," Kirk writes, "ought to be judged by its probable long-run consequences, not merely by temporary advantage or popularity" (20). Prudence is obligatory because of the inescapable imperfectability of man, and the fact that the flaws of human nature preclude the creation of any perfect political order, democratic or otherwise. "To seek for utopia," Kirk repeats, "is to end in disaster" (20). Indeed, given human imperfectability and the dangerous passions inherent in human nature, formal restraints upon political power, perhaps especially in democracies, are a *sine qua non* for the preservation of individual liberty.

Conservatives also believe, as Kirk points out, that freedom and property are closely linked. "Separate property from private possession," he notes, "and Leviathan becomes master of all" (21). And Kirk adds an observation that should resonate with Muslims today: "The conservative acknowledges that the possession of property fixes certain duties upon the possessor: he [the possessor] accepts those moral and legal obligations cheerfully" (22).[17] Man is a creation of God, Kirk understood, and men with property have a special obligation to use what God has given them in trust for the benefit of their less fortunate fellow men.

In addition, and perhaps especially important in the context of contemporary world events, is Kirk's emphasis on the traditional conservative respect for the "principle of variety" (20). Kirk's insistence on the importance of religious, political, and civilisational pluralism reflects the intent of the Qur'anic verse, "For every one of you We appointed a law and a way. And if God had pleased He would have made you a single people but (His plan is) to test you in what He has given you; so strive as in a race in all virtues" (5:48). Kirk detested uniformity, homogenisation, and standardisation, and regarded cultural variety as truly part of the divine order. This conservative empathy for non-European peoples, and reverence for the multiformity of God's handiwork, extends back to Edmund Burke himself, as exemplified in Burke's courageous opposition to the policies of repression of Warren Hastings, the British Governor of India, and Burke's support for both Muslims and Hindus against the tyranny of the British crown. Kirk himself wandered through the souqs of both Cairo and Marrakesh, and rejoiced in the way that those vibrant worlds linked the present to the past.

Finally, Kirk had much to say about United States foreign policy. In *The Politics of Prudence*, published in 1993 only a year before his death, Kirk offered sage advice about America's role in the world that most of the "conservative" impostors who currently wield power in Washington have categorically repudiated. A decade ago Kirk knew that the USA had come to bestride the world as a single colossus. But he asked the question that was fundamental then, and remains so today: "How should the United States employ the powers of its ascendancy? Are we Americans fulfilling a manifest destiny, the mission of recasting every nation and every culture in the American image?" (212). Any such homogenisation would constitute hell itself, Kirk believed, totally inimical as it was to his entire understanding of the critical importance of pluralism and variety in human affairs. Kirk pulled no punches in expressing his contempt for the "enthusiasts" who continue to maintain that the "political structure and the economic patterns of the United States will be emulated on every continent, forevermore" (213). In all of this, what is perhaps most remarkable is how totally ignored Kirk's insights have been by those who now hold power in Washington.

Kirk, the greatest of American conservatives, is almost frightening in his perspicacity. There is a law of nature, he wrote, that impels every living organism to preserve its identity against all attempts at appropriation or assimilation. That being the case, no one should be surprised that "men and nations resist desperately ... any attempt to assimilate their character to some other body social. This resistance is the first law of their being" (216). And then Kirk makes this striking observation: "There is one sure way to make a deadly enemy, and that is to propose to anybody, 'Submit yourself to me, and I will improve your condition by relieving you from the burden of your own identity and by reconstituting your substance in my own image'" (217). But such conservative insights are manifestly incomprehensible to those presently directing American foreign policy.

In summary, Kirk makes the point that a "soundly conservative foreign policy ... should be neither 'interventionist' nor 'isolationist': it should be prudent" (221). Its objective "should not be to secure the triumph everywhere of America's name and manners ... but instead the preservation of the true [American] national interest" (221). Kirk emphasised that the United States should accept "the diversity of economic and political institutions throughout the world" (221). Today, among most of those who pass themselves off as conservatives, such counsel is emphatically rejected.[18]

Let us turn now to the challenge of reinterpretation or revival of key Islamic concepts. Muslim intellectuals have for some time been grappling with this challenge, and have redoubled their efforts since 9/11. Americans should be aware of the efforts of such Muslim thinkers, and themselves come to understand the true meaning of some of the Islamic terms that are currently so ignorantly bandied about by the Western media.

Jihad and Qital

Especially in recent decades, perhaps no term has been more misunderstood by Muslims and non-Muslims alike than the word *jihad*. Among both Muslim extremists on the one hand and the general public in the West on the other, *jihad* has come to be associated with military conflict, and more broadly with compulsion and intolerance in general. However, and as Kreeft's observations suggest, all interpretations of *jihad* that place primary emphasis on violence are radically anti-Quranic. Nevertheless, such interpretations are everywhere, and now constitute major impediments to any new beginning in Muslim-Western relations.[19]

In the West, far too many commentators expostulate about Islam who have no knowledge of Arabic. In fact, it is a useful exercise to analyse the various meanings of *jihad* as offered in the two best Arabic-English dictionaries available, Hans Wehr's *A Dictionary of Modern Written Arabic* and Edward William Lane's *An Arabic-English Lexicon*. The Arabic root (*jim ha dal*) of the word *jihad* means variously to try, to endeavour, to strive, and to exert effort. In the four classes of verbs in which the root appears, only one (verb class three) incorporates any notion whatsoever of military activity. Even there, warfare is only a tertiary meaning. Both Wehr and Lane agree that the principal meaning of even verb form three is "to endeavour", or "to strive", in primarily moral or spiritual ways. Certainly, *jihad* has an obvious military aspect, but that military dimension is subsumed in a much larger whole.

Jihad has been historically understood by Muslims as of two different sorts, one far more important than the other. The "greater" *jihad* is the eternal struggle of each individual against temptation and the wiles of Satan. The "lesser" *jihad*, now much emphasised but downplayed in Islamic history, is the conduct of defensive war to protect the Islamic community. On the permissibility of defensive warfare only, the Qur'an is explicit: "And fight in the way of God against those who fight against you and be not aggressive; for surely God loves not the aggressors" (2:190). Fighting, the Qur'an explains, is permitted by Muslims only against people "who broke their oaths and sought to expel the Prophet and attacked you first" (9:13). When defensive religious war is unavoidable, the Qur'an makes clear that no advantage should be taken of the situation to amass booty: "Let those fight in the way of God who sell this world's goods for the Hereafter" (4:74). Above all, the Qur'an emphasises that peace is much to be preferred to military conflict: "If [one's enemies] incline to peace, incline you also to it and trust in God ... And if they intend to deceive you – then surely God is sufficient for you" (8:61, 62). In fact, the Qur'anic understanding of *jihad* has much in common with the Christian notion of "just war".[20]

Here, one should distinguish between the Qur'anic use of the term *jihad* on the one hand, and the word it employs to denominate fighting (*qital*) and killing (*qatl*) on the other. Linguistically, the Qur'an employs the word *jihad* in the vast majority of cases to describe actions that are moral rather than military. Although defensive military struggle has always been understood by Muslims to fall within the category of *jihad*, the usage of the term in the Qur'an is largely restricted to an advocacy of intellectual, moral, and missionary effort. The Qur'an denominates fighting, and/or killing, by most frequently avoiding the word *jihad* and using an entirely different root, namely *qaf ta lam*. A few examples of this very different usage will make my point.

For example, in Surah 2:190 the term *jihad* is not used. Rather, the verb form meaning fighting in the military sense is employed (*qatala*). The same is true in 2:191: the *qaf ta lam* root, meaning killing in verb form one and fighting in war in verb form three, are both employed (*tuqatiluhum* and *uqtuluhum* respectively). And in 2:193 and 2:217, *qatala* (or *qital*) is again the verb of choice. In 9:5 and 9:13, the same is true: the verb forms used, respectively meaning to "kill" and "fight", are derived from the same *qaf ta lam* root. The same is true in the cases of 4:74, 9:13, 9:36, and 22:38. And in every case where fighting or killing in war is endorsed, that endorsement is restricted by some moral condition. For example, in 2:190, after defensive warfare has been authorised, believers are cautioned "not to commit aggression" (*la ta'tadu*) because "Verily God does not like aggressors (*mu'tadin*)."

Contrast all of this with the Qur'anic use of the root *jim ha dal*. Thus, in 16:110 believers are urged to "struggle hard" (*jahidu*) and persevere under the burden of afflictions, and in 29:6 are told that "Whoever strives mightily (*jahada*) strives (*yujahidu*) for his own soul". In 29:8, the believers are reminded that "We have enjoined kindness to parents: but if they (either of them) endeavour (*jahadaka*) (to force) you to associate anything with Me in worship, obey them not." And in 29:69 they are told that "Those who strive (*jahidu*) in our (Cause) – We will certainly guide them to Our Paths." In 22:78 and 25:52 the *jim ha dal* root is also used in precisely the same sense of moral effort. At the same time, one should note that in 9:73 and 66:9, both late (Medinan) revelations, the Prophet is told by God to "Strive hard (*jahid*) against the unbelievers (*kuffar*)". This injunction can (and has) been interpreted in both military and moral senses. But the balance of what was truly intended by the use of *jihad* in its various forms seems clear enough on the grounds of both quantity and context.

To all of this, one might add that the notion of "holy war" (*al-harb al-muqaddasah*) is a relatively modern idea. There is no idea of "holy war" in the Qur'an, and it is not a concept developed by classical Muslim theologians. The focus on war in Islamic theology has traditionally been utilitarian: the question usually has been whether war is justified or not, and if so, under what conditions. In that theological literature one will search in vain for any denomination of war as holy. It may be especially important to remind oneself of these facts today (Abou El Fadl 2002: 19–20).

Hirabah

Given the all too common tendency to employ *jihad* and terrorism as synonyms, there is now perhaps no traditional Islamic concept that cries out louder for revival than that of *hirabah*.

Hirabah, designating "unholy war" and derived from the Arabic root *hariba*, meaning to be "furious" or "enraged", is a concept of seminal importance. *Hirabah*, not *jihad*, should be employed when describing any action that is clearly terrorist. *Jihad* might now best be largely restricted to describing non-military endeavours, and used especially in the context of the traditional Islamic understanding of the "greater *jihad*". Of course, *jihad* might continue to be used to denote what is clearly defensive warfare, but the fact that such warfare is defensive only, and why, needs to be clearly explained.

The Qur'an is categorical in its condemnation of terrorism, or *hirabah*:

[Verily] the punishment of those who wage war (*yuharibuna*) against God and his Messenger, and strive with might and main for mischief through the land, is: execution, or crucifixion, or the cutting off of hands and feet from opposite sides, or exile from the land: That is their disgrace in this world, and a heavy punishment is theirs in the hereafter. (5:33)

The medieval Arab commentators explained what they understood this Qur'anic condemnation of *hirabah* to mean. For example, the Spanish Maliki jurist Ibn al-Barr defines the committer of *hirabah* as "Anyone who disturbs free passage in the streets and renders them unsafe to travel, striving to spread corruption through the land by taking money, killing people, or violating what God has made it unlawful to violate, is guilty of *hirabah*."[21] Imam al-Nawawi states: "Whoever brandishes a weapon and terrorises the streets ... must be pursued by the authorities because if he is left unmolested his power will increase ... and corruption will spread."[22] And Ibn Qudamah defines *hirabah* as "the act of openly holding people up ... with weapons to take their money."[23] What is common to all these definitions, as Professor Sherman A. Jackson has pointed out, is that *hirabah* has traditionally been understood by Muslims to mean an effort to intimidate an entire civilian population, and the attempt to spread a sense of fear and helplessness in society.[24] Could one ask for better designations of what one today calls terrorism? And is it not precisely the realization of such social paralysis that groups like al-Qa'ida are attempting to accomplish?

In traditional Islamic parlance, *hirabah* means not only "unholy war", but also "warfare against society". As defined by Professor Khalid Abou El Fadl, it means "killing by stealth and targeting a defenceless victim to cause terror in society".[25] The concept of *hirabah* is closely connected with that of *fitnah*, which designates the disruption of established political and social order. *Fitnah*, like *hirabah*, was long considered by Islamic jurists to be among the crimes meriting the most severe of punishments. When Muslims refer to the activities of organisations allied with or sympathetic to Usama bin Ladin and al-Qa'ida – many of which use the word *jihad* to describe themselves and their activities – they would do well to describe those activities as *irhabiyyah* (terrorist) rather than as *jihadiyyah*.

Tajdif, Mufsidun, and Shaitaniyyah

There are assorted terms in traditional Islamic vocabulary in addition to *hirabah* that currently are attracting new attention from Muslims. Those terms include *tajdif, mufsidun*, and *shaitaniyyah*. Today, an increasing number of Muslims are employing this traditional vocabulary in an attempt to rethink their faith and to reclaim Islam from those extremists who are now so blackening its reputation.[26]

Of all allied understandings, the Islamic concept of *tajdif* has long been intimately associated with *hirabah*. *Tajdif* designates the blasphemy that results from the waging of unholy warfare by evildoers. *Tajdif* has traditionally been considered by Muslims as an act of apostasy punishable by death. The word *mufsidun* designates those who engage in *hirabah*, and who perpetuate what we today understand as terrorism. *Tajdif*, and the activities of *mufsidun*, have been understood by Muslims as examples of *shaitaniyyah*, or Satanic and anti-Islamic activity. Today, the fact is that increasing numbers of Muslim scholars and students of Islam, both in the West and the Islamic world, are beginning to use this old vocabulary to delegitimise terrorism. To the extent that this new (traditional) usage continues to spread, the better off the world will be.

Muslims Speak Out

Prominent Muslims throughout the world are beginning to discuss *hirabah*, and the substitution of the concept of *hirabah* for that of *jihad* in reference to terrorism. For example, Shaykh Yusuf al-Qaradawi of the United Arab Emirates categorically condemned the bombing in Bali in 2002 as a terrorist action, and said it represented "total barbarism". He stated that rather than an act of *jihad*, the Bali bombing constituted an "act of ... *hirabah* in juristic terms: a crime in Islam for which a severe punishment is specified without [any allowance] for the race, colour, nationality or religion of the culprit".[27] Similarly, condemning terrorism, and employing the word *hirabah* rather than *jihad* to describe it, Ezzedin Ibrahim, also of the UAE, states: "What occurred on 11 September 2001 is one of the most loathsome of crimes, which in Islam goes under the name of *al-hirabah*. *Hirabah* is the most abominable form of murder, in that it involves killing with terror and intimidation." Professor Akbar Ahmed of the American University in Washington, DC, describes contemporary events as constituting a "war of ideas within Islam", featuring pronouncements that are "clearly un-Islamic and even blasphemous toward the peaceful and compassionate God of the Qur'an ... al-Qa'ida's brand of suicide and mass murder and its fomenting of hatred among races, religions and cultures do not constitute godly or holy Jihad – but, in fact, constitute the heinous crime and sin of unholy Hiraba." Professor Ahmed emphasises that the act of *hirabah* committed on 9/11, through its "wanton killing of innocents – both non-Muslim and Muslim alike" as a means of "terrorizing [an] entire community", constituted the most "ungodly sort of 'war against society' and should be condemned as blasphemous and un-Islamic".[28] Radwan Masmoudi, President of the Center for the Study of Islam and Democracy in Washington, DC, states:

> The war against society and innocent civilians that Usama bin Laden is calling for is not *jihad*. To the contrary, it is a forbidden and un-Islamic war [*hirabah*] that is counter to all the values and teachings of Islam. [*Hirabah*] is a crime against innocent civilians and therefore a crime against humanity. In Islamic jurisprudence, there is no justification for the killing of innocent people.[29]

And Robert D. Crane echoes other prominent Muslims by noting:

> There is no such thing as Islamic terrorism, but there have always been Muslims who are terrorists. Today [such] alienated extremists ... are committing the most serious crime condemned by the Qur'an, which is the root of all other crimes, namely, arrogance ... They are committing the crime of *hirabah* ... There can be no greater evil and no greater sin.[30]

This condemnation of terrorism as *hirabah* builds on the more general denunciation of terrorism by Muslim leaders and scholars outside the United States that has been so much in evidence since 9/11. Many of them have cited the following passage from the Qur'an: "If anyone kills a human being for other than manslaughter or for spreading corruption on earth – it shall be as though he had killed all mankind; whereas, if anyone saves a life, it shall be as though he had saved the lives of all mankind" (6:51).[31]

Unfortunately, many of these condemnations of terrorism were made in languages other than English (principally Arabic and Urdu), and have only belatedly been translated into English. Even so, many have received little attention in the US media. This is the principal reason for the continuing misperception in the United States that Muslim leaders have given a green light to extremists by their supposed failure to categorically condemn terrorism.

The Islamic Illegitimacy of Contemporary Jihad

Today, Muslims may wish to remind themselves, and Westerners should understand, that in any acute emergency in which Muslim lives and lands were to be threatened and therefore defensive war were to be imperative, such defensive war – *jihad* – can legally be declared only by a recognised and legitimate ruler. Usama bin Ladin, or Ayman Zawahiri, or the various "resistance" groups that invoke military *jihad* in their own names, have (under traditional Islamic criteria) no right whatsoever to do so. Therefore, Usama bin Ladin's proclamation of a Jihad against the United States, "Jews", and "Crusaders" is a violation of Islamic law.[32] In this same vein, both Muslims and non-Muslims should understand that there are rules for military *jihad* and when it must be waged. These rules were codified by the first Caliph, Abu Bakr, and are considered authoritative by all traditional Sunnis. To the Islamic army he led, Abu Bakr prescribed the following: "Do not betray; do not carry grudges; do not deceive; do not mutilate; do not kill children; do not kill the elderly; do not kill women ... do not cut down fruit-bearing trees ... You will come upon [Christian monks], leave them to what they have dedicated their lives ...."[33]

Abu Bakr's rules for *jihad* are based on what is prescribed in the Qur'an and were endorsed by Muhammad. In the Qur'an, believers are enjoined "not to let the hatred of others ... make you swerve to wrong and depart from justice. Be just: that is next to piety" (5:8). And the Prophet himself said: "Attack in the name of God, but do not revert to treachery; do not kill a child; neither kill a woman; do not wish to confront the enemy."[34] Clearly, these sources leave no doubt that the military *jihad* proclaimed by some today constitutes not only *hirabah* but is illegal and even blasphemous according to traditional Islamic criteria.

Conservatism, Ecumenism, and the Future

Today, it is vital to understand that there is now in evidence a moderate Islamist movement throughout most of the Muslim world. This moderate Islamism insists above all upon democratic governance.[35] Moreover, it is supportive of traditional values and morality, and emphasises the importance of economic development, private property, and entrepreneurship.[36] The development of moderate Islamism, which remains anchored in traditional cultural values, provides great opportunity for dialogue between cultural traditionalists and conservatives, West and East. The good news is that this dialogue is already well under way. If a conflict of civilisations is to be avoided, it will surely be through conversation and dialogue that results will be achieved.

The Islamic revival, in its moderate and democratic form, has been considerably more successful than were the secular Arab nationalists in bringing women out of the home and into both politics and civil society. In common with American conservatives, the vast majority of moderate Islamists articulate an agenda that accords priority to the "permanent things", to the "wisdom of the ancestors", and to cultural orientations profoundly inimical to the secularist radicalism that Peter Kreeft deplores. Happily, the Vatican has led the West in engaging with this new reality. As long ago as the mid-1990s, Pope John Paul II made common cause with a number of Muslim delegations to the Cairo Conference on Population and the Beijing Conference on Women to oppose some of the egregious feminist and secularist proposals advanced by Western representatives.

Much of the return to an activist religious faith by Muslims worldwide should be understood by American conservatives to be good news. The Islamic revival has largely purged Muslim countries (with the notable exception of Syria) of the socialist nationalism once symbolised by Gamal Abdul Nasser of Egypt. Moderate Muslim activists have taken the initiative in reactivating that civil society, or "Third Sector", which Nasserite statism had done so much to destroy. Today, moderate Islamist intellectuals are spearheading discussion about limiting the power of the state and achieving an appropriate equilibrium between liberty and community. Everywhere, Islamist intellectuals are articulating notions of culture, tradition, and society strikingly congruent with the world-view of Russell Kirk and Robert Nisbet, and the scholarship of the distinguished American student of Third World societies, Grace Goodell of The Johns Hopkins University. The reassertion of conservatism in the Islamic world should be understood by American cultural traditionalists to constitute a golden opportunity to recruit allies among moderate Islamists in order more effectively to confront the radical secularism of late modernity that is now so prevalent everywhere.[37]

To these ends, an international association was established in 1997 consisting of distinguished Christian and Muslim scholars of conservative or traditionalist inclination committed to a common investigation of the "permanent things". That association, the Circle of Tradition and Progress, has held international symposia and workshops in Washington, DC, London, and Berlin. The objective of the Circle is to reintegrate Mediterranean and Arab Islam within that Western world of which it long constituted an important part. The Circle's goal is to accomplish this within the parameters of cultural conservatism, democratic governance, and individual liberty. The organisation's founding statement specifically cites Edmund Burke, Russell Kirk, Eric Voegelin, and Gerhart Niemeyer as providing much of its inspiration. The following excerpt from the Circle's Statement of Purpose may give a more substantive notion of what it is about:

> Implicit in the modernist project derived substantially from the European Enlightenment is an arrogant and naive insistence that human fulfilment can be achieved solely on materialistic bases, and a belief in the absolute autonomy of human reason and in man's presumed ability to transcend his moral and cultural systems in isolation from any belief in transcendence ... More broadly, the intention of the Circle is to foster intellectual activities designed to rectify the modern rupture between economics and ethics, reason and religion, and man and God. Above all, the Circle hopes to encourage greater understanding between religions and to contribute to reconciliation of peoples and to international cooperation.

In addition, the Circle's Statement of Purpose gives attention to geopolitics:

> We favour the conduct of international relations on a basis of respect for all of the world's civilisations. We oppose all attempts to export or impose cultural systems, to support dictatorial regimes, or to obstruct democratic transformation. It is our conviction that attempts to re-invent the Cold War with Muslims targeted as enemies of the West, or the West designated as an incorrigible enemy of Islam, are deplorable

and should be avoided. We are united in our belief that all such Manichean formulations will impede cooperation between Muslims and the West and are likely over time to have a dramatically negative impact on both international stability and world peace.[38]

Today, when a true "conflict of civilisations" appears only too possible, if it has not already begun, and when the radical secularism encapsulated in Western culture seems omnipresent, the principles of the Circle of Tradition and Progress constitute one reason to hope for a better future.

In this new century, it may be more important than ever before that all of the children of Abraham reject religious, cultural, and geostrategic polarisation. Indeed, it is now imperative for the monotheistic faiths to make common cause to address the similar challenges that confront them all. On this score as on so much else, Imam Abd al-Raouf offers good counsel. "We earnestly urge [our friends in the West] to go back to God, to turn their face to Him ... What was morally right for Noah, Abraham, Moses, Jesus and Muhammad must be the same for us whether we live in America, Europe, Asia, or Africa. We all should remember that we are brothers, members of the [same] human family. [Therefore] let us live together in peace."[39]

Notes

1   For their counsel or comments on aspects of this essay, I am grateful to Leonard J. Hochberg and Leonard P. Liggio.
2   For one judicious essay on terrorism, see Bernard Lewis, "License to Kill: Usama bin Laden's Declaration of Jihad", *Foreign Affairs*, November–December 1998. Lewis observes: "At no point do the basic texts of Islam enjoin terrorism and murder. At no point do they even consider the random slaughter of uninvolved bystanders." Lewis also takes note of Islam's generally excellent record of tolerance toward non-Muslim religious communities, especially when contrasted with medieval Christianity, where "evictions of Jews and ... Muslims [by Christians] were normal and frequent" (p. 19). It is unfortunate that this dispassionate essay was given so lurid a title.
3   For one of many examples of the theological perversities that now shape American domestic politics and influence the formulation of US foreign policy, see Alan Cooperman, "Bush's Remark About God Assailed", *Washington Post*, 22 November 2003, p. A6. This article discusses Southern Baptist and evangelical outrage over President George W. Bush's theologically accurate observation that Christians and Muslims worship the same God. Cooperman cites the vigorous disagreement with President Bush of the Revd Ted Haggard, President of the National Association of Evangelicals: "The Christian God encourages freedom, love, forgiveness, prosperity and health ... The Muslim God appears to value the opposite. The personalities of each God are evident in the cultures, civilisations, and dispositions of the people that serve them." To such comments by Haggard and others Cooperman reports the response of Sayyid M. Syeed, Secretary General of the Islamic Society of North America: "We read again and again in the Qur'an that our God is the God of Abraham, the God of Noah, [and] the God of Jesus. It

would not [enter] the mind of a Muslim that there is a different God [from the one] that Abraham or Jesus or Moses was praying to." But in fact the comments by Christian fundamentalists reported by Cooperman are mild when compared to others made by such evangelicals as the Revd Jerry Vines who has stated that Muhammad was a "demon possessed paedophile". For similarly extremist views, but from a neo-conservative perspective, see the online publication edited by David Horowitz, *Front Page Magazine*, at <www.frontpagemag.com> . All of this is truly surreal at a time when the United States government is so urgently soliciting the aid of the Islamic world in the ongoing "war against terrorism".

4   For a powerfully evocative portrait of a world very different from the one that we inhabit today, see Menocal 2002.

5   For discussion of some of those stereotypes and the urgent need to rethink received opinion, see Augustus Richard Norton, "Rethinking United States Policy Toward the Muslim World", *Current History*, February 1999, 51–8.

6   For one of many analyses indicating that a war of civilisations may now be well underway, see Patrick Seale, "Has the Bush Administration Declared War on Islam?", *Mafhoum Press Studies Review*, no. 70, 28 November 2003, at <http://www. mafhoum.com/press6/170P57.htm> .

7   It is now well established that, in most of the vast territories that fell under Islamic control after Muhammad's death in CE 632, it took three or four hundred years before a majority of the population converted to Islam.

8   Just as in Christianity, where "injustice, corruption and bloodletting have been committed in the name of a faith that teaches love, tenderness and sympathy", so in Islam, Abd al-Raouf notes, "one must make a distinction ... between Muslims in the ideal and Muslims as they actually behave" (Abd al-Raouf 1984: 21).

9   For one seminal work on the commonalities of that civilisation, see Fernand Braudel, *La Méditerranée et le monde méditerranéen à l'époque de Phillipe II* (Paris: Librairie Armand Colin, 1949).

10 For an analysis of how problematic the traditional notion is of a peninsular European continent and culture terminating neatly at the Bosphorus, see J. G. A. Pocock, "What Do We Mean By Europe?", *The Wilson Quarterly*, Winter 1997.

11 Liggio to Sullivan, electronic mail, 1 November 1998.

12 See David Gress, *From Plato to Nato: The Idea of the West and its Opponents* (New York: Free Press, 1998). Gress's discomfort with the category of Greco-Roman is due to the fact that he associates the putative ideals of classical Greece with the "radical" (Voltairean) rather than "sceptical" (Montesquieu, David Hume) Enlightenment, and with twentieth-century American liberalism. Gress maintains that since the Enlightenment the West has erred because it has used the myth of ancient Greece as a "replacement for Christianity" (p. 60). He follows Samuel P. Huntington in treating Islam as an alien and potentially enemy Other (pp. 527–34). For a critique of Gress, see Morton A. Kaplan, "What is the West?", *The World and I*, vol. 13, no. 12 (December 1998), pp. 14–15. Kaplan points out that classical Greek science was derived from North Africa and the Middle East, and that Christianity is hardly a Western invention. Kaplan also implicitly argues for retention of the category "Greco-Roman" as a proper designation of the essence of the West, and maintains that today the most dangerous enemies of the West are not outside it but "within its very bowels" in the form of irrationalism, relativism, and the collapse of faith.

13 Kreeft 1996: 98–102. For an echo of what Kreeft has to say by a prominent Muslim, see Khurshid Ahmad, "The Nature of Islamic Resurgence", in John L. Esposito (ed.), *Voices of Resurgent Islam* (Oxford: Oxford University Press, 1983).

14   Russell Kirk's most important book was perhaps his first, *The Conservative Mind: From Burke to Eliot*, published in five editions by Regnery Publishing between 1953 and 1995. This massive study should be considered required reading by anyone who wishes to understand true conservatism, as distinguished from today's counterfeit varieties.

15   The American Republican administration of President George W. Bush is following a policy of revolutionary internationalism that is diametrically opposed to all that is adduced here as the "Great Tradition" of conservative thought. And this is so because the former political Right in the United States has largely been captured by the so-called "neo-conservatives", ideologues all. For one excellent, if dated, discussion of the neo-conservatives, see Kirk 1993: 172–90. *The Politics of Prudence* is Kirk's last book, and distils the wisdom of a lifetime. Kirk denounced the neo-conservatives as "cultural and economic imperialists" (1993: 187), who failed to manipulate the elder and widely experienced President Bush.

16   In the Muslim world it may now be the radical Islamists who constitute the counterpart to the extremist and secular Western ideologues. Uncompromising, ideological Islamists have fallen into the same utopian trap as have the radical purveyors of ideology in the West. The fact that radical Islam claims to seek the establishment of true religion, while Western ideologues often reject religion entirely, should not be permitted to conceal the fact that ideologues both West and East are attempting what Eric Voegelin has described as the "immanentization of the eschaton": the impossible and enormously destructive endeavour to establish in this world what can only exist in the next. Radical Islamists would do well to ponder Kirk's observation that "the purpose of religious faith is the ordering of the soul, not the ordering of the state" (p. 210).

17   This comment by Kirk is at one with the Muslim understanding of stewardship. In its simplest form, this understanding identifies God as the owner of all things, and the legitimacy of man's temporary possession of property and wealth as contingent upon its use for individual and social betterment.

18   However, the contemporary picture is not all bleak. The new American journal of opinion, *The American Conservative*, has launched a vigorous campaign to recapture conservatism from neo-conservative and Likudnik interlopers. For one good example of the magazine's rhetorical vigour, see the issue of 1 December 2003. The cover carries a photograph of President George W. Bush below a caption reading, "Righteous Anger: The Conservative Case Against George W. Bush". And an article by Neil Clark not only criticises the "imperialism" and "Arabophobia" of the Bush administration but specifically evokes themes that are very close to those of Russell Kirk: "For the first time we have a US administration that talks of de-Arabizing the Middle East – the ultimate Perleian dream of each Arab nation governed by a clone of Ahmad Chalabi, bazaars replaced by shopping malls, and Arab hospitality (not good for business) replaced by Western corporate ethics" (p. 16). For additional evidence of contemporary conservative political incorrectness, see the website of Conservatives for Peace.com at <http://www.againstbombing.com/index.htm>.

19   For an ambitious but now dated overview of *jihad*, see Rudolph Peters, *Jihad in Classical and Modern Islam* (Princeton, NJ: Markus Wiener Publishers, 1966).

20   For the idea of just war in Christianity and Islam, see James Turner Johnson, *The Holy War Idea in Western and Islamic Traditions* (University Park: Pennsylvania State University Press, 1997). For an authoritative book demonstrating the fallaciousness of any notion that Islam has historically fostered violence, see Peter

Partner, *God of Battles: Holy Wars of Christianity and Islam* (Princeton, NJ: Princeton University Press, 1997).
21 *Al-Kaft fi Fiqh Ahl al-Medina al-Maliki* (Beirut: Dar al-Kutub al-'Ilmiyyah, 1997), pp. 582–3.
22 Al-Nawawi, *Kitab al-Majmu'*, 23 vols (Cairo: Dar Ihya' al-Turath al-'Arabi, 1995), 22: 227.
23 *Al-Mughni*, 14 vols (Beirut: Dar al-Kutub al-'Ilmiyyah, n. d.), 10: 315.
24 See Sherman A. Jackson, "Domestic Terrorism in the Islamic Legal Tradition", *Muslim World*, vol. 91 (Fall 2001), especially 295–7. This is the best scholarly article dealing with *hirabah* to date.
25 As quoted by Robert D. Crane, "*Hirabah* vs. *Jihad*", unpublished manuscript.
26 For one striking example of this sort of new thinking, see Lombard 2004.
27 As quoted in an undated communication from Jim Guirard to Antony T. Sullivan, 2002.
28 Ibid.
29 Electronic communication from Radwan Masmoudi to Jim Guirard, 15 November 2002.
30 Crane, "*Hirabah* vs. *Jihad*."
31 A Jewish sacred tradition likewise states that "if anyone causes a single soul to perish, Scripture regards him as though he had caused a whole world to perish, and if anyone saves a single soul, Scripture regards him as though he had saved a whole world" (*Mishnah Sanhedrin* 4: 5).
32 "Sheikh" Usama bin Ladin's statement is entitled "Jihad Against Jews and Crusaders" and is signed by Ayman al-Zawahiri, Abu Yasir Rifa'i, Ahmad Taha, Mir Hamzah, and Fazlur Rahman. Al-Zawahiri is designated as the "Amir of the Jihad Group in Egypt". Ahmad Taha states his affiliation as the "Egyptian Islamic Group". Mir Hamzah is identified as the "Secretary of the Jamiat-ul-Ulema-e-Pakistan", and Fazlur Rahman as "Amir of the Jihad Movement in Bangladesh". Concerning Americans, the statement does not mince words. Muslims are charged to "kill the Americans and their allies – civilian and military. [This is] an individual duty for every Muslim who can do it in any country in which it is possible to do it." For a devastating Muslim critique of this *fatwah*, see David Dukake, "The Myth of a Militant Islam", in Lombard 2004: 3–38.
33 *KhairAllah Tulfah*, Abu Bakr, vol. 12, p. 36.
34 See al-Waqidi, *Kitab al-Maghazi*, vol. 3, pp. 1117–18. For other examples of the Prophet's strictures on this score, see al-Tabari, *Jami' al-bayan 'an ta'wil ay al-Qur'an* (Beirut: Dar al-Fikr, 1955), vol. 2, p. 259. One *hadith* relating a command of Muhammad is the following: "Nafi' reported that the Prophet of God ... found women killed in some battles, and he condemned such acts and prohibited the killing of women and children." According to another *hadith* (related by the Caliph 'Umar), "whenever the Prophet of God ... sent out a force, he used to command it [as follows]: 'Do not commit theft; do not break vows; do not cut ears and noses; do not kill women and children'" (see Malik ibn Anas, *Muwatta*, trans. M. Rahimuddin [New Delhi: Taj, 1985, p. 200], *hadith* nos. 957 and 958). For reports of similar instructions by Muhammad prohibiting the killing of children, monks, and hermits and the mutilation of bodies, see Muslim, *Sahih*, vol. 5, pp. 46–50, and ibn Kathir, *Tafsir*, vol. 1, pp. 308–9.
35 For the best analysis to date of this development, see Noah Feldman, *After Jihad: America and the Struggle for Islamic Democracy* (New York: Farrar, Straus and Giroux, 2003). The arguments to the contrary by such publicists as Daniel Pipes are simply fallacious.

36   The Qur'an emphatically endorses the individual's right to hold private property, as long as all property owners understand that their "ownership" is in fact a trusteeship held from God, to which all things ultimately belong. The Qur'an and *hadith* also prescribe free trade and oppose price fixing. According to Islamic law, entrepreneurship is obligatory, both to satisfy immediate economic needs and to create capital. Indeed, to accumulate capital is considered to be of greater value than engaging in "extra" acts of worship. On this last point, see Abd al-Hayy al-Kattani, *Kitab Nizam al-Hukumah al-Nabasiyyah*, also known as *Al-Taratib al-Idariyyah* [The System of Prophetic Government] (Beirut, AH 1347), vol. 2, especially pp. 3 and 24.

37   On the possibility of forming an alliance between traditionalist Muslims and Christians to combat radical secularism, some comments by Allan Carlson, President of the Howard Centre for Family, Religion and Society, are suggestive. In a speech entitled "The Family of Faith Today: Shaping the Global Future", delivered in the Philippines on 27–28 March 1999, Mr Carlson reported: "During the 1997 United Nations Habitat conference in Nairobi, [a] ... coalition of conservative Christians and Orthodox Muslims took form, much to the consternation of the conference leaders."

38   See the *MESA Newsletter*, August 1997, p. 11. Signatories of the Statement include some prominent personalities in the Muslim Middle East and several distinguished scholars of Islam in the United States. Among the Muslims endorsing the ecumenical and culturally traditionalist principles adumbrated in the Statement are Kamal Abu al-Magd, Muhammad Amara, Tariq al-Bishri, Fahmi Huweidi, and Abdulwahab al-Massiri of Egypt, Sheikh Rachid al-Ghannoushi (Tunisia), and Munir Shafic (Jordan). Among the American signatories are David B. Burrell, Charles E. Butterworth, Louis J. Cantori, John L. Esposito, Leonard P. Liggio, Antony T. Sullivan, and John O. Voll.

39   Abd al-Raouf 1984: 67.

Chapter 10

From Clashing Civilisations to a Common Vision

Robert Dickson Crane

The Challenge

The Ring of Fire

The 9/11 terrorist attack on the symbols of US economic and military power at the beginning of the twenty-first century was a hell-sent gift to professional Islamophobes. They proclaimed that the much-vaunted clash of civilisations had now begun and that the only real civilisation, America, must win it decisively by any and every means. These Islamophobes, who fear Islam and regard it as a threat, range from the scholarly Bernard Lewis, who claims that Islam is simply a failed religion, to the think-tanker Daniel Pipes, who says that all Muslims are inherently violent, to the populist Franklin Graham, who says that the Prophet Muhammad, *salla Allahu 'alayhi wa sallam,* was a paedophile and that Islam is the incarnation of evil.

To Muslims in America it seemed that some Darth Vader had emerged from nowhere to attack America under the name of Islam. The initial reaction by the vast majority of non-Muslims in the fall of 2001 was anger against the perpetrators, but this was accompanied by ecumenical outreach to protect innocent Muslims from an expected backlash. Students of intra-civilisational dynamics and inter-civilisational clashes eventually began to explore the roots of extremism in all religions and civilisations, because terrorism growing out of hatred and even a drive for self-destruction goes far beyond the realms of economics and politics, as does also terroristic counter-terrorism.

During the succeeding year, however, the Islamophobes, backed by a phalanx of think-tanks and media moguls influenced by secular Zionism, managed to start turning this initial sympathy into a generalised hatred of Muslims as the root of all problems and a threat to civilisation. This is shown strikingly by the Pew Research Center poll taken in late June 2003, on whether Islam is more likely than other religions "to encourage violence among its believers". The percentage of those who said yes rose from only 25 per cent in March, 2002, to 44 per cent in June 2003, indicating that Islamophobia in the US almost doubled in one year.

A few weeks after 9/11, I was interviewed live by BBC on worldwide television to get my views on "why they hate us". The BBC was interested because I had just personally advised British Prime Minister Tony Blair on

Afghanistan and the causes of 9/11, and because I was not only a former US ambassador to the United Arab Emirates but at the same time was personally appointed by President Reagan in 1981 as an informal ambassador-at-large to the Islamist movements in North Africa and South West Asia. This bold initiative by President Reagan, incidentally, was no doubt a main reason why Secretary of State Alexander Haig, at the bidding of Henry Kissinger, fired me only three months after the appointment.

My answer to the BBC was that 9/11 was the desperate response by extremists who had been alienated by the repression of Muslims all over the world, especially in those areas that Daniel Pipes a decade earlier had dubbed the "ring of fire" all around the Muslim world. I explained that this ring of fire did not represent an attack by Muslims expanding outward to attack world civilisation, but resulted naturally from national liberation movements in Muslim-majority nations seeking independence from disintegrating, secular empires. Witness the Chechens' national liberation movement against the failed Soviet Empire, the battle by the Muslims of South East Europe against the nationalist remains of the Communist empire there, the *jihad* for self-determination and independence for Kashmir against the unravelling Indian Empire in South Asia, the ambitious struggle by the Uighur of south-west China against the declining central power in the Chinese Empire, and the struggle across North Africa, and especially in Algeria, against the dictatorships that remained after the hesitant retreat of European empires.

Then I started to add, "But, the heart of the worldwide liberation movement against imperial hegemony is in the very centre of the Muslim world against the American oppression of ... ", and those were my last words. The interviewer in London cut me off in mid-sentence. This was embarrassing on a worldwide hookup with perhaps tens of millions of listeners, because everyone knew exactly what I was about to say.

Of course, I was referring to the Palestinians. At the time, the world had not yet witnessed the invasion of Iraq, ostensibly to find weapons of mass destruction and stop Saddam's Hussain's supposed alliance with al-Qa'ida, or even to manage world oil prices. In a *Washington Post* op-ed piece on 12 August 2002, Henry Kissinger stated that the real reason for the invasion of Iraq was to institute a new international law to support America's "new world order". This was the first time that Kissinger had ever used this phrase, and this was one of the few times that any public figure ever mentioned Israel as a reason for imposing a new world order by unilateral pre-emption.

To blame 9/11 even remotely on secular Zionism in the Holy Land, and even to add the US occupation of Iraq in defence of Israel as a possible cause of terrorism, was absolutely forbidden in public. This is the one canon of political correctness that is never violated, except on the Internet. And Pipes' Campus Watch, initiated in 2003, was designed to close that last window of freedom, where objective observers can explain that America's unilateral counter-terrorism threatens to become the cause of what it is supposed to cure.

The "Clash of Civilisations": Distinguishing Between the Artificial and the Real

How can objective observers counter the Islamophobia that became so popular after 11 September 2001, and two years later was getting worse every day? We can begin by showing that the whole concept of a clash between or among civilisations is an artificial construct. This paradigm or framework of thought was designed by Samuel Huntington of Harvard University to show the potential conflict, but not the inevitability, of a clash between the culture of Western civilisation and the combined culture of a so-called Sino-Muslim civilisational alliance. The Islamophobes, however, welcomed this paradigm because it invoked a primordial Western fear of the invasions by Ghenghiz Khan and of the Muslims into Europe centuries ago.

This theory has two major problems. First, the battle between the West and the Rest is not between a secular America and the Muslim world. America is the least secular country on earth, despite the creeping secularisation of its public institutions and foreign policy. And, second, neither America nor the Muslim world is monolithic. Therefore, if there is to be a clash, it must be between only one part of one civilisation and one part of the other, between the reactionary extremism within the Muslim world and an equally reactionary extremism in America.

But, even this reactionary extremism within each civilisation is not monolithic. Perhaps the most powerful political force in the Bush Administration was a cabal of extremist neo-conservatives who wanted to conquer the world under the guise of bringing to it freedom and democracy. And they had forged an alliance of convenience with the radical Evangelical extremists who were willing to bring on a holocaust in the Holy Land in order to accelerate the return of Jesus, *'alayhi as-salam*.

The same dichotomy exists in the extremism within the Muslim community. We have political extremists who want worldly power under the guise of seeking justice, or else want merely to destroy all power in a frenzy of nihilism and hatred. And we have what we might call spiritual extremists who ask why we should bother to seek justice in the world when the world is about to end anyway.

The real clash is not between civilisations, but within each of them. Both within the Muslim world and within America, the clash is between the extremists of all types and the so-called moderates. And, increasingly, a clash is developing among the moderates between secular modernists and spiritual traditionalists. Among Muslims a clash is developing worldwide, but triggered especially by Muslims in America, between so-called liberal, or progressive Islam and traditional, or classical Islam. The same conflict is raging among non-Muslims, especially in America, between liberal modernism and the classical traditionalism of America's founders.

The Threat of "Liberal Islam"

Despite the alleged wisdom coming from the talking heads in the mainstream American media, perhaps the most dangerous threat over the long run to civilisation is extremism from the left, not from the right, from reactionary liberals, not from reactionary conservatives, however one wants to define these terms. In my view, there is no such thing as liberal or progressive Islam, and those who think there is may be the most dangerous extremists. Similarly, from the perspective of America's deeply spiritual Founders, the materialism and moral relativism infecting America's educational, political, and judicial institutions may be a more threatening form of extremism from within than is any threat from abroad.

The past century and a half in America can be summarised as a titanic conflict between the movement of secular modernism and the revolutionary traditionalism that gave rise to the "Great American Experiment" and has sustained it, despite all opposition, ever since. Militant secular humanists have set the framework for global ideological competition as a battle between secularism and transcendence, between the militant assertion of human power as the ultimate criterion for right and wrong and what we might call the traditionalist reverence for guidance from the transcendent nature of reality in divine revelation and natural law.

The same conflict has been growing, especially since 9/11, among Muslims. Modernism is an ideology, as distinct from modernity, which may be defined as the application of science and institutional reform to improve our material wellbeing. Modernism is the worship of the secular world by denying the purposefulness and sacredness of what God has created. It is the attempt to de-sacralise reality. I use the term "secular" or "secularism" in defining modernists not in the sense used by most Muslims from the Indian sub-continent as neutrality toward religion, but in the sense, almost universal among Americans, of hostility to any role of religion in public life.

Such hostility was almost inconceivable during the early decades of the American republic when the idea of a human society prospering or even existing without the guidance of God was inconceivable. The universal assumption was expressed by Thomas Jefferson, the framer of the American Declaration of Independence, who taught that no system of self-determination through representative government could succeed unless the people were properly educated; that education should consist primarily in teaching virtue; and that no people could long remain virtuous unless they acknowledged the source of truth in an absolute higher power and unless they applied in public life the wisdom that this higher power has imparted through all the world religions in divine revelation and natural law.

Modern secularists have tried to co-opt Jefferson as an alleged deist who thought that God created the universe but then immediately retired from the scene. In fact, he was a theist, who believed that God created the world and constantly sustains it out of love for every human person. His thousands of letters are now scheduled to be published, one volume every year for twenty years, as a result of a recent court order invalidating his last will and testament, which provided that his private correspondence never be made public. This gold mine of early American history is confirming him as one of the true representatives of traditionalist peoples of all faiths, whom he identified in his First Inaugural Address, 4 March 1801, as those who are "enlightened by a benign religion, professed, indeed, and practised in various forms, yet all of them inculcating honesty, truth, temperance, gratitude, and the love of man; acknowledging and adoring an overruling Providence, which by all its dispensations proves that it delights in the happiness of man here and his greater happiness hereafter."

The Founders of America condemned democracy because they associated it with the mobocracy of the French Revolution, which recognised no higher power than man himself. Instead they said that they were establishing a republic, which by definition recognises the higher sovereignty of God. They fought for freedom from oppression, as demonstrated in Patrick Henry's stirring call, now on the automobile plates of every car licensed in New Hampshire: "Give me freedom or give me death." Certainly many Palestinians share his commitment, as do most Muslims around the world almost as a condition for being a sincere Muslim.

Nevertheless, freedom was not an end in itself, but merely a means toward justice. The watchword throughout the founding of America was justice based on the inherent nature of the individual person as an expression of the divine Creator, who endowed every person with inherent responsibilities and inalienable rights. The Founding was based equally on the value of community and public life as a means to carry out these responsibilities and protect these rights. This is the meaning of the traditionalist movement that developed throughout the eighteenth century in England, and eventually gave rise to America and the Pledge of Allegiance, which calls for "one nation under God with liberty and justice for all".

Several conferences have been held by Muslims to dismiss this traditionalist thought as harmful to progress, or at best as irrelevant in the modern world. The first such conference after 9/11 was sponsored by the influential think-tank The Woodrow Wilson Center for Scholars and by the International Forum for Democratic Studies. The title of this conference, held on 25 September 2002, was simply "Liberal Islam". The keynote address, later published in the April 2003 issue of the prestigious *Journal of Democracy,* and delivered by Abdou Filali-Ansary, was entitled "What is Liberal Islam: the Sources of Enlightened Muslim Thought".

As a self-described Muslim moderate or modernising liberal, Dr Ansary divides Muslims into two groups, the first being "liberal", "reformist", or "modernising", and the second being "traditional", "fundamentalist", and "radical". The criterion he uses for distinguishing the two is epistemology or the study of how knowledge is acquired.

From my experience with self-proclaimed Muslims, or at least with some of the extremists among them, the liberal group questions the accessibility or even the existence of absolute truth. Speakers at well-known Muslim conferences on democracy have represented this position by insisting that Muslims stop talking about the "sovereignty of God", or even of *tawhid,* when discussing the coherence of diversity in the universe deriving from the Oneness of God. The basic tenet of the liberal Muslim is that the human mind creates truth and that it does not exist independently of man. In philosophy this is known as "positivism". This functionally atheist movement has given rise in recent decades to neo-conservatism, which is the opposite of American traditionalism. One of the neo-conservatives' highest priorities is to marginalize their traditionalist opponents, known as "paleo-conservatives".

According to Dr Ansary's deprecatory account, the liberal or modernist mindset contrasts with the traditional or fundamentalist mindset, which is mired in what he calls "the pre-modern epistemology". This, he says, is not so much literalist, which is the most common American definition of fundamentalism, as it is absolutist in the sense of its insistence that the purpose of the human mind is to seek absolute truth. He rightly condemns those who insist that they possess this truth, because such radical extremism would deny the search for knowledge that is incumbent on every human being as long as one lives.

Liberal Islam, in its oxymoronic manifestation, denies the validity of the search for truth. This is the hallmark of relativism. It is almost the same as saying that religion, all religion, is irrelevant at best, and that the modern Muslim must advance beyond the pre-modern mindset into the world of militant secularism. In effect, this argument is a call for secular fundamentalism as the permanent enemy of traditional wisdom and a call for a permanent clash of civilisations until a so-called enlightened Islam can be assimilated into the victory of Pax America.

By denying the essence of classical American thought and the identical essence of classical Islamic thought, the modernist advocates of "liberal Islam", or "progressive Islam", are opposing the revival of the best of Islam and the best of America. They are laying the groundwork for an ideological Armageddon between the forces of a paganising America and the rest of the world, which can result only in the worldwide collapse of all civilisation.

The Problematic of Liberal Islamists

Rivalling the advocates of "progressive Islam" are intellectual activists who are trying to develop the school of thought initiated almost a century ago by Hassan al-Banna in Egypt. These are known as the *ikhwan al-muslimun* or Muslim Brotherhood. These Muslims differ from the Muslim "progressives" in several important ways. First, they are not secular. They try to derive all their guidance from the two basic sources of Islam, the Qur'an and the Sunnah – or practice of the Prophet Muhammad(s). They try to apply this creatively in the modern world. Second, they are not pragmatists in the sense of justifying whatever means are most utilitarian in achieving their vision of a desirable global future. Instead they look to the wisdom of the past in order to revive the basic principles of the Islamic heritage and apply them to shape the future. In this sense they may be known as "constitutionalists" and even what is known as "strict constructionalists" in American legal philosophy, the Islamic constitution being the Qur'an.

This school of thought is neither positivist nor relativist and therefore can be accepted in principle by the vast majority of Muslims worldwide. The *ikhwan* are reformist, like the progressives, but also traditionalist in the sense of building on the best of the past. They recognise that real change in any civilisation can succeed only if it builds on the wisdom of tradition, because such change requires the support of the majority population who can understand new directions only within the framework of what they already know.

Perhaps the major intellectual drawback of the *ikhwan* is their tendency to use Western secular thought, which many of their leaders learned in American graduate schools, as the base case. But the *ikhwan* are no more monolithic than any other movement, in part because they have internalised the paradigmatic conflicts of their secular mentors in the West. Within this school of thought major differences have arisen between what at their extremes are known as socialists and libertarians.

Since the entire movement of the *ikhwan* originated and developed in reaction to colonial hegemony, and since economic exploitation was a major cause of their discontent, they focused as much on economic injustice as on political oppression. Their solution to the economic aspects of colonialism developed in academia during the mid-twentieth century largely under the influence of Karl Marx, though the original practitioners in Egypt during their short period of freedom under Nasser were staunch supporters of private property widely owned as the core principle of justice in the Islamic system of economic life. Their very successful enterprises, owned primarily or entirely by the employees, posed a severe threat to the statist policies of both the Egyptian and American governments, so the entrepreneurs among the *ikhwan* were all either executed or exiled. This failure to promote political freedom both nationally and worldwide through the development of *shari'ah*-based economic democracy was instrumental in directing the *ikhwan* to seek political power as the only road to justice. Increasing frustration in accomplishing this led a minority of them along a path to armed resistance.

The other trend in the *ikhwan* school of thought has been termed "enlightened Islamism" or even "liberal Islamism". The strategy of this movement of enlightened Islamism is to unite all the diverse politically oriented groups of Muslims on behalf of freedom. One of the most knowledgeable students of the *ikhwan* and an influential *ikhwan* activist, Professor Louis J. Cantori of the University of Maryland, calls for education of the citizen to "create a new set of values and a new set of expectations" so that "all the diverse parties would be looking to adhere to the principle of freedom from domination. We may be centralist, Marxist, and so on, but the one thing we agree on is the dignity and equality of the citizen."

The *ikhwan* movement appears to be splitting into two groups: those who support majoritarian democracy and those who call for the enlightened Islamism of republican democracy. At the extremes, these two groups represent radical egalitarianism and radical elitism. The dialogue between the two is led in the United States by the Center for the Study of Islam and Democracy (CSID), and in Britain by the International Forum for Islamic Dialogue (IFID), which works with its sister organisation in the UK, the Centre for the Study of Democracy. Professor Cantori is a founding member of the CSID's board and has sought to popularise what he terms "republican Islamism" through the IFID's influential journal *Islam 21: A Global Networking for Muslim Intellectuals and Activists.*

In the May 2003 issue of this journal, Professor Cantori presented this form of Islamism for counter-critique in his article, "Democracy from within Islam: A Republican Theory". He is not advocating republican Islam, but rather republican Islamism. He opposes liberal Islam as devoid of norms and values, but supports what he calls liberal Islamism. His point is that the Islamism of the Muslim Brotherhood has values, but they need to be applied in a liberal or enlightened way. Enlightened Islamism is liberal in the nineteenth-century sense of the term before it took on the connotation of socialist and/or libertine. Because liberal Islamism in this sense is conservative, he says that it is more appealing to most Muslims. He writes:

> It is conservative for three reasons. The first is that it reveres the past as possessing the traditions and religious values from which the virtue of the citizen is constructed (and not an imagined liberal utopian future). The second is that it instructs the individual into the responsibilities that he/she has for family and society (and not the individualism of liberalism). The third is that the ends of society are primarily moral purpose (and not individual happiness).

Cantori claims that this view of "republican democracy" is consistent with the thought that led up to the American Revolution as well as with Islam. This would be true, except that he fails to discuss the need for justice. This focus exclusively on political freedom perfectly mirrors the approach of President George W. Bush to world affairs. The President has used the word "justice" in reference to Iraq very sparingly, and then not in the sense of moral theology but only in the sense of "revenge". This approach ignores the economic injustices that serve as a chronic and growing cause of terrorism worldwide.

This exclusively political focus on freedom without normative content also ignores the emphasis by the founding generation of Americans on justice as their ultimate goal, for which freedom from domination was merely a means. For Muslims, this approach is fatally flawed because it ignores the rich tradition of Islamic law, which emphasises the core principle of Qur'anic revelation, expressed in such verses as "The Word of your Lord is perfected in truth and justice," and "And of those whom we have created are a people who guide with the truth and thereby do justice" (7:181).

Response

Justice and the Rule of Law

How do we move from clashes among and within civilisations to a common vision that can inspire a global civilisation of pluralist cooperation? This is possible only on the basis of ecumenical cooperation among the world religions. The one element common to them all is recognition of a higher source of truth beyond the authority of any person or human community. This recognition is the only rationale for recognising justice as a possible goal in social life. If human reason were the ultimate source of justice, then justice could not exist, because people would serve their own parochial interests by calling for different concepts of justice.

I once remarked to a leading Zionist rabbi in Washington, DC, Herzl Kranz, that what is needed in the Middle East is justice. He replied immediately, "Yes! Justice! We can achieve peace only through justice, by removing all the Arabs from Israel." He gave me the "bible" of radical Zionists, the book *They Must Go*, written by Meir Kahane not long before his assassination.

The most sophisticated concept of justice was developed over many centuries by the most brilliant minds in human history, by the great scholars of Islam. They developed it as a code of human responsibilities and rights that has never been matched since it went into eclipse six hundred years ago.

What is justice according to Islam? It is the legacy of God's messenger Muhammad. His legacy, like the legacy of all the Prophets of God, *'alayhi as-salam,* is the revival of the essence of all religion, which consists of four essentials. The Prophet Muhammad revitalised personal awareness and loving awe of God, which Muslims call *taqwa,* and a resulting commitment to truth and justice. These two essentials of faith in Islam and of every world religion reinforce each other. The neglect of either one can result in extremism. Without love and mercy, the pursuit of justice can result in cruelty and oppression. And without a commitment to establish a just society wherever one lives, one's love of God cannot have real meaning in the world.

The other two essentials are the basic philosophical principles known as *tawhid* and *mizan. Tawhid* refers to the concept that everything in the universe is interrelated with everything else in a coherent whole, and that this unity is the inevitable result of the Oneness of the Ultimate, the Creator of all, whom the Muslims and Arab Christians refer to as Allah, the non-Arab Christians call God, and the Jews call Elohim or Jehovah.

The second philosophical principle, known as *mizan,* comes from the first one. *Mizan* means balance. Since God created the universe as a balanced whole, as expressed throughout the Qur'an, a task of every human is to help perfect this balance by avoiding extremism. When one over-emphasises any one pursuit or goal in life, one can become an extremist by neglecting the others.

A framework for maintaining balance in life is provided by Islamic law and is its very purpose. This framework is a hierarchical system of human responsibilities and rights. For example, one has a responsibility to defend one's family and community, and one has an equal responsibility to respect individual human life. Those who kill innocents in the alleged defence of their community have clearly lost balance. This violates the design of Allah. It is extremist and therefore immoral.

The indignities of miserable poverty and cruel oppression can produce alienation, desperation, and extremism. Unfortunately, Muslims have suffered more than their share of both these causes and effects in the world, but this is no excuse for the resulting extremism. Regardless of how understandable it might be, extremism and the resulting violence are immoral and un-Islamic.

Extremism does not have to result from indignities, but it will unless there is a source and framework for hope. The source must be spiritual, based on *taqwa*. The framework must be a coherent body of human responsibilities and rights, based on a mutually reinforcing combination of divine guidance through revelation, *wahy*, and natural law, which Muslims call the *sunnatu Allahi* or signs of divine order in the universe. Without this intellectual framework, people wander in an intellectual void, and this, in turn, can produce a spiritual malaise.

Over the long run, the most productive initiative by the still largely silent majority of Muslims in marginalising Muslim extremists is to fill the intellectual and spiritual void that serves as an ocean in which the extremists can swim. This initiative must be undertaken at the grass-roots level, by such organisations as The Center for Understanding Islam, as well as by ecumenical think-tanks, and also in academia by the establishment of Muslim universities on a par with Oxford and Harvard. This initiative can provide the favourable environment needed for Muslims to ally with like-minded Christians and Jews in order to show that classical Islam and classical America are similar, even though many people do not understand or live up to the ideals common to both.

Teaching and emphasising that the founders of America and the great scholars of Islam shared the same vision is the best way to convince the extremists that their confrontational approach to the "other" is counter-productive. Recognising this commonality of purpose in life is the only way to overcome the threat mentality of those who are obsessed with conspiracy theories and think only about their own survival. Promoting an opportunity mentality of hope is the only way to convince the extremists that, in the long run, only those will prosper who can transcend their own self-centred interests in order to join with those who are no longer merely the "other" but now are members of a single pluralist community.

Shifting from a threat mentality to an opportunity mentality requires hopeful commitment to peace through justice in reliance on God. Justice is another word for the Will or Design of God, the *mashiyat*. It is also considered to be another term for the body of Islamic normative law. These norms or general principles, according to Islamic thought, provide the intellectual framework to understand and address all of reality.

The entire purpose of the Qur'an is implied in the last verse of Surat Ibrahim: "Here is a message for humankind. Let them take warning from it and let them know that He is [no other than] One God. Let persons of understanding take heed." Yusuf Ali comments: "Here is another aspect of the Truth of Unity. God being One, all justice is of one standard, for Truth is one, and we see it as one as soon as the scales of phenomenal diversity fall from our eyes. The one true Reality then emerges."

For the scholar, the best short introduction to this framework of Islamic thought may be found in the monograph, "*Usul al-Fiqh al-Islami*: Source Methodology in Islamic Jurisprudence", by Shaykh Taha Jabir al-'Alwani, who for more than fifteen years has been President of the Fiqh Council of North America, a member of the OIC Islamic Fiqh Academy in Jeddah, and a founding member of the Council of the Muslim World League in Mecca. This monograph, published in 1990, is a summation of his doctoral dissertation, completed in 1972 at al-Azhar University in Egypt. When a SWAT team invaded his house in the spring of 2002 as part of an investigation of the ultra-moderate International Institute of Islamic Thought, which he headed, his wife, Muna Abul Fadl, head of the Western Civilization Project at the International Institute of Islamic Thought and a former full professor of political science at al-Azhar, fled to Egypt and never returned.

For discussion among scholars, it is important to note that the art of Islamic normative law is part of the Islamic science of *'usul al-fiqh* or the roots of the *shari'ah*, and specifically was developed within the sub-context of *al-maslahah al-mursalah*, which addresses the good of the community. Within this discipline of *al-maslahah*, normative law was developed over the centuries by the use of three distinct methodologies. The first is *al-maslahah al-mu'tabarah*, which is based exclusively on an explicit *hukm* or ruling in the Qur'an or Sunnah. The second is based on *istislah*, which denotes restoration or reform, based on the root s-l-h, which means peace and prosperity through right order. This methodology is based on the values of Islam revealed in the Qur'an and Sunnah through induction from the parts to the whole. The third is based on *istihsan*. This comes from *hasana*, which means simply to be good, and is the most free-wheeling of the three. All reject *ra'i* or personal opinion in developing jurisprudential guidance and preserving the purity of divine revelation. These three can be mutually compatible and reinforcing, particularly in developing a framework not merely for law in a narrow sense but for public policy and for the development of Muslim think-tanks.

In order to fill the intellectual void both in the Muslim global community and in the minds of some Muslim intellectuals, Muslims need to emphasise the universal principles of Islamic normative law, known as the *maqasid al-shari'ah*, especially as developed by the greatest master of the art, Al-Shatibi, using the methodology of *istislah*. These principles spell out precisely the human rights that some sceptics have asserted do not exist in Islam. These *maqasid*, following the methodology instituted by the Prophet Muhammad and perfected in the architectonics pioneered six centuries ago by Al-Shatibi, are considered to consist of seven responsibilities, the practice of which actualise the corresponding human rights.

Al-Shatibi taught that the number of *maqasid* is flexible, as are the subordinate levels and architectonics of purpose, the *hajjiyat* and *tahsiniyat*, because the entire field of Islamic normative law is a product of *ijtihad* or intellectual effort. This commitment to *ijtihad*, which has been almost dead for six hundred years, is called for specifically in the Qur'an as the *jihad al-kabir*, "And strive with it [divine revelation] in a great jihad" (*Surat al-Furqan* 25:52).

The first *maqsud*, known as *haqq al-din*, provides the framework for the next six in the form of respect for a transcendent source of truth to guide human thought and action. Yusuf Ali notes, in reference to *Surat al-Baqarah* 2:193, that *din* is one of the most comprehensive terms in the Qur'an and can be translated simply as justice but with associated meanings in English expressed as duty and faith, all of which for a Muslim constitute religion. In his monumental translation and commentary (*tafsir*), Muhammad Asad translates *din* in this verse as "worship" of the ultimate being, God. Like many words in the Qur'an, the word *haqq* also contains many inherently associated meanings, including God, truth, and human rights. God instructs us in the Qur'an, "and the word of your Lord is perfected in truth and justice". Recognition of this absolute source of truth and of the responsibility to apply it in practice are needed to counter the temptations toward relativism and the resulting chaos, injustice, and tyranny that may result from the de-sacralisation of public life.

Each of these seven universal principles is essential to understand the next and succeeding ones. The first three operational principles, necessary to sustain existence, begin with *haqq al-nafs* or *haqq al-ruh*, which is the duty to respect the human person. The *ruh* or spirit of every person, created by God before or outside of the creation of the physical universe, is constantly in the presence of God, and, according to the Prophet Muhammad(s), is made in the image of God. This is the basis of the intimate relationship between God and the human person as expressed in the Qur'anic *ayah*, "We are closer to him than is his own jugular vein." The human soul or *nafs* is the decision-making element of the human person, and it is free to follow or reject the promptings of the *ruh*. When it uses the brain as part of the human person's physical element, the *jizm*, to reject inspiration from God directly or through one's own spirit, the soul is known as *al-nafs al-ammarah* or the commanding soul. The soul functions in ascending states of *taqwa* until it becomes the *nafs al-mutma'inah* in complete harmony or "oneness" with the divine.

This intimate relationship is also the basis of the prayer offered by the Prophet and by countless generations of Muslims for more than a thousand years: "*Allahumma, inni as'aluka hubbaka wa hubba man yuhibbuka wa hubba kulla 'amalin yuqarribuni ila hubbika*" – "O Allah! I ask You for Your love and for the love of those who love You. Grant that I may love every action that will bring me closer to Your love."

At the secondary level of this principle, known as *hajjiyat* or requirements, lies the duty to respect life, *haqq al-hayah*. This provides guidelines in the third-order *tahsinniyat* for what in modern parlance is called the doctrine of just war.

The next principle, *haqq al-nasl*, the third of the seven, is the duty to respect the nuclear family and the community at every level all the way to the community of humankind as an important expression of the person. This principle teaches that the sovereignty of the person, subject to the ultimate sovereignty of God, comes prior to and is superior to any alleged ultimate sovereignty of the secular invention known as the State.

This principle teaches also that a community at the level of the nation, which shares a common sense of the past, common values in the present, and common hopes for the future, such as the Palestinians, Kurds, Chechens, Kashmiris, the Uighur in China, and the Anzanians in the Sudan, has legal existence and therefore legal rights in international law. This is the opposite of the Western international law created by past empires, and perhaps only temporarily modified by the United Nations, which is based on the simple principle of "might makes right".

The third principle is *haqq al-mal*, which is the duty to respect the rights of private property in the means of production. This requires respect for institutions that broaden access to capital ownership as a universal human right and as an essential means to sustain respect for the human person and human community. This principle requires the perfection of existing institutions, especially those that maintain a monopoly of access to credit, in order to remove the barriers to universal property ownership so that wealth will be distributed through the production process rather than by stealing from the rich by forced redistribution to the poor. Such redistribution can never have more than a marginal effect in reducing the gap between the inordinately rich and the miserably poor, because the owners in a defective financial system need not and never will give up their economic and political power.

The next three universal principles in Islamic law concern primarily what we might call the quality of life. The first is *haqq al-hurriyah*, which requires respect for self-determination of both persons and communities through political freedom, including the concept that economic democracy is a precondition for the political democracy of representative government.

The secondary principles required to give meaning to the parent principle and carry it out in practice are *khilafah*, the ultimate responsibility of both the ruled and the ruler to God; *shurah*, the responsiveness of the rulers to the ruled through consultation, which must be institutionalised in order to be meaningful; *ijma'*, the duty of the opinion leaders to reach consensus on specific policy issues in order to participate in the process of *shurah*; and an independent judiciary.

This universal principle of Islam was observed only in the breach throughout much of Muslim history, and especially in the modern era. All of the great Islamic scholars were imprisoned, often for years and even decades, for teaching this requirement of political freedom. This speaks well for those who have tried to preserve the purity of divine revelation, but poorly for those who have pretended to practise it.

The second of these last three *maqasid* is *haqq al-karamah*, or respect for human dignity. The two most important *hajjiyat* for individual human dignity are religious freedom and gender equity. In traditional Islamic thought, freedom and equality are not ultimate ends but essential means to pursue the higher purposes inherent in the divine design of the Creator for every person.

The last universal or essential purpose at the root of Islamic jurisprudence, which can be sustained only by observance of the first six principles and also is essential to each of them, is *haqq al-'ilm* or respect for knowledge. Its second-order principles are freedom of thought, press, and assembly so that all persons can fulfil their purpose to seek knowledge wherever they can find it.

This framework for human rights is at the very core of Islam as a religion. Fortunately, this paradigm of law in its broadest sense of moral theology is now being revived by what still is a minority of courageous Muslims determined to fill the intellectual gap that has weakened the Muslim community or *ummah* for more than six hundred years, so that a spiritual renaissance in all faiths can transform the world.

Transcendent Identity

The key to advancement from parochial clash to common vision is what Dr Jeremy Henzell-Thomas calls the quest for a transcendent identity (Henzell-Thomas 2003). He warns that "mutual hostility and suspicion have been fuelled by the rhetoric of self-righteousness and rage, the psychological exploitation of fear, insecurity, and patriotic fervour, and even full-scale retreat into defensive isolation and identity crisis". The only reliable cure for "this war of barbarisms" is to work through both intra-faith and interfaith dialogue toward an "expanded sense of identity" by appealing to "that compassionate wisdom which does not delimit, negate, or abrogate, but which expands, affirms, and illumines". Every person is created with both a rational intellect of the brain and a higher intellect of the heart, which together form what in Islamic philosophy is known as the *'aql*. This equates with the *nous* in Orthodox Christianity and modern Catholic theology, which, if purified, knows God and the inner essence or principles of created things by means of direct apprehension or spiritual perception. Titus Burckhardt defines this *'aql* as the "universal principle of all intelligence, a principle which transcends the limiting conditions of the mind", a principle that is known, with some modern empirical justification, as the "heart".

Much of Dr Henzell-Thomas's essay explores the origin of words in various languages in order to show that modern derivations have lost the wisdom of their cognates and now reflect a divided world. Pursuing his line of thought, it is worth noting, for example, that there is no word for "sin" in Qur'anic Arabic, because Muslims focus on cause, not on effect, a practice that more Americans would do well to learn. In Islamic thought the actions that Christians call "sin" are caused ultimately by forgetting God. The very word for human, *al-insan*, comes from the root "to forget". This does not exclude the influence of non-corporeal beings, including the "Devil", in directing our attention away from God. Our need to be conscious of God is precisely why all religions call for frequent prayer and, in Eastern Orthodox mysticism, even for "constant prayer".

Although Dr Henzell-Thomas does not mention the fact that there is no word for "sin" in Qur'anic Arabic, he shows that the modern meaning of evil as the root of sin does not exist in the Greek word *hamartia*, which is normally translated as "sin" in English versions of the New Testament. The Greek original means "missing the mark" by being unbalanced on the side of excess and by losing focus on the right direction. This is basic to the Islamic term *mizan*, which attributes problems to lack of balance. As I learned while studying Arabic in Saudi Arabia in 1987–88, even the word for problem in Arabic, *mushkilah*, comes from the root *sh-ka-la*, which means internal disorder. The cure is the restoration of internal harmony and direction. This contrasts with the modern English concept of problem as an external obstacle that must be overcome or destroyed.

How can one transcend the duality syndrome that infects secular thought even to the extent that liberal Muslims consider science and religion to be separate fields of knowledge, and advocate that religion must be excluded from public life? How can one overcome the degradation of language and understanding whereby "righteousness", which means "being and acting in the right way", becomes "self-righteousness" and thereby loses the compassionate wisdom that seeks to expand and affirm? How can we overcome the modern tendency to reject the spiritual basis of goodness and thereby equate morality with moralism? How can we redress the conceptual perversion of the word "originality", which used to be regarded as an expression of our original nature emanating from the divine, but now is often reduced to the level of inventive conjectures, self-obsessed pretensions, flights of subjective fantasy, and mere shifts in fashion?

How do we deal with a secular world, in which "individuality" as the essence of human dignity becomes "individualism" with no meaning other than revolt against conformity; when acknowledgement of the "absolute" becomes "absolutism"; when the "authoritative" becomes "authoritarian"; when "science", which is the open-ended search for all knowledge, becomes "scientism" or the rejection of whatever cannot be proven in a test tube; when "forms" created by God become "formalisms" created by man; when "unity" becomes "uniformity"; "usefulness" becomes "utilitarianism"; "liberty" becomes "libertinism"; "modernity" becomes "modernism"; "religion" becomes "religiosity", and all these perversions of thought are employed to reject the validity of any and every spiritual quest?

Similarly, how can we transcend the pygmy minds of religious zealots who seek to create God in their own image, as Voltaire once put it, by limiting God within the formalisms of their own dogmas? The Qur'an informs us: "Glorified is He and exalted above what they describe" (*Surat al-An'am*, 6:100). How can we forget our innate awareness of God given to every person before or outside the beginning of time? Such self-inflicted amnesia, according to the Qur'an, is the ultimate source of evil. How can we worship instead the false god of secular materialism, the god of Mammon, with its gargantuan and insatiable appetite? How can we enter the larger space of our common identity as spiritual beings with a common origin and a common purpose?

Intercultural education is not the answer. Multiculturalism in American education does not address the common search for higher understanding, but teaches that there is no absolute truth, that everything is relative, and that no culture, including the traditionalist paradigm of America's founders, can have any objective value or meaning. Why? The reason quite simply is that religion is taught, if at all, merely as an anthropological or sociological exercise, not as a key to what it means to be human. The identity of human nature is off-limits as a subject of study, because this would involve teaching religion, without which human nature can have no value or meaning or even existence.

When public education is forbidden to address the essentials of religion, the only purpose of such education is to produce competent automatons with proven skills designed only to quantify and manage the material world in order to compete internationally in producing more bucks and better bombs. As Henzell-Thomas puts it, "This is the only way that government education can shore up a decaying system, the only way to make it look like it is working." Whether we realise it or not, the dominant current of secular fundamentalism is producing a new totalitarianism. As noted by the renowned student of the modern totalitarian phenomenon, Hannah Arendt: "The aim of totalitarian education has never been to instil convictions but to destroy the capacity to form any" (1968: 168).

We have entered a global crisis, of which global terrorism is only the most obvious symptom, because we have succeeded in shaping the world to match our governing world-view, which is a man-made environment that is increasingly mechanistic, atomised, soulless, and self-destructive. As Richard Tarnas says, there has been an epochal shift into absolute isolation from reality (1991: 441–5). This, in my view, is precisely why even the word "justice" has gone out of style. The pervasive de-sacralisation of all life may be leading to the end stage of a progressive destruction of holistic life, which begins in education and culminates in the chaos and subsequent totalitarianism of the "Lord of the Flies".

The culture war between liberals and conservatives, or progressives and traditionalists, or democrats and autocrats has now mutated into a violent symbiosis between secular relativists and religious totalitarians, who have joined in a marriage of convenience based on a solipsistic indifference to the "other" that amounts to pathological autism in its drive to conquer the world. In late February 2003, in his letter of resignation over the wisdom and legitimacy of President Bush's "fervent pursuit of war against Iraq", John Brady Kiesling, former political counsellor at the US Embassy in Athens, used the phrase the "global threat of American solipsism". The moral chaos sown by secular relativism is becoming the cultural soil in which religious totalitarianism springs forth and flourishes, choking off liberty and life itself.

Fortunately, God always leaves open the way to alternative futures and will lead us if we rely on His help. According to the Qur'anic teaching known as facilitation, God will remove barriers that hinder us from carrying out our free will, whether we are headed downward or upward. The enhancement of our free will downward is known as *istidraj* and upward as *yusra*: "With every difficulty there is relief" (*Surat al-Inshirah*, 94:5).

God permits challenges so that we can test and maximise our potential to do good, and He also permits and facilitates appropriate responses. The Qur'an emphasises again and again that no one is tested beyond one's abilities, because otherwise there would be no responsibility and no justice in this world or the next. Furthermore, "And verily the hereafter will be better for you than the present" (*Surat al-Duha*, 95:4).

The Roman Catholic priest and spiritual leader of the Trappist Order, Thomas Merton, with whom I corresponded as a member of the Franciscan Order during the Vietnam War, remarked shortly before he was accidentally electrocuted at a Buddhist gathering in Thailand during the war: "The purpose of every individual is to become the person that one is." Pope John Paul II developed this insight into what is called the theology of "personalism".

This spiritual identity that young people increasingly are seeking, not only outside mainline denominations of every religion but also within them, has always been the subject and object of the traditional wisdom, or *sophia perennis*. This is the timeless "primordial religion" underlying its various expressions in the form of different religions that have been established at different times and places to meet the specific needs of different communities. More than any other religion, Islam teaches this spiritual essence of all religions. The Qur'an explicitly confirms that God makes no distinction between any of His apostles or messengers (*Surat al-Baqarah*, 2:285).

The common identity of all persons consists in the idea common to all religions that the human being is created "in the image of God". As Dr Henzell-Thomas notes:

> This potential to embody the totality of divine attributes is an article of faith which is not of course solely Islamic, but is enshrined in the common Abrahamic tradition represented by the "People of the Book" (Jews, Christians, and Muslims), in the identity of *Atman* (the Self) and *Brahman* (the Absolute Reality) in the Vedanta tradition, [and] in the doctrine of the unity of the microcosm and the macrocosm in various esoteric traditions.

How does one actualise this vision of our common identity? This question of praxiology is the great challenge to humanity in an era when the lack of such a vision can result in universal self-destruction. The first requirement for every person in moving humankind away from clashing civilisations and toward a common vision is to commit oneself to one's own spiritual path in the knowledge that God has called each person to a path unique to him or her.

In hundreds of individual revelations, the Qur'an emphasises that diversity in the universe is a sign of the Oneness of its Creator, because otherwise there would be only meaningless uniformity. This is part of the holistic ontology of the *shari'ah* or Islamic law, which serves as the overarching framework of everything Islamic, both the spiritual and the mundane. Allah is One. Therefore the entire created order exists in the harmony of diversity in order to point to its Creator.

This diversity is part of the aesthetic of Islamic law, which teaches that the nature of transcendent reality, and of all being, is Beauty, which precedes and is independent of cognition. Beauty consists of unity, symmetry, harmony, depth of meaning, and breadth of applicability. The greatest beauty is the unitive principle of *tawhid*, or the coherence of the universe deriving from the Oneness of its Creator, because otherwise there could be no science and no human thought at all.

This diversity is also basic to the epistemology of Islamic law. All Creation worships Allah because He is one. The Qur'an states that even the stars and the trees bow down to Allah in ways that human beings do not understand. All knowledge is merely a derivative and an affirmation of the unitary harmony in everything that comes from Allah. Everything in creation is a sign, an *ayah*, of Allah designed to manifest the beauty and perfection of His will for our instruction. For example, the constant movement of the clouds shows the nature of the universe as a flux or state of constant change, so that we will seek the stability of peace only in Allah and in the permanent elements of existence that inform the spiritual life. Similarly, the variety of sunsets we see shows the diversity inherent in Allah's design for the universe, which in turn shows the uniqueness ordained for every individual person.

Both the clouds and the sunset, as well as every tree, have powerful lessons for every branch of knowledge, ranging from what Shaheed Isma'il al-Faruqi called the *fitric* or microcentric disciplines of physics and psychology, to the *ummatic* or macro-oriented disciplines of chemistry and sociology and politics, as well as for the study of transcendent religion, which is the master guide to both, and gives rise to the discipline of axiology or normative law, also known as transcendent law.

The Islamic word for human nature, *fitrah*, comes from the root *fa-ta-ra*, which means to split or cleave. This refers to the "splitting" of the Creation from the Creator and the subsequent emergence of separate particles from the singularity of the Big Bang. From this comes the study of modern physics, which now points to the law of non-local effects and the existence of super-luminal velocity, based on the shared "memory" of every particle in the universe from its origin in the divine singularity. This dimension of cause and effect independent of the limits that Albert Einstein postulated for the speed of light has always been basic to all religions.

From our primordial nature originating from the divine singularity, Allah, our identity is in essence the same as everyone else's, even though the diversity of forms is infinite. Dr Henzell-Thomas writes: "It is only our forgetfulness of our essential nature and its divine origin, and our heedlessness in failing to fulfil the burden of trust placed upon us that causes us to stray from our fully inclusive human identity." From this metaphysical awareness of *tawhid* as the governing principle of all Creation, and of unity in diversity as its expression, comes the understanding that precisely the commitment to a particular path gives us the means to encompass universalism. This understanding is the opposite of self-styled "universalists" who believe that adherence to a specific path and its formal requirements limits our ability to grasp universals. The traditionalist understanding in all faiths – which is rejected by the syncretists, who purport to take the best from all faiths and turn this into a new religion, and by many of the self-styled liberals – is that only through the mediation of forms, but not their elevation into formalisms, can the human being have access to what Muslims call the *haqq* or the Essential Truth, God.

According to Dr Henzell-Thomas, there is no contradiction between committing oneself to the forms or rituals of a particular spiritual path and pursuing of what is universal:

Following a path *exclusively* is totally reconcilable with the search for a universal identity, and, indeed, is the means to its attainment for countless spiritual seekers and spiritually developed beings from all religious traditions, but the *exclusivism* promoted by a defensive, backs-to-the-wall religiosity, which misappropriates God for a narrow community and denies that other paths are also expressions of the Self-disclosure of God, is necessarily a constriction of the heart, and is therefore incapable of encompassing divinity.

This openness to diversity as part of God's plan and to the legitimacy of faiths other than one's own enables one to go beyond the call for mere "tolerance" of the other. As the new Attorney General of the State of New Jersey once remarked to a gathering of Muslims and Sikhs and law enforcement officers on 12 June 2003, tolerance is what his mother asked him to exercise when she forced him to drink some vile liquid as medicine. Tolerance, as I have heard it used even in interfaith circles, is the attitude that I will not kill you now, but I will as soon as I get a good chance. This is similar to the Soviet use of the term "peaceful coexistence", which was clearly spelled out in the Communist legal journals as a stage prior to the worldwide victory of Communism.

The term "tolerance" comes from medieval toxicology and pharmacology, marking how much poison a body could "tolerate" before it would succumb to death. If we are to reach a common vision to avoid civilisational clash, we must obviously advance beyond tolerance. We must go beyond the arrogance of triumphalism, so common among fearful and reactionary people of all faiths, and beyond the static concept of "peaceful coexistence", to the higher calling of "peaceful cooperation".

Only through mutual self-understanding in interfaith dialogue can we undergo the mutual transformation that expands our own identity, and only through such transformation can we successfully promote mutual cooperation as a catalyst of justice. Commitment to spiritually informed and spiritually based justice is the only path that can lead to a common vision and to worldwide civilisational renewal. We pray that peace through justice will become a paradigm whose time has come. As the German philosopher Arthur Schopenhauer once noted: "All truth passes through three stages. First, it is ridiculed. Second, it is violently opposed. Third, it is accepted as self-evident."

Chapter 11

The Orphans of Modernity and the Clash of Civilisations[1]

Khaled Abou El Fadl

The Paradigm of Clashing Civilisations?

After 9/11 President Bush invited the world to choose sides: one had either to join the forces of good in the world, the upholders of civilisation and civility, or conversely, be counted among the evildoers. Having adopted this dichotomous world-view, the logical next step was to sort through the nations of the world and categorise them accordingly. Bush was perpetuating an old and well-established colonial habit. Colonialism divided the world into the civilised and the uncivilised, and declared that the white man's burden was to civilise the world, by force if necessary. It projected the exact same paradigm upon Islam. Accordingly, orientalists, who were often in the service of colonial powers, claimed that Islam divided the world into two abodes. They presumed that Muslims wished to convert the whole world, by force if necessary, to Islam. In reality, it was the coloniser, and not the colonised, that had adopted a missionary or crusading attitude *vis-à-vis* the other.

The absolutist and polarising policies of the US administration post-9/11 have led some commentators to speak of a "clash of fundamentalisms" – the fundamentalism of bin Ladin against that of Bush.[2] They hold that the current "war against terrorism" is being waged by two equally reactionary forces, each labouring under a dogmatic and essentialised world-view. This argument, however, is flawed because it is inaccurate to equate the morality of bin Ladin's and Bush's world-views. Regardless of how some aspects of the "war against terrorism" might be reminiscent of colonialism, the type of theology that drives bin Ladin is founded on a total disregard of any standards of civility or principles of humanity. Nevertheless, the rhetoric of the "war against terrorism", when coupled with a paradigm of clashing civilisations, does have the effect of perpetuating religious bigotry and of dehumanising the "other", however that "other" is defined.

Following 9/11, there has been a virtual avalanche of publications expressing unrestrained animosity to Islam as a religion and Muslims as a people. Two particularly sinister works that attempt to demonise all politically active Muslim individuals or organisations are Steven Emerson's *American Jihad: The Terrorists among Us*[3] and Daniel Pipes's *Militant Islam Reaches America*.[4]

I have no qualms in describing what took place on 11 September 2001 as the undoing of all that is civilised or decent. By any legal or moral measure, what took place was an act of immoral barbarism that exhibited a suicidal and destructive psychosis. The issue that concerns me here, however, is not the assessment of the immorality of the 9/11 attacks; rather, I am interested in assessing the morality and civility of our discourse in response to the attacks.

There are several aspects of our anti-terrorism policies that contribute to a symbolic leap from a declared "war against terrorism" to a "war against Islam". Initially, it is important to keep in mind that the moment we intimate that we in the West are civilised and Islam is barbaric, we effectively equate Islam and terrorism. The civilised West and uncivilised "other" is a frame of mind inherent in the very idea of the clash of civilisations because no one, not even Huntington and his supporters, truly believes the claim that the purportedly "clashing civilisations" are equal in moral merit or ethical value. Logically, it is possible for the good to clash with the good, but the socially constructed imagination will find this a theoretical possibility difficult to accept. If two civilisations are clashing, the natural assumption will be that one is good and the other is bad, and that we, whoever the "we" might be, are necessarily the good. In social psychology, this is often referred to as the binary instinct of "us" versus "them".

Since the US administration has asserted our goodness, then, by definition, whomever we clash with must necessarily be evil.[5] This is all the more so when we adopt paradigms such as "the axis of evil" or rhetorical concepts such as "rogue states". Such terms run counter to the idea of specific and individual liability and fault, and contribute to the idea of collective and generalisable fault. Effectively, what this type of language connotes is that there are bad nations of people, and not just guilty individuals. Again, at the symbolic and emotive level, this type of language contributes to an environment in which bigotry and prejudice thrive. When our leadership presumes itself capable of generalising about whole nations, branding them as evil, we set a normative example that encourages hate literature of the type we have witnessed recently.

If our response to criminal behaviour is less than principled, all we accomplish is to contribute to the diluting of the standards of justice and morality. Such dilution, in turn, contributes to the thriving of hateful discourses on Islam in which the paradigm of the clash of civilisations is exploited. Hate speech, like terrorism, is a form of barbarism, and we do not make a very convincing case for the civility of our culture if we respond to the barbarism of terror with the primitiveness of binary categories.

There are several methodological difficulties that ought to be considered when thinking about cultural values and the role they purportedly play in international relations. The first point pertains to what I will call "claims of lineage", the second pertains to "claims about the other", the third relates to "the enterprise of meaning", and the fourth addresses what I call "competence".

Claims of lineage

Proponents of the notion of the clash of civilisations seem to rely on an unfounded claim about the specificity and purity of particular values.

Accordingly, they are willing to classify particular values as squarely Judeo-Christian while others are Islamic. It is as if values have a genealogy that can be clearly and precisely ascertained, which then can be utilised in classifying what properly belongs to the West and what belongs to the Islamic "other". But the origin and lineage of values are as much a socio-historical construct as are claims about racial genealogical purity. Considering the numerous cultural interactions and cross-intellectual transmissions between the Muslim world and Europe, it is highly likely that every significant Western value has a measure of Muslim blood in it. Like racial categories, civilisational categories ought to be recognised as artificial political constructs that do not necessarily fit comfortably with socio-historical realities.

Claims about the "other"

Often the attempt to identify one's own civilisation and distinguish it from the "other" has much more to do with one's own aspirations than the reality of the "other". Put differently, descriptions of the "other", whoever the "other" may be, often tell us much more about the author of the description than the subject of the description.[6] For instance, if Westerners aspire to achieve a greater degree of democracy, or are anxious about their own shortcomings *vis-à-vis* women's rights, it is likely that they will invent an image of the Muslim "other" as the exact antithesis of their aspirations. By constructing the other in this way, one is able to be more satisfied and secure about one's own cultural achievements. The colonial images of the Orient – its exoticness, mystique, and harems – had much more to do with the anxieties and fantasies of the Western coloniser than they did with the sociological reality of the Orient.

The enterprise of meaning

There is a further problem with approaches that focus on civilisational paradigms and conflicts. Values, and their meaning in culture, are not constant or stable. They are continually shifting and mutating in response to a variety of influences and motivators. For instance, concepts such as *shurah* (government by consultation), the caliphate, or enjoining the good and forbidding the evil have had very different connotations from one century to another and one culture to another in Islamic history. Even when one is considering divinely revealed values, such values acquire meaning only within evolving and shifting contexts. When one speaks of Islamic justice, for instance, one is really speaking of various interpretive enterprises that existed at different times in Islamic history, which gave the notion of justice in Islam a variety of connotations.[7] And when commentators speak of a civilisational conflict between the West and Islam, there is a further creative or inventive process engaged in by the commentators themselves. Since meaning is the product of cumulative enterprises that generate communities of meaning, a student of Huntington cannot speak in terms of an Islamic notion of justice or an Islamic notion of human liberty. The most that this student can do is to speak of prevailing meanings within specific communities of interpretation. Thus, the student might, for example, speak in terms of a Mu'tazali notion of justice or an Ash'ari notion of justice.

Competence

Put simply, who is competent to say which of the competing communities of meaning is representative of the values of a civilisation? It is imperative to keep in mind that when students of Huntington claim that Islamic civilisation stands for a particular proposition, they are selecting what, in their minds, is the community that best represents Islamic civilisation. For example, the interpretive community to which someone like Muhammad 'Abduh belongs may assert "y". Meanwhile, bin Ladin and his interpretive community may assert "x". By claiming that Islamic civilisation stands for "x" but not "y", Huntington's students are making a choice about representation. Again, this choice might have much more to do with the choice-makers, such as Huntington's students, than with the actual dynamics of Islamic societies.

These cautionary points show that claims of civilisational conflict are fraught with conceptual pitfalls. They are likely to degenerate into powerful vehicles for the expression of prejudice. As such, they tend to promote misunderstandings and conflict. It is no wonder that when one examines the arguments of Western proponents of the clash of civilisations, one finds that they invariably ascribe most of what they perceive to be good and desirable to the West, and most what of they find distasteful or objectionable to Islam or Islamic civilisation. As a means of maintaining an air of impartiality, they often condescendingly assert that the values of the "other", foreign and unacceptable as they might be for Westerners, ought to be respected. What for Westerners might be considered egregious violations of human rights must be considered bearable for Muslims because Muslims have a distinctly different set of social and cultural expectations from the Judeo-Christian West.[8]

The effect of the doctrinal commitment to the paradigm of clashing civilisations only serves to obfuscate the real dynamics that are, in fact, taking place in Islam. There are significant tensions within contemporary Islam that are bound to impact materially upon the world today. Bin Ladin's terrorism is not the product of a system of thought that he single-handedly invented. Rather, his violence is an integral part of the struggle between interpretive communities over who gets to speak for Islam and how. He has emerged from what can appropriately be described as a state of civilisational dissonance – a state of social schizophrenia in which the challenge of modernity and alienation from Islamic historical experience play the predominant roles.

Orphans of Modernity

The real challenge that confronts Muslim intellectuals is that political interests have come to dominate public discourse to the point that moral investigation and thinking have been marginalised in modern Islam. In the age of postcolonialism, Muslims have become preoccupied with the attempt to remedy a collective feeling of powerlessness, often by engaging in sensational acts of power symbolism. The normative imperatives and intellectual subtleties of the Islamic moral tradition are rendered subservient to political expedience. Elsewhere, I have described this contemporary doctrinal dynamic as the predominance of the theology of power in modern Islam, and it is this theology that is a direct contributor to the emergence of highly radicalised Islamic groups.[9] Far from being authentic expressions of inherited Islamic paradigms, or a natural outgrowth of the classical tradition, these are thoroughly a by-product of colonialism and modernity. Such groups ignore the Islamic civilisational experience, with all its richness and diversity, and reduce Islam to a single dynamic – that of power. They tend to define Islam as an ideology of nationalistic defiance *vis-à-vis* the hegemony of the Western world. Therefore, instead of Islam being a moral vision given to humanity, it becomes constructed into the antithesis of the West. In the world constructed by these groups, there is no Islam; there is only opposition to the West.

Illegitimate means are consistently justified by invoking higher ends. In essence, what prevails is an aggravated siege mentality that suspends the moral principles of the religion in pursuit of the vindications of political power. In this siege mentality, there is no room for analytical or critical thought, and there is no room for seriously engaging the Islamic intellectual heritage.

While national liberation movements such as that of the Palestinian or Algerian resistance resorted to guerrilla or non-conventional warfare, modern-day terrorism of the variety promoted by bin Ladin is rooted in a different ideological paradigm, a theology that can be described as puritan, supremacist, and thoroughly opportunistic in nature. This theology is the by-product of the emergence and eventual primacy of a syncretistic orientation that unites Wahhabism and Salafism in modern Islam.

Wahhabism

The foundations of Wahhabi theology were set in place by the eighteenth-century evangelist Muhammad ibn Abd al-Wahhab (d. 1792). With a puritanical zeal, Abd al-Wahhab sought to rid Islam of all the corruptions that he believed had crept into the religion – corruptions that included mysticism and rationalism. Wahhabism resisted the indeterminacy of the modern age by escaping to a strict literalism in which the text became the sole source of legitimacy. Wahhabism exhibited extreme hostility to all forms of intellectualism, mysticism, and sectarianism within Islam. The Wahhabi creed also considered any form of moral thought that was not entirely dependent on the text a form of idolatry, and treated humanistic fields of knowledge, especially philosophy, as "the sciences of the devil".

According to the Wahhabi creed, it was imperative to return to a presumed pristine, simple, and straightforward Islam, which was believed to be entirely reclaimable by a literal implementation of the commands and precedents of the Prophet, and by a strict adherence to correct ritual practice. Wahhabism also rejected any attempt to interpret the divine law from a historical, contextual perspective; in fact, it treated the vast majority of Islamic history as a corruption of, or aberration from, true and authentic Islam. The dialectical and indeterminate hermeneutics of the classical jurisprudential tradition were considered corruptions of the purity of the faith and law. Furthermore, Wahhabism became very intolerant of the long-established Islamic practice of considering a variety of schools of thought to be equally orthodox, and attempted to narrow considerably the range of issues upon which Muslims may legitimately disagree. Orthodoxy was narrowly defined, and Abd al-Wahhab himself was fond of creating long lists of beliefs and acts which he considered deviant and heretical innovations whose adoption or commission would immediately render a Muslim an unbeliever.

Wahhabi ideology was resuscitated in the early twentieth century under the leadership of Abd al-Aziz ibn Sa'ud, who adopted the puritanical theology of the Wahhabis and allied himself with the tribes of Najd, thereby establishing the nascent beginnings of what would become Saudi Arabia. Importantly, the Wahhabi rebellions of the nineteenth and twentieth centuries were very bloody because the Wahhabis indiscriminately slaughtered Muslims, especially those belonging to the Shi'ite sect. This led several mainstream jurists to describe the Wahhabis as a fanatical fringe group. Interestingly, the Wahhabis introduced practices into Islam that were unprecedented and which considerably expanded the intrusive powers of the state. For instance, the Wahhabis set the first reported precedent of taking roll call at prayers. They prepared lists of the inhabitants of a city and called off the names during the five daily prayers in the mosque. Anyone absent without a sufficient excuse was flogged. Perhaps the most extreme form of Wahhabi fanaticism took place recently, on 11 March 2002, when the *mutawwa'in* (religious police) prevented schoolgirls from exiting a burning school in Mecca, or from being rescued by their parents or firemen, because they were not "properly covered". At least fifteen girls are reported to have burned to death as a result.[10]

Saudi Arabia aggressively promoted Wahhabi thought around the Muslim world, especially after 1975, with the sharp rise in oil prices. In the 1950s and '60s, Saudi Arabia was coming under considerable pressure from republican and Arab nationalist regimes, which tended to consider the Saudi system archaic and reactionary. In the 1970s, Saudi Arabia finally possessed the financial means to address its legitimacy concerns. The Wahhabis either had to alter their own system of belief to make it more consistent with the convictions of other Muslims, or they had to spread aggressively their convictions to the rest of the Muslim world. They chose the latter option.

Salafism

Wahhabism, however, did not spread in the modern Muslim world under its own banner, but under that of Salafism. It is important to note that even the term "Wahhabism" is considered derogatory to the followers of Abd al-Wahhab since Wahhabis prefer to see themselves as the representatives of Islamic orthodoxy. According to its adherents, Wahhabism is not a school of thought within Islam, but is Islam itself, and the only possible Islam. The fact that Wahhabism rejected the use of a school label gave it a rather diffuse quality and made many of its doctrines and methodologies eminently transferable. Salafism was a far more credible paradigm in Islam than Wahhabism; in many ways, it was an ideal vehicle for Wahhabism. Therefore, in their literature, Wahhabi clerics have consistently described themselves as Salafis, and not Wahhabis.

Salafism is a creed founded in the late nineteenth century by Muslim reformers such as Muhammad 'Abduh, al-Afghani, al-Shawkani, al-San'ani, and Rashid Rida. Salafism appealed to a very basic concept in Islam, namely, that Muslims ought to follow the rightly guided precedent of the Prophet and his companions (*al-salaf al-salih*). Methodologically, Salafism was nearly identical to Wahhabism, except that Wahhabism is far less tolerant of diversity and differences of opinions. In many ways, Salafism was intuitively undeniable, partly because of its epistemological premise. The founders of Salafism maintained that on all issues Muslims ought to return to the original textual sources of the Qur'an and the *sunnah* (precedent) of the Prophet. In doing so, Muslims ought to reinterpret the original sources in the light of modern needs and demands without being slavishly bound to the interpretive precedents of earlier Muslim generations.

As originally conceived, Salafism was not necessarily anti-intellectual, but like Wahhabism it did tend to be uninterested in history. By emphasising a presumed golden age in Islam, the adherents of Salafism idealised the time of the Prophet and his companions, and ignored or demonised the balance of Islamic history. Furthermore, by rejecting juristic precedents and undervaluing tradition as a source of authoritativeness, Salafism adopted a form of egalitarianism that contributed to a real vacuum of authority in contemporary Islam. According to Salafism, anyone was considered qualified to return to the original sources and speak for the divine will. However, unlike Wahhabism, Salafism was not hostile to the juristic tradition or the practice of various competing schools of thought. In addition, Salafism was not consistently hostile to mysticism or Sufism.

Importantly, Salafism was largely founded by Muslim nationalists who were eager to read the values of modernity into the original sources of Islam. Hence, Salafism was not necessarily anti-Western. In fact, its founders strove to project contemporary institutions such as democracy, constitutionalism, or socialism onto the foundational texts and to justify the paradigm of the modern nation state within Islam. In this sense, Salafism, as originally conceived, betrayed a degree of opportunism.

By the mid-twentieth century, it had become clear that Salafism had drifted into stifling apologetics. Salafist apologists responded to the intellectual challenges of modernity by adopting pietistic fictions about the Islamic traditions; such fictions eschewed any critical evaluation of Islamic doctrines and celebrated the presumed perfection of Islam. A common apological device was to argue that any worthwhile modern institution was first invented by Muslims. Thus, Islam liberated women, created a democracy, endorsed pluralism, protected human rights and guaranteed social security long before these institutions ever existed in the West. The main effect of apologetics was to contribute to a sense of intellectual self-sufficiency that often descended into moral arrogance.

"Salafabism"

Wahhabism proceeded to co-opt the language and symbolisms of Salafism in the 1970s until the two had become practically indistinguishable. Both theologies imagined a golden age in Islam; this entailed belief in a historical utopia that is entirely retrievable and reproducible in contemporary Islam. Both remained uninterested in critical historical inquiry and responded to the challenge of modernity by escaping to the secure haven of the text. And both advocated a form of egalitarianism and anti-elitism to the point that they came to consider intellectualism and rational moral insight to be inaccessible, and thus corruptions of the purity of the Islamic message. These similarities facilitated the Wahhabi co-option of Salafism. Wahhabism, from its very inception, and Salafism, especially after it entered its apologetic phase, were infested with a kind of supremacist thinking that prevails until today. To simplify matters, I will call this unity of Wahhabism with the worst that is in Salafism, Salafabism.

The consistent characteristic of Salafabism is a supremacist puritanism that compensates for feelings of disempowerment with a distinct sense of self-righteous arrogance *vis-à-vis* the nondescript "other" – whether the "other" is the West, non-believers in general, or even Muslim women. Instead of simple apologetics, Salafabism responds to the feelings of powerlessness and defeat with uncompromising and arrogant symbolic displays of power, not only against non-Muslims, but even more so against fellow Muslims. Salafabism anchored itself in the confident security of texts. But so far from respecting the integrity of the text, Salafabism is abusive of it. As a hermeneutic orientation, it empowers its adherents to project their socio-political frustrations and insecurities onto the text. Religious texts consistently become as whips to be exploited by a select class of readers in order to affirm reactionary power dynamics in society (Abou El Fadl 2001).

The adherents of Salafabism no longer concerned themselves with co-opting or claiming Western institutions as their own. Under the guise of reclaiming the true and real Islam, they proceeded to define Islam as the exact antithesis of the West. Apologetic attempts at proving Islam's compatibility with the West were dismissed as inherently defeatist. Salafabists argued that colonialism had ingrained into Muslims a lack of self-pride or dignity, convincing them of the inferiority of their religion. This has trapped Muslims into an endless and futile race to appease the West by proving Islam's worthiness. According to this model, there are only two paths in life: the path of God (the straight path) and the path of Satan (the crooked path). In attempting to integrate and co-opt Western ideas such as feminism, democracy, or human rights, Muslims have fallen prey to the temptations of Satan by accepting ungodly innovations (*bida'*, sing. *bid'ah*). Islam is the only straight path in life, and must be pursued regardless of what others think and of how it impacts on their rights and well-being.

Salafabists insist that only the mechanics and technicalities of Islamic law define morality. This legalistic way of life is considered inherently superior to all others, and the followers of any other way are regarded as infidels (*kuffar*), hypocrites (*munafiqun*), or iniquitous (*fasiqun*). Lives that are lived outside the divine law are inherently unlawful and therefore an offence.

Usama bin Ladin

Bin Ladin, like most extremist Muslims, belongs to the orientation I have called Salafabist. Although raised in a Wahhabi environment, bin Ladin is not strictly speaking part of that creed. Wahhabism is distinctly introverted: it primarily asserts power over other Muslims. This reflects its obsession with orthodoxy and correct ritualistic practice. Militant puritan groups, however, are both introverted and extroverted: they attempt to assert power over both Muslims and non-Muslims. As populist movements, they are a reaction to the disempowerment most Muslims have suffered in the modern age at the hands of harshly despotic governments and interventionist foreign powers. Fuelled by the supremacist and puritan creed of Salafabism, these groups become uncompromisingly fanatical.

The existence of this puritan orientation in Islam is hardly surprising. All religious systems have suffered at one time or another from absolutist extremism, and Islam is no exception. There were extremists such as the Qaramites and Assassins, for example, whose terror became their very *raison d'être*, and who earned unmitigated infamy in the writings of Muslim historians, theologians, and jurists. After centuries of bloodshed, these two groups learned moderation, and they continue to exist in small numbers in North Africa and Iraq. The lesson taught by Islamic history is that extremist groups are ejected from the mainstream of Islam; they are marginalised and eventually treated as a heretical aberration.

The problem, however, is that the traditional institutions of Islam that have historically acted to marginalise extremist creeds no longer exist. This is what makes the events of 9/11 so significant for the future of Islam. Those events symbolise the culmination of a process that has been in the making for the past two centuries. After 9/11 and the bloodletting that followed, the question is: now that we have witnessed the sheer amount of senseless destruction that the children of this orientation are capable of producing and the type of world they are capable of instigating, will Muslims be able to marginalise Salafabism and render it, like many of the arrogant movements that preceded it, a historical curiosity? In this regard, the paradigm of the clash of civilisations helps neither Muslims nor non-Muslims in understanding the modern Islamic experience. Moreover, to the extent that this paradigm invents an Islamic authenticity at odds with the West, it simply aggravates the siege mentality in the Muslim world.

In past decades, when Muslim intellectuals attempted a critical engagement with their tradition and a search for the moral and humanistic aspects of their heritage, they were invariably confronted by the spectre of post-colonialism;

their efforts were evaluated purely in terms of whether they appeased or displeased the West, and they were accepted or rejected by many Muslims accordingly. The fact is that the paradigm of the clash of civilisations, by promoting a binary view of Islam and the West, only serves to empower puritan orientations within modern Islam, such as that of the Salafabists and their child, bin Ladin.

Notes

1   Edited version, reproduced with permission from the author and the journal *Global Dialogue* (ed. Paul Theodoulou), vol. 4, no. 2 (Spring 2002), issue on "The Impact of September 11", 1–16.
2   See, for example, Tariq Ali, *The Clash of Fundamentalisms: Crusades, Jihads and Modernity* (London: Verso Press, 2002).
3   Steven Emerson, *America's Jihad: The Terrorists among Us* (New York: Simon and Schuster, 2002).
4   Daniel Pipes, *Militant Islam Reaches America* (New York: W. W. Norton, 2002).
5   Huntington's claim that his clash of civilisations paradigm is value-neutral is disingenuous.
6   For an analysis of this process, see Khaled Abou El Fadl, "Islamic Law and Ambivalent Scholarship", *Michigan Law Review* (2002).
7   For a detailed study of the role of authorial enterprise, communities of interpretation, and Islamic law, see Abou El Fadl 2001.
8   This is the gist of Huntington's argument about the wrongfulness of believing in universal Western values; see Huntington 1996: 308–12.
9   Khaled Abou El Fadl, "Islam and the Theology of Power", *Middle East Report*, 221 (Winter 2001), 28–33.
10 See "Saudi Police 'Stopped' Fire Rescue", BBC news report, 15 March 2002. I confirmed this incident in a conversation with the father of one of the girls who was killed. The Saudi authorities initially said they would investigate, but a day later they denied that the incident had occurred.

PART THREE

JEWISH, CHRISTIAN, AND MUSLIM RESPONSES TO RELIGIOUS DIVERSITY

They shall sit every man under his vine and under his fig tree; and none shall make them afraid: for the mouth of the Lord of hosts hath spoken it.
For all people will walk every one in the name of his god, and we will walk in the name of the Lord our God for ever and ever.

Micah 4:4–5

The stranger who lives with you shall be treated like the native-born. Love him as yourself, for you were strangers in the land of Egypt. I am the Lord your God.

Leviticus 19:34

The pious of the nations have a share in the world to come.

Babylonian Talmud Sanhedrin 13

Peter began: "I now see how true it is that God has no favourites, but that in every nation anyone who is Godfearing and does what is right is acceptable to Him."

Acts 34–5

And of His signs is the creation of the heavens and the earth and the diversity of your tongues and colours.

Qur'an 30:22

To each community among you have We appointed a law and a way of life. And if God had so willed, He could have made you one community: but [He willed it otherwise] in order to test you by means of what He has bestowed upon you.

Qur'an 5:48

We have appointed for every community a way of worship that they shall perform. Therefore do not allow yourself to be drawn into disputes about this ... God will judge between you on the Day of Resurrection concerning that about which you used to differ.
Qur'an 22:67–9

Truly those who believe, and the Jews, and the Christians, and the Sabaeans – whoever believes in God and the Last Day and performs virtuous deeds – surely their reward is with their Lord, and no fear shall come upon them, neither shall they grieve.

Qur'an 2:62

The lamps are many, but the light is the same. It comes from beyond.
Shaykh Jalal al-Din Rumi

When you know your way and opinions to be true, you have the right to say, "My way is right and the best." But you do not have the right to say, "Only my way is right."
Said Nursi

Chapter 12

September 11: The Case Against Us All[1]

Tony Bayfield

In the summer of 2001, I was invited to give the Younghusband Lecture, an annual event sponsored by the World Congress of Faiths. In my mind it was to be an academic paper on the dangers of fundamentalism. In October, a few weeks after the catastrophe in the United States, I found myself, along with twenty other "faith leaders" sitting round the table at No. 10 Downing Street, getting more and more irritated by the collective politeness and rather pallid blessings bestowed upon the Prime Minister. When it came to my turn to speak, I think I caused some offence by saying that, given the scenes daily on our televisions from New York, Belfast, Kashmir, and Israel, it was little short of miraculous that the Prime Minister had not written off all religion and religious leaders as a dangerous waste of space and wasn't it about time that we all stood up against the fundamentalists within our respective traditions and stood together in affirmation of the shared values we claimed to believe in.

Over the following months, the situation in Israel/Palestine became more and more the focus of my concern for reasons that are obvious. I became increasingly inarticulate and less and less clear what I wanted or felt able to say. In the nick of time – maybe I should say the old nick of time – I found a way out of my dilemma. What follows, however, is full of anguish and anger – anguish and anger which terrified me during the process of writing and giving the lecture.

This isn't a lecture in the conventional sense, still less a learned paper. But I have chosen to publish it exactly as it was given. If it has any merit, it has merit as it was written and given rather than dying the death of a thousand qualifications and footnotes.

There are footnotes, but almost all of them are of a particular kind. After the lecture, there were responses and discussion, and I realised that there were times when I had used shorthand or made points that were simply not understood. What the footnotes seek to do is to explain a little more what was clearly not understood on first hearing – and, just occasionally, to defend either Satan or me when we felt particularly badly treated.

One final point. This is a lecture about Judaism, Christianity, and Islam. As I said before the lecture, I have singled out the three Abrahamic faiths because I think there are features that are peculiar to this particular trinity of which I am a member. But I have no wish to make listeners or readers of other faiths feel excluded and some of the charges apply far beyond the three faiths on trial. Fundamentalism has become a universal scar across the world's religions. There is no reason why only Jews, Christians, and Muslims should feel attacked and insulted by what follows.

There is a famous passage in a somewhat esoteric tractate of the Talmud called *Eruvin*, with which I have been working recently.[2] It is marvellous stuff, which will be familiar to some here. It's about two "schools" – Pharisaic, early rabbinic – founded by two older contemporaries of Jesus called Hillel and Shammai. They were in dispute about a matter of *halakhah*, Jewish law, and both sides maintained that they alone were right. After three years the situation was finally resolved only by a *bat kol*, a heavenly voice, which declared: "these and these [both views] are the words of the living God." But, said the voice, there are some matters, such as matters of law, where we have to have a definitive ruling even though both views are "God's truth". Because we are forced in this instance to make a decision, we will follow the school of Hillel. Why, asks the Talmud? Because the members of the school of Hillel were kind and modest, and studied the rulings of both sides, and mentioned the school of Shammai before the school of Hillel and humility, not actively seeking greatness and the power to impose that goes with it, and not being over-anxious to win at all costs – all virtues that deserve the highest reward.

It is a marvellous passage and it is one that I, as a progressive Jew, read as an essential seed of a most profound concept – that different groups hear the voice of the living God in different ways; that only on very limited occasions is it necessary to make a definitive ruling. For the most part, we can and must live with the fact that not only do Jews, Christians, and Muslims all hear the words of the living God but that we often hear them in different ways. Even when there has to be a single way of doing things that does not invalidate the truth of the other, what matters is humility and respect, and not seeking cheap victories, or the power to impose our view.

It is truly marvellous stuff.

But a few days ago I noticed that this particular section of Talmud ends immediately after the passage I have just quoted with another famous passage:

> Our rabbis taught that for two-and-a-half years the school of Shammai and the school of Hillel were in dispute again, the former asserting that it would have been better for us if human beings had not been created, and the latter maintaining that it is better for us to have been created. Finally, they took a vote and decided that it would have been better for us had we not been created. But, since we have been created, we should reflect on our past deeds and make amends or, as some say, examine our future actions.[3]

The Talmud is a literary work. It appears at first glance simply to be the record of debates that took place over a period of some hundreds of years, roughly connected by theme. But that isn't so. It is a record of discussions and debates over some hundreds of years, but very carefully and thoughtfully edited to reflect an overriding argument, to provide an added overall dimension. So it is quite legitimate to ask why the editors of this section chose to end a sublime, tolerant, exalted view of human debate and dispute, a section advancing an insight so profound about the fragmentary, partial nature of revelation and truth as perceived by human beings, with something which punctures these exalted ideals and brings us down to earth with such a harsh, discordant note of deflation and despondency.

I think there is little option but to conclude that they did so because they knew that we would find the internalisation of such a modest and humble view of what each of us holds dear, to be extraordinarily hard. In fact, they knew that we would fail repeatedly to acknowledge that "these and these are both the words of the living God"; that we would not listen respectfully to each other and restrain our desire to "win"; that we would become hopelessly entangled in the dilemma of distinguishing that which is relative from that which is universal; that we would become obsessed by the desire to justify ourselves amidst the inevitable dirtying of hands when exercising power; that we would fail the challenge to be humble and self-critical, and therefore it would have been better had we not been set the challenge of life in the first place.

As one who simply cannot live up to the standards demanded of me by that passage in the Talmud, as one who has to exercise leadership within the Jewish community, as one who constantly gets his hands dirty because he believes he has to, as one who shares the terror and anger and sense of betrayal, and sense of being repeatedly and deliberately misrepresented and misunderstood, and experiences the internal conflicts of shame and guilt of most Jews at this time, I simply cannot begin to speak in the spirit of that heavenly voice because I don't in my innermost heart really believe it. I have never empathised with the note of deflation and despair at the end of that section of Talmud before, but there are times now when I do. As Rabbi Tony Bayfield, professional head of the Reform Movement in Britain, I am too angry, too fearful, too hurt, too conflicted and despairing to say anything constructive to you, but yet I know there is something that must be said.

I hope you will give me the benefit of the doubt, show me a little compassion in what I am about to do. Even, if I show you and me no compassion at all.[4]

As I am sure you know, the word *Satan*, Satan, or *ha-Satan*, the Satan, is relatively rare in the Hebrew Bible. It is used in a number of ways and developed in different ways within later Jewish, Christian, and Muslim traditions. There is, however, no doubt that one of the meanings of *Satan* in the Hebrew Scriptures is adversary, prosecuting counsel. *Satan* was the angel who presented before God the case against.[5] The only way that I can escape from my inner conflict and emotional turmoil is to address you, to address us in the guise of the prosecuting angel. It adds hubris as well as cowardice and intellectual dishonesty to my many other sins, but remember that I am not playing Satan, just a humble barrister ("a humble barrister", now there is an oxymoron for you!).

When those two planes smashed murderously and deliberately into the Twin Towers of the World Trade Centre on 11 September 2001, one of the most horrifying things that should have been apparent in an appalling, horrifying event was the failure, the absolute failure of Judaism, Christianity, and Islam. Dear God, it should have been apparent before in a hundred terrifying, excruciating[6] scenes over the last seventy years. I won't, at this point, name them because if you do know what they are, my case is proved, and if you really don't know what they are, if you can only see scenes which condemn another faith not your own, then my case is doubly proved.

Indictment I
My first indictment is the failure to recognise that Judaism, Christianity, and Islam are siblings, yet continue to act out the worst features of sibling rivalry that even the most dysfunctional family could possibly muster.

Let me remind you that you are each the child of Abraham, and that rabbinic Judaism, Christianity, and Islam all share either the same scriptures, or versions of the same scriptures. Yet you do not act with the love that normal, reasonably well-adjusted siblings show towards each other. Nor do you recognise the feelings of jealousy and rivalry that normal siblings also experience, and have to recognise, if they are to move forward in a constructive way. Where you are so remarkably alike, both in your strengths and in your faults, you show no acknowledgment of this fact. Have you any idea of the similarities between today's Muslims in Britain and Jews in Britain a century ago – not just socially and economically, but in the way you view your sacred scriptures and in your attitudes to the discipline of religious law? Yet you experience all of the murderous and violent feelings of dysfunctional siblings and don't recognise it.
 Let me quote, your Honour, a Jewish scholar, Alan Segal:

> Judaism and Christianity designed two different ways of understanding their universal missions ... When Christianity promulgated its doctrine of the salvation of all believers, it understood itself to be the universal proselytising religion for world salvation. By contrast, Judaism understood itself to be a kingdom of priests in a culturally plural world ... Their different histories do not alter the fact of their birth as twins in the last years of Judean statehood. They are both truly Rebecca's children, but unlike Jacob and Esau, they have no need to dispute their birthright. It can belong to both of them together.[7]

Siblings. No need to dispute their birthright. So, why the patronising and the stereotyping and the scarcely concealed distaste?[8]
 Why, dear Christians, do you rush to use the language of your own greatest infamy – holocaust, Nazis, genocide – to describe the behaviour of Jews in Israel and Palestine today?[9] Are you so desperate to prove that Jews are no better than anyone else, no better than you? Do you have any idea of how hurtful and offensive such language is? I suspect you do. And, my dear Jews, do you really think that the past excuses you your continuing contempt for the New Testament as a book of revelation and experience of the Divine, your failure to hold Christian holy places as sacred as your own? You use terms like "*goyim*" with such contempt; many of you refuse to discuss matters of theology with your siblings;[10] will not enter a church even for a funeral mass; drink wine produced by your own sisters and brothers lest you be drawn into apostasy through socialising.[11]

Nor have I finished my first indictment there. It was Louis IX, "Saint" Louis, King of France, who burnt Jewish books in Paris and then set out on Crusade to attack his Muslim siblings as well. It was in Christian France in 2002 that Muslims attacked synagogues and Christians in their droves voted for Le Pen in a show of Islamophobia that shook even Britain – evidently reminding our Home Secretary of the hordes of Muslim and Hindu bogeymen who threaten to "swamp" us here as well.

Let me continue, from a Jewish prayer book no less: "Ishmael, my brother, how long shall we fight each other? My brother, from times bygone, my brother – Hagar's son, my brother the wandering one. Time is running out, put hatred to sleep." If ever words were empty, these are them. If ever words were poisonous, they are those in the Saudi press reviving the blood libel which, dear Christian sibling, you invented to demonise the Jew and which is but one example of the wholesale export of the vocabulary of Christian anti-Semitism into the Islamic world in the last decade.[12] Only siblings could show such enduring, murderous hatred.

Indictment II
None of you have confronted the challenges of your own scriptures.

However you wriggle, and however you squirm, there are passages in the Qur'an, which have licensed misguided Muslims to claim the superiority of Islam and to use accounts of rebellious Jewish tribes to support anti-Jewish sentiments. There are passages that have been used to justify the *fatwah* to hound people and call for their murder, the proclamation of Jihad as bloody holy war, the imposition of cruel and violent punishments, and the support of governments that set Muslim against Muslim, Sunnis against Shi'ites, and fund and sponsor terrorism. It is no use you saying that people who interpret the Qur'an in those terms are interpreting it wrongly. Your brilliant and uplifting sacred texts have been misused and abused, and you have done nothing effective to stop it.

Exactly the same is true of the New Testament text, which still serves as a vehicle for those who would argue in favour of Christian superiority and supercession, who would seek to deny their siblings their share of the birthright and inheritance. You cannot reasonably suggest that the very text of the New Testament as it is read so often without explanation is kind to your Jewish sisters and brothers, the heirs of the Pharisees. And let me remind you of that most dangerous of passages in the Gospel of St John (8:44) which describes Jews as children of the devil – your devil, not *Satan*!

And, finally, back to the Jews. Let me refer you to the story of Pinchas, which you read with such reverence and often so little commentary publicly, each year. Pinchas who took the law into his own hands and murdered a Jew and a non-Jew. Pinchas who was rewarded for extra-judicial murder with hereditary priesthood. Remember Yigal Amir who took the law into his own hands and murdered Yitzhak Rabin in the name of Judaism. Remember Baruch Goldstein who rose in the night after reading the book of Esther and murdered Muslims at prayer.[13]

Each of you has failed to confront the real challenges of your Scriptures, the terrifying passages, and the passages that can be used to license the murder of siblings.

Remember the story of Abraham and Sarah and Hagar and Ishmael in the Hebrew Bible. The very text prefigures the desperate, sinful struggle based upon ignoble fears, jealousies, and passions that you have read instead as license and justification.[14]

Indictment III
You have been seduced by Greco-Roman and later notions of imperialism into thinking that you alone are "the way and the truth and the life", into thinking that your story is the only story, into thinking not only that yours is the only family on earth but that you are the only child who is loved by God, the only child who really matters, the only child who is the true heir of Abraham.

Where is the modesty? Where is the humility? You make truth claims as if you were God. Is it not enough that each of you has the most wonderful story, a fragment of history touched by God? Is it not enough that each of you has a precious strand of the covenant made originally through Noah with the whole of humanity?[15] Why have you been insatiable? Why do you continue to fight battles against each other for power and control over the whole world? Why do you still fight the Crusades? Were they not monstrous and appalling enough? Your Honour, do I really need to detail what Karen Armstrong has called the "contempt for Islam" (1991: 40) that has disfigured the thinking even of liberal Western intellectuals in the twentieth century – the support of colonialism from Algiers to Damascus, the fantasies, the stereotypes, the belittling. Today you reap huge anger, radicalisation, the desire for revenge – are you surprised? But does that make it right?

When will your misguided lust for empire and power end? Why is it not possible for Christian and Muslim to be content with what they have? Why do you need to own the whole world, which is actually God's? Why can the three of you not allow each other to be – with Christian or post-Christian lands in which Muslims and Jews are respected minorities; Muslim lands with Christians and Jews as respected and unpersecuted minorities; and Jews in their tiny land, side by side with a Palestinian land, in which minorities can live without fear or hindrance – in which Palestinians do not still openly or secretly covet Tel Aviv and in which dreams of a Greater Israel are simply shameful memories.

Indictment IV
Since the 1960s we have seen the rise of the most disfiguring feature on the face of world religion, and particularly amongst you three, that even I can remember in my long and distinguished career. It is called "fundamentalism".

Before you start protesting that Judaism or Islam cannot be fundamentalist, let me tell you that fundamentalism has little or nothing to do with a literal reading of scripture. Though fundamentalism has its origins, I accept, in a series of pamphlets written in the United States ninety years ago, I am not talking pamphlets. If religion is not about facing up to the challenges of the present; if it is not about leading people resolutely into a future, into a world in which nature in every sense is transformed, in which justice rolls down like waters and righteousness as an everlasting torrent; if it is not about building a world in which every human being can sit under their vine and under their fig tree and no one will terrorise them; if it is not about creating a world in which, as the prophet Micah says, each person walks in the way of their God, a God who is Herself a manifestation of that which is shared, unnameable and Without End; if it is not about that true peace which fills the world as the waters cover the sea – then it has no meaning and no value. Yet fundamentalists are afraid of the present and terrified of the future; fainthearted in the face of their mission, they run away from the challenge of reality. They build an imaginary world which they think resembles the Christianity of the New Testament, or eighth-century Islam, or eighteenth-century Poland, but which doesn't, and has no authenticity. Fundamentalists, in their fear and in their insecurity claim to have a monopoly on truth and more, they seek to seize power and so impose their authority on others. It is a desperate and disastrous phenomenon.[16]

It has led to fifteen or twenty thousand[17] fundamentalist Jews clinging to land which must, in justice, become part of the State of Palestine. It has led to coalition governments in Israel, which reflect neither the democratic will, nor the ideals of Judaism.

It has led to a situation in the United States where the Churches have been captured and seduced by men like Pat Buchanan, and have become a major obstacle to American participation in aid, in development, in the eradication of Third World poverty.

Fundamentalism has led to the defacing and defaming of everything that is good and just and life-enhancing in Islam so that the term "Muslim fundamentalist" now, tragically, seems synonymous with "Muslim" in the minds of many ordinary people in the West, fuelling the present scandal of Islamophobia and bringing libel, pain, discrimination, and suffering to ordinary Muslims in Britain.

Brainwashing young, deprived, and discriminated-against young people into thinking that becoming a suicide bomber and killing innocent civilians – men, women, and children – is not what Islam is about even *in extremis*.

Terrorism can never, never be justified, and fundamentalism has scarred the reputation of religion in a way that makes my task, Your Honour, so delightfully easy. The failure of Jewish, Christian, and Muslim leaders alike to denounce fundamentalism and to stand together in affirmation of shared values, in particular, values relating to the sanctity of life and the central role of religion to challenge power, not to seize it for coercive purposes – that is my penultimate indictment.

Indictment V
You have indulged in the rape of the Third World.

There is no doubt that the Christian and post-Christian West is carrying out a
process of exploitation of the Third World, which is a scandal and a disgrace.
Whole swathes of the world have been exploited economically, primarily for
the benefit of developed countries. Whole swathes of the world have been left
to deal with the legacy of colonialism and imperialism. Whole swathes of the
world have been exploited by the Abrahamic faiths which showed no respect
whatsoever for the faiths of the indigenous peoples. His Honour once implored
you to "take care of your own soul and another person's body, not your own
body and another person's soul".[18] You took no notice and did the reverse.

  You have made globalisation a nightmare by making it an instrument, not
for spreading education and welfare and eliminating hunger, but for trampling
the brotherhood and sisterhood of humanity, each person's precious
individuality, under foot. You have sought to impose democracy, free trade,
and human rights primarily to win economic and political advantage. You
have resisted democracy, free trade, and human rights, protesting that they are
part of Western imperialism, because they threaten your hegemony and stand
as an implied criticism of your culture.

  That exploitation, that cynicism, that venality, that failure of responsibility,
that use of alliances for strategic and economic reasons even if it has meant
supporting oppressive regimes with no regard for human rights, whether they
be defined by Judaism, Christianity, or Islam, has sown seeds in which
fundamentalism, fanaticism, and terrorism – absolutely and completely
unjustified though they are – have as a terrible matter of fact found fertile
breeding grounds in which they too can abuse and betray the starving, the
uneducated, the defenceless, and the impoverished.

  There is my indictment. For many centuries you could, to some extent at
least, have been excused – "Father forgive them for they know not what they
do"; you were the *tinok shenishba*, the child blinded by the limited values of the
world around you. But since the emergence of the global village, since the
development of universal communications, since the unlearned lessons of
world war, since the *tremendum* of the Shoah – there can be no alibi. You
reveal only arrogance. You show no humility. You have not been prepared to
be even moderately self-critical, let alone radically self-critical, which alone
could save you. You have performed small acts of goodness and kindness, but
you have failed when it comes to the big picture and the tough issues. You
speak of peace, but you train children to hate and arm them with terrible
weapons.

  You do not know who you are – siblings, siblings, siblings. You treat each
other abominably, yet you have no insight at all into the origins of your
murderous feelings towards each other, which you deny even as you are
exhibiting them. You allow your Scriptures to be the mandate for violence,
hatred, and contempt. You have been seduced by political notions of empire
into the conquest of land and souls. You have allowed fundamentalists and
fanatics to perform your dirty work and fulfil your base ambitions. You have

raped and exploited the Third World and created the conditions in which despair and terror are rife.

Now you will instantly resort to self-justification, or pay lip service to my criticisms, whilst mounting an uncompromising defence and justification of your conduct in your heart.

Your Honour, your children out there – Jews, Christians, and Muslims – are suffering and dying, yet their leaders are fiddling the books of *cheshbon nefesh*, of true accounting, whilst the three Abrahamic faiths, their cities, their people, and their souls burn. September 11th did indeed change the world forever. It finally made apparent the abject failure of religion, the farce of religion, the moral bankruptcy of religion. Your Honour, I rest my case.

Satan slumps into his seat with a hypocritical inner smile of satisfaction. Or is the awful smile mine? Has he indeed, cruelly but necessarily, spoken the words of Adonai, of Allah, of Christ, of the living God? Or has he been a vehicle too clever by half for saying what a Jew and a Christian and a Muslim must say in public for themselves?

Better to have been created or not created?[19] I cannot believe that I am so depressed that I can even contemplate the Talmudic answer. But it is the qualification to that answer with which I will end: "We should reflect on our past deeds or, as some say, examine our future actions." I am so desperate that I do not think that there is any point in calling upon us to reflect upon our past deeds, such is the extent to which we are bound up with our own stories and our own telling of history. The only thing we can do is to examine our future actions and, starting from this very moment, resolve to act to save our faiths and the world.

Notes

1 This paper was first given as the Younghusband Lecture, which is an annual event in memory of Sir Francis Younghusband, founder of the World Congress of Faiths. This lecture was delivered at the Sternberg Centre for Judaism, London, on 3 May 2002, and is reproduced with the author's permission from the journal *Interreligious Insight*, vol. 1, no. 1 (January 2003), 20–33.

2 Babylonian Talmud, Tractate *Eruvin* 13b (Soncino English edition starts bottom p. 85).

3 Ibid., pp. 86–7.

4 I am not sure how much it is necessary to explain. My anger comes from the fact that I think that Israel has been grossly misrepresented in much of the world's press, not the least in Britain. It is monstrous that people should question the right of the State of Israel to exist, or deny its right to protect its citizens against a vile and inhuman terrorist assault. That is not to deny that Israel has been drawn into a situation in which the totally unacceptable has occurred – the continued occupation of someone else's land, the denial of human rights, the killing and maiming of innocents, collective punishment, and a host of other related actions. I stand by both the preceding sentences. One of the problems of speaking as a Jew in Britain

today is that people repeatedly take comments out of context and use those comments to reinforce positions with which one totally disagrees. Another was summed up for me by a journalist in *The Independent* who described me as being like two people. I don't think that schizophrenia is the correct diagnosis of my present mental state, but depression may well be – the anger and the anguish being symptoms. I hope this is of some use in explaining further why I adopted the device that I am now about to explain.

5   See for instance *ha-Satan*, the adversary at the beginning of the book of Job.

6   Yes, an intended choice of word!

7   Alan F. Segal, *Rebecca's Children: Judaism and Christianity in the Roman World* (Cambridge, MA, and London: Harvard University Press, 1986), pp. 180–81.

8   *Satan* would say that Christians are especially prone to adopt a patronising tone, hinting at those awful Jews, and less-than-civilised Muslims, who do not share the Christian understanding and propensity for peace, reconciliation, and self-sacrificing love. He would add that the French Ambassador to Britain, in privately describing Israel as "a shitty little country", illustrated perfectly the word "distaste".

9   I was fascinated that a member of the audience rushed to the defence of Christianity, ascribing responsibility for the Final Solution solely to the tiny group who attended the Wannsee Conference. First, don't we get the governments we deserve? Second, I am of course aware that Nazi anti-Semitism and Christian anti-Judaism are not the same thing. But there is an overwhelming body of literature which demonstrates conclusively that Nazi anti-Semitism could never have wrought the horror it did without countless centuries of Christian anti-Judaism. *Satan* would ask whether people really thought that the Shoah was the shining culmination of Western Christian civilisation?

10   For instance, Joseph B. Soloveichik, one of the most revered Jewish thinkers of the twentieth century.

11   This is the reason why wine produced by gentiles is not regarded by some Jews as kosher.

12   Someone objected that the Saudis could not be guilty of anti-Semitism since they are themselves Semites. I think that is an obtuse point to make. One of my Muslim friends says that a decade ago there was little or no anti-Semitism or, if you prefer, anti-Judaism amongst Muslims. Today, he goes on, it is rife. All of the old libels have been taken on board – only a matter of days ago, there was an outburst of chanting and rioting and use of the blood libel in, of all places, San Francisco. The belief that September 11 could not have been perpetrated by Muslims, but must have been a Mossad plot, part of the international Israeli-Jewish conspiracy to discredit and destroy Islam, is, my Muslim friend tells me, widespread. Objection overruled!

13   A member of the audience told me that I was being unfair in singling out the Jewish fanatics by name – implying that they are only a handful of individuals – whilst implying that Muslim and Christian fanatics were too many to name. But somebody else told me that I was generalising. All I can say is that I wasn't trying to make light of Jewish culpability and *Satan's* imprecision was more to do with having a thirty-minute, not a thirty-day, trial than with my Jewish bias getting in the way.

14   What is being said here is that the very text of the Hebrew Bible is deeply uncomfortable for Muslims and quite understandably makes them feel excluded and set apart. Much of Jewish interpretation of this passage simply seeks to justify that which cannot and should not be justified.

15   The point was rightly made that the covenant with Noah is not part of Muslim tradition. However, *Satan* stands by his assertion that God has a covenantal relationship with all humanity and the Jewish relationship, the Christian relationship, and the Muslim relationship are all subsets, and do not imply either the superiority of one or the inferiority of the other.

16   One of the objections raised at this point was that not all fundamentalists are dangerous and not all are fanatics. Furthermore, we cannot be held responsible for the dangerous fanatics in our respective faith traditions. *Satan* would reply that all fundamentalists *as defined by him* are dangerous, or potentially dangerous. More importantly, he would be caustic in the extreme at the denial of responsibility. He would quote the Jews: "All Israel are sureties one for another." He would quote the Christians: "Never send to know for whom the bell tolls" (John Donne). He would quote the Muslims: " Whosoever of you sees an evil action, let him change it with his hand; and if he is not able to do so, then with his tongue; and if he is not able to do so, then with his heart – and that is the weakest of faith" (an-Nawawi, *Forty Hadith*, no. 34).

17   There are, I believe, some 200 000 settlers. However, many are there, not for ideological reasons (at least not their own), but for economic reasons, lured there by government subsidies and cheap housing. The figure of 15 000 or 20 000 refers to those who are there for ideological reasons. The overwhelming majority are not a real obstacle to peace since they would, presumably, readily accept rehousing, provided only that they did not lose out economically. It is the minority of fundamentalists, fanatics, and ideologues who hold both peoples to ransom as *Satan* asserts.

18   A well-known Hasidic aphorism.

19   Some people told me that the end of the lecture was hard to understand. I have re-read it. Provided that one realises that I have gone back to near the beginning, to the second passage from the Talmud, I hope that it is now clear. I do not think that rehearsing our respective cases and retelling history is actually going to yield very much. Our only salvation lies in asking where, and on the basis of which shared values, can we go constructively, together from here.

Chapter 13

Towards a Jewish Theology of Trilateral Dialogue[1]

Norman Solomon

Introduction

The construction of a Jewish theology of trilateral dialogue starts with an easy task but leads to a hard one. The easy one is to affirm some of the values and doctrines to be found within Christianity and Islam, and to create a "theological space" in which these other faiths may be allowed a positive role in the divine plan. This is a well-rehearsed theme in Jewish tradition, expounded within even the most conservative circles.

But when this little mountain has been climbed a big one looms behind it. The traditional assumption, undisputed in pre-modern times, was that Judaism constituted the only fully authentic expression of divine revelation, the comprehensive and absolute truth. Acknowledgment of the value and truth contained in other faiths was at best patronising, tied to the assumption that one day all would come to realise the superior truth of Torah. The traditional texts do not make for a "dialogue of equals".

I will take the soft option first, and describe traditional ways of "making theological space" for Christianity and Islam. After that, I shall explore the possibility that the dialogue might somehow become a dialogue of equals.

Traditional Ways of Making Space for the Other

The Hebrew Scriptures are contemptuously dismissive of the religious cults of the surrounding peoples and especially of the previous inhabitants of the land of Israel: "And you shall break down their altars, and dash in pieces their pillars, and burn their Asherim with fire; and you shall hew down the graven images of their gods; and you shall destroy their name out of that place" (Deuteronomy 12:3).

This attitude to "idol worship" has never changed. It continues to challenge Jews, Christians, and Muslims in their relationship with Hindus and others who direct their worship through images; indeed, Jews and Muslims are uncomfortable even with Christian use of images and icons in worship.

Nevertheless, by late biblical times Israelites realised that there were other people in the world who worshipped the one, unseen God. Such people form the category of *yir'ei Hashem* (God-fearers, *cf.* Psalm 115:11); perhaps it is to them that the verse "From the rising of the sun to its setting the name of the Lord is praised" (Psalm 113:3) refers.

By the third century CE, when the sages were defining Judaism and classifying the *mitzvot* (commandments), they accorded the status of *ger toshav* ("resident alien", cf. Leviticus 25) to individuals who, whilst not identifying themselves with the Jewish people by commitment to the Sinai Covenant, abandoned idolatry. This recognition was formalised as the Noahide Covenant, consisting of seven commandments (*sheva mitzvot*): Laws (that is, to establish courts of justice), (the prohibitions of) Idolatry, Blasphemy, Sexual Immorality, Bloodshed, Theft, and (cutting) the Limb from a Living Animal (certain types of cruelty to animals?).[2]

Tosefta, which is our earliest source for this "code", interprets each of these "commandments" in some detail, and the discussion is taken still further in the Talmud [3] and other rabbinic writings, where serious attempts are made to anchor the whole system in Scripture, particularly Genesis 9.[4]

Some scholars regard the Seven Commandments as a summary of natural law.[5] David Novak has argued that they constitute a "theological-juridical theory rather than a functioning body of laws administered by Jews for gentiles actually living under their suzerainty at any time in history"; they are presented by the rabbis as "pre-Sinaitic law perpetually binding on gentiles", and their precise formulation reflects "a period in Jewish history when the line of demarcation between Jews and gentiles was fully drawn, and when Jews were required to determine those moral standards which were inherently right" (Novak 1983: 34). This would have happened when the split between Judaism and Christianity was forcing strong lines of demarcation to be drawn.

Modern writers often state that the Seven Commandments include "belief in God"; this is careless representation of either the prohibition of idolatry or that of blasphemy. None of the extant early versions of the *sheva mitzvot* expressly demands belief in God. Why is this? Most probably because the rabbis were far more concerned with the rejection of idolatry than with formulating definitions of God. An explicit demand for belief in God would have required some understanding, some definition, of God, and this was precisely the area into which the rabbis did not wish to enter. They asked only that the worship of idols cease and the worship of God be taken seriously and treated with respect; there was to be no emphasis on the substantive content of belief in God. Precise descriptions of the nature of God did not matter, holiness of life did. In conformity with this view, the third-century Palestinian Rabbi Yohanan declared: "Whoever denies idolatry is called *yehudi* (a Jew)."[6] Novak is mistaken when he claims that Rabbi Isaac, who places the prohibition of idolatry first in his list, holds that "God's absolute authority over man is the beginning of the Noahide law and its foundation."[7] It is the rejection of idolatry, and the respect for God-talk and worship, not the recognition of a defined divine authority, which is the foundation of Noahide law as conceived by the rabbis.

Maimonides held that a gentile ought to adopt the Noahide laws not merely because they are rational but through acceptance of the fact that God had commanded them in Scripture.[8] He did not doubt that the human intellect, used with integrity, would lead one to belief in the authenticity of the biblical text and tradition, hence to the assumption that correct belief would accompany moral virtue.

On 26 October 1773 Moses Mendelssohn initiated a correspondence on this theme with Rabbi Jacob Emden of Altona (1697–1776):

> And to me these matters are difficult … that all the inhabitants of the earth from the rising to the setting of the sun are doomed, except us … unless they believe in the Torah which was given to us an inheritance to the congregation of Jacob alone, especially concerning a matter not at all explicit in the Torah … what will those nations do upon whom the light of the Torah has not shone at all?[9]

Mendelssohn, rather than Maimonides and Emden, has become the model for subsequent Jewish thinking, and writers such as David Hartman have readily adopted the Covenant with Noah as the "theological space" within which to accommodate people of other faiths, notwithstanding their rejection of Scripture or rabbinic interpretation.

Attempts have been made to implement the Noahide concept on a practical level. The Kabbalist rabbi Elia Benamozegh of Leghorn (1823–1900), for instance, persuaded a Catholic would-be convert to Judaism, Aimé Pallière, to adopt Noahism rather than full-blown Judaism. Pallière championed Noahism until the end of his life in 1949; he attracted interest rather than followers.[10] In the late twentieth century a number of Southern Baptists and others in the USA converted to a form of Noahism with some measure of Jewish encouragement; Aaron Lichtenstein observed that "the worst hardship borne by practising Noahites is the lack of fellowship."[11] An organisation of "B'nai Noah" with some thousands of followers is based at Athens, Tennessee, where its Emmanuel Study Centre publishes a bimonthly journal, *The Gap*.

Closer to the mainstream of Jewish religious activity is the impetus the *sheva mitzvot* concept gives to Jews to accept moral responsibility in society in general, for it demands that support and encouragement be given to "the nations" to uphold at least this standard. A notable instance of this was a series of public addresses and interventions by the Hassidic leader Menahem Mendel Schneersohn (the "Lubavitcher Rebbe") of New York (1902–94) in which he expounded the Noahide laws in relation to the needs of contemporary society. This included an exchange of letters with President Reagan in 1986, in which he commended the president for "giving valuable support to the dissemination of the Seven Noahide Laws, so basic to any society worthy of its name".[12]

Some generations before the formulation of the Noahide Laws, rabbis Joshua and Gamaliel II had debated whether unconverted gentiles "have a portion in the world to come"; subsequent Jewish tradition has endorsed Joshua's view that "the righteous of all nations have a share in the world to come."[13] This doctrine is a rabbinic assertion of the ability of every human being, even *unconverted*, to find favour in the eyes of God; Judaism does not have an equivalent to *extra ecclesiam non est salus* (there is no salvation outside the Church).[14] However, it leaves undefined what constitutes a "righteous" person; some rabbis would exclude from this category anyone who denied the authenticity of Scripture or of the rabbinic tradition of interpretation.

The reports of this debate between Joshua and Gamaliel do not use the term "saved", but the relatively cumbersome expression "have a portion in the world to come". Quite possibly this reflects a rejection of the perceived Christian presupposition that people are somehow "condemned" until "saved" by a special act of cosmic redemption which must be believed in to be efficacious.

Diogenes Laertius (second century CE) attributed to both Socrates and Thales the saying: "I thank Tyche that I was born a human being and not an animal, a man and not a woman, a Greek and not a barbarian."[15] This striking utterance rebounded across cultural barriers, modifying its meaning, and illuminating thereby the differences between the cultures.

Paul, for instance, had already said (Galatians 3:28): "There is no such thing as Jew and Greek, slave and freeman, male and female; for you are all one person in Christ Jesus." Scholars differ radically in their interpretations of Paul's words. Still, the context of "faith versus law" in which the remark is set means that it is and was popularly understood as meaning that faith, or belief (whether or not that means propositional belief) in Christ Jesus was that which saved – belief, not deeds. Belief, according to Paul, is the criterion of God's favour, and it is the line of demarcation between the issue of Abraham and other people.

A rabbinic variant runs: "I call to witness heaven and earth, that whether *goy* (gentile) or Jew, whether man or woman, whether manservant or maidservant, it is entirely according to the deeds of the individual that the heavenly spirit rests upon him."[16] This sentence cannot have been the model for Galatians 3:28, for none of its many versions is early enough. Rather, it is a comment, a reaction. The rabbis countered Paul (whether or not they were directly aware of his words) with the statement that "all is in accordance with the deeds of the individual" – a view firmly in accord with the prophet Ezekiel's stress on the concept of individual responsibility.[17]

Historical Development, *praeparatio evangelica*

Another way to accommodate Christianity and Islam within Jewish theology, to find "theological space" for them, is hinted at by Sa'adia Gaon (882–942),[18] and more fully developed by Judah Halevi (c. 1075–1141) and Moses Maimonides (1135/8–1204). Islam and Christianity are in error, but can be accommodated as part of the divine design to bring the nations gradually to God. The other monotheistic religions, says Halevi, "serve to introduce and pave the way for the expected Messiah, who is the fruition, and they will all become his fruit".[19]

In a paragraph censored from the printed editions of his *Mishneh Torah* Maimonides rejects the truth-claims of Christianity and Islam on the basis that they fail to meet the criterion of consistency with the Torah of Moses. Despite this, he assigns both Christianity and Islam a role in the process of world redemption:

> The teachings of him of Nazareth (Jesus) and of the man of Ishmael (Mohammed) who arose after him help to bring all mankind to perfection, so that they may serve God with one consent. For insofar as the whole world is full of talk of the Messiah, of words of Holy Writ and of the Commandments – these words have spread to the ends of the earth, even if many deny their binding character at the present time. When the Messiah comes all will return from their errors.[20]

Several medieval Jewish thinkers, unlike the rabbis of the Talmud, were familiar with Christian and Muslim texts, and offered comment, whether by way of defence or instruction. Sometimes this is found in the context of the forced "disputations" which elicited from Jews much keen apologetic.[21]

The Provençal rabbi Menahem ha-Meiri (d. *c.* 1315) coined the expression *umot hagedurot bedarkei hadatot* ("nations bound by the ways of religion") to avoid identification of Christians in his own time with pagan idolaters, and used this category to justify what was probably already a customary relaxation of certain rabbinic laws.[22] This enabled a positive evaluation if not of the doctrines, at least of the way of life, of Christians.

The acknowledgement that some truth may be found in other religions is as far as most were prepared to go in the "age of faith", when religions rested on their absolute truth-claims. The concept is common to Judaism, Christianity, and Islam. It seems to have arisen first in Christianity, when Christians attempted to explain their relationship with Judaism. Since Christianity sought to "prove" itself by claiming to "fulfil" the Hebrew Scriptures, it developed a hermeneutic of those scriptures as *praeparatio evangelica*, "preparation for the good news". That is, the Israelites and the Jews who succeeded them were "on the way", but had not completed the journey. Muhammad, the "seal of the prophets", accomplished the same sort of "completion" for Islam, leaving Judaism and Christianity as steps on the way to full Islam. It is hardly surprising to find that medieval Jewish thinkers adopted the same condescending attitude towards Christianity and Islam.

Authentic, but Culture-Bound, Prophecy

Was it not possible to move beyond "condescension" to an acknowledgment that authenticity might be found in the "other"? This is hardly what the Spanish Jewish poet and philosopher Solomon ibn Gabirol (*c.* 1020–58) had in mind when he penned the lines:

> Thy glory is not diminished by those worshipping others beside Thee,
> For they all but aim to come to Thee.[23]

For he continues:

> And all of them imagine they have attained their desire, but they have
> laboured in vain.
> Only Thy servants are discerning, and walk in the right way.

The further step was however taken by an admirer of Ibn Gabirol, the Jewish
neo-Platonist Netanel ibn Fayyumi (d. *c.* 1164), leader of the Jews of Yemen,
who adopted into a Jewish context ideas current amongst the Sufi brethren, the
Ikhwan as-Safa'. Netanel asserts the authenticity of the prophecy of
Muhammad, as revealed in the Qur'an, and at least the possibility that there
are additional authentic revelations (he does not mention Christianity).

Here are the steps by which Netanel establishes his contention that the
prophecy of Muhammad is authentic:

> The first creation of God was the Universal Intellect ... its exuberant joy
> and happiness caused an overflow, and thus there emanated from it the
> Universal Soul. (2, 94)[24]

> Through the necessity of His wisdom ... He mercifully vouchsafed unto
> mortals a revelation from the holy world – the world of the Universal Soul
> – which originated from the overflow of its holy cause, the Universal
> Intellect – which in turn goes back to its originator – may He be exalted!
> This ... expressed itself in an individual man whose spirit is free from the
> impurity of nature and is disciplined in the noblest science and the purest
> works ... [a] prophet. (95)

> Know then ... nothing prevents God from sending into His world
> whomsoever He wishes, since the world of holiness sends forth emanations
> unceasingly ... Even before the revelation of the Law he sent prophets to
> the nations ... and again after its revelation nothing prevented Him from
> sending to them whom He wishes so that the world might not remain
> without religion. (103–4)

> Mohammed was a prophet to them but not to those who preceded (sc. were
> prior to) them in the knowledge of God. (105)[25]

> He permitted to every people something He forbade to others. (107)

> He sends a prophet to every people according to their language. (109)[26]

Netanel interprets revelation in a "naturalistic" fashion. It is a universal
phenomenon, of which Muhammad is a specific instance. He parallels his
philosophical arguments with a skilful use of Jewish midrashic material.

Netanel's position differs radically from the *praeparatio* stance of
Maimonides and others. Maimonides, for all his acknowledgment of the
purity of Islamic monotheism and the historic function of Islam in preparing
for the Messiah, crudely refers to Muhammad as *ha-meshugga* (an impostor).
Netanel is neither casual nor tongue in cheek in his assessment of Muhammad;
his affirmation of Muhammad's prophetic authenticity is not an *ad hoc* or *ad
hominem* argument, but a key statement within an extensively elaborated
philosophical system which carries the social implication of respect for the heirs
of the prophets, these heirs being the "imams, administrators, the learned and
the wise".[27]

Netanel, unsurprisingly for a man of his time, maintains the absolute superiority of the revelation through Moses – superior because the Israelites were on a sufficiently high spiritual plane to receive it. What is nevertheless remarkable is his acceptance of plural revelations and of the culture-boundedness of revelation. In this, he is far more a philosopher for our time than was the celebrated Maimonides.

Away from Religious Absolutism and Essentialism

In 1973 the Viennese-born Reform rabbi and philosopher Ignaz Maybaum (1897–1976), by then long-resident in England, published a volume entitled *Trialogue between Jew, Christian and Muslim*. Maybaum, building on the work of his mentor Franz Rosenzweig, sees the tasks of Judaism, Christianity, and Islam as complementary. Christianity, in his view, develops the spiritual aspect of religion, Islam its political dimension; Judaism alone maintains the essential balance to correct the excesses of the other two. The characteristic forms taken by Christianity and Islam are not arbitrary, but fit them for their historic missions in the process of world redemption.

This simplistic account of the characters of the three religions is grossly misleading; each has occurred in a wide range of forms, spiritual, authoritarian, both or neither. Judaism, for instance, manifests itself both in extreme other-worldly guise, as amongst the twelfth-century Hasidei Ashkenaz, and in authoritarian guise, as amongst some of the contemporary Orthodox. Maybaum knows this full well, so dismisses such manifestations of Judaism as "not really Jewish", but intrusions of Christianity and Islam respectively; in his view, only liberal Judaism is truly Jewish. It is unclear what he thinks about the numerous forms of Christianity and Islam that do not correspond to his stereotypes. This stereotyping of religions, as that of such concepts as "Hebrew thought" and "Greek thought", must be categorically rejected. It is closely akin to the "essentialism" which, through racial or ethnic stereotyping, has wrought such grave damage in our societies. The historical reality is that there is not one "ideal" Judaism (or Christianity or Islam) out there, but a rich and varied tradition comprising many Judaisms.

Moreover, the Rosenzweig/Maybaum line does not escape the triumphalism and condescension inherent in the medieval theologies. This is perhaps most obvious when one considers Rosenzweig's oft-cited argument that Christians need Jesus as "son of God" to bring them "to the Father", whereas Jews do not need Jesus because they are already "with the Father"[28]. Why, after two thousand years of Christianity, should a difference remain, and why should Christians, many of whom come from families devoted to Christianity for centuries, find it necessary to convert to their religion with the aid of an approachable mediator, whereas Jews, even totally secular ones, are thought to have an easy familiarity with God from birth?

Rosenzweig's remark was probably apt at the time it was made; Jewish apologetics demanded such a rebuttal of persistent Christian attempts to belittle Judaism and convert Jews to Christianity. Moreover, this was an age of essentialism, when Harnack and Baeck could respectively dogmatise about exactly what a "true" Christian or Jew was,[29] selectively ignoring the realities of their respective communities. Rosenzweig was following Judah Halevi, whose poetry he loved and translated; Halevi maintained that the Jewish race as such had a distinctive spiritual quality. Such a doctrine may have passed in the eleventh century (Halevi himself had "transposed" it from the Muslim philosopher Al-Qassim's self-understanding as a Shi'ite), but is surely no longer acceptable at a time when the world has learned to reject racism.

Conclusion

The organisers of this symposium have spoken of a "narrative purpose which binds diverse essays and contributors together". I interpret this as the attempt to reformulate our religious traditions in terms of Enlightenment/(post-) modern understanding and to demonstrate their relevance to the contemporary situation. Those of us who are engaged in interfaith dialogue have discovered that this is a common enterprise, not specific to any one faith group. It is in this discovery that I find a way to articulate a theology of trilateral dialogue which maintains continuity with earlier strands in Jewish teaching, but does not make extravagant claims of truth or superiority on behalf of Judaism.

The underlying principles are as follows:

1   It is impossible, historically, to establish a single, "ideal", or "authentic" form of any religion. Traditions within each of the three religions are too diverse to permit this.
2   This diversity is not a fault, but a sign of the spiritual creativity of each faith, of its continuous "dialogue with God".
3   The diverse forms are expressions of faith occasioned by the diversity of human personalities and cultures.

Do these assumptions relativise religious faith unduly? Certainly, they demand that we abandon the absolutist claims of our predecessors. This demand does not arise primarily from within the interfaith dialogue itself, but from the critical impact of modernity, not least of historical studies, on all traditional expressions of religion.

Although diverse forms of expression of faith come about because of the diversity of human personalities and cultures, each individual is rooted to a particular time, place, and community. I, as an individual, find myself within a particular community and derive my sense of identity, my forms of expression, my strength, from that location. So far as I am concerned there is nothing "relative" about this; I am quite unambiguously located in a particular time, place, and community. I cannot "negotiate" my location; it is an objective fact. (This is not to deny that there might be circumstances in which I would decide to move.) I recognise that you, too, are unambiguously located in a time, place, and community. When we both accept this situation, we can engage in a dialogue without threatening or feeling threatened.

In the dialogue, there is mutual recognition that we are in different "places", without any one of those places being specially privileged. The beginning of dialogue is simply to disclose to ourselves and to each other what these places are. We must discover ourselves as individuals, not as representatives of religious establishments. In the dialogue:

1   There will be openness to the diversity within each tradition.
2   There will be discussion of relationships, including frank acknowledgement of past hurts, with the aim of fostering mutual trust.
3   There will be recognition of common problems arising from the confrontation with modernity. This will include not only the theological issues about God, revelation, redemption, and the like, but also social and political issues. When the problems are seen as shared, we can explore them together, drawing critically on the resources of all our traditions.

What I have outlined here is a truly creative dialogue. There is of course need for dialogue at less creative levels. There is dialogue amongst representatives of religious establishments; this can produce guidelines for better relationships. There is dialogue amongst unreformed fundamentalists; this is certainly better than harangue or violence directed at one another. And individuals who take part in either can move on to something better, for no one remains unchanged in dialogue.

Paul van Buren (1995) has spoken of Jews and Christians "travelling together". This metaphor, which must be extended at least to Muslims, aptly describes the adventure of dialogue.

Notes

1   This paper was given at the OJEC (The Council of Christians and Jews in the Netherlands) Conference, Amsterdam, 14 November 2000.
2   Tosefta *Avoda Zara* 9: 4. Some scholars have claimed to discover a hint of the *sheva mitzvot* in Acts 15: 29; this is far-fetched and anachronistic. The Tosefta is an early rabbinic supplement to and commentary on the Mishna, perhaps originating in the mid to late third century.
3   Babylonian Talmud, *Sanhedrin* 55b onwards.
4   See Novak (1983), chap. 1, and Novak (1989), chap. 1.
5   See Novak's interesting discussion (1983: 231 f.) of Samuel Atlas' suggestion that the distinction between the Noahide law of robbery and the Jewish law of robbery was the rabbis' way of making a conceptual distinction between natural and covenantal law. N. Rakover, "The 'Law' and the Noahides", *Jewish Law Association Studies* (Scholars Press: Atlanta, 1990), pp. 169–80, explores the differences between Noahide and Jewish law, and finds it helpful to understand Noahide law as "a sort of natural human law" (p. 172).
6   Babylonian Talmud, *Megilla* 13a.
7   Novak (1983: 108), referring to Babylonian Talmud *Sanhedrin* 56b.
8   Maimonides, *Mishneh Torah Hilkhot Melakhim*, 8: 11. For a full discussion, see Novak 1983: chap. 10.

9 Moses Mendelssohn *Gesammelte Schriften* XVI, pp. 178–80. I have used Novak's translation (1983: 370).

10 E. Benamozegh, *Morale juive et morale chrétienne* (1867). Benamozegh's magnum opus first appeared in Paris in 1914 under the title *Israël et l'humanité* and a new and revised edition was published by Albin Michel, Paris, in 1961. Marco Morselli's Italian translation, *Israele e l'umanità*, was published by Casa Editrice Marietti, Genoa, in 1990. Pallière's main work is *Le Sanctuaire Inconnu*; the most recent English version is *The Unknown Sanctuary*, trans. L. W. Wise (New York, 1985).

11 See Aaron Lichtenstein's "Who Cares About The Seven Laws Of Noah? A Status Report", *Jewish Law Association Studies* IV (Atlanta, GA: Scholars Press, 1990), pp. 181–90. See also Lichtenstein's own book *The Seven Laws of Noah*, 2nd edn (New York: Rabbi Jacob Joseph School Press, 1986).

12 It would be useful to have a bibliography of Lubavitch writings on the Noahide Laws. There are numerous pamphlets and addresses, and even a "moral video" directed to non-Jews. *An Abbreviated Code of Jewish Law for non-Jews* is also said to be in preparation. In fact, compilations of this sort already exist, for instance the Joel Schwartz' Hebrew *OR LE'AMIM* Devar Yerushalayim (Jerusalem, 1984), and Solomon Schonfeld's *The Universal Bible* (London, 1955).

13 Babylonian Talmud, *Sanhedrin* 13.

14 Augustine *De Bapt.* iv, c, xcii, 24. Cf Cyprian's earlier *habere non potest Deum patrem qui ecclesiam non habet matrem* in *De Cath. Eccl. Unitate*, vi.

15 Diogenes Laertius 1:33. See Martin Hengel, *Jews, Greeks and Barbarians* (London: SCM Press, 1980), p. 78 and chapter 7, for an exploration of the idea of racial superiority in the Hellenistic world.

16 The version I have translated is that in *Yalkut Shimoni* on Judges 5. See also Tosefta *Berakhot* 7: 18; Jerusalem Talmud *Berakhot* 9: 2; Babylonian Talmud *Menahot* 43b.

17 Ezekiel 18. See P. Joyce, *Divine Initiative and Human Response in Ezekiel*, Supplement Series 51 of the *Journal for the Study of the Old Testament* (Sheffield, 1989).

18 Sa'adia ben Joseph, *Kitab fi al-Amanat wa-al-I'tiqadat* (Arabic), vol. 2, chap. 5. Rosenblatt's translation has been republished as Samuel Rosenblatt (trans.), *The Book of Beliefs and Opinions* (New Haven, CT, and London: Yale University Press, 1989). Sa'adia is of course highly critical of Christological doctrine, but this does not blind him to the positive aspects of Christianity.

19 Judah Halevi, *The Kuzari*, trans. Hartwig Hirschfeld, 2nd edn (New York: Schocken Books, 1964).

20 Maimonides, *Mishné Torah Melakhim* 11.

21 See Hyam Maccoby (ed. and trans.), *Judaism on Trial: Jewish–Christian Disputations in the Middle Ages* (London: Associated University Presses, 1982; republished, Oxford: Littman Library, 1992). Samuel Krauss, ed. William Horbury, *A Handbook to the History of Christian-Jewish Controversy from the Earliest Times to 1789* (Tübingen: Mohr, 1996). Daniel Lasker, *Jewish Philosophical Polemics against Christianity in the Middle Ages* (New York: Ktav/Anti-Defamation League of B'nai B'rith, 1977).

22 Meiri's views are expressed in his talmudic commentaries, especially that on *Avoda Zara*. For an English language account and discussion, see Katz, op. cit., chapter 10.

23   Solomon Ibn Gabirol, *Keter Malkhut* #8. Translated by Israel Zangwill, in Israel Zangwill, *Selected Religious Poems of Solomon Ibn Gabirol* (Philadelphia, PA: Jewish Publication Society of America, 1923), 85/6.

24   References here are to Ibn Fayyumi 1907. The best edition of the Judeo-Arabic text, with a Hebrew translation and notes, is Y. Kafih's second version, *Bustan el-Uqul: Gan ha-Sekhalim* (Jerusalem: Halikhot Am Israel, 5744/1984).

25   Ibn Fayyumi assumes that older equals better.

26   Cf. Qur'an, Surah 14:4.

27   Ibn Fayyumi 1907: 51; Arabic text, op. cit., p. 31.

28   Franz Rosenzweig, *The Star of Redemption*, 2nd German edition (1930), trans. William Hallo (Notre Dame, WI, and London: University of Notre Dame, 1970), Part 3, Book 2, pp. 350 and 396, and Maybaum's comments, p. 86 f.

29   Adolf von Harnack's original lectures *Das Wesen des Christentums* were given in Berlin in 1899–1900 and Leo Baeck's response, *Das Wesen des Judentums* (The Essence of Judaism), was published in 1905.

Chapter 14

Christians and People of Other Faiths

Marcus Braybrooke

Introduction

Recent events have highlighted the importance of interfaith dialogue. We have to get to know each other and learn to respect one another's beliefs and religious practices if we are to live together in one society and as a world community.

On 11 September 2001 – that fateful day – a young Muslim from Pakistan was evacuated from the World Trade Centre where he worked. He saw a dark cloud coming towards him. Trying to escape, he fell. A Hasidic Jew held out his hand, saying, "Brother, there's a cloud of glass coming at us, grab my hand, let's get the heck out of here."

People of all faiths have held hands to support and comfort each other and to join together in prayer. We need to continue to hold hands as we shape a more just and peaceful society.

I do not, however, want to concentrate on the practical contribution that interfaith dialogue and cooperation can make to peace and social justice, which I have discussed elsewhere (Braybrooke 1992 and 1998), but to suggest that we also need to move beyond tolerance and understanding to a recognition that each faith has a precious gift to share with the world. We not only need to understand other people's beliefs and practices; we can also, while remaining true to our own faith commitment, learn from others. We should see religious diversity as an enrichment, not a problem.

Some time ago, Rabbi Dr Shaye J. D. Cohen, speaking to Christians and Jews said: "It is not enough simply to believe in tolerance, not enough simply to allow the other's existence. What we need is a theology on each side to validate the other's existence" (1997: 326). In recent years a growing number of Christians have come to recognise the spiritual riches of other faiths and to abandon old exclusive attitudes. This is very much a process in operation so there are few agreed conclusions and much variety of emphasis among Christians of different churches and traditions.

This rethinking has involved looking again at what the Bible says and taking a fresh look at some Christian doctrines. Inevitably, the rethinking is conditioned by what has gone before, so it is necessary first to consider the assumptions of the majority of Catholic and Protestant Christians in Western Europe in the late nineteenth and early twentieth century – many of whom hoped that the world would be won for Christ in a generation. These assumptions, which the influential Methodist thinker Kenneth Cracknell calls the "inherited entail", were so pervasive, that it is necessary to acknowledge them and then to see why they are unsatisfactory before trying to develop a new perspective.

The Inherited Entail

First, Cracknell mentions the *theological exclusiveness* of the Church, which has a long history. Some would trace it back to the New Testament and sayings, such as "No one comes to the Father but through me" (John 14:6), or:

> This Jesus is the stone rejected by the builders, which has become the keystone – and you are the builders. There is no salvation in anyone else at all, for there is no other name under heaven granted to men by which we may receive salvation. (Acts 4:11–12 NEB)

This exclusiveness is also enshrined in Church statements. From a decree of the Council of Florence (1438–45):

> The Holy Roman Church firmly believes, professes and proclaims that none of those who are outside the Catholic church – not only pagans, but Jews also, heretics, and schismatics – can have part in eternal life, but will go into eternal fire, "which was prepared for the devil and his angels", unless they are gathered into that Church before the end of life.[1]

More recently, it was said at the Congress on World Mission, held in Chicago in 1960, that "in the years since the war, more than one billion souls have passed into eternity and more than half of these went to the torment of hell fire without even hearing of Jesus Christ, who he was, or why he died on the cross of Calvary."[2]

Second, Cracknell recalls the *missionary background*. He quotes from the *Form of Agreement,* drawn up by the Serampore missionaries, Carey, Marshman, and Ward, on 5 October 1805:

> But while we mourn over their miserable condition [that is, of the "poor idolaters" among whom they were working], we should not be discouraged as though their recovery were impossible. He who raised the Scottish and brutalised Britons to sit in heavenly places in Christ Jesus, can raise these slaves of superstition, purify their hearts by faith, and make them worshippers of the one God in spirit and in truth. The promises are fully sufficient to remove our doubts, and to make us anticipate that not very distant period when he will famish all the gods of India, and cause those very idolaters to cast their idols to the moles and bats, and renounce for ever the work of their own hands. (Cracknell 1986: 18–19)

As Cracknell says, and has himself shown in his fine study *Justice, Courtesy and Love: Theologians and Missionaries Encountering World Religions, 1846– 1914,* some missionaries took a more sympathetic attitude to the religions which they encountered. We should also beware of judging previous generations by our own standards, nor overlook the heroism of many missionaries and the contribution that many of them made to Asian and African societies. Cracknell's point, however, is that the missionaries and their many supporters were "programmed to see the darkest and basest side of the religions and cultures among which they ministered" (1995: 20).

Third, Cracknell draws attention to the *cultural assumptions of imperialism.* Hardly anyone in Europe or North America had any doubt about the cultural superiority of Western civilisation. As Thomas Babington Macaulay, who was the Law member of the Governor General of India's Executive Council, wrote in what is known as "Macaulay's Minute", "A single shelf of a good European library was worth the whole native literature of India and Arabia" (Cracknell 1995: 22). Western civilisation was also perceived as "Christian" civilisation. In 1828, for example, William Huskisson told the House of Commons: "In every quarter of the globe we have planted the seeds of freedom, civilisation, and Christianity." The converse of this arrogance was "the belittling of everything that was strange as alien and exotic, childish, and laughable, belonging to the infancy of the human race" (ibid., 23).

Christians today may not be brought up with this "entail"! But it has coloured the debate in recent years because many of the thinkers who have struggled for a new relationship have had to free themselves from this inheritance.

Questioning Traditional Teaching

In the twentieth century a growing number of Christians questioned the dominant view that only those who believe in Jesus, or are members of the Church, can be "saved and go to heaven". They did so for a variety of reasons:

1 The biblical material is ambiguous. Commonly quoted verses, such as John 14:6, or Acts 4:12, to which we will return, need to be read in context and balanced by other passages of Scripture. The Hebrew prophet Malachi (1:11) said: "From furthest East to furthest West my name is great among the nations. Everywhere fragrant sacrifice and pure gifts are offered in my name." Jesus is reported as saying that gentiles will share in the kingdom of God, and in the parable of the sheep and the goats, people are judged by how they behave (Matthew 25:31).

2 The Christian tradition is not monochrome. The second-century Christian apologist Justin Martyr hoped to meet Plato in heaven. On the walls of some Orthodox monasteries one can see paintings of Plato and Aristotle alongside Isaiah and Jeremiah. In the Middle Ages, Nicholas of Cusa, who was a mathematician and an influential philosopher as well as a cardinal, suggested that behind all religious differences, there was one universal religion – even if it did include belief in the Trinity and the Mass!

In the seventeenth century, Robert de Nobili, an Italian Jesuit of a good family, who settled in Madurai in South India, started to wear the orange robe of a *sannyasi*. When he taught the Christian faith in South India, he said, "The law which I preach is the law of the true God, which from ancient times was by his command proclaimed in these countries by *sannyasis* and saints."[3]

3 The belief that millions who have never heard the gospel are condemned to eternal damnation is to many Christians incompatible with a belief in a God of Love. John Hick has written, "Can we then accept the conclusion that the God of love who seeks to save all people has nevertheless ordained that men and women must be saved in such a way that only a small minority can in fact receive this salvation?" (1973: 122).

4 Personal contact with people of other faiths has led Christians to acknowledge the goodness and holiness of many people who are not Christian. Sir Francis Younghusband, who founded the World Congress of Faiths, said in a radio talk:

> I have come into the most intimate contact with adherents of all the great religions, Hindus, Muslims, Buddhists and Confucians. I have been dependent upon them for my life. I have had deep converse with them on their religions ... It has forced me down to the essentials of my own Christianity and made me see a beauty there I had not known till then. It also forced me to see a beauty in the depths of their religion. (Braybrooke 1996: 19)

5 Some Christians have found beauty and inspiration in the scriptures of other religions, and there are many anthologies that bring together readings and prayers from the great faiths.[4] Indeed, some Christians in India include readings from the Buddhist and Hindu scriptures in their own worship.

6 Critical scholarship has questioned whether all the sayings of Jesus, especially in John's gospel, are the actual words of Jesus. Traditional understanding of the Christological claims of the New Testament and of the Church have also been questioned by some contemporary theologians.[5]

7 The practical need to combat racism and prejudice, and to create more harmonious societies and a more peaceful world, has also been an important incentive for seeking cooperation with people of other faiths. Paul Knitter has written that "concern for the widespread suffering that grips humanity and threatens the planet can and must be the 'common cause' for all religions" (1995: 21).[6]

For these and other reasons, there is now a vigorous debate in the Churches about the appropriate attitude that Christians should adopt towards people of other faiths.

Different Christian Attitudes to Other Faiths

The views of Christians on the relation of Christianity to other faiths are, following Alan Race, sometimes categorised as "exclusive", "inclusive", and "pluralist". It is recognised that these are very broad terms and that it is hard to pigeonhole particular scholars. Even so, the terms are quite useful and reference is often made to them.[7]

The *exclusive* view is that the Gospel is the only source of authentic knowledge of God. Jesus is the only Saviour. The uniqueness of Jesus Christ is affirmed and salvation is only available through his atoning death. Karl Barth and Emil Brunner are well-known exponents of this position as well as the influential missionary theologian Hendrik Kraemer who wrote: "If we are ever to know what true and divinely willed religion is, we can do this only through God's revelation in Jesus Christ and nothing else" (Race 1983: 23).

Inclusivism is the view that there is some knowledge of God outside the Christian church, although God's "supreme" or "final" revelation is in Jesus Christ. There is also the hope that good people who are not Christian will be "saved" by God, despite their lack of Christian faith. The second-century apologist Justin Martyr, whom we have already mentioned, wrote:

> It is our belief that those men who strive to do the good which is enjoined on us have a share in God; according to our traditional belief they will by God's grace share his dwelling. And it is our conviction that this holds good in principle for all men ... Christ is the divine Word in whom the whole human race share, and those who live according to the light of their knowledge are Christians, even if they are considered as being godless.[8]

A rather similar position is adopted by many Christians today, as, for example, by the contemporary Jesuit scholar Fr Jacques Dupuis, who says, "Salvation is at work everywhere, but in the concrete figure of the crucified Christ the work of salvation is seen to be accomplished" (1997: 328).

Pluralism is the view that no one religion can claim a monopoly on divine revelation. All religions point to the Divine mystery who or which is the source of all religious life. For example, the historian Arnold Toynbee wrote:

> I think that it is possible for us, while holding that our own convictions are true and right, to recognise that, in some measure, all the higher religions are also revelations of what is true and right. They also come from God, and each presents some facet of God's truth. (1957: 111)

Alan Race includes in this group William Hocking, an American philosopher, Ernest Troeltsch, a German theologian, and John Hick, a British philosopher and theologian, whose writings have been especially influential. Hick, in his *God and the Universe of Faiths,* called for a Copernican revolution in theology, involving a shift from the "dogma that Christianity is at the centre to the realisation that it is *God* who is at the centre, and that all religions of mankind, including our own, serve and revolve around him" (1973: 131). Hick's views are partly based on the mystical awareness that the Ultimate exceeds all our thoughts and speculation. Religions point beyond themselves to the Divine Mystery. He also produces philosophical arguments suggesting that the varying personal and non-personal forms in which God is known are "all alike divine phenomena formed by the impact of God upon the plurality of human consciousness" (cited in Race 1983: 37).

Interpretation of Scripture

These varying approaches are reflected in the way Scripture is interpreted, and it is worth giving more attention to some of the verses already mentioned to show that the "exclusive" attitude is not necessarily that of Scripture.

The Prologue to St John's Gospel, which affirms the incarnation of the Word in Jesus Christ, may also be understood to link the incarnation to the universal self-revelation of God. Because this view is unfamiliar, it is worth quoting a number of writers who make this connection, for example, Archbishop William Temple, who wrote:

> By the Word of God – that is to say by Jesus Christ – Isaiah and Plato and Zoroaster and Buddha and Confucius conceived and uttered such truths as they declared. There is only one divine light; and every man in his measure is enlightened by it.[9]

John Hick writes:

> The different religions have their different names for God acting savingly towards humankind ... If selecting from our Christian language, we call God-acting-towards-humankind the Logos, then we must say that *all* salvation, within all religions, is the work of the Logos, and that under their various images and symbols men and women in different cultures may encounter the Logos and find salvation ... The life of Jesus was one point at which the Logos – that is God-in-relation-to-man – has acted; and it is the only point that savingly concerns the Christian; but we are not called upon, nor are we entitled, to make the negative assertion that the Logos has not acted and is not acting anywhere else in human life. (1980: 75)

Raimundo Panikkar, a Christian who has a deep knowledge of Hinduism, takes a similar position:

> The Christ the Christian comes to proclaim is Christ *present, active, unknown,* and *hidden within Hinduism.* The same Christ who lives and acts in the Hindu is the one whom the Christian recognises as Jesus of Nazareth. This Christ present, active, unknown and hidden may be called "Iswara", "Bhagavan", or even "Krishna", "Narayana", or "Siva".[10]

Kenneth Cracknell himself adds a reminder that religion is deeply ambiguous and can mask as well as reveal the light. He then suggests that:

> If it is truly the case that all human beings are created in and through the eternal Word, the *Logos,* we can hardly suppose that it can be the view of the author of the Fourth Gospel that because the Word has become flesh and lived among us, that

primary relationship has come to an end. On the contrary, the argument must surely be "how much more" are all human beings likely to be related to God through the one who is now risen and ascended. (1986: 107)

These views may find support in John 1:9. This says that the light, which is the Word of God "was in being, light absolute, enlightening every man born into the world". At least that is the marginal reading in the New English Bible and agrees with the translation of the King James Authorised Version of the Bible. It suggests that the Light of God is eternally present, enlightening every person who is ever born. As the nineteenth-century Anglican scholar Bishop Westcott wrote,

> The words must be taken simply as they stand. No man is wholly destitute of the illumination of "the Light". In nature, and life, and conscience it makes itself felt in various degrees to all. The Word is the spiritual Sun ... This truth is recognised here by St John, but he does not (like Philo) dwell upon it. Before the fact of the incarnation it falls into the background.[11]

The same words can, however, be translated, as they are in the main text of the New English Bible, "The real light which enlightens every man was even then coming into the world", which applies the words specifically to the incarnation. This, argues the New Testament scholar C. K. Barrett, is the meaning, and the verse should not be used to support belief in a universal revelation:

> When the prologue is interpreted in terms of Hellenistic religion, and the Logos (word) thought of in Stoic manner, it is natural to see in the present verse a reference to a general illumination of all men [*sic*] by the divine Reason, which was subsequently deepened by the more complete manifestation of the Logos in the incarnation ... Whether John's words do in fact bear this meaning is open to doubt. In the next verse he emphasises that "the world did not recognise him" – there was no natural and universal knowledge of the light. It was those who received Christ who received authority to become children of God. In the rest of the gospel the function of light is judgement; when it shines some come to it, others do not. It is not true that all men have a natural affinity with the light.[12]

The question is at what point does John start to speak of the incarnation – at verse 9 or earlier? The Greek allows for both translations and interpretations. Even John 14:6, in which Jesus claims to be the "Way, the Truth and the Life" may not be so exclusive as it is usually understood. The Dutch Catholic theologian Arnulf Camps writes:

> Religions are not first and foremost institutionalised systems but Ways. Aren't the Old and New Testaments full of talk about the Way of the Lord? Weren't the first Christians called followers of the Way? (Acts 9:2). Doesn't the first Sura of the Koran talk about the straight Way? Doesn't Hinduism know three Ways to salvation? Doesn't Buddhism talk about the Eightfold Path? Here it seems to me, we have a good starting-point for dialogue. (1983: 84)

The term "way" was also common not only in the Judaism of the first century, but in Stoicism, Platonism, Hermetic, and Mandean literature, as well as in Gnostic dualism. Cracknell suggests that for those who are Christian theologians "other religious traditions are counterparts to Christianity" (1986: 79). They set their followers ideals and encourage them in moments of crisis. They claim to relate to the "way" of the universe – the cosmic order in which individuals are to find their own ways. Yet, Cracknell continues, "The Christian community believed then, as it must still do, that this Way of God has been most clearly discerned in the way that Jesus followed – the path of rejection and suffering, of abandonment and death" (1986: 85).

Another verse often quoted to support an exclusive view is Acts 4:12: "Salvation is found in no one else, for there is no other name under heaven given to men by which we must be saved." The verse is the climax of the narrative in chapters 3 and 4, which begins with a healing miracle. Peter has said to the man who was lame from birth, "in the name of Jesus Christ, walk" (Acts 3:6). Peter then explains to the people: "It is Jesus' name and the faith that comes through him that has given this complete healing to him, as you can see" (3:16). Peter's address to the people alarmed the religious leaders. He was taken before the high priest and asked: "By what power or what name did you do this?" Peter answered that the healing was by "the name of Jesus Christ of Nazareth". The word translated here as "salvation" could also be translated "healing", and of course the two are closely linked. Yet, if Peter's answer is translated: "There is no healing in any one else at all ... there is no other name ... by which we must be healed", it relates more closely to the context of a miracle of healing.

There must also be doubt whether Peter would so early make such a staggering claim for the unique salvific role of Jesus. It seems a statement of Lucan theology. Further, as Kenneth Cracknell says, even if Jesus is the name through whom the Christian experiences salvation, "this does not preclude the possibility that the grace and love which Jesus represents for us might be found under the names of the other religious traditions" (1986: 10).

It is clear that those Christians who reject an exclusive interpretation of John 14:6 and Acts 4:12 in no way wish to minimise the Christian claim that the revelation and saving power of God is experienced in Jesus Christ, but they are open to the possibility that a knowledge of God's saving love may also be experienced in other communities of faith.

Balancing Particularity and Universality

This leads to the wider discussion of how to do justice both to the particularity of religions and to what they have in common, and, for the Christian, of how to hold together belief in the unique revelation of God in Jesus Christ and affirmation of God's universal activity and care for all people.

At the 1893 World Parliament of Religions, which was held in Chicago, Swami Vivekananda, one of the Hindu participants said, "We accept all religions as true" (Barrows 1893: II, 977). In this, Vivekananda was echoing the teaching of his master Sri Ramakrishna, who claimed to have reached the same mystical experience of unity with the Divine by following various spiritual paths. From this, Ramakrishna argued that the differences between religions were merely a matter of the language and the cultural conditioning of different mystics. Ramakrishna's claims have occasioned wide discussion about the nature of mystical experience. Walter Stace, in his *The Teachings of the Mystics*, supported Ramakrishna's claim: "The same mystical experience may be interpreted by a Christian in terms of Christian beliefs and by a Buddhist in terms of Buddhist beliefs."[13] The Indian philosopher Sarvepalli Radhakrishnan also said, "The seers describe their experiences with an impressive unanimity. They are near to one another on mountains farthest apart."[14]

This view, however, has been disputed. R. C. Zaehner, who was Spalding Professor of Eastern Religions and Ethics at Oxford, argued, in his *Mysticism, Sacred and Profane,* that there are different types of mystical experience. My own feeling, as I have suggested elsewhere, is that there are differences of mystical experience, but, unlike Zaehner, I hesitate to assert that the theistic experience is higher than the monistic experience.[15]

Vivekananda's words at the 1893 World Parliament of Religions were a particular challenge to Christianity. The nineteenth century was the great age of Christian mission – especially by Protestant churches – in Asia and Africa. Christian triumphalism, with its claim to the unique and final revelation of God, was also evident amongst many in Chicago. In place of such aggressive Christian evangelism, Vivekananda seized the moral high ground by implying that the missionaries' call for conversions was irrelevant and narrow-minded. Instead Vivekananda appealed for universal tolerance. In his reply to the welcome, part of which has already been quoted, he declared:

> I am proud to belong to a religion which has taught the world both tolerance and universal acceptance. We believe not only in universal toleration, but we accept all religions as true. I am proud to belong to a nation which has sheltered the persecuted and the refugees of all religions and all nations of the earth. (Barrows 1893: II, 102)

The importance of mutual respect between members of different religions is now widely recognised. Yet the relation of religions to each other is still a subject of vigorous debate. At least at the level of their teachings and practices there are significant differences between religions. For example, some religions claim that human beings have only one life on earth, others suggest that the soul comes back again and again in different bodies. There is sharp disagreement on whether God has a Son. Religious rituals are very varied. Is there a common or unifying spiritual experience? Can we indeed speak of universal human experiences?

My own view is that there is one God who made and loves all people and seeks from them an answering love and obedience. The great religions of the world are channels of that divine love and human responses to it. Because they are human responses, all are flawed. I do not think religions are all the same. Rather they are shaped by a creative experience of the Divine and by centuries of tradition and reflection. Each religion, as the American Catholic Robert Edward Whitson put it, is therefore "unique and universal: unique in that the core of each is a distinct central experience – not to be found elsewhere – and universal in that this core experience is of supreme significance for all men" (1963: 97). Each religion has a particular message or "gospel" for the whole world. As we learn from each other, our understanding of the Divine Mystery will grow. There are, in my view, more and less adequate pictures of God and understandings of the divine purpose. For example, traditional Christian teaching about hell – especially as a punishment for non-believers who never heard of Jesus – cannot be squared with belief in a God who loves all human beings.

Fr Bede Griffiths, a Catholic priest who explored the meeting of Christianity and Hinduism at his ashram in South India, expressed a similar approach when he wrote:

> The Buddha, Krishna, Christ – each is a unique revelation of God, of the divine Mystery, and each has to be understood in its historical context, in its own peculiar mode of thought ... each revelation is therefore complementary to the other, and indeed in each religion we find a tendency to stress first one aspect of the Godhead and then another, always seeking that equilibrium in which the ultimate truth will be found. (1976: 86–7)

Yet his views may seem inadequate to many Christians who believe that Jesus is the unique and only Son of God and Saviour of the world. The New Testament claim is that the Word of God was incarnate in Jesus Christ, and that in him, God is made known. The experience of faith is to have been met by the grace and love of God in Jesus Christ. The question is whether that experience is only in Jesus. A number of Christian thinkers acknowledge that members of other faiths may have a similar experience of divine grace and forgiveness, but some, like Karl Rahner, will claim that it is in fact an experience of Christ, although he is not known by name. Cardinal Arinze, who is President of the Pontifical Council for Interreligious Dialogue, affirms: "all human beings are included in the great and unique design of God in Jesus Christ, even when they are not aware of it."[16] That is to say there is one saving act – the death of Christ – for all people, but there are those who benefit from it without conscious faith in Jesus Christ.

Cardinal Francis Arinze's remarks raise questions about how Christians understand the work of Christ, often known as the Atonement. A traditional belief is that Jesus Christ died on the cross for the sins of the whole world. If that is thought of as an objective event, which altered humanity's standing in relation to God, then the belief itself implies that it is significant for all people. An alternative understanding of the meaning of the death of Jesus is to think of it in a more personal and subjective way. By his willingness to die on the cross, Jesus showed that there is no limit to God's love for us. To believe this is to experience an inner change that frees the believer from fear and by deepening his or her compassion makes the believer sorry for his or her selfishness and lack of love. In gratitude the believer makes a self-offering to the service of the Lord.

For myself, the story of Jesus' death on the cross is the place where I have known most vividly the unlimited love and forgiveness of God, which has helped to free me from self-doubt and fear and has enabled me to grow in love for others. I am glad to witness to this divine mercy and long for others to experience such forgiveness and peace for themselves. I do not, however, feel the need to pass judgement on the spiritual journey and experience of others. The interfaith sharing for which I long, of which there is still too little, is to speak to each other of our experience of the grace of God – "telling one another our beautiful names for God." As the blind man in St John's Gospel says, "One thing I know, that whereas I was blind *now* I see" (9:25). If others can say the same, then we should rejoice together and learn from each other's story.

Some Christians, especially in the Orthodox Churches, have tried to balance the particular work of Christ and the universal love of God by emphasising the role of the Holy Spirit. His Beatitude Archbishop Anastasios of Tirana in a striking passage, wrote:

> "Present everywhere and filling all things", in the words of the prayer preceding almost all Orthodox services, the Holy Spirit continues to act for the sanctification of all persons and the fulfilment and completion of the salvation of the whole world: as the Spirit of holiness transferring the breath, love, and power of the trinitarian God to human existence and the universe: as the Spirit of power, dynamically renewing the atmosphere in which human beings live and breathe (it is the Holy Spirit who burns up whatever is rotten – concepts, ideas, institutions, customs, demonic structures – and offers new energy for the transforming and renewing of all things in creation); as the Spirit of truth, working and inspiring human beings in their longing and search for truth in any religious setting, every aspect of truth, including scientific, related to human life (this revelation of truth culminates in the decisive knowledge of the mystery of Christ who is the truth *par excellence* and it is the Spirit who reveals Christ); as the Spirit of peace calming the hearts and helping to create new relationships among human beings, bringing understanding and reconciliation to the whole of humankind; as the Spirit of justice giving inspiration and power for people to long and struggle for peace.[17]

Seeing the Other as a Fellow Pilgrim

We should learn to see members of other faiths as fellow pilgrims. There are all too many people in our world who have little awareness of spiritual realities, and religious communities have a responsibility to make known their teachings. It is entirely proper to witness to one's experience of divine mercy. There is nothing to apologise for mission if it is such witness. It is natural to tell others of good discoveries we have made. If, however, mission becomes religious recruiting or proselytism, it fails to reflect God's own respect for human freedom and it is likely to be resented and to become divisive. People should, however, be free to change their religion if they feel this will help their spiritual growth, although those who change their religion, or who wish to marry a member of another faith community, often experience strong opposition and rejection.

When there is so much conflict in the world, often inflamed by religious differences, theological discussion may seem rather remote. But the more practical work of trying to remove prejudice and build up understanding, as well as encouraging communal harmony and cooperation will, in the long run, only be successful if we change the image of the other, so that we no longer see them as "heathen" or "unsaved" or "non-Christians", but as fellow pilgrims and children of the One God.

A common liturgical response at Christian services is "Lord, have mercy upon us". Who do we mean by us? Members of the same congregation, members of the same denomination, all Christians, or all humanity? If we mean anything less than all people, our compassion fails to reflect the love and mercy of God "Who makes his sun rise on good and bad alike, and sends the rain on the honest and the dishonest" (Matthew 5:45).

Notes

1 Quoted in Cracknell 1986: 9.
2 Quoted in John Hick 1973: 121.
3 Quoted by Stephen Neil, *A History of Christian Missions* (Harmondsworth: Penguin Books, 1964), p. 185.
4 See, for example, *World Scripture,* ed. Andrew Wilson (St Paul, MN: Paragon House, 1991); *Universal Wisdom,* ed. Bede Griffiths (San Francisco, CA: HarperCollins, 1994); *Bridge of Stars,* ed. Marcus Braybrooke (London: Duncan Baird, 2001).
5 I discuss these issues more fully in my *Time to Meet* (1990), pp. 84–90.
6 See also the writings of Hans Küng.
7 See Race 1983 (rev. edn, 1993), and Race 2001.
8 Justin Martyr, *Apology* 46, 1–4.
9 William Temple, *Readings in St John's Gospel* (London: St Martin's Library Edition, Macmillan, 1961), p. 9.
10 Author's italics, article in *New Blackfriars*, 1969. See also E. H. Cousins, *Christ of the 21st century* (Shaftesbury: Element, 1992), pp. 73–104.
11 B. F. Westcott, *The Gospel According to St John* (Edinburgh: John Murray, 1908), pp. 13–14.
12 *The Gospel According to St John* (London: SPCK, 196), p. 134.
13 Walter Stace, *The Teachings of the Mystics* (New York: New American Library, 1960), p. 12.
14 S. Radhakrishnan, "Fragments of a Confession" in *The Philosophy of Sarvepalli Radhakrishnan*, ed. Paul Arthur Schilpp (New York: Tudor Publishing, 1992), p. 62.
15 See further my *Spiritual Experience That Crosses Religious Divisions,* 2nd series Occasional Paper 20 (Oxford: Religious Experience Research Centre, 1999), *passim.*
16 "The Christian Commitment to Interreligious Dialogue", *L'Osservatore Romano,* 17 July 1989, para 3 and para 9.
17 *Current Dialogue*, WCC, n. 26 (June 1994), p. 46.

Chapter 15

Mystery and Plural Faiths: Religious Diversity as Expression of the Quest for a *Deus Absconditus*

Frank Julian Gelli

Deity, Diversity, and Mystery

The existence on planet Earth of a plurality of faiths and religious beliefs, many apparently irreconcilable with each other, is a fact. The matter of God's existence is not a fact in the same sense, of course. Religions can be the object of empirical and phenomenological study in a way in which their object obviously cannot. Fortunately for me, however, this problem can be bracketed. I am an Anglican priest. This nails my colours firmly to the mast. My contribution is necessarily from a Christian religious perspective. But I am also a committed Islamophile – and not a little interested in Zen Buddhism too. I happen to believe that the religious diversities we discern in the shared world that we inhabit are expressions of a salutary, dynamic mystery – the same divine mystery in which believers rejoice and which they worship and seek to serve. I see no contradiction in connecting this mystery with the revealed, scriptural God who transcends the world and who is indeed also immanent in it. God the Creator pervades His creation; He is, I would like to put it, actively efficient in nature in innumerable ways, but He is eminently so through the agency of a key part of His creation: humanity. The selfsame God is also actively present and involved in the world through that rich mix, that variety of manifestations – practices, activities, rituals, and beliefs – which we all know as "religions".

However, before I set forth the argument that is my title – the mystery of a *Deus Absconditus* as both a validation of, and an invitation to, faith pluralism – I shall briefly consider a few difficulties.

Three Difficulties

Difficulty number one: Historically revealed, monotheistic faiths like Judaism, Christianity, and Islam make universalist, "exclusivist" claims which appear *prima facie* incompatible with a genuine acceptance of faith pluralism. It is one thing to accept the "brute fact" of the existence of other faiths. It is quite another to acknowledge such faiths as valuable in themselves, as a

227

manifestation and expression of divine providence, and not simply as necessary nuisances, or errant children, or mere conversion material. Historically speaking, there is little doubt what the main thrust of the church's attitude has been. For example, the third collect for Good Friday in the Anglican Book of Common Prayer lumps together "Jews, Turks, Infidels, and Heretics", and goes on to pray: "Fetch them home, blessed Lord, to Thy flock, that they may be saved amongst the remnant of true Israelites, and be made one fold under one Shepherd, Jesus Christ our Lord." So much for religious pluralism.

Difficulty number two: Doctrinal differences. Almost anyone who has engaged in any conversation with Muslims about religion will at some stage have been confronted with pointed questions about key Christian doctrines such as the Incarnation and the Trinity. Not only do Muslims not share them – in my experience, they find them objectionable, even offensive, non-monotheistic ideas. They are felt to be so because, on the strength of certain Qur'anic passages, they appear to contradict the belief in the absolute oneness of God, so central to the Islamic revelation.

On the Christian side, the person and prophetic status of Muhammad, so intimately bound up with Muslim belief, has hitherto presented perhaps the biggest stumbling block to a positive evaluation of the Islamic faith.

Difficulty number three: This has to do with very deep-seated, personal emotional attitudes. Naturally, such emotions partly flow out of an awareness of the two previous points. Actually, they amount to much more than that. Muslim memories seem to stretch very far into the past. Historical figures and events which are rather nebulous and remote in the mind of most Western people may not be quite so to the Muslim self-consciousness. Having recently taught a group of Muslim postgraduate students, I was struck by the extent to which not just the Crusades, but episodes like the capture of Constantinople, the Spanish *reconquista*, the siege of Vienna by the Turks, and so on were discussed and *felt* with the same intense sense of personal relevance and involvement as, say, the thorny issue of Palestine is today.

For their part, Christians have become all too aware, especially after 9/11, not only of the current, popular association of some Islamic fringes with violence and terrorism, but also of the apparent vigour, the fervour, and the renewed dynamism that Islam today presents to the world. European converts to Islam can be met in increasing numbers, in all ranks and levels of society. For instance, two Italian ambassadors to Saudi Arabia during the last ten years have converted to Islam. Predictably, these perceptions may, and often do result in fear, loathing, and hostility by insecure Christians towards Muslims. That is a mindset hardly conducive to a genuine acceptance of the other faith in the sense that is under discussion.

Clearly, all these three painful problems must be addressed. It is also clear to me that each difficulty is not susceptible of the same type of response. For example, it can be argued that tricky questions of doctrine demand the technical knowledge and expertise that only professional theologians are supposed to have. Such matters would therefore best be dealt with in the context of academic examination and debate. That may or may not be right. I would myself contend that the most straightforward way of conveying the meaning of the Christian belief in the Incarnation – the Word of God made flesh – is to "explain" it not as a piece of peculiar Church dogma shot through with Greek metaphysics, but as a supreme, cosmic act of divine love for humanity. The true story of the Neapolitan slum priest, Father Borrelli, told in Morris West's wonderful *Children of the Sun*, seems to me as effective an illustration as possible of what the Incarnation does mean. Stated in mere verbal terms, this may not impress the unimpressable, but my point is that it is the self-sacrificial love of scores of Christian men and women down the centuries that both embodies and witnesses that incarnate love in action. Should someone tartly comment, "Very well, but you still will not win Muslims over with that simplistic line," I would happily reply, "I am not sure about the 'simplistic'. *Simplex sigillum veri.* Isn't simplicity a mark of truth?" But of course, the Father Borrelli story may not "win over" anyone, but so what? That is not my aim. Religious pluralism – I deliberately leave the expression undefined, because I am not a believer in the necessary virtue of having definitions – is not about winning people over to your own religion, is it? Conversation, yes. Conversion, no.

My latter point is directly connected with the first difficulty. By and large, mainline Christian churches no longer subscribe to the crude, insensitive proselytising attitudes of the past. The third Good Friday collect is hardly ever used these days. Some Christians would put that down to failure of nerve or enfeeblement. In the context of the subject of this chapter, though, I submit that such a shift in emphasis is best construed as corresponding to a growth in tolerance and spiritual maturity. Scalp-hunting – proselytism – is not the only, not even the best way, of witnessing to divine truth.

The healing of memories is surely a long-term process. And, of course, memories are like an iceberg: the submerged, subconscious part is by far the largest and the most lethal. Ancestral fears of the other, be he Turk or Crusader, accumulated over centuries, will not vanish overnight as a result of multi-faith dialogue. Yet, I suggest that images, such as the recent, courageous one of Pope John Paul II, kissing the Qur'an and praying in a mosque at Damascus, provide the sort of talismanic templates that are needed for the healing process.

Lastly, the person of the Prophet Muhammad. Here I am going to be very bold and very brief. I *know* this difficulty can be solved – at least spiritually. I know that, because I have experienced it myself. It is possible for a Christian to learn to value and love Islam's "seal of the Prophets". At least I can show how I have done it. A forthcoming book of mine, which may be entitled *The Mahdi's Return*, will illustrate the way in which I have achieved that.

Deus Revelatus and *Deus Absconditus*

Perhaps the heart of the matter resides in an overemphasis on a theology of a *Deus Revelatus*. This is, for Christians, the God who has revealed Himself to humankind in Jesus Christ. Reformers like Martin Luther saw such a self-disclosed divinity as one who is always gracious to men for the sake of their salvation. Very well. But another aspect of such a positively revealed, Scripture-based model of God is that the Christian believer finds Christ reported in the New Testament as making for himself absolute claims such as, "I am the Way, the Truth, and the Life. No one comes to the Father except through Me" (John 14:6). Tricky matters of Gospel hermeneutics aside, it would be difficult, again, to reconcile this passage with the idea of authentic faith pluralism.

Alongside the stress on the image and words of a *Deus Revelatus* – a revealed God whose utterances and commands seem to rule out an authentic acceptance of other faiths – however, I wish to suggest, we ought to place the idea of a *Deus Absconditus*, a hidden God. This is, I hasten to say, a biblical expression. In Isaiah (or, for the fastidious, Deutero-Isaiah) 45:15, we read: "Verily, Thou art a God that hidest Thyself, O God of Israel, the Saviour." What a splendid, bracing paradox! The God who reveals Himself through His prophet is by the same prophet proclaimed as a God who hides Himself.

It is notable how this paradoxical prophetic utterance is itself set within a wider paradox. A foreigner, a non-Jew, the Median king Cyrus, conqueror of Persia, is exalted as Messiah, God's own anointed. It is this ostensibly heathen ruler who will free the Israelites from Babylonian captivity and rebuild Jerusalem. It seems that Isaiah here is saying that the Gentiles will come to recognise Israel's God, hitherto unknown to them, as their God too, and through this recognition and faith the entire earth will be recreated. The nations of the world are shown as saying – or, rather, uttering an exclamation to this saving God, who acts through Cyrus – "Truly, you are a hidden God!" The divine plans, the Lord's redemptive acts, are concealed from human eyes; they are hidden even beneath the very unexpected figure of a conquering pagan king, Cyrus.

Martin Luther seems to have felt the image of a hidden God disturbing. I, on the contrary, find the idea exceedingly exciting. It seems to me a stimulating, fertile metaphor.

God and Mystery

The quest for the Hidden God perhaps can be said to arise necessarily out of an awareness of the limitations of ordinary human knowledge concerning the divine. A thinker as bold as Spinoza can confidently maintain that "the human mind has an adequate knowledge of the eternal and infinite essence of God" (*Ethics*, II, 47). But another, previous great Jewish mind, Maimonides, argues, much more in accordance with the teachings of the Hebrew Bible, that we must always deny that we have grasped the essence of the divine. Maimonides well understood the need for religion to preserve a basic sense of the mystery and infinity of God. St Thomas Aquinas too teaches that human language "fails to represent adequately what God is" (*Summa*, I, 13:2). Relevant scriptural references to God appear to bear out the views of Maimonides and Aquinas here. Terms like "incomparable" (2 Sam. 7:22), "invisible" (John 1:18), "inscrutable" (Isa. 40:28), "infinite" (I Kings 8:27), "eternal" (Isa. 57:15), "omniscient" (1 John 3:20), and so on, may be cited to indicate how that is the case.

Quest and Insight

In the passage from the prophet Isaiah, which has provided me with the key category of the *Deus Absconditus*, the nations outside the Abrahamic covenant, the Gentiles, are described as suddenly brought to the startling recognition of the God of Israel. Such a god was initially – speaking for a moment from a purely phenomenological standpoint – one tribal deity amongst others. Now the heathen perceive him as the universal Lord, their own God too. This realisation takes place through the grand agency, against the dramatic background of human history, of the pagan king Cyrus. "That's it!" I like to imagine a hypothetical bystander of good will exclaim: "I've got it! Truly, you are a hidden God! And my God too."

Insights into the splendid realisation of a universal, unitary God of all who transcends human diversities – my *Deus Absconditus* – can occur, I am inclined to say, in a variety of ways. Those familiar with the techniques of Zen masters, for example, will be aware of the *koan* procedure, whereby a seemingly simple but baffling question ("Does a dog have a Buddha-nature?") posed by a master to a pupil is used to generate a train of deep mental puzzlement which may eventually result in the desired *satori*, enlightenment. Zen training, of course, despite its deceptive spontaneity, is a structured, rigorous affair.

From my own experience, though, I am convinced that such epiphanic intuitions can come about in other more natural, effortless, unexpected, and humble ways, outside institutional frameworks like *dojos*, meditation halls, churches, monasteries, and so on. I suspect readers may find this a strange, self-regarding admission, but one of my own turning-points took place in an ordinary, cosily cluttered flat near a place called Haji Bairam, in the city of Ankara, Turkey. What was it about? It would be perverse of me to withhold further information, although I suspect it will not strike many as cognitively very satisfactory. It was a smile, a natural, beautiful, thoughtful but lovely smile, smiled by a girl, a student of theology at Ankara University, called Ayshe. God's grace was, I am convinced of it, at work through that smile. That was the moment when my own "that's it!" took place. The penny dropped. The light dawned. Ayshe's smile did not turn me into a card-carrying Muslim, no, but it certainly made me luminously aware, made me feel certain that the difference between her faith and my own amounted to no more than a thread.

In *The Parliament of the Birds*, by the renowned Persian mystic, Farid Uddin Attar, the birds undertake a quest for their king, an elusive, remote, half-glimpsed entity, the Simurgh. The overt, obvious pantheism of the conclusion clearly detracts from the fascinating narrative, interlarded with parables, anecdotes, and confessions, all meant to symbolise the various stations, ranks, and degrees of the mystic's ascent towards God. The dissatisfaction I felt at the doctrinaire dénouement in the *Parliament* confirms for me the importance of keeping the quest unending, so to speak. The Hidden God to whom a plurality of faiths points is best approximated in an asymptotic way. Genuine religious believers and seekers of all persuasions engaging in the search are aware of drawing closer and closer to Him on their earthly pilgrimage. As to actually reaching the final goal – spelling out its full meaning in our partial, limited human language – well, this side of eternity we would be wise to refrain from blabbering too much about it, lest we fall into one of the many traps and pitfalls that await fools, fundamentalists, and the unwary alike.

Humans naturally believe in God, although sometimes they also have doubts. God, both known and unknown, self-disclosed and yet essentially hidden, draws us irresistibly, by the power of His infinite bounty and grace, towards Himself. The search for union with the Divine takes place, of course, in our common, shared – relatively insignificant on a cosmic scale – little planet that we call Earth. People of other faiths, whose perspective on the object of the search may vary from ours, should be seen as fellow-travellers towards the same hidden/revealed goal. We ought to respect them, listen carefully to what they have to say, learn from them when it is necessary, engage in mutual collaboration on objectives that are common, whenever that is possible, and, above all, love them.

Pluralism and Love

Yes, love them. Perhaps this statement will sound rather pious or predictable, coming from a Christian. If so, I am very sorry about it, but ultimately I see no other way. The question of a plurality of faiths in an increasingly polarised world can be tackled at various levels and in many ways, some distinctly better than others. For instance, the idea of religions in dialogue seems intrinsically preferable, morally and spiritually, than that of religions in collision. It is good to talk. Never mind how occasionally we might feel a sense of weariness or even downright boredom at the waffle emanating from some well-meaning interfaith characters. In the Christian Church we used to speak of ecumenical bores. Now, perhaps, such worthy individuals are being overtaken by interfaith bores. Yet, I am, despite myself, forced to admit than even jaw-jaw is better than war-war. I hope I have at least partly succeeded in suggesting how the image of the *Deus Absconditus* can stimulate sincere seekers of many faiths to pursue a spiritual quest that carries with it a recognition of the high value of religious pluralism as a stage in the search for divine truth. But the "love thing", to paraphrase President Reagan, still remains vitally important. A little story, based on one told by that fine master of worldwide spirituality, the late Anthony De Mello, SJ, perhaps will bring out what I mean.

There was a man once whose garden was invaded by dandelions. You know what I mean: that common plant of the genus *Taraxacum*, with jagged leaves and a large bright yellow flower on a hollow stalk, followed by a globular head of seeds with downy tufts. Those tufts can be felt to be a real nuisance if you happen to have a very large number of dandelions in your garden. So the man tried to get rid of the dandelions. He tried every kind of treatment. Nothing seemed to work. He wrote letters to various experts, the media, even the ministry of agriculture, the lot. It made no difference to the outcome: whatever he tried, the dandelions were still there.

Eventually, in despair, the man turned to a neighbour, an affable, wise old codger who seemed very good at keeping his own garden patch in good order. "What shall I do?" the man asked with real anxiety. "These dandelions are driving me crazy. I have tried everything. Please, advise me."

The old fellow, his blue eyes sparkling with knowledge and wisdom and humour, smiled pleasantly at him and said, "I suggest you learn to love them."

Chapter 16

Religious Pluralism and Islam in a Polarised World

Murad Wilfried Hofmann

The Issue

In the sheer number of civilian victims – how else to measure the human catastrophe? – the 9/11 disaster is not among the very worst massacres in recent world history. Post-"9/11" lore indicates that much by referring to downtown New York as "ground zero", a terminology of nuclear warfare vividly echoing the mass killing of 274 000 Japanese civilians at Hiroshima and Nagasaki. And since we are dealing with State terrorism here, we might also recall the virtual extinction of the American Indians, slave trading, Dresden, Auschwitz, and Srebrenica.

Yet if the events of 11 September 2001 are measured by their long-term repercussions and their impact on the American psyche, they may certainly prove to be as momentous as any previous crimes in which a massive number of victims died. In fact, on that day US citizens learned two painful lessons that had previously escaped them: (i) that "God's Own Country" is vulnerable, and (ii) that there are many people "out there" who passionately hate much of what North America stands for.

This knowledge would have been useful if it had moved the American public to analyse the situation by identifying the causes of terrorism and the ensuing aims. Alas, both the American government and the media missed this unique chance. As in the case of the Holocaust – and with much of the same motivation – these pertinent questions were not asked, as if to seek to explain meant to condone.[1] Instead, in typical American fashion, the US administration claimed the moral high ground by reducing its "analysis" to the distinction between good (we) and evil (them). As after Pearl Harbour, the American moral majority threatened to come down like a ton of bricks on anyone who could be labelled a terrorist. (One obvious outcome of this approach was of course that Israel is hardly ever mentioned in the context of 9/11.)

The European scene was markedly different. In London, Paris, and Berlin the point was immediately made that peace – that is, the absence of violence – is the fruit of *justice*. Governments and pundits were quick to admit that injustice and poverty – which is itself a special form of injustice – were part of the equation, and this view was shared by many Muslims, who were troubled by what has happened, or is happening, in Algeria, Tunisia, Bosnia, Kosovo,

Egypt, Palestine, Chechnya, and Kashmir. The European media did not overlook the fact that Usama bin Ladin himself had severely condemned suppressive and hypocritical Muslim governments. Even so, one can easily predict that terrorism will not stop before justice is brought to the Palestinian people by giving them statehood, dismantling the illegal Israeli settlements, offering the right of return to Palestinian expatriates, and making East Jerusalem their capital.

The events of 9/11 may have been analysed differently on either side of the Atlantic, but the immediate result was the same: FEAR. Indeed, the entire Occident is now mortally afraid of what some Muslim(s) might do next. A black beard – formerly considered progressive *à la* Che Guevara – now suffices as grounds for arresting an Indian Sikh or an Arab Christian as a potential Muslim terrorist. And even the appearance of innocence is deemed suspicious, a sure sign that the suspect is a "sleeper".

Immediately after 9/11, the fear of further "Islamic terrorism" coincided with the simultaneous fear of civil unrest as a result of physical attacks against Western Muslims and their property. This concern moved the most unlikely people, such as President Bush and Chancellor Schröder, to visit mosques, to read the Qur'an, or to make sweepingly favourable statements about Islam as a peaceful world religion. To hear politicians say that "Terrorism has no religion" made everybody feel fair and reasonable.

However, once the danger of civic unrest had been averted, Western politicians and clerics reverted to the overriding theme of an Islamic threat. Prototypically, Cardinal Karl Lehmann of Mayence, president of the Conference of Catholic Bishops in Germany, insinuated on television that there was something wrong with Islam after all: had this religion skipped, or had it still to experience, its rationalist "Enlightenment"? His colleague in Cologne, Cardinal Joachim Meisner, interviewed by a popular magazine, went even further: he bluntly accused Muslims of being tolerant *vis-à-vis* other religions and ideologies for tactical reasons only, while they remained a minority.[2]

These attitudes of fear and suspicion, not only towards Muslims but also towards Islam as such, are alarming in view of the fact that the occasions for a real "clash of civilizations" are on the increase in a globalising world, in which, as during the previous century, worldwide migration is likely to remain uni-directional. For political, economic, and educational reasons people will continue to move from East to West and from South to North, not into but away from the Muslim world. Indeed, Islam still seems to be spreading in the United States and Europe.

Of the 30 million Muslims in Europe, including Albanians, Azeris, Bosnians, Chechens, and Tatars, 15 million live in Central and Western Europe, mainly in France (North Africans), Britain (Indo-Pakistanis), and Germany (Turks). In Germany, in the year 2000, 2578 mosques were counted. In the United States, too, the growth of Islam, especially among Afro-Americans, is phenomenal. In fact, 45 per cent of the entire world population of Muslims are currently living as minorities in non-Muslim countries. In the last resort one thus must deal with the widespread fear that these compact masses of Muslim foreigners, with their high birth-rates, may sooner or later overwhelm the religious and cultural traditions of the indigenous populations.

Alas, as part of a vicious circle, many Muslims in the West are nourishing this suspicion through reverse discrimination. In order to escape *assimilation*, they even refuse *integration*, and thus foster subcultural Muslim islands as a form of spiritual self-ghettoization. The annual convention of the UK Islamic Mission in Sheffield, on 20 August 2000, attended by some 4000 Muslims, was virtually conducted in the Urdu language because nearly all of them were of Indo-Pakistani origin. This not only excluded non-Urdu-speaking British Muslims; it presented Islam as an utterly *foreign* religion.

Under such circumstances, even if less extreme, more and more Europeans will start wondering what will happen to their way of life if these seemingly strange, backward, and "fanatically religious" Muslims were one day to obtain the majority? If they assume, as many do, that a Muslim majority would systematically deny minority rights, they are likely to fight tooth and nail against any further Islamic expansion in their neighbourhood – whatever the law may say. That the Muslims are nowhere ever likely to become a majority is in fact irrelevant: fear is no less real for being totally irrational.

No wonder then that Muslims, everywhere in Europe, are now facing emotional reactions, mostly spontaneous, but more and more organised, threatening to build into a veritable backlash against all things Islamic. In Germany, fanatical "evangelical" Christians have already begun to launch anti-Islamic campaigns for a "Germany free of Islam". Right-wing extremists, especially in former Communist East Germany, are allergic to anything foreign, that is, "un-German". In Hesse, in the region of Frankfurt, state elections have been won with chauvinistic slogans. Recent state elections in North-Rhine-Westphalia were also symptomatic of the general anti-pluralistic mood, for there the Christian Democratic opposition party rhymed the catch phrase *Kinder statt Inder* (children instead of Indians), suggesting that Germany does not need foreign computer experts and that German culture is the *leading culture* (*Leitkultur*) to which every immigrant should be obliged to conform. Incidentally, the events of 9/11 did not create, but merely reinforced, these phenomena.

Against this worrying background, it should be obvious that discussing the traditional Islamic jurisprudence of religious pluralism is no mere exercise in nostalgia. On the contrary, it is highly relevant today to show that the Muslim world has a great multi-religious record, as in Andalusia and Sicily; that pluralism never was a major issue for Muslims; that in places where the Muslim world continues to be multi-religious, as in Egypt, communal problems of a truly religious nature are rare. This topic is indeed exceedingly relevant in view of the fact that, unconsciously, much of the anxiety about Islam is based on the unspoken assumption that the Muslims might drop their soft and pluralistic approach if they were ever to become a majority in any Western country or region. In other words, as a precondition for the defence of *Muslim* minorities – Muslim *dhimmi*, so to speak – it is essential that Western media and those who

exert an influence on public opinion should be made aware of the true Islamic
model of religious pluralism. The better Muslims are at this task, the better are
the chances for Islam *everywhere*.

The Qur'anic Model of Pluralism

The Islamic model of religious pluralism is of course based on both the Qur'an
and the Sunnah, or example of the Prophet Muhammad. But for the purpose
of demonstrating the Islamic standpoint to Western people, it is advisable to
base one's arguments exclusively on the Qur'an. While all Occidental people
can check Muslim allegations based on the Qur'an, they cannot possibly do the
same with arguments based on the *hadith*, or sayings of the Prophet. Luckily,
this approach is without drawbacks because all the important points that need
to be made here can be taken from the Qur'an.

*Muslims believe that not only Muslims but every good and God-abiding person
can go to heaven*

It is clearly stated: "Those who believe [in the Qur'an] and those who follow
the Jewish faith, and the Christians and the Sabiaeans, any who believe in God
and the Last Day and do good deeds, shall have their reward with their God
(2:62)." The same message can be deduced from verse 111 of the same Surah:
"Send not away those who call on their Lord morning and evening, seeking His
face (6:52)." Muhammad Asad was correct in pointing out that this refers to
people of *any* religion (Asad 1980: 179, n. 41).

Allah and Whoever is worshipped as God by others are identical

Muslims are instructed to say: "We believe in the revelation which has come
down to us and in that which has come down to you; our God and your God is
one and the same, and it is to Him we [all] submit" (29:46). This point is
especially important in view of the fact that even the President of one of the
Lutheran Churches in Hesse and Nassau, Professor Peter Steinacker, recently
denied it publicly. Of course, he confused the Oneness of God/Allah with the
differing *images* of God held by Muslims, Jews, and Christians. Concepts of
Him are one thing; He is another.

*God has guaranteed the existence of more than one religion for as long as the
world lasts*

This can be deduced from Surah 22:67: "Those who believe [in the Qur'an],
those who follow the Jewish faith, and the Sabiaeans, Christians, Magians, and
Polytheists – Allah will judge between them on the Day of Judgment" [that is,
not earlier].

In fact, God repeatedly makes it clear that religious pluralism corresponds to
His will (42:8), and that it is He who gave every community its direction of

prayer (*qiblah*; 2:148) and its ritual (22:67). "Had God so willed, He would indeed have guided all mankind aright" (13:31; 16:9; 16:93) and would have made them one single community (11:118; 42:8). The *Surat al-Ma'idah* (5:48) is a virtual manifesto of religious pluralism and therefore, in this context, by far the best Muslim argument:

> To every one of you We gave a law and way of life. And if God had so willed, He could surely have made you all one single community. But [He willed otherwise] in order to test you through what He has given you. Therefore, compete with each other in doing good works. To God you all must return. Then He will make you truly understand all about that which you used to differ.

This verse is no less than a *structural guarantee* for the survival of more than one religion, and every Muslim should know it by heart.

Muslims are expected to be not only tolerant but respectful of other religions

Since religious pluralism is God's will, this means that tolerance of members of other denominations is a minimum requirement for Muslims. This is best expressed in *Surat al-Baqarah* (2:256): "There is no compulsion in religion", meaning that it is both useless and forbidden to try and coerce people in matters of belief: "So let believe whoever wills, and let disbelieve whoever wills" (18:29).

That is why Muslims can say, as in *Surat al-Kafirun*, without any second thought: "To you your religion, and for me mine" (109:6). There can be no second thought since, as we can gather from 30:22 and 49:13, pluralism in races, colours, languages, and religions is part of human nature: *fitrah*. It is in keeping with these basic principles that Muslims are urged not to engage in religious disputes (42:15), not to judge or condemn non-Muslims (6:52), and to speak kindly with them.

We can sum up: the Qur'anic model considers religious pluralism not only as normal but as beneficial; it treats faith as a personal affair, and discourages religious dispute – all elements that non-Muslims should find reassuring.

However, this beautiful posture of tolerance in a divinely ordained pluralistic universe is marred when our adversaries and, alas, some Muslims as well, claim, first of all, that "Islam alone is God's religion" and, second, that this religion is bound to be "victorious" over all others.

The first idea, expressed, for instance, in *Surat al-'Imran* (3:19), is based on a misunderstanding of the term "Islam" both here and elsewhere. When the Qur'an says "*Inna ad-din 'ind' Allah al-Islam*", "Islam" has to be understood as it was at the beginning of the Qur'anic revelation, that is, as "submission" or "self-surrender". It would be an anachronism to read such verses as if they referred to the world religion as it was subsequently to become. Thus 3:19, and correspondingly 3:85, are to be read: "The only true religion in the sight of Allah is submission to Him."

The second idea is based on several identical verses which, like 48:28, seem to predict that Islam will *prevail* over every religion, in the sense of replacing them

– which would be a contradiction of what is stated elsewhere, for example, in 5:48. The verb in question (*zahara 'ala*) can, however, also be understood as "to outshine". In that case, the light of Islam, thanks to its higher intensity, shines so strongly that it *outshines* every other religion. Prevailing, in this sense, does not imply that what is outshone no longer exists. One should therefore read 48:28 as follows: "It is He Who has sent His messengers with guidance and the religion of truth to make it shine over all religion."

Nor is the Islamic model diminished by the fact that the Qur'an mainly encourages friendship between Muslims, not between Muslims and non-Muslims (3:118 ff.; 2:120). This is only natural – there is simply more affinity between people who consider themselves as brothers and sisters (49:10; 3:103). Religious pluralism does not imply wishy-washy social uniformity.

Comparing Theory and Practice

When Muslims point out attractive aspects of their religion, it is usually dismissed as sheer *theory* and contrasted with ugly behaviour in *practice*. Indeed, it is hardly surprising that Muslims have frequently failed to live up to the Qur'anic model described above when one considers how far advanced it is. In fact, the Islamic model for the protection of religious minorities preceded the Western one by some 1300 years. But we have to compare apples with apples, and not with pears.

The Catholic Church, in direct opposition to the idea of tolerance and plurality, was guided until quite recently – that is, up to the convening of the Second Vatican Council – by its fateful doctrine *extra ecclesiam nulla salus* – "There is no salvation outside the Church." Thus Christianity not only globalised its ill-conceived notions of hereditary sin and the related universal need of "salvation"; the Church presented itself as the only remedy for the problem it had constructed. This feeling both of superiority and mission led to the most atrocious internecine warfare between Christians themselves, first between Catholics and Orthodox (as at the Sack of Constantinople in 1204), and after the Reformation between Protestants and Catholics. The 30 Years War (1618–48) left Germany with a population decimated to merely six million and produced another vicious doctrine called "*cuius regio, eius religio*" "He who governs determines the religion of the population." One cannot imagine a worse, wholesale violation of the lofty Qur'anic norm of "*la iqraha fi-d-din*" – "Let there be no compulsion in matters of faith."

Countless are the sorrows, countless are the victims of those two doctrines, which, in a secular version, are still very much alive in the French idea of *mission civilisatrice* and the American idea of "God's Own Nation".

The Crusades and the so-called Spanish *Reconquista*, terminated by the Fall of Granada in 1492, present us with practical examples of the very antithesis of the Islamic ideal of religious pluralism. However, we would be mistaken if we believed that Crusading ever stopped. In a secular fashion, it was continued during the entire process of colonisation, from Napoleon's Egyptian campaign via the American Indian wars to the Zionist occupation of Palestine. Today it runs under the name of globalisation.

It was not my purpose to mention these sad examples of Occidental savagery in order to adopt a "holier than thou" posture, nor do I wish to revel in protest and indignation. Rather, we must keep the intolerance of Western religious history in mind in order to understand contemporary Western thinking. In concrete terms, it is quite obvious that many Western people cannot even conceive of Muslim tolerance because they know nothing of the sort from their own history. In other words, Western people innocently assume that the Muslims, if only they could, would act exactly as the Crusaders had done when, for instance, they conquered the holy city of Jerusalem.

Thus Western institutionalised intolerance in the past has become, via collective memory, a psychological barrier for more tolerance today. Once again, fear is at the controls.

Islamic Jurisprudence of Pluralism

It is therefore extremely important that Muslims in the West know their own history well enough to impress Western minds with Islamic tolerance not only in theory but also in practice. Everybody should be acquainted with 'Umar ibn al-Khattab's respect and protection of the Christians in the Near East and the fruitful coexistence of Islam, Judaism, and Christianity both in Muslim Spain and in the Ottoman Empire.

Also contemporary examples of Muslim religious tolerance should be pointed out: the existence of fourteen million Copts in Egypt after 1300 years of Muslim rule; the peaceful coexistence of a large Muslim majority in Malaysia with prosperous Indian and Chinese minorities; the flourishing of Jewish communities in Muslim countries.

If, in the process, Muslims are confronted with individual cases of religious discrimination, mainly during the medieval period, they should be the first ones to admit it. It is well known that the Crusades, the *Reconquista*, and the Ottoman campaigns in Central Europe resulted in much bitterness and abuse on both sides. Typical of many jurists (*fuqaha*) of his time, an-Nawawi wrote, for instance, in his *Minhaj at-Talibin* that "an infidel who has to pay his poll-tax should be treated by the tax collector with disdain", that infidels are forbidden to build churches in new Muslim towns, may not ride a horse, and "must not sound the bells of their churches".[3] Others wanted to forbid Christians from eating pork, drinking alcohol, or displaying crosses. Some even based such attitudes on the Qur'an, for instance, by reading *Surat at-Tawbah* (9:29), as "Fight the infidels ... until they pay the *jizyah* tax with willing submission and are humbled" (or brought low, or feel subdued), while it would have been better to read the same verse as "Fight the infidels ... until, having surrendered, they pay their poll-tax with a willing hand" (or, in another interpretation, "within their means").

All Muslims in the West should know how Islamic jurisprudence (*fiqh*) deals with the rights of religious minorities (*siyar*). These Islamic norms were also so advanced that they have not yet been superseded by any modern legislation or convention.

That this aspect of jurisprudence sprang from a normative custom among pre-Islamic Arab tribes still strikes one as extraordinary: under their iron code of hospitality, any member of a tribe, women as well, could – at least temporarily – give political asylum to whomsoever they wished, and this had to be respected by the entire tribe (*al-aman al-ma'ruf*). Following the relevant Qur'anic instructions, this institution in Islam developed into a permanent treaty relationship (*al-aman al-mu'abbad*) between the State and its non-Muslim residents from the *ahl al-kitab*,[4] the so-called *dhimmi* (protected minority).

Under this status, religious minorities in the Muslim world enjoyed virtual autonomy and self-administration in religious affairs, including personal status, family affairs, inheritance, and criminal law (if the offence was committed within the community of the minority). In modern terms, this means that members of a religious minority were exempt from the legal monopoly that sovereign States usually exercise over all people in their territory. Consequently Jews could lend money on interest, and Christians could buy, sell, and consume pork and wine. At the same time, as promised by Muhammad (s) to the Christians in Najran in 631 CE, these minorities enjoyed the protection of their lives, property, lands, faith, churches, and all their possessions, just like the Muslim majority.[5] In fact, according to al-Bukhari, the Prophet of Islam once said: "One who hurts a *dhimmi* hurts me, and one who hurts me, hurts Allah."

In fact the *dhimmi* were treated differently only in three respects:

1　They were exempt from military service;
2　In consideration thereof they paid an annual poll-tax (not necessarily higher than *zakat*, the tax paid by Muslims); and
3　They were precluded from becoming head of State.

This model for the coexistence of different religious communities was so liberal that in the nationalistic nineteenth century it even promoted Greek, Serbian, and Bulgarian separatism. No doubt, if adhered to, it could still facilitate the solution of the seemingly intractable ethno-religious conflicts in the Balkans.

Nevertheless, Islamic law is frequently criticised for supposedly making the *dhimmi* second-class citizens. There is, however, nothing to prevent even further improvements in minority rights if the Qur'anic protection of non-Muslims is seen not as the *maximum*, but as the *minimum*, to be granted. This being the case, non-Muslims could be offered full citizenship, provided that they are willing to serve in the armed forces (though even then, the office of head of State should remain reserved for Muslims).

To sum up: the commitment of Muslims to religious pluralism is not a tactical posture, for their divine law demands it. They can therefore be counted on to grant the very minority rights that they claim for themselves.

A Word of Caution

If the Muslim model for the coexistence of religions is well explained, Western anxieties about how Muslims would behave if they were ever to attain majority status might subside considerably. But this alone will not do the trick. Anxiety breeding aggression is bound to linger as long as Muslim minorities are seen to be aspiring to political power.

This point was recently made quite forcefully by the Tunisian Shaykh Rashid al-Ghannouchi, who lives in exile in London. He urged Muslim minorities not to run for government, nor to seek to gain wealth and influence, but rather to focus on social work in order first to secure their presence. These are his words: "If these Muslim minorities, at this point, adopt the ideas of Islamic governance laid out by Sayyid Qutb and others, they will have signed their own death warrant."

Al-Ghannouchi makes it quite clear that social work deserves priority over political work since what is achieved socially is more permanent. That is why he calls on Muslims everywhere to give up the idea of Islamic political parties and focus instead on building civil society with democratic institutions, and this, he says, must begin at the grass-roots level.[6]

Prospects

There are optimists who believe that the problem of religious strife will soon be settled by means of human rights legislation, the science of religions, and the ecumenical movement. Will the Islamic model be realised in the West, by the West? I am less certain.

It is of course true that the family of nations, after the Second World War, has seen a multitude of legislative efforts, both nationally and internationally, to guarantee the freedom of religion, both as regards belief and public worship. The beautiful texts in the national constitutions, in the United Nations declarations, and in regional human rights conventions are well known. Recently, a group of Wise Men has elaborated yet another "Human Rights Charter of the European Union", with a view to "giving a soul to Europe" and drafting a European Constitution.

The problem here is that texts do not necessarily change mentalities, and besides, bureaucracies can easily sabotage norms in the process of application. Why else would Muslims still need to fight for the acceptance of *hijab*, Islamic schooling, the call to prayer, *halal* food, and Islamic burial rites? There is no shortage of august legal texts, but how many people abide by them?

As if Ibn Hazm had never lived (see Aasi 1999), the nineteenth century claimed the birth of a new science: the science of religions (in the plural). Ever since, universities have been swamped with professorships in comparative religion, philosophy of religion, sociology of religion, psychology of religion, religious anthropology, and phenomenology of religion. Alas, just as religion entered the world of academia in a big way, it departed from the hearts and minds of society. Religion was no longer studied by *religious* people, such as

Ibn Hazm, Ibn Battuta, or Ibn Khaldun. In fact, religion proper (that is, theology) ceased to be a scientific subject and was contemptuously left to the unscientific minds of theologians.

It is true that the science of religions, as a matter of principle, treats all religions as equal, including Islam: as equally manmade and equally illusory. All the key figures – Auguste Comte, Ludwig Feuerbach, Friedrich Schleiermacher, Max Müller, Karl Marx, Sigmund Freud, Charles Darwin, Friedrich Nietzsche, William James, Max Weber, Emile Durkheim, Carl Gustav Jung, Edmund Husserl, Max Scheler, and Martin Heidegger – somehow or other drained the religious (Rudolf Otto's notion of the numinous) from what continued to be labelled "religion".

The problem with this secularist attitude is that while it provides tolerance, it withholds recognition, or acceptance. The difference is crucial because tolerance, when granted from above, is graciously exercised towards a thing or a person deemed unworthy of respect. That is why the Muslims must never be content with mere toleration. They should rather argue that, in the words of Johann Wolfgang von Goethe, "tolerance should be a transitional attitude only. It must lead to acceptance. Mere toleration amounts to an insult."[7]

The world ecumenical movement has undoubtedly made great progress during the last one hundred years. This is due above all due to self-criticism within Christianity, starting with Adolf von Harnack and continued by people such as Adolf Schlatter, Paul Tillich, John Hick, Hans Küng, Matthew Fox, and Gerd Lüdemann. By questioning the Trinity, the divine nature of Jesus, and the authenticity of most of the New Testament, they have inevitably brought about an ecumenical *rapprochement* of sorts. But the result we now see is *theological relativism,* and this is almost as harmful as *secular relativism,* based on cultural anthropology.

Thank God the choice is not between passionate slaughter and passionate embrace, for there is a third option, which is that of clear-headed peaceful competition. If everyone were to reduce his *shahadah*, or profession of faith, to its first part, letting drop his attachment to a particular revelation (and thus culture), all would end up in the very non-committal Deism that was so fashionable in the eighteenth century among people like Frederick the Great of Prussia, Voltaire, Lessing, and Goethe. It is one thing to admit that somebody else's religion contains a certain amount of truth and beauty – as his, or her, way to "salvation". It is another thing simultaneously to deny that the truth of one's own religion outshines all others. Even if our gold is of 24 carats, we may also apply the word "gold" to other people's jewellery of only 16 carats.

The problem facing the ecumenical movement is, however, not cognitive but moral: a religion can only fulfil its function of taming human passions if it is believed to be true beyond any doubt. True relativism and true morality exclude each other. The Muslims should therefore adhere to their divine model of religious pluralism, which allows them to *accept* other religions, while maintaining the profile of their own. The Islamic message is integration, not assimilation. The Muslims in the West want to be a recognisable building block for a spiritually renewed Western society. The only way they can fulfil this function is by remaining what they are.

Notes

1 A notable exception to the overall rule is, and was, Paul Findley, whose books *They Dare to Speak Out* (1985) and *Silent No More* (2001) amount to a devastating critique of American Near Eastern policy.
2 *Die Bunte*, no. 47 (2001), p. 50.
3 English translation (Lahore: Law Publishing Company, 1914), pp. 467–9.
4 The People of the Book, those to whom a divine Scripture had been revealed: Jews and Christians.
5 Abu Yusuf, *Kitab al-Kharaj* (Cairo, 1922), p. 72 f.
6 Rashid al-Ghannouchi, "Islamic Movements: Self-criticism and Reconsideration", *Palestine Times*, no. 94 (April 1999), quoted from MSANEWS on the Internet, 14 April 1999, < http://www.ptimes.com >.
7 Goethe, *Complete Works: Maxime und Reflexionen,* no. 121.

Chapter 17

Ecumenical Islam: A Muslim Response to Religious Pluralism[1]

Roger Boase

The Present Context

In the increasingly interdependent world in which we now live, the coexistence of different religious, cultural, and ethnic groups poses an existential problem that our ancestors never had to confront. For the first time in history the general outlook of a large number of people in the "Westernised" world is dogmatically secular. Yet, as a result of the rapid expansion of the mass media, Internet and email communication, immigration, cheap travel, tourism, and other factors associated with the process of globalisation, we are faced with the daily spectacle of racial, cultural, and religious multiplicity. This is particularly true in the cosmopolitan cities of Britain, Europe and the USA, where citizens, motivated as much by self-interest as by altruistic motives, have had to learn to tolerate and even welcome diversity. Thus the word "pluralism" has come to be used by social scientists not as a neutral term synonymous with diversity, but as an evaluative or loaded concept similar to multiculturalism.

There are three main attitudes to this phenomenon of religious diversity. First, there are those who see it as a threat to their religious beliefs. Such people, who include conservative exclusivists, on the one hand, and militant extremists, on the other, insist upon doctrinal uniformity, claiming exclusive validity for their beliefs and practices. Those who see themselves as holy warriors, or crusaders, or the instruments of God's retribution clearly belong to this category.

Second, there are those who see diversity as a blessing, as a sign of God's abundant generosity. Such people are aware of the need for mutual understanding and seek to engage in dialogue with members of other faith communities; for them religious pluralism is both an outlook on life and an inspirational ideal. They would say that no person who is intellectually honest would claim that his or her religion has exclusive validity. Several theologians have followed this route in the interests of world peace; they have sought to explain that the great world faiths share a common global ethic (see Küng and Kuschel 1993). A growing number of people, some whom we might call inclusivists rather than pluralists, fall within this broad category.

Third, there are those who are so indoctrinated with cynical modern values that they take this phenomenon of religious diversity as another indication that religion itself is an anachronism. In the words of Hossein Nasr, "the very plurality of religious forms has been used by some as an argument against the validity of all religions" (Nasr 1972: 126). In the opinion of these dogmatic secularists, religion merely makes people superstitious and fanatical.[2] This has been the point of view of secular humanists since the time of Voltaire. For such people, "religion is the poison in the blood ... The problem's name is God."[3]

The suicide attacks against the Pentagon and the World Trade Centre on 11 September 2001, in which people of many nations and faiths died, including several hundred Muslims, could be viewed as a devastating assault on the concepts of multiculturalism and religious pluralism. I say this for two reasons. First of all, anyone who would defend or condone this atrocity would be totally opposed to the vision of a pluralist society, and the same is obviously true of the perpetrators. Second, relations between Muslims and non-Muslims have been seriously damaged as a consequence of what happened. In the new climate of mistrust, prejudice against Islam is openly expressed in the media, and many of those who have been identified by their dress or general appearance as Muslims have been vilified and victimised. Indeed, many people even regard this crime as proof that Islam is incompatible with civilised values, interpreting it as a fulfilment of Samuel Huntington's prophetic warnings of a clash of civilisations (Huntington 1996).

It needs to be said, however, that the military responses to 9/11 have made matters much worse. In the Qur'an there are two passages that we should reflect upon: "Since good and evil are not equal, repel evil with what is better: then he between whom and thee was enmity will become as it were thy friend and intimate" (41:34), and "And let not hatred of any people lead you into the sin of deviating from justice" (5:8).

"Let us not become the evil we deplore," said one of the clergymen who spoke at the memorial service for the victims of 9/11.[4] It was wrong to bomb Afghanistan, one of the poorest countries on earth, especially at a time of drought, when millions of people were on the verge of starvation, without even first engaging in diplomacy. It was also unwise because, by doing so, the USA lost the moral ascendancy and the sympathy that they needed to win hearts and minds in the "war against terrorism",[5] and increased "the likelihood of an on-going and continuous confrontation of cultures, that will not only divide the world but shatter the internal cohesion of our increasingly multi-cultural societies."[6] It is easier, after all, to destroy nations than to rebuild them. Sir Michael Howard and others suggested that, instead of dignifying the terrorists with the status of belligerents, the 9/11 attacks should instead have been treated as a crime against the international community to be dealt with by means of a police operation to hunt down the criminals and bring them to justice before an international court.[7]

Furthermore, the US military interventions in Afghanistan[8] and Iraq and the introduction of anti-terrorist legislation that curtails civil liberties have set dangerous precedents for other nations, such as India, Israel, and Russia, fighting their own "wars on terror". More worrying still, the US government may no longer be in a position to restrain other nations if and when they launch similar military offensives.

It is a mistake to believe that if we merely increase our expenditure on arms and surveillance technology, we will somehow guarantee our security. Those who think in this way have learnt nothing from the events of 9/11. In the words of one of Israel's most influential journalists, "The terrorism of suicide bombings was borne of despair and there is no military solution to despair."[9] In many of the world's trouble spots, Muslims have been tortured, killed, and denied their most basic rights. It is estimated that in the first six months after the end of the first Gulf War 110 000 Iraqi children had died from polluted drinking water, malnutrition, cancer caused by depleted uranium, and other health problems caused by the war.[10] In many parts of the world young Muslim men resort to violence and no longer heed the voice of reason and moderation because they feel marginalized and have nothing to lose. And they seek to give legitimacy to their actions by means of an exclusivist and militant perversion of Islam, without realising that this is the Islamic mirror-image of the racist ideology of those who persuaded Philip III to expel some 600 000 Muslims, or descendants of Muslims, from Spain in the seventeenth century (Boase 2002), or of those responsible for more recent and more revolting examples of religious and ethnic cleansing.

Although recent events have aroused curiosity about Islam, Islam is still the most misunderstood of the major world religions. Conspiracy theories about Islam have been widely propagated. Public paranoia and religious prejudice have been nurtured by a spectacular growth in pulp fiction with titles such as *The Enemy Within* or *Armageddon*.[11] Another related misconception is that Islam is incompatible with the principles of democracy. This is simply a modern version of the old orientalist theory of Islamic despotism, and again unfortunately it is a fallacy to which some fanatical Islamists subscribe.[12] So the real dichotomy is not between Muslims and non-Muslims, but between extremists and exclusivists, on the one hand, and inclusivists and pluralists, on the other.

In Search of the Common Ground between Christianity and Islam

If we seriously wish to engage in dialogue, it is not advisable to adopt confrontational language. President Bush, for example, is fond of paraphrasing Christ's words, "He that is not with me is against me" (Matthew 12:30; Luke 11:23). But these words should not be taken out of context. Whatever certain Christians may say, Jesus was not an exclusivist: he was simply saying that we have to make a commitment to serve God and take a stand against evil – that we can only be truly human, or humane, when we seek to become the servants of God's love and compassion.[13]

Although Christian theology is harder to reconcile with the concept of religious pluralism than either Judaism or Islam, in recent years the need to engage in interfaith dialogue has impelled some Christian theologians to move in that direction. The ecumenical theologian John Hick recently published an article summarising much of his life's work, entitled "Is Christianity the only true religion?" (Hick 2001). The majority of Christians would probably still consider this an unusual question; they would answer yes, citing the famous words that Jesus is reported to have said: "I am the way, the truth, and the life; no one comes to the Father, but by me" (John 14:6). However, more and more Christians today are abandoning the exclusivist point of view. The Vatican acknowledges – and has done since the Second Vatican Council in 1965 – that other religions "often reflect a ray of that Truth which enlightens all men",[14] while at the same time still maintaining that Christ alone is the mediator and way of salvation. More recently, in 1991, a Vatican document has stated that those who do not acknowledge Jesus Christ as their saviour may yet be "saved" if they follow the dictates of their conscience and "what is good in their own religious traditions".[15] The Jesuit Jacques Dupuis has gone further and has proposed the heretical opinion that other religious traditions might actually be considered "ways, means and channels of salvation willed and devised by God for their followers".[16] Dupuis maintains that God's Word and His Spirit are present in other religions and are not limited to the historical event of the Incarnation of Jesus Christ: "The action of the Word as such exceeds that of the Word incarnate in his glorified humanity" (Dupuis 2001b: 1521). Many New Testament scholars have even openly dared to affirm that, on the basis of the first three Gospels, it cannot be said that Jesus himself ever claimed to be God incarnate; in the words of the late Archbishop Michael Ramsey, "Jesus did not claim deity for himself."[17]

Hick has pointed out that the Lord's Prayer, the Christian equivalent of the *Fatihah,* the opening Surah of the Qur'an, and the one prayer that we know was certainly communicated by Jesus to his disciples, summarising his message to mankind, contains no reference to the central dogmas of Christianity – the Divine Incarnation, the Atonement, and the Trinity (Hick 1991: 5). Mindful of the fact that these dogmas are the chief barriers to interfaith dialogue, especially between Jews, Christians, and Muslims, Hick has redefined these dogmas as theological theories, or metaphors, rather than divinely revealed truths. If one believes that only Christianity was founded by God in person, and that only Christ is the doorway to eternal life, then it must follow that all the other world religions are in some way defective or inferior. By deliberately undermining Christianity's claim to unique superiority, Hick's strategy has been to open up the way to what he calls "a genuine religious pluralism" (1991: 17).

Hick has advocated a "Copernican revolution in theology", which would place God, rather than Christ, at the centre of our pluralistic religious universe (1973: 130–31; cf. 1993: 167–85) – a proposition that to Sufi mystics is hardly revolutionary. He would regard the great world faiths as "equally valid ways of conceiving, experiencing, and responding in life to the ultimate reality that we call God" (1995: ix). He cites, with approval, the words of the great spiritual master Shaykh Jalal al-Din Rumi: "The lamps are many, but the light is the same. It comes from beyond."[18] The late Frithjof Schuon, a modern Sufi shaykh, says much the same thing: "it is metaphysically impossible that any form should possess a unique value to the exclusion of other forms; for a form, by definition, cannot be unique and exclusive" (1953: 34); "every religious message is a Message of the Absolute", and therefore "a given religion in reality sums up all religions and all religion is to be found in a given religion, because Truth is one" (1991: 73–5). In other words, all sacred forms are imbued, in varying degrees, with God's Spirit because they are reflections of the Absolute, or different languages expressing the same Truth. As the mystic al-Junayd says, "The colour of water is the colour of its receptacle."

The chief difference between a traditionalist, such as Schuon or Nasr, and a pluralist, such as Hick, is that the former would regard different religions as different manifestations of – rather than different human responses to – the Absolute or the Real. Although many Muslims would reject Schuon's universalism, if one takes a closer look at the Qur'an and the sayings of the Prophet Muhammad, one will find that Islam is far more ecumenical and comprehensive than other revealed Scriptures, offering Jews, Christians, and all those committed to a sacred tradition a global framework for cooperation, a genuine basis for mutual understanding, and the best answer to the challenge of religious diversity.

Ecumenical Islam

At first sight it might seem odd to apply the word "ecumenical" to Islam, especially when one considers that this term was used at the Council of Nicaea in 325 CE when the Aryan (and subsequently Muslim) view of Jesus as a human "creature" was condemned as heretical. Yet, if we recognise that it derives from the Greek word *oikoumene*, meaning "belonging to the whole inhabited world", it will become apparent that this word is certainly applicable to Islam, for the Prophet Muhammad "was sent as a mercy to the worlds", *Rahmat lil 'alamin* (Qur'an, 21: 107), that is to say, to all peoples in all places. The same is true of the word "catholic", from the Greek *katholikos,* universal. In the words of Syed Ameer Ali, "The catholicity of Islam, its expansiveness, and its charity toward all moral creeds, has been utterly mistaken, perverted, or wilfully concealed by the bigotry of rival religions" (1965: 175). As Seyyed Hossein Nasr says, "universalism is in fact, in the deepest sense, the very *raison d'être* of Islam" (2000: 216). Jonathan Sacks has suggested that "universalism is an inadequate response to tribalism, and no less dangerous" (2002: 50) because it leads to the belief in one truth to which everyone must be converted, by force if necessary. This may be true of political ideologies, such as Communism, or the cultural uniformity and cynical materialism that are the by-products of globalisation. But this is not my understanding of universalism in either a spiritual or an ethical sense.

Some non-Muslim authors are prepared to concede that the Qur'an offers a charter for interfaith dialogue (Gaudeul 1990: 14–17), but they do not give an adequate account of this "charter" because their preconceptions about Islam prevent them from perceiving the broader framework upon which it rests.[19] I would suggest that the ecumenical message of Islam may be defined under the following headings: (i) the recognition that each one of us possesses a religious instinct, or primordial religion (*din al-fitrah*); (ii) the right attitude to God – that of an obedient servant (*'abdallah*); (iii) the right attitude to God's creation

– that of a custodian (*khalifah*); (iv) the right attitude to others – as equals deserving courtesy and respect; (v) the universality of revelation – that no community on Earth has been denied spiritual guidance; (vi) the special status of Jews and Christians as monotheists; and (vii) the duty to engage in dialogue with people of all other faiths and to compete with them in doing good. The future of humanity and even the future of the planet may depend upon our ability to convey this practical spiritual wisdom and to refute the distorted image of Islam that prevails in the mind of the general public.

Much of the Qur'an is taken up with advice on how the Prophet Muhammad and, by extension, every Muslim should engage in dialogue with members of other faith communities, in particular with Jews and Christians, the inheritors of the Semitic religious tradition, or *ahl al-kitab* – the people of Scripture. It has been rightly said: "a Muslim who deliberately rejects encounter with those of other faiths and other ways of thinking, or even opposes and fights against them, betrays God's cause."[20] During the lifetime of the Prophet Muhammad, learned discussions took place between Jewish rabbis and Muslims. We also know that when a delegation of Christians from Najran in South Yemen visited the Prophet in Medina, a religious debate took place and the Christians performed their prayers in the mosque. The Prophet Muhammad's role as a political arbitrator skilled in the art of diplomacy is well known. It was in this capacity that he was invited to settle a feud between two tribes, the Aws and the Khazraj, thus enabling his followers to escape persecution in Mecca by migrating to Medina. But his far more important role as a spiritual arbitrator is often overlooked.

Qur'anic Interfaith Principles

The following seven principles of interfaith dialogue may be extracted from the Qur'an:

The first principle is that "there shall be no compulsion in matters of faith" (2:256). This disproves the fallacy that Islam imposes on the non-Muslim the choice between conversion and the sword.

The second principle is that we should not ridicule the beliefs of others: "But do not revile those whom they invoke instead of God, lest they revile God out of spite, and in ignorance: for We have made the deeds of every people seem fair to them. In time, they must return to their Lord, and then He will make them understand what they have done" (6:108).[21] People are naturally attached to those beliefs implanted in them from childhood. Therefore we should not injure their feelings, and provoke unnecessary antagonism, by mocking the objects of their veneration. Besides, no mortal has it in his power to cause another person to believe unless God graces that person with His guidance. All we can do is set an example in our own conduct.

The third principle, a corollary to the above, is that we should not associate with those who ridicule our faith: "Do not take for your friends such as mock at your faith and make a jest of it ... but fear God, if you are believers: for, when you call to prayer, they mock at it and make a jest of it – simply because they are people who do not use their reason" (5:57–8).[22] Those who enjoy the company of such people are hypocrites (*munafiqun*) "who would deceive God, whereas they deceive none but themselves" (2:9; cf. 4:142).

The fourth principle is that, when we address those who do not share our beliefs, we should speak with courtesy, tact, and self-restraint, and refrain from discussing our beliefs with those who are unwilling to listen: "And do not argue with the followers of earlier revelation otherwise than in a most kindly manner" (29:46; cf. 17:53, 16:125–8); "And bear with patience what they say, and part from them with a fair leave-taking" (15:88).

The fifth principle is that we should invite people to use their reason, appealing to the intellect (*al-'aql*) to judge the truth of God's words, because there is no contradiction between faith and reason: "O People of Scripture, why do you argue about Abraham, seeing that the Torah and the Gospels were not revealed till long after him? Will you not, then, use your reason?" (3:65).

It is unreasonable to claim that paradise is reserved for the practitioners of any single religion: "And they claim, 'None shall ever enter paradise unless he be a Jew' – or, 'a Christian.' Such are their wishful beliefs! Say: 'Produce some evidence for what you are claiming, if what you say is true!' " (2:111).

The sixth principle is that we should avoid engaging in idle speculation about the nature of God, or the truth of God's revelations: "Only those who disbelieve dispute the truth of God's messages (*ayat*). But let it not deceive thee that they seem to be able to do as they please on earth" (40:4; cf. 22:8); "Accursed be the conjecturers who are dazed in perplexity" (51: 10–11).

Since the Qur'an is a regarded as a revealed Book, Muslims are not free to accept the truth of some verses and reject the truth of others, as the Jews of Medina wished to do (2:85). Nor should those without knowledge venture to interpret the Qur'an in their own arbitrary way:

> Now those whose hearts are given to swerving from the truth go after that part of it [the Qur'an] which has been expressed in allegory, seeking [to create] dissension, and seeking [to arrive at] its final meaning; but none but God knows its final meaning. Hence those who are deeply rooted in knowledge say: "We believe in it; it is all from our Lord, although none takes heed, save those endowed with insight." (3:7–8)

If we perceive apparent contradictions in the Qur'an, these are due to our lack of insight. Therefore the Holy Prophet has said: "To dispute about the Qur'an is infidelity" (*Mishkat-ul-Masabih,* I, 275). He is also reported to have said: "Preach what you know [of the Qur'an], and entrust what you do not know to one who knows it" (Ibid., I, p. 274).

Since God cannot be comprehended by human reason, it is wrong to attempt to define His nature: "Utterly remote, in His glory, is the Lord of the heavens and the earth – the Lord in almightiness enthroned – from all that they may attribute to Him by way of definition" (43:82; cf. 6:103). "Think about the creation," says the Prophet, "but do not think about the Creator." The Persian mystic Abu 'l Majd Sana'i expresses this idea beautifully:

> Whatever comes to your mind that I am that – I am not that!
> Whatever has room in your understanding that I would be like this – I am not like this!
> Whatever has room in your understanding is all something created –
> In reality know, O servant, that I am the Creator. (Schimmel 1994: 226–7)

Muslims are therefore advised to shun the company of those who enter into false discourses about the nature of God and His revelations "until they embark on another topic" (6:68).

The seventh principle is that the followers of different religious traditions should compete with one another in piety: "Compete with one another in doing good works, for to God you will all return, and He will inform you about that wherein you differ" (5:48).

Islam as Ancient Wisdom

It was not the Prophet Muhammad's intention to establish a new religion; like Jesus, his aim was to renew and recapitulate the teachings of those prophets, or messengers, who had preceded him. The word *muslim* means one who seeks to do the will of God.[23] According to one of the Prophet's sayings, every human being is born a Muslim: "Every child is born in the *fitrah* [the natural state], and it is his parents who make him into a Jew or a Christian."[24] In this context, the word "parents" has the wider meaning of "social influences" or "social environment". Hence we may infer that – to quote the words of the late Professor Isma'il al-Faruqi – "the historical religions are out-growths of *din al-fitrah*, containing within them differing amounts or degrees of it" (1998: 139).

Every human being possesses an innate disposition to worship God and to discriminate between right and wrong (Qur'an 30:30). Those who heed that instinct are being true to their nature; those who deny it are "the iniquitous, who break their bond with God after it has been established" (2:26–7) – they conceal or cover up the truth within themselves and are ungrateful for God's gifts, both the idea of concealment and ingratitude being inherent in the word for unbelievers, *al-kafirun* (Haeri 1985: 16). They have become enslaved to the lower soul, "the soul commanding to evil" (*an-nafs al-ammarah bi's-su'*, 12:53), and have blocked their ears to the voice of conscience, "the blaming soul" (*an-nafs al-lawwamah*, 75:2). By training and controlling the lower instincts and the whims of the ego, the soul may be purified until it obeys the voice of conscience and reaches the state of "the soul at peace" (*an-nafs mutma'innah*, 89:27) when the soul is no longer divided against itself.

This inner struggle, which the Prophet Muhammad called the "greater *jihad*", has been experienced and studied by mystics everywhere. Sufi masters often compare this transformation to breaking in a wild horse so that it can bring the rider to his goal (Schimmel 1975: 112–13). The *nafs*, or ego, is sometimes compared with a donkey, for there is a saying of the Prophet Muhammad: "Your *nafs* is your donkey! Don't be a donkey to your *nafs!*" (Nazim Qibrisi 1980: 17). Buddhists use the parable of tracking down, catching, and taming a wild ox. All spiritual teachers are agreed that the ego is the chief obstacle to spiritual progress. Sufis have said that egotism, including attachment to dogmas, is "the worst of all the veils" (Lewisohn 1995: 296), the source of infidelity (*kufr*), idolatry, and dualism (*shirk*). In a commentary on Shabistari's *Garden of Mystery,* it is even said that the soul, or *nafs,* is "an infidel, utterly devoid of faith, who, disguised as a Muslim, has turned thousands of other people into infidels, heretics, and hypocrites; its artifice and guile are beyond all bound and measure" (Lewisohn 1995: 301). Spiritual teachers in every mystical tradition speak of the way in which the mind may be crippled by psychological appetites, such as fears and desires, and the craving for security.[25]

Spiritual knowledge is *re*-cognition, a memory of what we already know, and to remember in Latin is *recordare,* indicating a return to the heart, *cor* (Schuon 1981: 240): "The Arabic word for intellect *al-'aql* is related to the word 'to bind', for it is that which binds man to his Origin" (Nasr 1989: 12). Similarly religion, from the Latin *religare,* is that which binds each one of us to God through a sacred revelation, and to our fellow creatures as members of a sacred community. As the Qur'an explains, the rope that links us to God also links us to one another: "And hold fast, all together, unto the bond with God, and do not draw apart from one another" (3:103). We are commanded by God to care for two categories of neighbours: "the neighbour who is near, and the neighbour who is a stranger" (4:36). Our neighbours today, increasingly, are those who are strangers. We live among strangers and strangers live among us. But, as fellow inhabitants of this "global village", we are all neighbours and we should treat each other as neighbours.[26]

Since the word *Islam* means "submission", from the same root as *salam,* "peace", a Muslim is a person who attempts to find inner peace in the remembrance of God, which is why in the Qur'an the disciples of Jesus bear witness that they are Muslims, meaning that they have surrendered themselves to God (3:53): "He guides to Himself all those who turn to Him – those who believe, and whose hearts find their rest in the remembrance of God – for, verily, in the remembrance of God hearts do find their rest" (13:27–8). Unfortunately this wisdom has been forgotten by most people, or distorted beyond recognition. Today, when the conspiracy theory of a global Islamic threat seems to have been vindicated, it is widely believed that terrorism and Islam are synonymous, and that Islam poses a threat to civilisation.[27] Many journalists have inflamed anti-Muslim sentiments by disseminating a distorted image of Islam, although it has to be admitted that some "Islamists" will probably agree with the views attributed to them. Daniel Johnson, for example, makes the extraordinary assertion that Islam is the only Abrahamic religion that has a tradition of "suicide as a path to Paradise", and claims that, according to the Qur'an – which he quotes out of context – Jews and Christians will be "mustered into Gehenna".[28] "We have reason to be suspicious of Islam and to treat it differently from the other major religions," writes Julie

Burchill.[29] Even some of the most solid scholarly works on Islam are tainted by this bias.[30]

If Islam were really, as some suppose, a religion of fire and sword, why would "the true slaves of the Most Merciful" be defined in the Qur'an as "those who walk gently on earth and who, when the ignorant address them, say 'Peace' " (25:63)? Why would Muslims be admonished to greet one another, on all occasions, with the words, *As-salamu 'alaykum wa rahmatullah wa barakatahu,* "Peace be with you and God's mercy and blessings"? It is clearly stated that "God does not love aggressors" (2:190), and that war is only permitted in self-defence.

Muslims are taught to dedicate themselves constantly to God's service with the words, *Bismillah ar-rahman ar-rahim,* "In the name of God, the most Merciful, the most Compassionate" – words that are repeated several times during every prayer. Any action, if it is performed in God's name, may become a form of worship. Therefore, as the Buddhist Marco Pallis says, "in the Active Life when fully integrated all acts without exception are ritual in character" (Pallis 1991: 48). This means that there should be no separation between the sacred and the profane, between the religious and the political, or even between work and play. Pallis even asserts that the dominant model of Western society in which such a division of interests prevails is degenerate (1991: 49).

Nature and Natural Diversity as a Sacred Trust

The bond that links us to God gives us a special relationship with the rest of God's creation, which is that of a custodian, vicegerent, or *khalifah*. It is this role that links together all people of faith. By failing to care for the natural world, human beings are betraying the covenant made by the children of Adam to acknowledge their Lord (7:172). As the Prince of Wales said, in "A Reflection on the Reith Lectures for the Year 2000", we have failed to live up to this "sacred trust between mankind and our Creator, under which we accept our duty of stewardship for the earth" because this principle has "become smothered by almost impenetrable layers of scientific rationalism" (Charles 2001: 13). In other words, we have forgotten what it means to be human because we have forgotten our status in the divine scheme of things as God's servants and deputies. Concern for nature and the protection of bio-diversity and the earth's resources from the destructive effects of greed, wastefulness, and pollution should unify the whole of humanity in the search for common solutions.

Human beings have betrayed God's trust by seeking to dominate and plunder nature without any regard for the long-term effects. The spiritual value of worldly things is generally overlooked because the contemporary secular scientific mentality lacks a sense of the sacred. The world has become desanctified and, as a result, humankind has become impoverished and dehumanised. In the words of the late Philip Sherrard, an Orthodox Christian, "we do not have any respect, let alone reverence for the world of nature because we do not fundamentally have any respect, let alone reverence for ourselves ... Our contemporary crisis is really our own depravity writ large" (1992: 9). In the words of the Qur'an, "Corruption has appeared on land and sea because of what human hands have done" (30:41).

People have become enslaved by greed and discontent, fostered by imaginary needs that tend to expand into "rights". There is a failure to recognise the need for self-restraint. As the poet and farmer Wendell Berry says, mental appetites "can be far more gross and capacious than physical ones. Only humans squander and hoard, murder and pillage because of notions" (1991: xxvii). The environment cannot be properly protected without an awareness of the sanctity of all things, and this awareness cannot be acquired without the rediscovery of the sacred within ourselves (Nasr 1993: 145; cf. Nasr 1998). Disharmony between Man and God has led to disharmony between Man and Nature. Human beings have thus become trebly alienated. Those who have no respect for nature and who assume that they alone have sovereign power are guilty of arrogance and ingratitude. It has been said that "God Himself is the ultimate environment" (Nasr 1993: 131) because the created world is a book of signs (*ayat*) which point to the Creator, or a mirror reflecting God's Attributes: "We shall show them Our signs in the horizons and within themselves, so that it will become clear to them that this [revelation] is indeed the truth" (41:53). "I was a hidden treasure and I loved to be known," says God in a well-known *hadith*, "and so I created the world."

The right relationship between humans and their natural environment must be based on the recognition that we do not really own anything: "No! I swear by this land, and thou art a lodger in this land ... " (90:1). Similarly, in the Old Testament, God warns Moses that the Israelites cannot claim rights of ownership to the Promised Land since all of us are merely tenants, temporary lodgers in the land that we must share as best we can: "The land shall not be sold forever: for the land is Mine; for ye are strangers and sojourners with Me" (Leviticus 25:23). Moses, as reported in the Qur'an, passed on this command to his people: "Indeed all the earth belongs to God: He bequeaths it to such of His servants as He pleases" (7:128). In a metaphysical sense, we are all strangers and travellers on earth, and, strictly speaking, one ought to say that, since God is the real Owner, we merely enjoy the usufruct of things.

If a person owns some land which can be cultivated, it is his or her duty to make use of it by planting crops or trees, because, to leave land uncultivated is tantamount to rejecting and wasting God's bounty. "If anyone has land," the Prophet said, "he should cultivate it, or lend it to his brother for cultivation, or otherwise release it from his ownership" (al-Qaradawi 1985: 278). The cultivation of the soil might even be called a form of charity: "There is no Muslim who grows a plant or sows a seed, then birds or a man or an animal eat of it, but it is charity for him" (*Mishkat*, I, p. 249). Uncultivated land is similar to hoarded wealth because, in both cases, the owner and the community are deprived of its beneficent use (9:34). For this reason waste land (*al-mawat*) that belongs to no one can be claimed by the first person who cultivates it (*Mishkat*, II, p. 307).

The sin of wastefulness and the duty to share one's wealth with the poor are repeatedly mentioned in the Qur'an: "O Children of Adam! Beautify yourselves for every act of worship, and eat and drink, but do not waste: verily, He does not love the wasteful!" (7:31; cf. 6:14). The Prophet Muhammad used to practise moderation and economy in all things. It is reported by Ibn 'Umar that he approached Sa'ad while he was performing his ablutions, and said: "What is this wastefulness?" Sa'ad answered: "Is there wastefulness in water?" "Yes," said the Prophet, "even if you are beside a flowing river." This shows that even if there is an abundance of a certain commodity, we should not take more than what is necessary. A very similar story is reported about Gandhi.[31]

Since everything that we enjoy on earth is really a loan from God, the rich are exhorted to remember that, in supervising their wealth, they are acting as God's trustees: "Spend on others out of that of which He has made you trustees: for those of you who believe and spend freely [in charity] shall have a great reward" (57:7). One does not need to be rich to be charitable because every act of kindness to man or beast is a form of charity: "One assists a man in riding his beast or in lifting his provisions to the back of the animal, this is charity; and a good word and every step which one takes in walking over to prayer is charity; and showing the way is charity."[32]

Religious Diversity and the Universality of Revelation

Just as biological diversity is divinely ordained, so multiplicity of every kind – religious, cultural, or ethnic – is part of God's magnificent design:

> And among His wonders is the creation of the heavens and the earth, and the diversity of your tongues and colours: for in this, behold, there are messages indeed for those endowed with knowledge. (30:22)
> To each [community] among you have We appointed a law and a way of life. And if God had so willed, He could have made you one community: but [He willed it otherwise] in order to test you by means of what He has bestowed upon you. So vie with each other to excel in goodness and moral virtue. (5:48)

In Gandi's words, "Revelation is the exclusive property of no nation, no tribe" (1962: 25).

This means that, by the gift of reason, we have to decide for ourselves what is the right way, and avoid becoming involved in religious disputes:

> We have appointed for every community a way of worship that they shall perform. Therefore do not allow yourself to be drawn into disputes about this, but summon [them] to your Lord, for you follow right guidance. And if they wrangle with you, say: "God knows very well what you are doing." God will judge between you on the Day of Resurrection concerning that about which you used to differ. (22:67–9)

Islam accepts the legitimacy of all earlier revelations, teaching veneration for all prophets since the time of Adam. The Qur'an repeatedly stresses that all peoples on earth have had their prophets and messengers. In other words, prophetic guidance is not limited to any one community, period, or civilisation.

So Muslims – if they are true to their faith – do not claim a monopoly of spiritual truth, or a monopoly of revelation:

> And indeed, within every community have We raised up an apostle [with this message]: "Worship God and shun the powers of evil" (16:36).
> Nothing is said to you that was not said by Us to apostles before you. (41:43)
> Say: "We believe in God, and in that which has been bestowed from on high upon us, and that which has been bestowed upon Abraham and Ishmael and Isaac and Jacob and their descendants, and that which has been vouchsafed by their Lord to Moses and Jesus and all the prophets: *we make no distinction between any of them*. And to Him do we surrender ourselves" (3:84, emphasis added).

Since only some of God's apostles are mentioned in the Qur'an (40:78), the Buddha and the avatars of the Hindus are not necessarily excluded.

Jewish-Christian-Muslim Relations

In the *Sahifat al-Madinah*, sometimes called the Constitution of Medina, the Prophet Muhammad legislated for a multi-religious society, based on equality, tolerance, and justice, many centuries before such an idea existed in Europe. Indeed, early Muslim society was more pluralistic in a religious sense than some Muslim societies today. Under the terms of this document each religious and ethnic group enjoyed complete cultural and legal autonomy. The Jews were not required to pay any tax, nor was there any clause demanding their subjection. They were bound by the same duties as the other parties to the contract; together they formed a single community, or *ummah*, a word that today is generally used only with reference to the Muslim community. Belief in One God was regarded as a sufficient basis for cooperation:

> To the Jew who follows us belongs help and equality. He shall not be wronged nor his enemies aided. The Jews must bear their expenses and the Muslims their expenses. Each must help the other against anyone who attacks the people of this document. They must seek mutual advice and consultation, and loyalty is a protection against treachery. (Peters 1990: I, 217)

This tradition of tolerance was continued by the Caliph 'Umar, who, when he entered Jerusalem in 638 CE, obtained permission to pray in the Church of the Holy Sepulchre, but decided instead to pray outside for fear that his action would be taken as a precedent to convert the church into a mosque. Not only did he guarantee security and freedom of worship to the Christian inhabitants but he also showed equal respect to the Jews. He personally supervised the cleansing of the Temple Mount when the first Jewish families returned to the Old City, and interceded on their behalf against the Christians who were strongly opposed to the Jewish resettlement.[33]

In the present climate of mistrust and tension between Jews and Muslims, it is important to emphasise that they have a common spiritual heritage. In the Qur'an, Jews and Christians are not told to renounce their beliefs, but to heed the advice of their own revealed Scripture (5:44–7). The Prophet Muhammad had taught his followers to greet one another in the Jewish manner with the words "Peace be with you", to cover their heads in prayer, and to perform similar ablutions. He had issued dietary restrictions acceptable to Jews, which would have satisfied what rabbis demanded of strangers admitted to live among them: the prohibition against the eating of pork, or blood, or any animal that had been strangled, sacrificed to idols, or had met a natural death. He had strongly recommended the practice of circumcision. Until the Banu al-Nadir were banished in 3 AH, the Prophet had a Jewish secretary, 'Abdullah ibn Salam, and five years later he married a Jewish girl, Safiyyah, whose first husband and father, both leaders of the Banu al-Nadir, had been implacable enemies of the Prophet. She remained devoted to the Prophet and when he was sick and dying, stepped forward and said: "O Prophet of God, I surely wish that what you suffer from might be in me rather than in you." Furthermore, the Prophet belonged to a clan of the Quraysh, a tribe claiming descent from Abraham's son Ishmael.

The paradoxical doctrinal accretions that have become central to Christianity – the Incarnation, the Trinity, the Atonement, and Original Sin – are alien to both Judaism and Islam: "They surely conceal the truth who say, 'Behold, God is the Messiah, son of Mary.' The Messiah [himself] said, 'O children of Israel, worship God [alone], who is my Lord as well as your Lord'" (5:72). That "the son of God" may be understood as a figure of speech is indicated by the words that Jesus is reported to have said to Mary after the Crucifixion: "I ascend to my Father and your Father, and my God and your God" (John 20:17). Similarly, Jesus says in the Qur'an in two different verses: "God is my Lord and your Lord; so worship Him: this is a straight path" (3:51; 19:36; cf. 5:117).

The title "son of God" is mentioned twice by the Angel Gabriel in Luke's Gospel (1:31–2; 1:35), but it is not said that Jesus *was* the "son of God", but merely that the child will be *called* the son of God, suggesting that this was an honorary title. As Geza Vermes says, "Whereas every Jew was called son of God, the title came to be given preferably to the just man, and in a very special sense to the most righteous of all men, the Messiah son of David."[34] Muslims tend to reject the metaphor of a filial kinship between the Creator and His creatures as verging on the blasphemous: "He begets not, and neither is He begotten; and there is nothing that could be compared with Him" (112:3–4). This is the only reason why some Muslims might have reservations about reciting the first line of the Lord's Prayer: "Our Father which art in heaven".

In Islam deeds take priority over doctrines. There are certain central beliefs that must be accepted, but God will judge us by our intentions and actions, including prayer, fasting, and charity:

> True piety does not consist in turning your faces towards the east and the west, but truly pious is he who believes in God, and the Last Day, and the Angels, and the Scriptures, and the Prophets, and spends his substance – however much he may cherish it – upon his near of kin, and the orphans, and the needy, and the wayfarer, and the beggars, and for the freeing of human beings from bondage, and is constant

in prayer, and pays the alms tax [the purifying dues, or *zakat*]; and truly pious are they who keep their promises when they promise; and are patient in misfortune and hardship and time of peril: it is they who have proved themselves true, and it is they who fear God. (2:177)

The above definition of piety is not exclusively Muslim because the five requirements of faith – belief in God, the Day of Judgement, the Angels, the Scriptures, and the Prophets – are shared by Jews and Christians, and the duty to pray, to give in charity, and to keep one's word are universally accepted by those who follow a sacred tradition.[35]

Incidentally, the fact that freeing a slave is mentioned here and elsewhere (cf. 90:11) as a meritorious action proves, if proof were needed, that Islam discourages slavery.[36] All people are to be treated as equals and with equal justice, without regard for class, race, nationality, age, or gender. The only real hierarchy is that which is based on piety and spiritual rank. In the mosque there are no places reserved for dignitaries; all men stand shoulder to shoulder, whether they are princes or paupers, and at the time of the pilgrimage, all men and women wear an identical piece of white cloth. The Holy Prophet is reported to have said: "There is no superiority for an Arab over a non-Arab, neither a black over a white or white over a black except in piety. Indeed the noblest among you is the one who is most conscious of God." While the Prophet was on his Farewell Pilgrimage, he said: "O people, listen and obey, even if an Abyssinian slave is in command over you, so long as he leads you according to the Book of God."[37]

This, of course, does not mean that all men and women are born equal, nor does it mean that they receive equal rewards either here or in the hereafter; they differ in their intellectual abilities and natural talents, and they differ from one another in their willingness to use their potentialities. Some people have been blessed with more of God's bounty than others, but each will be judged by what he or she does with what God has generously provided: "He [God] ... has raised some of you by degrees above others, so that He might try you by means of what He has bestowed upon you" (6:15).

In Islam the rich do not merely have a duty to distribute some of their wealth to the poor, but the poor have a right to a share of their wealth. Now, however, as a result of globalisation and a growing burden of debt, the gap between the rich nations of the world and the poor grows ever wider. It is estimated that the combined wealth of the ten richest people in Britain is equivalent to the wealth of twenty-three of the world's poorest countries with a joint population of 174 million people, and the wealth of the world's three richest families is equal to that of 600 million people living in the world's poorest countries.[38] Eighty countries have per capita incomes lower than a decade ago, and sixty countries have grown steadily poorer since 1980. Two billion people now suffer from malnutrition, a figure which is likely to double in three or four decades. Meanwhile, obesity in the West has become a serious health problem, even among children.[39] As a result of these inequalities in the distribution of wealth, we have a global economic system that is incompatible with freedom, self-sufficiency, democracy, security, and the conservation of the earth's resources, and this leads to "a widespread perception of economic injustice that threatens not merely global stability but America's moral leadership".[40]

Conclusion

What is to be done to remedy this depressing state of affairs? Hans Küng has attempted to elaborate a global ethic (Küng and Kuschel 1993: 23f). Other Christians have sought to devise a globally responsible pluralistic theology (Knitter 1995). Muslims, on the whole, have failed to respond to this challenge, despite the fact that, by means of the Qur'an, they are well equipped to do so.

As we have shown, the Qur'an contains a charter for global dialogue and cooperation. Muslims need to implement this charter and demonstrate that extremism is contrary to Islam.[41] The Prophet Muhammad is reported to have said: "The differences of opinion among the learned within my community are [a sign of God's] grace." It is this Islamic tradition of tolerance that has to be revived, for those who cannot appreciate pluralism within their own religious community will certainly not be able to value religious pluralism.[42]

The dialogue of cultures or civilisations must begin with education. School children in every country should be exposed to the teachings of the major world religions and they should learn about their cultural indebtedness to other religions and civilisations.[43] Everywhere the curricula should be expanded to include the study of the classical works of both Muslims and non-Muslims.

On the political level, as Muhammad Asad – the son of a rabbi – has said, Jerusalem is the key to world peace because it is "a symbol of the wider community of all believers in the One God" (1987: 169). It was to Jerusalem that Muslims first turned in prayer and it was from there that the Prophet Muhammad made his visionary ascent to heaven.

Global dialogue at every level is the best way of preventing extremists from hijacking Islam or any other religion as an innocent victim.[44] Muslims in particular have a duty to share with the world the practical spiritual wisdom that they have inherited, instead of allowing misconceptions to generate a "them and us" mentality that is already leading to a polarisation of the world. Those who espouse a doctrine of cultural superiority and religious exclusivism are merely fanning the flames of war.

Notes

1   This essay is based on a paper presented at the 3rd Annual Conference of the Association of Muslim Social Scientists (AMSS), *Unity and Diversity: Islam, Muslims, and the Challenge of Pluralism*, held at the Diplomatic Academy, Westminster University, London, 20–21 October 2001. I have used some material from this essay in "Hatred and Revenge: Religious Pluralism Under Assault", *Middle East Affairs Journal*, vol. 7, nos 3–4 (Summer/Fall 2001), 43–50, and *World Faiths Encounter*, no. 22 (July 2002), 21–7.

2   The Christian scholar Kenneth Cragg, playing the devil's advocate, writes: "The enormities of which bigotries can be guilty send many into despair, crying 'A plague on all your houses.' Are they not all – as has been said – 'licensed insanities' whose licence, if ever valid, should now be rescinded?" (Cragg 2002: 13).

3   Salman Rushdie, concerning the massacre of Muslims in Gujerat, *The Guardian*, 9 March 2002.

4   Fergal Keane, "Public Enemy Number One?", *The Independent Review*, 4 February 2003, 4–5.

5   I use inverted commas because it is not really a war and, in any case, one cannot wage war against an abstract noun.

6   Professor Michael Howard, lecture given at the Royal United Services Institute, London, summarised in *The Independent* (2 November 2001).

7   Howard said in the same lecture: "To 'declare war' on terrorists, or even more illiterately, on 'terrorism' is at once to accord them a status and dignity that they seek and which they do not deserve."

8   In Afghanistan the combined toll of victims may never be known. See research by Marc W. Herold <www.cursor.org/stories/noncounters.htm>, and "3500 Civilians Killed in Afghanistan by US Bombs", 10 December 2001. In Iraq, according to a study published in *The Lancet*, reported by Jeremy Laurance and Colin Brown in *The Independent* (29 October 2004), over 100 000 Iraqis have lost their lives since the launch of the Second Gulf War in March 2003.

9   Words of Nahum Barnea, cited by Ian Gilmour, Lord Gilmour of Craigmillar, former Secretary of State for Defence, "Let there be justice for all, Mr Bush", *The Observer*, 31 March 2002.

10 See Thomas W. Zavrel, "Epidemiology and Risk: Health Effects of War and Sanctions on the Population of Iraq" <http://www.meaus.com/94-epidemology-iraq-2004.htm>.

11 Dr Anas al-Shaikh Ali is writing a book on this subject, which he discussed in a talk entitled "Islamophobia in Popular Culture", addressed to the Association of Muslim Researchers, London, 16 June 2001.

12 Plans to dominate the Middle East may eventually be foiled by Muslim democracy; see Jim Lobe, "Muslim Democracy Foils Bush's Imperial Plans", AlterNet, 3 March 2003. If the political aspirations of Iraqis are thwarted, this will result in further violence and extremism, as in Algeria and Palestine.

13 The exclusivist views of many of President Bush's strongest supporters are well known. Franklin Graham, son of the celebrated evangelical preacher Billy Graham, said on 26 March 2003 that when people ask him about Islam, "I let them know I don't believe in their God" (Deborah Caldwell, "Poised and Ready", BeliefNet, 27 March 2003). The Revd Jerry Vines, on the eve of the Southern Baptist Convention in St Louis in 2002, told several thousand delegates that Islam's Allah is not the same as the God worshipped by Christians, and he added: "And I will tell you Allah is not Jehovah, either. Jehovah's not going to turn you into a terrorist" (Mark O'Keefe, "Plans Under Way for Christianizing the Enemy", Newhouse News, 27 March 2003). Daniel Pipes, another influential Islamophobe, has the following statement on his website: "Individual Islamists may appear law-abiding and reasonable, but they are part of a totalitarian movement, and as such, all must be considered potential killers."

14 *Declaration on the Relation of the Church to Non-Christian Religions* (*Nostra Aetate*, 1965) <http://listserv.american.edu/catholic/church/vaticanii/nostra-aetate.html>.

15 *Reflections and Orientations on Interreligious Dialogue and the Proclamation of the Gospel of Jesus*, Pontifical Council for Interreligious Dialogue and Congregation for the Evangelization of Peoples, Pentecost 1991, section 29.

16 Dupuis 2001a: 1985. The views expressed by Father Dupuis here, and in his book *Towards a Christian Theology of Religious Pluralism* (1997), concerning a plurality of ways of salvation were condemned as heretical by the Congregation for the Doctrine of the Faith in a *Notification* approved by the Pope on 24 November 2000.

17 See *Jesus and the Living Past* (Oxford: Oxford University Press, 1980).

18 Hick 1989: 233; Hick 1985: 108; *cf.* Nicholson's edition of the *Mathnawi*, III, v. 1259, and Legenhausen's comments above, p. 67.

19 An outline of Islamic pluralism vaguely similar to mine may be found in Aslan (1998: 187–96).

20 M. Salim Abdullah, "What Shall be the Answer to Contemporary Islamic Fundamentalism?" in Küng and Moltmann 1992: 71.

21 Cf. "No men shall deride [other] men: it may well be that those [whom they deride] are better than themselves; and no women [shall deride other] women ... And neither shall you defame one another, nor insult one another" (49:11).

22 Cf. "He has enjoined upon you in this divine writ that whenever you hear people deny the truth of God's messages and mock at them, you shall not sit with them until they engage in some other talk – or else you will become like them" (4:140).

23 Muhammad Asad, in his rendering of the Qur'an into English, generally avoids the words "Muslim" and "Islam" because of the modern ideological connotations that these words have acquired in the mind of the average reader. This is what he told me in a private conversation in Tangier.

24 Malik ibn Anas, *Al-Muwatta: The First Formulation of Islamic Law*, trans. Aisha Abdurrahman Bewley (Granada, Spain: Madina Press, 1992), 16.16.53.

25 Cf. *The Penguin Krishnamurti Reader*, ed. Mary Lutyens (Harmondsworth: Penguin Books, 1970).

26 Dr Muzammil H. Siddiqi made this point in a lecture entitled "An Islamic Approach to Pluralism", at a Jewish-Christian-Muslim Interfaith Dialogue event at the University of South Carolina in Columbia on 29 November 2001.

27 Even before 11 September 2001 more than half of those surveyed in an opinion poll in the USA thought that Islam supported terrorism (Findley 2001: 88, and his chapter on "Terrorism and Defamation").

28 "War to the death between America and Islamic terrorists", *The Daily Telegraph*, 12 September 2001, p. 18.

29 Article from *The Guardian*, 18 August 2001, cited in *Q-News*, no. 335 (September 2001), p. 32.

30 A good example is Peter Partner, *God of Battles: Holy Wars of Christianity and Islam* (Princeton, NJ: Princeton University Press, 1998), reviewed by me in *The American Journal of Islamic Social Sciences*, vol. 17, no. 1 (2000), 101–3.

31 Mahatma Gandhi was staying with the first Indian Prime Minister, Mr Nehru, in the city of Allahabad. In the morning Gandhi was washing his face and hands. Mr Nehru was pouring water from the jug as they talked about the problems of India. As they were deeply engaged in serious discussion, Gandhi forgot that he was washing; before he had finished washing his face, the jug became empty. So Mr Nehru said, "Wait a minute and I will fetch another jug of water for you." Gandhi said, "What! You mean I have used all that jugful of water without finishing washing my face? How wasteful of me! I use only one jug of water every morning." He stopped talking; tears flowed from his eyes. Mr Nehru was shocked. "Why are you crying, what has happened, why are you worried about water? In my city of

Allahabad there are three great rivers, the Ganges, the Jumna, and the Saraswati, you don't need to worry about water here!" Gandhi said, "You are right, you have three great rivers in your town, but my share in those rivers is only one jug of water a morning and no more", cited by Satish Kumar, in *Save the Earth*, ed. Jonathan Porritt (London: Dorling Kindersley, 1992), p. 132.

32 Maulana Muhammad Ali, *A Manual of Hadith*, 2nd edn (London and Dublin: Curzon Press, 1978), p. 210.

33 Norman Stillman, *The Jews of Arab Lands: A History and Source Book* (Philadelphia, PA: Jewish Publication Society of America, 1979), pp. 154–5.

34 *Jesus the Jew: A Historian's Reading of the Gospels*, 2nd edn (London: SCM Press, 1983), p. 195.

35 In two other passages (discussed by Mahmoud Ayoub below, pp. 277–8), belief in God, belief in the Day of Judgement, and righteous action are the only three elements mentioned as essential for those who would earn God's favour (62, 5:69).

36 See W. 'Arafat, "The Attitude of Islam to Slavery", *The Islamic Quarterly*, 10 (1966), 12–18; and Momin 2001: 130.

37 Zakaria Bashier, *Sunshine at Madinah* (Leicester: The Islamic Foundation, 1990), p. 125.

38 Cited in Rumman Ahmed, "My Identity and Me: An Exploration of Multiple Identities and their Contribution towards a Faith Position", *World Faiths Encounter*, 28 (March 2001), 50.

39 Robert D. Crane cites these statistics in a paper entitled "The New Pagan Empire", Editorial in the Spring 2003 issue of the *Middle East Affairs Journal*. He notes that in three years, 1997–2000, the wealth of the Forbes 400 richest Americans grew by a daily average of $1 920 000 each. Cf. <www.forbes.com>.

40 See Crane, "The New Pagan Empire" (op. cit.).

41 Some polemical booklets distributed in mosques, if read by non-Muslims, would merely confirm anti-Muslim prejudices. In some English translations of the Qur'an, the words "like the Jews" and "like the Christians" have been added in parenthesis in the opening Surah to define two categories of transgressors, as if this is implied by the text, when in fact the majority of traditional scholars strongly reject this interpretation.

42 Bhikhu Parekh made this point with reference to cultural groups (2000: 337). Much of what he says about multiculturalism is also true of religious pluralism. On the subject of moderation, see Yusuf al-Qaradawi's essay on "Extremism" in Kurzman 1998: 196–204; and Abdel Haleem 1999: 59–81.

43 A useful sourcebook for teachers, covering many aspects of Islamic culture, is *The Legacy of Muslim Spain*, ed. Salma Khadra Jayyusi (Leiden: E. J. Brill, 1992); it contains an article by me on "Arab Influences on European Love-Poetry" (pp. 457–82).

44 See interview with Shaykh Hamza Yusuf Hanson in *The Guardian*, 8 October 2001.

Chapter 18

The Challenge of Pluralism and the Middle Way of Islam[1]

Jeremy Henzell-Thomas

There is a story from a classic of Islamic spirituality[2] about four quarrelling travellers, a Persian, a Turk, an Arab, and a Greek, who argue about how best to spend a single coin, which is the only piece of money they have between them. They all desire grapes, but they do not realise this because each speaks a different language. A traveller hears them quarrelling and buys them a bunch of grapes.

Everybody is in a state of yearning, because there is an inner need existing in all of us, a basic urge to remember our original state of unity, but we give it different names and have different ideas of what it may be. The traveller-linguist in the story represents the sage, the man or woman of spiritual insight, who knows that the other travellers all yearn for the same thing. Such a person is the harmoniser or peacemaker, who is able to resolve the misunderstanding and strife between the travellers and fulfil all their needs with a single coin. The single coin is, of course, *tawhid*, the divine unity, which is the ground of all diversity.

There is a special need at this time, in the midst of all the rhetoric about the clash of civilisations, to issue a strong warning about the consequences of exaggerating differences. More than ever, we need traveller-linguists who can translate from one "language" into another to bring to light the *convergence* of people's deepest aspirations.

I would like to challenge the dangerous doctrine of the clash of civilisations by finding common ground between the Anglo-Saxon spirit and Islamic values and virtues in the idea of the "middle way". According to the late President of Bosnia, 'Alija 'Ali Izetbegovic,[3] the source of this convergence is an Englishman, the thirteenth-century philosopher Roger Bacon, who "set the entire structure of English philosophical thought on two separate foundations": inward experience, which leads to spiritual insight, and observation and experimentation, which is the basis of modern science. Bacon never attempted to reduce everything to either a scientific or a religious outlook, but sought to establish a balance between the two: "This aspect of Bacon's genius is considered by most Englishmen as the most authentic expression of English thought and feeling."

President Izetbegovic then adds that there is "another important fact about Roger Bacon which has never been sufficiently studied and recognised: the father of English philosophy and science was a student of Arabic." Indeed, he lectured at Oxford in Arab clothes. He was strongly influenced by Islamic thinkers, especially by Ibn Sina, and to this influence can be attributed the character of Bacon's thought and, through him, perhaps the origin of the middle way as an important guiding principle in English life. He stressed the need for balance: balance between reason, observation, and science, on the one hand, and faith, on the other; balance between individual freedoms and rights, and wider responsibilities within society; balance between utilitarian morality, or pragmatism, and the highest ideals; and balance between a practical concern with the everyday needs and a hunger for transcendence.

Another Bacon, Sir Francis Bacon, is well known as one of the fathers of the scientific revolution in England, a champion of empiricism who held that we must purge the mind of prejudice, conditioning, false notions, and unanalysed authority – what he called the "Idols of the human mind" which distort and discolour the true nature of things – and rely instead on direct experience, observation, and "true induction" as methods of gaining sound knowledge.[4]

It has recently been argued that "multi-racialism can thrive only within the context of a common culture."[5] Such a view might seem to accord with the view of the Greek philosopher Heraclitus, quoted by Sir Francis Bacon in support of his ideas, that the limitations of the human mind cause us to seek truth within the confines of our own "lesser worlds" rather than in the "greater or common world". However, it is the grossest form of reductionism to equate the "lesser worlds" with the assumed "parochialism" represented by the imported cultures of immigrant ethnic minorities, and to equate the "greater common world" with a common nationalistic identity, as if the latter is any less parochial. There is a greater common world than the "common culture" of Englishness, whatever that may be, to which critics of multiculturalism say that all races in England must subscribe. The "greater common world" is greater too than the assumption of shared values in the self-referential rhetoric about preserving "our way of life" in the West. While many people of all faiths and cultures would agree that there are certain core values in Western civilisation which are worth defending, along with certain core values in other cultures, to suggest that there is some kind of monolithic "way of life" in the West is an illusion, and is an example of the very "fundamentalism" which is so often attributed to Islam.

The "greater common world" is greater even than the increasingly connected global community, which already transcends dwindling national boundaries. It is a world that Francis Bacon associates with what he calls the *Ideals* of the Divine, not the *Idols* of the human mind. It is the inclusive world of our true nature (*fitrah*) as fully rounded human beings, and it can have countless cultural expressions.

I do not wish to exaggerate the common ground that can be found in the Anglo-Saxon world and Islam. For one thing, it can easily be shown that the balance between the religious and the scientific outlooks began to be seriously disturbed with the onset of the scientific revolution in the seventeenth century, and we know what has happened now: a profound and pervasive loss of the sense of the sacred in Western culture wrought by scientific materialism, or scientism. By limiting science to experimentation, the original balance between inward experience and external observation, which was central to Bacon's vision, was destroyed. The Western mind became externalised, focused only on observable and quantifiable realities. Inward experience, the source of a deeper science or wisdom, was no longer to be trusted; the capacity for contemplation was neglected, and the very idea of revelation, of a Book "for those who believe in the Unseen" (2:4), beyond the reach of human perception, was denied.

The displayed Book of Nature, too, was divested of its *significance*, in the sense that its beautiful and majestic signs (*ayat*), symbols (*rumuz*), and similitudes (*amthal*) – whether in the "far horizons" or within ourselves – were no longer seen as pointing beyond themselves to the existence of an infinite and merciful Creator who had invested everything with "due measure and proportion", but only as phenomena referring to nothing outside their own self-sufficient laws and mechanisms.

At the heart of the concept of the middle way is the principle of fairness, the "fair play" so integral to the English conception of good character. The English word "fair" has two meanings: the first is "just, equitable, reasonable", and the second is "beautiful". But the meaning of its original Germanic root is "fitting", that which is the right size, in the correct ratio or proportion. The range of meanings of this word "fair" reflect a truly Islamic concept, the idea that to be just is to "do what is beautiful" (*ihsan*), to act in accordance with our original nature (*fitrah*), which God has shaped in "just proportions" (Qur'an 82:7) as a "fitting" reflection of divine order and harmony. Indeed, "Everything have We created in due measure and proportion" (54:49). So, a fair and just society is a beautiful society, and, in the words of a famous *hadith*, "God is Beauty and delights in the beautiful."

The most obvious expression of diversity is the underlying elemental polarity in the whole of creation, for, as the Qur'an says, "everything have We created in pairs" (51:49), and "We have created you all out of a male and a female" (49:13). The dance of this polarity is the excitement we call "love", for "among His wonders is this: He creates for you mates out of your own kind, so that you might incline towards them, and He engenders love and tenderness between you: in this, behold, there are messages indeed for people who think!" (30:21). God has created the world and everything in it as a system of polarities so that we may pass beyond these opposites to the essential Unity that is both our original identity and our ultimate goal as human beings. Every person, however, is free to derive from the polarity underlying the fabric of the universe the exact opposite lesson. We see this in the tendency of people to see reality in black and white, a propensity to see the world in terms of mutually hostile and competing civilisations, an us-versus-them ideology that self-righteously attributes rightness and goodness only to its own perspective.

The tendency to dichotomise reality in this way appears to be inherent in the way the brain works, because if you were able to see simultaneously all the grey areas, all the possible contradictions to any position, every ambiguity, and every conceivable point of view, you would be paralysed, incapable of any decisive action, or overwhelmed by confusion. There has to be some selection of input and output.

The tendency to debate, or engage in an adversarial argument, is ingrained in us because we inhabit a world of duality, and this tendency is reinforced by the gift of language, given to man alone by God, when He "imparted unto Adam the names of all things" (2:31). On one level this is the capacity for differentiating and naming things through the faculty of conceptual thought. On another level completely, "the letter", as al-Niffari, says, "is a veil" that separates us from unity precisely because it is a tool for manifesting endless diversity and multiplicity.[6]

But, unlike computers, human beings have the means to reconcile opposites, to encompass creative paradox, to be comfortable with diversity and difference. That is because as well as being given the Names that enable us to differentiate, we are also endowed with *fitrah*, that innate disposition which enables us to remember the unity of our primordial condition. And it is only through constant remembrance that we can purify our own hearts. In the words of the *hadith qudsi*,[7] "Neither the heavens nor the earth encompass me, but the heart of my faithful servant does encompass me." It is only in the human heart that opposites can be reconciled, that diversity and unity coexist.

True respect for diversity, so vital in today's interdependent world, is predicated on real dialogue, on the development of a relationship based on mutual engagement, not the mere exchange of clichés about the "celebration of diversity". As Diana Eck has said, interfaith dialogue, which is the first principle of pluralism, is a process of mutual transformation, for by understanding the "other", we may understand ourselves better (1993). As the Prophet Muhammad (s) said, "He who knows his own self, knows his Lord."

Tolerance is a starting-point in the development of a pluralistic society, and it is often upheld, along with empiricism, pragmatism, and the balance between individual liberty and the rule of law, as a characteristically English – and wider Anglo-Saxon – virtue. There may be some truth in this, and it is certainly the case that, despite the undeniable reality of unparalleled levels of institutional Islamophobia in Britain today,[8] there are millions of ordinary Britons who are essentially fair-minded, just, and tolerant people, who do not want to live in a divided society.

It is important not to fall into the jingoistic trap of equating particular virtues with national identities. Fair play is not a monopoly of the English. As I have already indicated, the semantic field encompassed by the English word "fair" has clear correspondences with the Arabic *ihsan*, righteousness or charity, from *husn*, beauty. Similarly, the root of the Arabic word *'adl*, justice, has the sense of proportion and symmetry. We need to look for such equivalences in order to discover the common underlying language represented by universal semantic fields. We must always come back to the single coin of the innate disposition of the human being, and not be tempted into invidious comparisons designed to promote particular communities at the expense of others.

Diana Eck warns against the danger of confusing pluralism with relativism. While relativism presupposes a stance of openness, pluralism presupposes both openness and commitment. We need to be aware of the "cynical intellectual sleight of hand" through which "some critics have linked pluralism with a valueless relativism" (1993: 193). This is a favourite ploy of those who seek to discredit pluralism by suggesting that it encourages a view of the world in which anything goes. Jacques Barzun has said, in his monumental survey of Western civilisation from 1500 to the present day, that "in the realm of ethics, the most blatant absurdity of the day is wrapped up in the bogey word *Relativism*. Its current misapplication is a serious error ... Nine out of ten times, the outcry against Relativism is mechanical" (2001: 760–61). Barzun maintains that the term has become "a cliché that stands for the cause of every laxity", and it would be easy to produce examples of past and present fulminations against relativism as the very ground of hedonism and self-indulgence, and a slippery slope of cunning casuistry and satanic whisperings, taking us further and further away from the certainty of eternal truths and absolute values.

The problem here is that we need to distinguish between relativism and the root of the word, which gives us "relativity" and "relationship". The usual charge against relativism is that the relativist denies that there is a fixed right or wrong, and that relativism and conscience are therefore diametrically opposed. However, as Eck points out, the "thoughtful relativist" is a "close cousin" of the pluralist (1993: 194), someone who is able to "relate" to people of other communities and able to show how absolutism can give rise to bigotry and oppressive dogma.

Muslims should recall that one of the founding principles of Islamic civilisation was a spirit of intellectual curiosity and scientific inquiry, which Muslim scholars communicated to the Christian, Greek, and Jewish communities living in their midst. It is stated in the Qur'an that Muslims are "a community of the middle way" (2:143), suggesting, according to Muhammad Asad, "a call to moderation in every aspect of life" and "a denial of the view that there is an inherent conflict between the spirit and the flesh" (1980a: 30). A closed, exclusive, puritanical, hostile, and inward-looking version of Islam, which regards all non-Muslims as enemies and refuses to engage with the rest of humankind, corresponds with no period of greatness in Islam and will bring none.

Notes

1   This paper integrates, revises and abridges material from the author's Opening Plenary Address and his Concluding Remarks at the 3rd Annual Conference of the Association of Muslim Social Scientists (AMSS), *Unity and Diversity: Islam, Muslims, and the Challenge of Pluralism*, held at the Diplomatic Academy, Westminster University, London, 20–21 October 2001; AMSS Occasional Paper Series, 1 (Richmond, Surrey, 2002).

2   Jalalal-Din Rumi, *Mathnawi*, II, 3681 ff.

3   On the resemblances between the Anglo-Saxon "middle way" and the "third way of Islam", see Izetbegovic 1994: 271–86; cf. Abdal Hakim Murad, "British and Muslim", *American Muslim Network*, no. 7 (November 2001), based on a lecture given to a conference of British converts on 17 September 1997.

4   See Francis Bacon's "The Four Idols" (originally in *Novum Organum*) in *Plato's Heirs: Classic Essays*, ed. James D. Lester (Lincolnwood, Illinois: NTC Publishing Group, 1996), pp. 53–63.

5   Sir Richard Body, *England for the English* (London: New European Publications, 2001), p. 181.

6   *The Mawaqif and Mukhatabat of Muhammad Ibn 'Abdi 'l-Jabbar al-Niffari*, trans. and ed. A. J. Arberry (Cambridge: Cambridge University Press, 1935), p. 111.

7   A saying reported by the Prophet Muhammad, but spoken by God in the first person.

8   In the UK the Media and Popular Culture Watch project at the Forum Against Islamophobia and Racism (FAIR) is monitoring incidences of Islamophobia in the media and entertainment industries.

Chapter 19

The Qur'an and Religious Pluralism[1]

Mahmoud M. Ayoub

Introduction

The Qur'an was revealed at a time when the principle of universalism in human civilisation and religious culture had become normative for religious thought and worship. It must be viewed both as a timeless divine revelation as well as an important historic event in human civilisation. While no committed Muslim would deny my first assertion, many have insisted on the transcendent character of the Qur'an, thus limiting or altogether denying the fact that the Qur'an is inextricably bound to human history. The Qur'an spoke directly to both the spiritual and social situation of humankind at large and to the situation of the Arabs of the Arabian Peninsula. Speaking of the mission of the Prophet Muhammad, God says, "We have not sent you except as a mercy for all beings" (21:107), and He commands Muhammad thus: "Say: 'O humankind, I am the messenger of God to you all'" (7:158).

The Qur'an, it may thus be concluded, came to speak to all of humanity. However, it came to speak not in a vacuum, but within a historical context. Hence, its immediate objective was the moral and religious situation of the Arabs of the Prophet's time. It must therefore be further concluded that although we can always hear the Qur'an speaking anew to our own particular situation, its own historical context must not be obscured behind its universal and timeless dimension.

Human Diversity

Humanity began as one and must remain one, but it is unity in diversity. This diversity, moreover, is not due to the gradual degeneration of human society from an ideal or utopian state. Nor is it the result of a lack of divine guidance or human understanding. Rather, religious diversity is a normal human situation. It is the consequence of the diversity of human cultures, languages, races, and different environments. The Qur'an states:

> Humankind was all one community. Then God sent prophets as bearers of good tidings and warners. He sent down with them the Book with the truth in order that it may judge among men concerning that in which they differ. But none differ concerning it, save those who were given the scriptures after manifest signs had come to them, being envious of one another. God guides aright by His permission those

273

who have faith to the truth, concerning which they differed. God guides whom He wills to the straight way.[2]

Here the Qur'an does not use the term "books", that is to say, the plurality of scriptures, but the Book in general, the Book which is the heavenly archetype of all divine revelations, and of which all true scriptures are but earthly exemplars.

God communicated His revelation to the prophets in order that they may judge on His behalf among human communities concerning their moral and religious differences. But differences, and hence disunity, arose only through one of the most universal of human failings: not the original sin of disobedience, but envy and hostility, which are natural human weaknesses arising from insecurity and wilful arrogance.

Here we have the synthesis of this Qur'anic dialectic: it is unity in diversity. Unity is the essence of our understanding of the oneness of God, *tawhid*, as expressed in the profession of faith (*shahadah*), *There is no god except Allah*. It is also the basis of the essential unity of all creation and of humankind. But diversity is a necessary consequence of geography, of language, or of what we may positively call the rich variety of human civilisations.

What the Qur'an decries is not diversity but discord or conflict. It decries what it calls, in Surah 2:213, *baghi*, meaning hostility, insolence, or envy among human individuals and societies. Difference is good, but conflict is evil. This is, in my view, what the Qur'an is saying to us all, Muslims and non-Muslims.

A Pluralistic World

The Qur'an presents the thesis of unity within the framework of religious and cultural pluralism. For the first time in human history, we now live in a pluralistic world, a world increasingly unified by our modern means of instant communication. Yet this pluralistic world is not as open to forms of religious or cultural globalism as many think. The common view now is that the world is shrinking into a global village. If this were really true, it would mean the utter impoverishment of human cultures as they all merge into an indistinct mass of cultural uniformity. The fallacy of the notion of the global village can be seen from the conflicts that often arise within one city, and indeed within one district in a city, among people belonging to different ethnic, religious, and ideological identities.

The world, it is to be hoped, is not heading towards a global village. Globalisation, in all its cultural and economic forms, is the latest stage of Western neo-imperialism. For those committed to a sacred tradition such as Islam it is both a threat and a challenge. What we should be aiming for, as the Qur'an enjoins, is acceptance and appreciation of the plurality of cultures and religions, but within the unity of faith in the one God.

Pluralism does not necessarily mean a tower of Babel, where everyone speaks a different language with no possibility of communicating with, or understanding, one another. Rather, underlying religious pluralism must be a unity of purpose and open dialogue. Here again we have the Qur'anic answer, that is, unity of faith, where wisdom and fair dialogue ought to bring together the communities of different religions and cultures into a harmony of faith and purpose. From the Qur'anic point of view, this unity operates within a historical continuity of divine revelation, beginning with Adam and ending with Muhammad. Although revelation ended with the Qur'an, divine guidance continues in the proper interpretation and implementation of sacred scriptures. This kind of divine inspiration will continue till the end of time.

Messengers and Prophets

We did aforetime send messengers before you. Of them, there are some whose story We have related to you, and some whose story We have not related to you.

(40:78)

The Qur'an mentions only twenty-five prophets. Five of these are called *Ulu al-'Azm* (prophets of power or strong resolve): they were sent by God as messengers not only to their own people but to all humankind.[3]

The verse just cited implies that there is an indefinite number of messengers and prophets about whom we are not informed. In fact, the Islamic tradition, with the usual exaggeration of the popular piety of every religious tradition, puts the number of prophets from Adam to Muhammad at 124 000. Does this mean that just because God did not tell us about these prophets we should not try to identify at least some of them? The criterion for such an undertaking is, according to the Qur'an, the message of the truth of divine transcendence, with its moral and spiritual meaning for human life and history. This truth is the essence of the messages of all the prophets of God.

There is no great difficulty in identifying such prophets in the monotheistic traditions, namely Judaism, original Zoroastrianism, Christianity, and Arabia before Islam. But this task becomes far more complex in the case of the wisdom religions of India and China, and the native traditions of Africa and the Americas. The Qur'anic framework is the principle that *there is no community but that a warner was sent to it* to warn it in its own language (10:47; cf. 4:41; 16:36).

We Muslims must look at the great religious figures – prophets, philosophers, and the great teachers of human history – and discover how they fit into this broad Islamic framework. This is a challenge that Muslims have not yet faced in any meaningful way. It must, however, be observed that the strong interest of early Muslim scholars in the study of other religions and sects could have served as the impetus and framework of a universal Islamic theology of prophethood and revelation. Let me, in any case, make a tentative attempt at identifying some of the extra-Qur'anic and extra-biblical prophets and sages.

Non-Islamic Faiths

There is no doubt that Zarathustra's original message was not a message of absolute dualism. That is to say, Ahura Masda, the "Wise Lord", and Ahriman, the evil spirit, were not thought by the prophet Zarathustra to be equal powers, one of good and the other of evil. Rather, the power of good will in the end prevail, but evil is necessary for the good truly to manifest itself.

The hymns of Zarathustra[4] present also a strict monotheistic ethical system. It repudiates lying or falsehood. It looks forward to a universal resurrection and final judgement, when the righteous will be rewarded with the bliss of paradise and the wicked chastised with the torments of hell. But the end of the drama of human history will be the ultimate purification and salvation of all beings. Hell will then be used to enlarge the earth. Undoubtedly, therefore, Zoroastrianism belongs to the long process of divine revelation and Zarathustra was certainly one of the prophets sent by God.

The Buddha, of whom Zarathustra may have been a near contemporary, rejected the Hindu gods in whose name the brahminical priesthood dominated Indian society. Instead, he preached an ethical and spiritual philosophy that was clearly based on the transcendent reality of *dharma*, the universal and timeless principle, or norm, underlying all phenomena of being and becoming.[5] Furthermore, the Buddha's teachings made Buddhism a truly universal religion. Therefore, the Buddha must be seen as part of the ongoing progress of humanity towards knowledge of the one God.

This process, however, did not always move in a continuously linear progression. There is always somewhere the voice of God speaking to humanity, but at times this voice becomes obscured by the vain imaginings of arrogant and misguided groups or individuals. This is the price of the freedom that God gave humankind. Otherwise, if human beings were angels without freedom, they would not sin.

Human beings have the special prerogative of being capable of both sin and righteousness. Like Adam, all human beings must strive for a prophetic existence, but not for prophethood itself. This is because prophethood is not a status that can be achieved through individual effort. It is a divine election: "God knows best where He places His message" (6:124).

In the *Rig Veda*, the few hymns addressed to the god Varuna are some of the most beautiful devotional prayers in religious literature. They are addressed to the one and only God, who is merciful and a just judge of human actions and inner thoughts. He thus punishes the wicked and rewards the good. The hymns in question, therefore, invoke His mercy and beg His forgiveness. Unfortunately, these ideals were quickly eclipsed by the politics of the Arian conquests of India. Thus, the great god Indra, who was perhaps an ancient war hero, soon overshadowed Varuna, the Lord of mercy and forgiveness.

The Jews, according to the well-known Islamic reformer Sayyid Rashid Rida (d. 1935), must be regarded throughout their ancient history as the people who were charged with being the guardians of *tawhid*, at least in the Middle East and the Mediterranean basin.[6] Perhaps because of this special privilege, the Jews became too particularistic, viewing themselves as God's only chosen people. Nonetheless, they remained the sole guardians of ethical monotheism until the coming of Christianity (or Islam, many would argue).

It must further be observed that, although Christians, by the middle of the fourth century, had established the dogma of the Trinity, no one can seriously question their faith in the one God. Christians have been wrestling with this theological doctrine, or as the Church has always insisted, divine mystery, for the last 2000 years without reaching a universally recognised formulation of it. Nevertheless, the Qur'an insists that Christianity, Islam, and Judaism are all religions honouring and worshipping the one and only God. God uses human beings to uphold knowledge of Him. He uses not only prophets, but communities as well, to safeguard the remembrance of His name in His houses, and these houses of God include synagogues, churches, mosques, and monasteries (22:40). In another verse of the same Surah, the various major religious communities that existed at the time of the revelation of the Qur'an are listed.[7]

It is noteworthy that *those who have associated other gods with God* are not identified with any of the other communities, but are in a category by themselves. They are in fact mentioned after the Muslims, Jews, Christians, Sabaeans, and Zoroastrians. This classification assumes a process of progressive revelation from which only open idolatry is excluded. Still, in the end, it leaves final judgement as to the truth or falsehood of any religion to God.

The verse just cited is not an isolated one. The Qur'an states:

> Had your Lord so willed, He would have made humankind one community. But He made them different in order to try you with that which He had given you. Vie then with one another in the performance of righteous works. To God shall be your return and He will inform you concerning that about which you had differed. (5:48)

Here, too, the idea that human diversity is a divinely instituted, or at least divinely sanctioned, phenomenon is clearly affirmed. Likewise, this verse asserts that the ultimate judgement with regard to the differences among humankind will be for God to make on the Day of Resurrection.

The Qur'anic Affirmation

Islam dealt with the issue of religious diversity and unity of faith in Medina in the most concrete fashion, as the Prophet had to deal with both the Jewish tribes of Medina and the Christian community of Najran. There is one verse that appears in the first major Medinan Surah, and which is then repeated verbatim, in the last but one major Surah to be revealed to the Prophet before his death. This is, to my knowledge, the only verse repeated in exactly the same words in the Qur'an. The fact that this verse occurs at the beginning and end of the Prophet's political career means that neither the words nor the purport of these two identical verses were abrogated. The verse in question reads: "Surely those who have faith, the Jews, the Christians, and the Sabaeans, whoever accepts faith in God and the Last Day and performs good deeds, those shall have their reward with their Lord; no fear shall come upon them nor will they grieve" (2:62, 5:69).

Muslims have, since the rise of the Islamic caliphate, strenuously attempted to negate this clear and twice-repeated Qur'anic assertion. They have always resorted to two important verses that, in some ways, complete one another. The first declares: "Surely the true faith before God is *islam*" (3:19). The second asserts: "Anyone who seeks a faith other than *islam*, it will not be accepted from him" (3:85). Here we see clearly the clash between the Qur'anic view of religious pluralism and the conservative and narrow world-view of Muslim jurists. This is because the Qur'an undoubtedly means by the term *islam*, in both verses, not the legal Islamic identity of Muslims, but the way of total submission to God, which is open to all the people of faith from Adam to the end of time.

It is important before we discuss this problem in some detail to observe that most of the verses in the Qur'an dealing with the religious communities, particularly with the Christians, do not fall in the category of legislative verses (*ayat al-ahkam*) and therefore cannot be subject to abrogation. An exception to this rule is verse 29 of Surah 9, the well-known *Jizya* verse. This is a legislative verse, as it regulates political and social relations between the Muslim community and the peoples of the Book (Jews and Christians). Other Qur'anic verses dealing with the two monotheistic faith communities belong to the genre called narrative verses. That is to say, they are moral and religious statements, but do not legislate any rulings, as in the case of the verse under discussion.

The two verses in Surah 3, which assert that the only faith acceptable to God is *islam*, raise the important question just mentioned, namely, what is the proper, or at least more likely interpretation, of the term *islam* in these two verses? If we say that there is no difference between Islam as the name of an institutionalized religious law, and *islam* as the total submission of the will of the creature to the will of the Creator, then one must in the end negate the other. This also means that all references in the Qur'an to the *islam* of all the prophets from Adam to Muhammad are meaningless. Furthermore, this means that no other manifest or institutionalised religion will be acceptable to God except the legalistic and ritualistic Islam that has been practised by Muslims for the last 1500 years. This would mean that all the Qur'anic verses asserting the plurality of religion and unity of faith are empty words.

Islam as Universal Attitude

Islam is not, according to the Qur'an and early Prophetic tradition, the name of a religion. Rather, it signifies the attitude of the entire creation before God. The term *islam*, in this sense, applies to the heavens and the earth and all that is in them, to humankind and to everything that God created. This is the first and universal plane of the meaning of the term *islam*. On another plane, *islam* applies to any human beings who profess faith in the one God and seek to obey

God in all that they do and say. It is in this sense that the Qur'an speaks of Noah, Abraham, Moses, and Jesus and his disciples, as Muslims.

This does not mean that Jesus and all the people of faith from the beginning of human history and until the coming of Islam as an institutionalized religion observed the rituals of Islam and lived in accordance with its juridical and social principles and customs. Nevertheless, Jesus, for example, is presented in the hagiography of popular Muslim piety known as *Qisas al-Anbiya'* (Tales of the Prophets) as though he were one of the Prophet's companions (*sahabah*), making his ablutions (*wudu'*), facing the *qiblah*, and offering the regular Islamic prayers. Of course, in this narrow sense, neither Jesus, nor any of the people of faith in God before Muhammad were Muslims. But in their attitude of total obedience to God, Jesus and all the prophets of God and their followers were *muslims*, submitters to God.

The Qur'an clearly distinguishes between Islam as an institutionalized religion and *islam* as the framework of true faith (*iman*) and righteous living (*ihsan*). The verse which most explicitly draws this distinction is the well-known *ayat al-A'rab* (the "Verse of the Bedouins", Surah 49:14), where the nomadic Arab tribesmen are challenged in their assertion, "We have accepted faith", and told instead to say, "We have become Muslims", for true faith had not yet entered their hearts.

In addition, this verse raises the issue of diversity and unity within the Muslim community, one of the most grievous problems it faces today. To be more specific: can any Muslim, in the name of a legal or theological school or ideology, declare another Muslim who may not agree with him to be a rejecter of faith (*kafir*)? The Qur'an emphatically asserts: "Do not say to one who offers you the salutation of peace (*salam*), 'You are not a believer'" (4:94). Many Muslims today are not willing to accept pluralism within their own community, let alone the pluralism of religions within a unity of faith.

The third and most concrete plane of *islam* is the Islam of a given community, following a particular divine law, revealed to a particular prophet. In the case of Islam, it is the sacred law (*shari'ah*) revealed to the Prophet Muhammad. This is not to deny that this institutionalised Islam is continuous with the essential *islam* of all the people of faith both before and after Muhammad. Rather, the religion of Islam, like all revealed religions before it, is a concrete manifestation of this primordial and universal *islam*.

This in fact is the logic of the dialectic of the Qur'anic world-view, the dialectic of unity in diversity. This dialectic in no way negates the continuity of revelation, from the words that "Adam received from his Lord" to the Qur'an of the Prophet Muhammad. Nor does it deny the continuity of revelation vouchsafed to all the prophets with the inspiration of righteous people in every age to interpret and implement God's revelations in their lives and the lives of their peoples.

This basic distinction between prophetic revelation, which ended with Muhammad, and the continuous divine guidance of the entire humanity in its quest for God and the good, is typified in the *shahadah*, which is the basis of the Islamic faith. It is the witness of all things to the oneness of God. The added affirmation, or second *shahadah*, "*Muhammad is the Messenger of God*", is what distinguishes Muslims from the people of other faiths. For this special affirmation applies to Muslims who follow the law of the Prophet Muhammad, those who offer the five daily prayers, fast during the month of Ramadan, and observe all the obligations (*fara'id*) which he instituted on behalf of God.

This Qur'anic world-view, moreover, presents Muslims with the greatest challenge of their faith. It is the challenge to seek a true fellowship of faith with the other religions and their faith communities on the basis of this Qur'anic dialectic.

The Challenge of the Qur'an

I shall end this discussion with the following few conclusions.

The first is that, neither the Qur'an nor the Prophetic tradition demands of Jews and Christians that they give up their religious identity and become Muslims unless they freely choose to do so. The basis of this religious freedom in Islam is the categorical Qur'anic assertion that "*there is no coercion in religion*" (*la ikraha fi al-din*; 2:256).

Second, the Qur'an and Prophetic tradition not only enjoin Muslims but also the followers of other faiths to engage in meaningful dialogue, cooperation, and agreement on basic principles. This is what the Qur'an calls "*a word of common assent*" (*kalimatan sawa'*), namely, that "*we worship no one except God and ... we do not take one another as lords beside God*" (3:64).[8] This important call to a unity of faith across the diversity of religions is far more relevant to our time than it was to the time of the Prophet and his people. It goes far beyond the issue of whether Christians actually worship their monks or not. One of the Companions of the Prophet, 'Adi ibn Hatim, who was formerly a Christian, said to the Prophet: "But the Jews and the Christians do not worship their Rabbis and their monks." The Prophet said, "Do not they legislate for them and they accept their legislation?" This is tantamount to worshipping them because worship in Islam is obedience, and if one obeys anyone other than God, then it is as though one worships him instead of God.

It is important in this regard to observe that Karaism, a movement within Judaism which arose after Islam, may be regarded as an answer to this call. The Karaite movement continues to this day to call other Jews to return to the law of God as revealed in the Torah, and rejects Rabbinic Judaism. It is with this Rabbinic Judaism that the Qur'an was concerned and with which the Muslim community has been struggling ever since.

Judaism, as it has been observed for nearly 2000 years, is Rabbinic Judaism. Although Rabbinic Judaism is continuous with biblical Judaism, the latter has been completely superseded by the former. This is perhaps the reason behind the Qur'anic call for the people of the Torah, wherein, it is said, there is "guidance and light" (5:44), to judge by what God has revealed in it. For the same reason, the Qur'an calls upon the people of the Gospel to "judge in accordance with what God has revealed therein" (5:47).

To the extent that Eastern Christians, more than other peoples, have tried to harmonise their faith in God with moral living and humility before God, they are considered to be the "*nearest in amity*" to Muslims (5:82–5). This special relation with the Christians does not close the door to dialogue with other religious communities. In fact, the legal designation of *ahl al-kitab* (peoples of the Book) has been quite fluid. It came to include more and more communities as Muslims came to know more and more religious traditions.

To conclude: what then is the challenge that the Qur'an presents to us today? The challenge is this, that we all have faith in God and compete with one another in righteous works. It follows from this challenge that all people of faith respect one another and that they believe in all of God's revelations.

The Qur'an presents the followers of all three monotheistic religions not only with a great challenge, but with a great promise as well. The promise is this: "Were the people of the Book to abide by the Torah, the Gospel, and that which was sent down to them from their Lord [the Qur'an], they would have provisions from above them and from beneath their feet" (5:65–6).[9]

Notes

1 This chapter is reproduced with the permission of the author and the journal *Global Dialogue* (ed. Paul Theodoulou), vol. 2, no. 1 (Winter 2000), issue on "The New Universe of Faiths", but it has been abbreviated. An earlier version appeared in *Encounters*, vol. 3, no. 2 (September 1997), 103–18.
2 Surah 2:213. For different interpretations of this verse, see Ayoub 1984: vol. 1, pp. 215–18.
3 They are Noah, Abraham, Moses, Jesus, and Muhammad. As for Adam, the Qur'an states, "We found no resolve in him" (20: 115).
4 These are the ancient Yasnas, translated into English as *The Hymns of Zarathustra* by M. Henning (London: J. Murray, 1952).
5 See the penetrating study of *dharma* as the transcendent reality by Smith 1967.
6 See Rida's commentary on Surah 5:82, *Tafsir al-Manar*, vol. 6 (Egypt: Dar al-Manar, 1954).
7 Surah 22:17 reads: "Surely those who have accepted faith, those who are Jews, the Sabaeans, the Christians, the Magians, and those who have associated other gods with God, God will judge among them on the Day of Resurrection. God is witness over all things".
8 This verse follows the only heated debate between the Prophet and the Christians, which is alluded to in the *mubahalah* verse, 3:61.
9 This means that they would eat of the bounties of the skies through rain and the rich yields of the earth.

POSTSCRIPT

Blessed are the peacemakers: for they shall be called the children of God.

Matthew 5:3

Peace I leave with you, my peace I give unto you: not as the world giveth, give I unto you. Let not the heart be troubled, neither let it be afraid.

John 14:27

He guides to Himself all those who turn to Him – those who believe, and whose hearts find their rest in the remembrance of God – for, verily, in the remembrance of God hearts do find their rest.

Qur'an 13:27–8

The true slaves of the Most Merciful are those who walk gently on earth and who, when the ignorant address them, say "Peace".

Qur'an 25:63

Peace is not merely a distant goal that we seek, but a means by which we arrive at that goal.

Dr Martin Luther King Jr

Permission [to fight] is given to those against whom war is wrongfully waged ... those who have been driven from their homelands against all right for no other reason than their saying, "Our Lord is God!" For if God had not enabled people to defend themselves against one another, monasteries and synagogues and mosques – in all of which God's name is abundantly extolled – would certainly have been destroyed.

Qur'an 22:39–40

The name of the one God must become increasingly what it is: a name of peace and a summons to peace.

Novo Millennio Ineunte

No peace among the nations without peace among the religions.

Hans Küng

If peace were as profitable as war, we would have peace.

Pope Paul VI

Chapter 20

The Failure of War[1]

Wendell Berry

If you know even as little history as I do, it is hard not to doubt the efficacy of modern war as a solution to any problem except that of retribution – the "justice" of exchanging one damage for another. Apologists for war will insist that war answers the problem of national self-defence. But the doubter, in reply, will ask to what extent the cost even of a successful war of national defence – in life, money, material, foods, health, and (inevitably) freedom – may amount to a national defeat. National defence through war always involves some degree of national defeat. This paradox has been with us from the very beginning of the American republic. Militarisation in defence of freedom reduces the freedom of the defenders. There is a fundamental inconsistency between war and freedom.

In a modern war, fought with modern weapons and on the modern scale, neither side can limit to "the enemy" the damage that it does. These wars damage the world. We know enough by now to know that you cannot damage a part of the world without damaging all of it. Modern war has not only made it impossible to kill "combatants" without killing "non-combatants"; it has made it impossible to damage your enemy without damaging yourself. That many have considered the increasing unacceptability of modern warfare is shown by the language of the propaganda surrounding it. Modern wars have characteristically been fought to end war; they have been fought in the name of peace. Our most terrible weapons have been made, ostensibly, to preserve and assure the peace of the world. "All we want is peace," we say as we increase relentlessly our capacity to make war.

Yet after a century in which we have fought two wars to end war and several more to prevent war and preserve peace, and in which scientific and technological progress has made war ever more terrible and less controllable, we still, by policy, give no consideration to non-violent means of national defence. We do indeed make much of diplomacy and diplomatic relations, but by diplomacy we mean invariably ultimatums for peace backed by the threat of war. It is always understood that we stand ready to kill those with whom we are "peacefully negotiating".

Our century of war, militarism, and political terror has produced great – and successful – advocates of true peace, among whom Mohandas Gandhi and Martin Luther King, Jr, are the paramount examples. The considerable success that they achieved testifies to the presence, in the midst of violence, of an authentic and powerful desire for peace and, more important, of the proven will to make the necessary sacrifices. But so far as our government is concerned, these men and their great and authenticating accomplishments might as well never have existed. To achieve peace by peaceable means is not yet our goal. We cling to the hopeless paradox of making peace by making war.

Which is to say that we cling in our public life to a brutal hypocrisy. In our century of almost universal violence of humans against fellow humans, and against our natural and cultural commonwealth, hypocrisy has been inescapable because our opposition to violence has been selective or merely fashionable. Some of us who approve of our monstrous military budget and our peacekeeping wars none the less deplore "domestic violence" and think that our society can be pacified by "gun control". Some of us are against capital punishment but for abortion. Some of us are against abortion but for capital punishment.

One does not have to know very much or think very far in order to see the moral absurdity upon which we have erected our sanctioned enterprises of violence. Abortion-as-birth-control is justified as a "right", which can establish itself only by denying all the rights of another person, which is the most primitive intent of warfare. Capital punishment sinks us all to the same level of primal belligerence, at which an act of violence is avenged by another act of violence. What the justifiers of these acts ignore is the fact – well-established by the history of feuds, let alone the history of war – that violence breeds violence. Acts of violence committed in "justice" or in affirmation of "rights" or in defence of "peace" do not end violence. They prepare and justify its continuation.

The most dangerous superstition of the parties of violence is the idea that sanctioned violence can prevent or control unsanctioned violence. But if violence is "just" in one instance as determined by the state, why might it not also be "just" in another instance, as determined by an individual? How can a society that justifies capital punishment and warfare prevent its justifications from being extended to assassination and terrorism? If a government perceives that some causes are so important as to justify the killing of children, how can it hope to prevent the contagion of its logic spreading to its citizens – or to its citizens' children?

If we give to these small absurdities the magnitude of international relations, we produce, unsurprisingly, some much larger absurdities. What could be more absurd, to begin with, than our attitude of high moral outrage against other nations for manufacturing the selfsame weapons that we manufacture? The difference, as our leaders say, is that we will use these weapons virtuously, whereas our enemies will use them maliciously – a proposition that too readily conforms to a proposition of much less dignity: we will use them in our interest, whereas our enemies will use them in theirs. Or we must say, at least, that the issue of virtue in war is as obscure, ambiguous, and troubling as Abraham Lincoln found to be the issue of prayer in war: "Both [the North and the South] read the same bible, and pray to the same God, and each invokes his aid against the other ... The prayers of both could not be answered – that of neither could be answered fully."

Recent American wars, having been both "foreign" and "limited", have been fought under the assumption that little or no personal sacrifice is required.

In "foreign" wars, we do not directly experience the damage that we inflict upon the enemy. We hear and see this damage reported in the news, but we are not affected. These limited, "foreign" wars require that some of our young people should be killed or crippled, and that some families should grieve, but these "casualties" are so widely distributed among our population as hardly to be noticed.

Otherwise, we do not feel ourselves to be involved. We pay taxes to support the war, but that is nothing new, for we pay war taxes also in time of "peace". We experience no shortages, we suffer no rationing, we endure no limitations. We earn, borrow, spend, and consume in wartime as in peacetime. And of course no sacrifice is required of those large economic interests that now principally constitute our economy. No corporation will be required to submit to any limitation or to sacrifice a dollar. On the contrary, war is the great cure-all and opportunity of our corporate economy, which subsists and thrives upon war. War ended the Great Depression of the 1930s, and we have maintained a war economy – an economy, one might justly say, of general violence – ever since, sacrificing to it an enormous economic and ecological wealth, including, as designated victims, the farmers and the industrial working class. And so great costs are involved in our fixation on war, but the costs are "externalised" as "acceptable losses". And here we see how progress in war, progress in technology, and progress in the industrial economy are parallel to one another – or, very often, are merely identical.

Romantic nationalists, which is to say most apologists for war, always imply in their public speeches a mathematics or an accounting of war. Thus by its suffering in the Civil War, the North is said to have "paid for" the emancipation of the slaves and the preservation of the Union. Thus we may speak of our liberty as having been "bought" by the bloodshed of patriots. I am fully aware of the truth in such statements. I know that I am one of many who have benefited from painful sacrifices made by other people, and I would not like to be ungrateful. Moreover, I am a patriot myself and I know that the time may come for any of us when we must make extreme sacrifices for the sake of liberty – a fact confirmed by the fates of Gandhi and King.

But still I am suspicious of this kind of accounting. For one reason, it is necessarily done by the living on behalf of the dead. And I think we must be careful about too easily accepting, or being too easily grateful for, sacrifices made by others, especially if we have made none ourselves. For another reason, though our leaders in war always assume that there is an acceptable price, there is never a previously stated level of acceptability. The acceptable price, finally, is whatever is paid.

It is easy to see the similarity between this accounting of the price of war and our usual accounting of "the price of progress". We seem to have agreed that whatever has been (or will be) paid for so-called progress is an acceptable price. If that price includes the diminishment of privacy and the increase of government secrecy, so be it. If it means a radical reduction in the number of small businesses and the virtual destruction of the farm population, so be it. If it means the devastation of whole regions by extractive industries, so be it. If it means that a mere handful of people should own more billions of wealth than is owned by all of the world's poor, so be it.

But let us have the candour to acknowledge that what we call "the economy" or "the free market" is less and less distinguishable from warfare. For about half of the last century, we worried about world conquest by international communism. Now with less worry (so far) we are witnessing world conquest by international capitalism. Though its political means are milder (so far) than those of communism, this newly internationalised capitalism may prove even more destructive of human cultures and communities, of freedom, and of nature. Its tendency is just as much toward total dominance and control. Confronting this conquest, ratified and licensed by the new international trade agreements, no place and no community in the world may consider itself safe from some form of plunder. More and more people all over the world are recognising that this is so, and they are saying that world conquest of any kind is wrong, period.

They are doing more than that. They are saying that local conquest also is wrong, and wherever it is taking place local people are joining together to oppose it. All over my own state of Kentucky this opposition is growing – from the West, where the exiled people of the Land Between the Lakes are struggling to save their homeland from bureaucratic depredation, to the East, where the native people of the mountains are still struggling to preserve their land from destruction by absentee corporations.

To have an economy that is warlike, that aims at conquest and that destroys virtually everything that it is dependent on, placing no value on the health of nature or of human communities, is absurd enough. It is even more absurd that this economy, that in some respects is so much at one with our military industries and programmes, is in other respects directly in conflict with our professed aim of national defence.

It seems only reasonable, only sane, to suppose that a gigantic programme of preparedness for national defence should be founded first of all upon a principle of national and even regional economic independence. A nation determined to defend itself and its freedoms should be prepared, and always preparing, to live from its own resources and from the work and the skills of its own people. But that is not what we are doing in the United States today. What we are doing is squandering in the most prodigal manner the natural and human resources of the nation.

At present, in the face of declining finite sources of fossil fuel energies, we have virtually no energy policy, either for conservation or for the development of safe and clean alternative sources. At present, our energy policy simply is to use all that we have. Moreover, in the face of a growing population needing to be fed, we have virtually no policy for land conservation and no policy of just compensation to the primary producers of food. Our agricultural policy is to use up everything that we have, while depending increasingly on imported food, energy, technology, and labour.

Those are just two examples of our general indifference to our own needs. We thus are elaborating a surely dangerous contradiction between our militant nationalism and our espousal of the international "free market" ideology. How do we escape from this absurdity?

I don't think there is an easy answer. Obviously, we would be less absurd if we took better care of things. We would be less absurd if we founded our public policies upon an honest description of our needs and our predicament, rather than upon fantastical descriptions of our wishes. We would be less absurd if our leaders would consider in good faith the proven alternatives to violence. Such things are easy to say, but we are disposed, somewhat by culture and somewhat by nature, to solve our problems by violence, and even to enjoy doing so. And yet by now all of us must at least have suspected that our right to live, to be free, and to be at peace is not guaranteed by any act of violence. It can be guaranteed only by our willingness that all other persons should live, be free, and be at peace – and by our willingness to use or give our own lives to make that possible. To be incapable of such willingness is merely to resign ourselves to the absurdity we are in; and yet, if you are like me, you are unsure to what extent you are capable of it.

Here is the other question that I have been leading toward, one that the predicament of modern warfare forces upon us: how many deaths of other people's children by bombing or starvation are we willing to accept in order that we may be free, affluent, and (supposedly) at peace? To that question I answer: none. Please, no children. Don't kill any children for my benefit. If that is your answer too, then you must know that we have not come to rest, far from it. For surely we must feel ourselves swarmed about with more questions that are urgent, personal, and intimidating.

But perhaps also we feel ourselves beginning to be free, facing at last in our own selves the greatest challenge ever laid before us, the most comprehensive vision of human progress, the best advice, and the least obeyed:

> Love your enemies, bless them that curse you, do good to them that hate you, and pray for them which despitefully use you and persecute you; that ye may be the children of your Father which is in heaven: for He maketh His sun to rise on the evil and the good, and sendeth rain on the just and on the unjust. (Luke 6:27)

Note

1   Reprinted with permission from *Yes! A Journal of Positive Futures* (Winter 2002 issue), PO Box 10818, Bainbridge Island, WA 98110. Subscriptions: 800/937–4451. Web: <www.yesmagazine.org> .

Bibliography

Aasi, Ghulam Haider (1999), *Muslim Understanding of Other Religions – A Study of Ibn Hazm's Kitab al-Fasl fi al-Milal wa al-Ahwa' wa al-Nihal*, Islamabad: International Institute of Islamic Thought.

Abd al-Raouf, Muhammad (1984), *A Muslim's Reflections on Democratic Capitalism*, Washington, DC: American Enterprise Institute.

Abdel Haleem, Muhammad (1999), *Understanding the Qur'an: Themes and Style*, London: I. B. Tauris.

Abou El Fadl, Khaled (2001), *Speaking in God's Name: Authority, Islamic Law, and Women*, Oxford: Oneworld.

—— (2002), *The Place of Tolerance in Islam*, Boston, MA: Beacon Press.

AbuSulayman, AbdulHamid (1993), *Towards an Islamic Theory of International Relations: New Directions for Methodology and Thought*, 2nd rev. edn, Herndon, VA: International Institute of Islamic Thought.

el-Affendi, Abdelwahab (ed.) (2001), *Rethinking Islam and Modernity*, Leicester: The Islamic Foundation and the Maghreb Centre for Research and Translation.

Ahmad, Imad-ad-Dean, and Ahmed Yousef (eds) (1998), *Islam and the West: A Dialog*, Beltsville, MD: United Association for Studies and Research and American Muslim Foundation.

Ahmad, Khurshid (1995), "Islam and the West: Confrontation or Cooperation?", *The Muslim World*, January–April.

Ahmed, Akbar S. (1988), *Discovering Islam: Making Sense of Muslim History and Society*, London: Routledge & Kegan Paul (rev. 2002).

—— (1992), *Postmodernism and Islam: Predicament and Promise*, London: Routledge.

—— (1999), *Islam Today: A Short Introduction to the Muslim World*, London: I. B. Tauris (rev. 2002).

—— (2003), *Islam Under Siege: Living Dangerously in a Post-Honor World*, Cambridge: Polity Press.

Ahmed, Akbar, and Lawrence Rosen (2001), "Islam, Academe, and Freedom of the Mind", *The Chronicle of Higher Education*, 2 November.

Akram, Ejaz (2002), "Religion as the Source of Reconciliation among Civilizations", *American Journal of Islamic Social Sciences*, vol. 19, no. 2, 34–45.

Ali, Syed Ameer (1965), *The Spirit of Islam: A History of the Evolution and Ideals of Islam with a Life of the Prophet*, London: Methuen.

Arendt, Hannah (1968), *Totalitarianism*, New York: Harcourt Brace Jovanovich.

Armstrong, Karen (2000), *The Battle for God: Fundamentalism in Judaism, Christianity and Islam*, London: HarperCollins.

Asad, Muhammad (trans.) (1980), *The Message of the Qur'an*, Gibraltar: Dar al-Andalus.

—— (1987), *This Law of Ours and Other Essays*, Gibraltar: Dar al-Andalus.

Asani, Ali S. (2002), "On Pluralism, Intolerance, and the Qur'an", *The American Scholar*, vol. 71, no. 1, 52–60.

Aslan, Adnan (1998), *Religious Pluralism in Christian and Islamic Philosophy: The Thought of John Hick and Seyyed Hossein Nasr*, Richmond, Surrey: Curzon Press.

Ayoub, Mahmoud M. (1984), *The Qur'an and Its Interpreters*, Albany: State University of New York Press.

—— (1997), "Nearest in Amity: Christians in the Qur'an and Contemporary Exegetical Tradition", *Islam and Christian-Muslim Relations*, vol. 8: 145–64.

Barber, Benjamin R. (1995), *Jihad vs. McWorld*, New York: Times Books.

Barney, Gerald O. (ed.) (1999), *Threshold 2000: Critical Issues and Spiritual Values for a Global Age*, Michigan: CoNexus Press, Millennium Institute.

Barrows, John Henry (ed.) (1893), *The World's Parliament of Religions*, 2 vols, Chicago, IL: Parliament Publishing Company.

Barzun, Jacques (2001), *From Dawn to Decadence. 1500 to the Present: 500 Years of Western Civilisation*, London: HarperCollins.

Bauman, Zygmunt (1998), *Globalization: The Human Consequences*, Cambridge: Polity Press.

Bayfield, Tony, and Marcus Braybrooke (eds) (1992), *Dialogue with a Difference: The Manor House Group Experience*, London: SCM Press.

Berger, Peter (1979), *The Heretical Imperative*, Garden City, NJ: Doubleday.

Berry, Wendell (1991), *Standing on Earth: Selected Essays*, Ipswich, Suffolk: Golgonooza Press.

—— (2003), "Futility of War: A Citizen's Response", *Resurgence*, no. 218 (May/June), 8–11.

Boase, Roger (2002), "The Muslim Expulsion from Spain", *History Today*, vol. 52, no. 4, 21–7.

Bodansky, Y. (1999), *Bin Laden: The Man who Declared War on America*, Roseville, CA: Prima Publishing Co.

Boullata, Issa J. (1995), "*Fa-stabiqu'l-khayrat*: A Quranic Principle of Interfaith Relations", in *Christian-Muslim Encounters*, ed. Yvonne Yazbeck Haddad and Wadi Z. Haddad, Gainesville: University Press of Florida.

Braibanti, Ralph (1999), *Islam and the West: Common Cause or Clash?* Washington, DC: Georgetown University, Occasional Paper Series, The Center for Muslim-Christian Understanding.

Braybrooke, Marcus (1990), *Time to Meet*, London: SCM Press.

—— (1992), *Pilgrimage of Hope: One Hundred Years of Global Interfaith Dialogue*, London: SCM Press.

—— (1996), *A Wider Vision*, Oxford: Oneworld.

—— (1998), *Faith and Interfaith in a Global Age*, Grand Rapids, MI: CoNexus Press; Oxford: Braybrooke Press.

—— (2002), *What We Can Learn From Islam: The Struggle for True Religion*, Arlesford, Hampshire: John Hunt.

Braybrooke, Marcus, and Kamran Mofid (2005), *Sustaining the Common Good: Bringing Economics and Theology Together. A Theologian and an Economist in Dialogue*, London: Shepheard-Walwyn.

Byrne, Peter (1995), *Prolegomena to Religious Pluralism: Reference and Realism in Religion*, New York: St. Martin's Press.

Camps, Arnulf (1983), *Partners in Dialogue: Christianity and Other World Religions*, Maryknoll, NY: Orbis Books.

Champion, Françoise (1999), "The Diversity of Religious Pluralism", *MOST Journal on Multicultural Societies*, vol. 1, no. 2, <http://www.unesco.org/most/v11n2cha.htm>.

Charles, Prince of Wales (1994), "Islam and the West", *Islamica: The Journal of the Islamic Society of the London School of Economics*, vol. 1, no. 4 (January), 4–8.

—— (2001), "A Reflection on the Reith Lectures for the Year 2000", *Temenos Academy Review*, vol. 4, 13–18.

Chittick, W. C. (1983): *The Sufi Path of Knowledge: The Spiritual Teachings of Rumi*, Albany: State University of New York Press.

—— (1994), *Imaginal Worlds: Ibn al-Arabi and the Problem of Religious Diversity*, Albany: State University of New York Press.

Cohen, Shaye J. D. (1997), "The Unfinished Agenda of Jewish-Christian Dialogue", *Journal of Ecumenical Studies*, vol. 34, no. 3 (Summer).

Coward, Harold (2000), *Pluralism in the World Religions*, Oxford: Oneworld.

Cox, Harvey (1966), *The Secular City*, New York: Macmillan.

—— (1988), *Many Mansions*, Boston, MA: Beacon Press.

Cracknell, Kenneth (1986), *Towards a New Relationship: Christians and People of Other Faith*, London: Epworth Press.

—— (1995), *Justice, Courtesy and Love: Theologians and Missionaries Encountering World Religions, 1846–1914*, London: Epworth Press.

Cragg, Kenneth (2002), *Am I Not Your Lord? Human Meaning in Divine Question*, London: Melisende.

D'Arcy, May (1998), *Pluralism and the Religions*, London: Cassel.

Dawe, D. G., and J. B. Carman (eds) (1980), *Christian Faith in a Religiously Plural World*, Maryknoll, NY: Orbis.

D'Costa, Gavin (1986), *Theology and Religious Pluralism*, Oxford: Basil Blackwell.

—— (ed.) (1990), *Christian Uniqueness Reconsidered: The Myth of a Pluralistic Theology of Religions*, Maryknoll, NY: Orbis.

Donovan, Peter (1993), "The Intolerance of Religious Pluralism", *Religious Studies*, vol. 29, 217–29.

Dupuis, Jacques (1997), *Towards a Christian Theology of Religious Pluralism*, Maryknoll, NY: Orbis Books.

—— (2001a), "Christianity and Other Religions: From Confrontation to Encounter: The Storm of the Spirit", *The Tablet*, 20 October.

—— (2001b), "From Confrontation to Encounter: God is Always Greater", *The Tablet*, 27 October.

Eck, Diana L. (1993), *Encountering God: A Spiritual Journey from Bozeman to Benaras*, Boston, MA: Beacon Press.

—— (2002), *A New Religious America: How A "Christian Country" Has Become the World's Most Religiously Diverse Nation*, New York: Harper-SanFrancisco, a Division of HarperCollins.

Ehrlich, Stanlaw, and Graham Wooton (eds) (1980), *Three Faces of Pluralism: Political, Ethical, and Religious*, London: Gower.

Esack, Farid (1997), *Qur'an, Liberation & Pluralism: An Islamic Perspective of Interreligious Solidarity against Oppression*, Oxford: Oneworld.

Esposito, John L. (1992), *The Islamic Threat: Myth or a Reality?*, New York: Oxford University Press.

—— (2002), *Unholy War: Terror in the Name of Islam*, New York: Oxford University Press.

Falk, Richard (1999), *Predatory Globalization: A Critique*, Cambridge: Polity Press.

—— (2000), *Human Rights Horizons: The Pursuit of Justice in a Globalizing World*, New York and London: Routledge.

al-Faruqi, Ismail Raji (1998), *Islam and Other Faiths*, ed. Ataullah Siddiqui, Markfield, Leicester: The Islamic Foundation.

Findley, Paul (1985), *They Dare to Speak Out: People and Institutions Confront Israel's Lobby*, Westport, CT: Lawrence Hill.

—— (2001), *Silent No More – Confronting America's False Images of Islam*, Beltsville, MD: Amana.

Flannery, Austin P. (ed.) (1975), *Documents of Vatican II*, Grand Rapids, MI: William B. Eerdman.

Forward, Martin (2001), *Inter-religious Dialogue: A Short Introduction*, Oxford: Oneworld.

Friedman, Thomas (2000), *The Lexus and the Olive Tree: Understanding Globalization*, London: HarperCollins.

Fukuyama, Francis (1992), *The End of History and the Last Man*, London: Hamish Hamilton.

Fuller, Graham E., and Ian O. Lesser (1995), *A Sense of Siege: The Geopolitics of Islam and the West*, Boulder, CO: Westview/RAND.

Gandhi, Mahatma K. (1962), *All Religions are True*, ed. Anand T. Hingorani, Bombay: Bharatiya Vidya Bhavan.

Garaudy, Roger (1977), *Pour un dialogue des civilisations: L'Occident est un accident*, Paris: Éditions Denoël.

Gaudeul, Jean-Marie (1990), *Encounters and Clashes: Islam and Christianity in History*, Rome: Pontificio Istituto di Studi Arabi e Islamici.

Giddens, Anthony (1990), *The Consequences of Modernity*, Cambridge: Polity Press.

—— (2000), *Runaway World: How Globalisation Is Reshaping Our Lives*, London: Routledge.

Glyn, Patrick (1999), *God: The Evidence – The Reconciliation of Faith and Reason in a Postsecular World*, Rocklin, CA: Forum: Prima Publishing.

Griffiths, Bede (1976), *Return to the Centre*, London: Collins.

Haeri, Shaykh Fadhlalla (1985), *Journey of the Universe as Expounded in the Qur'an*, London: Kegan Paul International.

Halliday, Fred (1996), *Islam and the Myth of Confrontation*, London: I. B. Tauris.

—— (2002), *Two Hours that Shook the World: September 11, 2001: Causes and Consequences*, London: Saqi Books.

Halsell, Grace (1986), *Prophecy and Politics: Militant Evangelists on the Road to Nuclear War*, Westport, CT: Lawrence Hill and Co.

—— (1999), *Forcing God's Hand – Why Millions Pray for a Quick Rapture – and Destruction of Planet Earth*, Washington, DC: Crossroads Int. Publishing.

Hamnett, Ian (ed.) (1990), *Religious Pluralism and Unbelief*, London: Routledge.

Henzell-Thomas, Jeremy (2003), "Passing Between the Clashing Rocks: The Heroic Quest for a Transcendent Identity", 32nd Annual Conference of the Association of Muslim Social Scientists (AMSS), Indiana University, Bloomington, IN, 26–28 September 2003.

Herzog, Roman (1999), *Preventing the Clash of Civilizations: A Peace Strategy for the Twenty-First Century*, London: Palgrave Macmillan.

Hick, John (1973), *God and the Universe of Faiths*, London: Macmillan.

—— (1980), *God Has Many Names*, London: Macmillan.

—— (1985), *Problems of Religious Pluralism*, New York: St. Martin's Press.

—— (1989), *An Interpretation of Religion*, New Haven, CT: Yale University Press.

—— (1991), "Islam and Christian Monotheism", in *Islam in a World of Diverse Faiths*, ed. Dan Cohn-Sherbok, London: Macmillan.

—— (ed.) (1993), *The Myth of God Incarnate*, 2nd edn, London: SCM Press (1st edn 1977).

—— (1995), *The Rainbow of Faiths: Critical Dialogues on Religious Pluralism*, London: SCM Press.

—— (1997), "The Epistemological Challenge of Religious Pluralism", *Faith and Philosophy, Journal of the Society of Christian Philosophers*, vol. 14, no. 3 (July 1997).

—— (2001), "Is Christianity the Only True Religion?", *World Faiths Encounter*, no. 28, 3–11.

Hick, John, and Paul F. Knitter (eds) (1987), *The Myth of Christian Uniqueness*, Maryknoll, NY: Orbis.

Hofmann, Murad (1997), *Islam: The Alternative*, 2nd edn, Beltsville, MD: Amana.

—— (2001a), *Religion on the Rise: Islam in the Third Millennium*, Beltsville, MD: Amana.

—— (2001b), *Modern Islamic Polity in the Making*, Islamabad: Institute of Policy Studies.

Huntington, Samuel P. (1996), *The Clash of Civilizations and the Remaking of World Order*, New York: Simon and Schuster.

Ibn Fayyumi, Netanel (1907), *The Garden of Wisdom*, trans. D. Levine, New York: Columbia University Press (repr. 1966).

Ibn Khaldun (1967), *The Muqaddimah: An Introduction to History*, trans. Franz Rosenthal, 3 vols (New York, 1958), abridged in one volume by N. J. Dawood, London: Routledge & Kegan Paul.

Izetbegovic, 'Alija 'Ali (1994), *Islam between East and West*, rev. edn (1st edn 1984), Indianapolis, IN: American Trust Publications.

Johnstone, Douglas, and Cynthia Sampson (eds) (1994), *Religion, the Missing Dimension of Statecraft*, New York: Oxford University Press.

Kaldor, Mary (1999), *New and Old Wars: Organized Violence in a Global Era*, Cambridge: Polity Press.

Kaplan, Robert (1997), *The End of the Earth: From Togo to Turkmenistan, from Iran to Cambodia, a Journey to the Frontiers of Anarchy*, New York: Vintage Books.

Kassam, Karim-Aly S. (1997), "The Clash of Civilizations: The Selling of Fear", *Islam in America*, vol. 3, no. 4.

Kelsay, John, and Sumner B. Twiss (eds) (1994), *Religion and Human Rights*, New York: The Project on Religion and Human Rights.

Kepel, Gilles (2002), *Jihad: The Trail of Political Islam*, London: I. B. Tauris.

Khatami, Muhammad (1998), "Dialogue of Civilizations", New York: United Nations General Assembly, 24 September.

King, Martin Luther (1967), *Where Do We Go From Here? Chaos or Community*, Boston, MA: Beacon Press.

Kirk, Russell A. (1993), *The Politics of Prudence*, Bryn Mawr, PA: Intercollegiate Studies Institute.

Knitter, Paul F. (1985), *No Other Name? A Critical Survey of Christian Attitudes Toward the World Religions*, Maryknoll, NY: Orbis.

—— (1995), *One Earth Many Religions: Multifaith Dialogue and Global Responsibility*, Maryknoll, NY: Orbis.

Kolly, Tim (ed.) (2002), *Globalization: Prospects for Peace, Prosperity and World Order*, Chicago, IL: McCormick Tribune Foundation.

Kottak, Conrad Phillip (2000), *Cultural Anthropology*, Boston, MA: McGraw-Hill, Higher Education.

Koylu, Mustafa (1999), "Possibilities and Conditions for Christian-Muslim Dialogue: A Muslim Perspective", *Encounters*, vol. 5, no. 2 (September), 179–97.

Kreeft, Peter (1996), *Ecumenical Jihad*, San Francisco: Ignatius Press.

Küng, Hans (1986), *Christianity and the World's Religions*, New York: Doubleday.

—— (ed.) (1996), *Yes to a Global Ethic*, London: SCM Press.

—— (1997), *A Global Ethic for Politics and Economics*, London: SCM Press.

—— (2003), "A Global Ethic: Development and Goals", *Interreligious Insight*, vol. 1, no. 1 (January), 8–19.

Küng, Hans, and Karl-Josef Kuschel (eds) (1993), *A Global Ethic: The Declaration of the Parliament of the World's Religions*, trans. John Bowden, London: SCM Press.

Küng, Hans, and Jürgen Moltmann (eds) (1992), *Fundamentalism as an Ecumenical Challenge*, London: SCM Press.

Kurzman, Charles (ed.) (1998), *Liberal Islam: A Sourcebook*, New York: Oxford University Press.

Legenhausen, Muhammad (1999), *Islam and Religious Pluralism*, London: Al-Hoda.

—— (2000), *Contemporary Topics of Islamic Thought*, Tehran: Al-Hoda.

Lewis, Bernard (1998), *The Multiple Identities of the Middle East*, New York: Schocken Books.

—— (2002), *What Went Wrong? Western Impact and Middle Eastern Response*, New York: Oxford University Press.

—— (2003), *The Crisis of Islam: Holy War and Unholy Terror*, London: Weidenfeld & Nicolson.

Lewisohn, Leonard (1995), *Beyond Faith and Infidelity: The Sufi Poetry and Teachings of Mahmud Shabistari*, Richmond, Surrey: Curzon Press.

Lombard, Joseph E. B. (ed.) (2004), *Islam, Fundamentalism, and the Betrayal of Tradition: Essays by Western Muslim Scholars*, Bloomington, IN: World Wisdom.

Magonet, Jonathan (2003), *Talking to the Other: A Jewish Experience of Dialogue with Christians and Muslims*, London: I. B. Tauris.

Majdalawi, Rudwan, and Faruq 'Abd al-Haqq (1995), *Maqasid al-Shari'ah: The Nature, History, and Application of Holistic Law*, Damascus, Syria: The Abu Nur Center.

Malik, Aftab Ahmad (ed.) (2003), *The Empire and the Crescent: Global Implications for a New American Century*, Bristol: Amal Press.

Marti, Felix (2001), *Clash of Civilizations or Intercultural Dialogue?*, New York: Global Education Associates.

McAuliffe, Jane Dammen (1991), *Qur'anic Christians: An Analysis of Classical and Modern Exegesis*, Cambridge: Cambridge University Press.

Menocal, María Rosa (2002), *The Ornament of the World: How Muslims, Jews, and Christians Created a Culture of Tolerance in Medieval Spain*, Boston, MA: Little Brown.

Micklethwait, John, and Adrian Wooldridge (2000), *A Future Perfect: The Challenge and Hidden Promise of Globalization*, New York: Times Books.

Mische, Patricia M., and Melissa Merkling (eds) (2001), *Towards a Global Civilization? The Contribution of Religions*, New York: Peter Lang.

Mishkat-ul-Masabih. An English Translation with Arabic Text of Selection of Ahadis from the Highly Voluminous Works of Bokhari, Muslim, and Other Traditionalists of Repute, ed. and trans. Al-Haj Maulana Fazlul Karim, 4 vols, Lahore: n.d. [1979].

Mittelman, James (2000), *The Globalization Syndrome: Transformation and Resistance*, Princeton, NJ: Princeton University Press.

Mofid, Kamran (2002), *Globalisation for the Common Good*, London: Shepheard-Walwyn.

Momin, Abdur-Rahman (2001), "Pluralism and Multiculturalism: An Islamic Perspective", *American Journal of Islamic Social Sciences*, vol. 18, no. 2, 115–46.

Moucarry, Chawkat (2001), *Faith to Faith: Christianity and Islam in Dialogue*, Leicester: Inter-Varsity Press.

Nasr, Seyyed Hossein (1972), *Sufi Essays*, London: Allen and Unwin.
—— (1987), *Traditional Islam in the Modern World*, London: Kegan Paul International.
—— (1989), *Knowledge and the Sacred*, Albany: State University of New York Press.
—— (1993), *The Need for a Sacred Science*, Richmond, Surrey: Curzon Press.
—— (1996), *Religion and the Order of Nature*, New York: Oxford University Press.
—— (1998), *The Spiritual and Religious Dimensions of the Environmental Crisis*, London: Temenos Academy.
—— (2000), "Islamic-Christian Dialogue: Problems and Obstacles to be Pondered and Overcome", *Islam and Christian-Muslim Relations*, vol. 11, 213–27.
Nazim Qibrisi, Shaykh [Muhammad] (1980), *Mercy Oceans: The Teachings of Maulana Abdullah al-Faizi ad-Daghestani*, talks recorded in Damascus, 1980.
Neusner, Jacob, and Tamara Sonn (1999), *Comparing Religions Through Law: Judaism and Islam*, London: Routledge.
Novak, David (1983), *The Image of the Non-Jew in Judaism*, New York and Toronto: Edward Mellen Press.
—— (1989), *Jewish-Christian Dialogue*, New York: Oxford University Press.
Pallis, Marco (1991), *The Way and the Mountain*, rev. edn, London: Peter Owen.
Parekh, Bhikhu (2000), *Rethinking Multiculturalism: Cultural Diversity and Political Theory*, Basingstoke: Palgrave.
Peters, F. E. (1990), *Judaism, Christianity, and Islam*, 3 vols, Princeton, NJ: Princeton University Press.
—— (1997), "*Alius* or *Alter*: The Qur'anic Definition of Christians and Christianity", *Islam and Christian-Muslim Relations*, vol. 8, 165–76.
Peterson, Michael, William Hasker, David Basinger, and Bruce R. Reichenbach (1991), *Reason and Religious Belief: An Introduction to the Philosophy of Religion*, New York: Oxford University Press.
Picco, Giandomenico (2001), "A Dialogue Among Civilizations", in *Seton Hall Journal of Diplomacy and International Relations*, 2, 5–10.
Pilger, John (2002), *The New Rulers of the World*, London: Verso.
al-Qaradawi, Yusuf (1985), *The Lawful and Prohibited in Islam*, trans. Kamal el-Helbawy, M. Moinuddin Siddiqui, and Syed Shukry, London: Shorouk International.
Race, Alan (1983), *Christians and Religious Pluralism: Patterns in the Christian Theology of Religions*, Maryknoll, NY: Orbis (rev. edn, 1993).
—— (2001), *Interfaith Encounter: The Twin Tracks of Theology and Dialogue*, London: SCM Press.
Race, Alan, and Ingrid Shafer (eds) (2002), *Religions in Dialogue: From Theocracy to Democracy*, Aldershot, Hants: Ashgate.
Rashid, Ahmad (2000), *Taliban: Islam, Oil and the New Great Game in Central Asia*, London: I. B. Tauris.
Robinson, Neal (1991), *Christ in Islam and Christianity*, London: Macmillan.

Rosenfeld, Jean E (2002), *The Religion of Usamah bin Ladin: Terror as the Hand of God*, Los Angeles, CA: UCLA Center for the Study of Religion.
Rouner, Leroy S. (ed.) (1984), *Religious Pluralism*, Notre Dame, IN: University of Notre Dame Press.
—— (1988), *Human Rights and the World's Religions*, Notre Dame, IN: University of Notre Dame Press.
Rumi, Jalal al-Din (1972), *Discourses,* trans. A. J. Arberry, New York: Samuel Weiser.
Sachedina, Abdulazziz (2001), *The Islamic Roots of Democratic Pluralism*, New York: Oxford University Press.
Sacks, Jonathan (2002), *The Dignity of Difference: How to Avoid the Clash of Civilizations*, London: Continuum.
Schimmel, Annemarie (1975), *Mystical Dimensions of Islam*, Chapel Hill: University of North Carolina Press.
Schuon, Frithjof (1953), *The Transcendent Unity of Religions*, trans. Peter Townsend, London: Faber & Faber (rev. edn, New York: Harper, 1975).
—— (1981), *Esoterism as Principle and as Way*, Pates Manor, Bedfont, Middlesex: Perennial Books.
—— (1991), *The Essential Writings*, ed. Seyyed Hossein Nasr, Shaftesbury: Element Books.
Segesvary, Victor (2000), *Dialogue of Civilization: An Introductory Civilizational Analysis*, Lanham, MD: United Press of America.
Shah-Kazemi, Reza (1993), *Paths to Transcendence: Spiritual Realization according to Shankara, Ibn Arabi, and Meister Eckhart*, Albany: State University of New York Press.
—— (2002), "The Metaphysics of Interfaith Dialogue: Sufi Perspectives on the Universality of the Qur'anic Message", in *Paths to the Heart: Sufism and the Christian East*, ed. James S. Cutsinger, Bloomington, IN: World Wisdom.
—— (2004), *The Other in the Light of the One – Unity, Universality and Dialogue based on Sufi exegesis of the Holy Qur'an*, Oxford: Oxford University Press.
Sherrard, Philip (1992), *Human Image: World Image*, Ipswich, Suffolk: Golgonooza Press.
Sherwin, Byron L., and Harold Kasimow (eds) (1999), *John Paul II and Interreligious Dialogue*, Maryknoll, NY: Orbis Press.
Siddiqi, Ataullah (2002), "*Believing* and *Belonging* in a Pluralist Society – Exploring Resources in Islamic Traditions", in David A. Hart (ed.), *Multi-Faith Britain*, London: O Books, pp. 23–33.
Smith, Huston (2001), *Why Religion Matters: The Fate of the Human Spirit in an Age of Disbelief*, New York: HarperSanFrancisco, a Division of HarperCollins.
Smith, Wilfred Cantwell (1967), *Questions of Religious Truth*, New York: Scribner's.
—— (1981), *Towards a World Theology: Faith and the Comparative History of Religion*, Philadelphia, PA: Westminster Press.
Smock, David R. (ed.) (2002), *Interfaith Dialogue and Peacebuilding*, Washington, DC: United States Institute of Peace Press.

Sullivan, Antony T. (2003), "New Frontiers in the Ecumenical Jihad Against Terrorism: Terrorism, Jihad, and the Struggle for New Understandings", *The American Muslim* (January–February).

Swidler, Leonard (ed.) (1992), *Muslims in Dialogue: The Evolution of a Dialogue*, Lampeter, Dyfed, Wales: The Edwin Mellen Press.

—— (ed.) (1998), *For All Life: Toward a Universal Declaration of a Global Ethic*, Oregon: White Cloud Press.

Tarnas, Richard (1991), *The Passion of the Western Mind: Understanding the Ideas That Have Shaped Our World View*, New York: Random House.

Testas, Abdelaziz (2003), "Models of Cultural Exclusion and Civilizational Clashes: A Comparison between Huntington and Siddiqi", *Islam and Christian-Muslim Relations*, vol. 14, no. 2: 175–87.

Toynbee, Arnold (1957), *Christianity Among the Religions of the World*, New York: Scribner's.

Twiss, Sumner B., and Bruce Grelle (eds) (1998), *Explorations in Global Ethics: Comparative Religious Ethics and Interreligious Dialogue*, Boulder, CO: Westview Press.

Van Buren, Paul M. (1995), *A Theology of the Jewish-Christian Reality*, 3 vols, Lanham, MD: University Press of America.

Watt, William Montgomery (1991), *Muslim-Christian Encounters: Perceptions and Misperceptions*, London: Routledge.

Whitson, Robert Edward (1963), *The Coming Convergence of the World Religions*, New York: Columbia University Press.

Wuthnow, Robert (2001), *After Heaven: Spirituality in America since the 1950s*, Berkeley, CA: University of California Press.

Index